ORGANIZATIONAL RISK FACTORS FOR
JOB STRESS

EDITED BY
STEVEN L. SAUTER AND
LAWRENCE R. MURPHY

AMERICAN PSYCHOLOGICAL ASSOCIATION

WASHINGTON, DC

Published by
American Psychological Association
750 First Street, NE
Washington, DC 20002

Copies may be ordered from
APA Order Department
P.O. Box 2710
Hyattsville, MD 20784

In the United Kingdom and Europe, copies may be ordered from
American Psychological Association
3 Henrietta Street
Covent Garden, London
WC2E 8LU England

Typeset in Century Schoolbook by Easton Publishing Services, Inc., Easton, MD

Cover designer: Minker Design, Bethesda, MD
Printer: Kirby Lithographic Co., Inc., Arlington, VA
Technical/production editor: Miria Liliana Riahi

Library of Congress Cataloging-in-Publication Data
Organizational risk factors for job stress / edited by Steven L. Sauter
  and Lawrence R. Murphy.
      p.   cm.
    Includes bibliographical references and index.
    ISBN 1-55798-297-X (softcover)
    1. Job stress. 2. Quality of work life. 3. Work environment.
  4. Employees—Health risk assessment. I. Sauter, Steven L.
  II. Murphy, Lawrence R.
  HF5548.85.O74   1995
  158.7—dc20   95-31599
                                                                    CIP

British Library Cataloguing-in-Publication Data
A CIP record is available from the British Library.

Printed in the United States of America
First edition

Contents

Contributors

Pamela K. Adelmann, *Northwestern University, Evanston, IL*
John R. Aiello, *Rutgers University, New Brunswick, NJ*
John P. Allegrante, *Columbia University Teachers College, New York*
Randal Beaton, *University of Washington, Seattle*
Pascale Carayon, *University of Wisconsin at Madison*
Peter Y. Chen, *Ohio University, Athens*
Michael D. Class, *University of Illinois at Chicago*
Eric W. Farmer, *Defence Research Agency, Farnborough, Hants, UK*
Gloria Fisher, *Mississippi College, Clinton*
Deborah M. Flynn, *Nipissing University, North Bay, Ontario, Canada*
Jane Y. Fong, *Rogers and Associates, Atascadero, CA*
Traci L. Galinsky, *National Institute for Occupational Safety and Health, Cincinnati, OH*
Robert F. M. Herber, *University of Amsterdam, The Netherlands*
Irene L. D. Houtman, *TNO Prevention and Health, Leiden, The Netherlands*
Dennis T. Jaffe, *Saybrook Institute, San Francisco*
Monica Jarrett, *University of Washington, Seattle*
Steven M. Jex, *Central Michigan University, Mount Pleasant*
Bill Jones, *Carleton University, Ottawa, Canada*
Ger J. Keijsers, *Dutch Institute for the Working Environment, Amsterdam, The Netherlands*
E. Kevin Kelloway, *University of Guelph, Ontario, Canada*
Kathryn J. Kolb, *Rutgers University, New Brunswick, NJ*
Michiel A. J. Kompier, *TNO Institute of Prevention and Health, Leiden, The Netherlands*
Symen Kuiper, *University of Amsterdam, The Netherlands*
Paul A. Landsbergis, *Cornell University Medical College, New York*
Marlene P. Lukaszewski, *Western Connecticut State University, Danbury*
Nancy J. McIntosh, *University of South Florida, St. Petersburg*
Theo F. Meijman, *University of Groningen, The Netherlands*
John L. Michela, *University of Waterloo, Ontario, Canada*
Dinis Reis Miranda, *University Hospital, Groningen, The Netherlands*
Lawrence R. Murphy, *National Institute for Occupational Safety and Health, Cincinnati, OH*
Shirley Murphy, *University of Washington, Seattle*
Christopher S. Pan, *National Institute for Occupational Safety and Health, Cincinnati, OH*
Thomas G. Pickering, *Cornell University Medical College, New York*
Kenneth Pike, *University of Washington, Seattle*
Sally A. Radmacher, *Missouri Western State College, St. Joseph*
Dennis A. Revicki, *Battelle Center for Public Health Policy and Research, Arlington, VA*
Jaesoon Rhee, *Columbia University, New York*
Robert H. Rosen, *Healthy Companies, Washington, DC*
Herman Rongen, *University of Utrecht, The Netherlands*
Steven L. Sauter, *National Institute for Occupational Safety and Health, Cincinnati, OH*

Wilmar B. Schaufeli, *Utrecht University, The Netherlands*
Lawrence M. Schleifer, *Rockville, MD*
Peter L. Schnall, *Center for Social Epidemiology, Los Angeles*
Irvin Schonfeld, *City University of New York*
Joseph E. Schwartz, *State University of New York, Stonybrook*
Elizabeth M. Semko, *Jackson State University, MS*
Charles L. Sheridan, *University of Missouri, Kansas City*
Marian K. Silverman, *Owens Corning, Toledo, OH*
Carlla S. Smith, *Bowling Green State University, OH*
Paul E. Spector, *University of South Florida, St. Petersburg*
David J. Sternbach, *Fogel Foundation, Washington, DC*
Andrew J. Tattersall, *University of Wales College of Cardiff, UK*
Marjolijn van der Velde, *University of Illinois at Chicago*
Max van Dormolen, *University of Amsterdam, The Netherlands*
F. John Wade, *Jackson State University, MS*
Katherine Warren, *Cornell University Medical College, New York*
Theodore W. Whitley, *East Carolina University School of Medicine, Greenville, NC*
Fang Xia, *Columbia University, New York*

Foreword

The purpose of work is to develop ourselves and to provide economic sustenance. The work we do must nourish our lives if we are to do good work. Work, indeed, is central to our lives. Yet, despite these positive attributes of work, organizational stress seems to be on the rise. There is a large gap between what people want and need from work and what they are actually receiving.

In today's workplace, people and their organizations are not working well together. There is a jumble of friction, misperceptions of roles and responsibilities, and steadily deteriorating relationships. People are being asked to do more work, in less time, with fewer resources. Employees and employers are feeling the pain and consequences of this strain: Workers are more stressed and dissatisfied with their work; many organizations are unhealthy, unproductive places of employment; and the employee—employer relationship is more fragile and less predictable than ever before.

American organizations have a long history of underestimating the cost and potential of people in the workplace. One of the primary reasons is that many organizations tend to create work policies on the basis of the belief that work is something to be extracted from people—as though they were a kind of fuel to be burned up and reduced to waste—instead of on the belief that work is something people need and want to do. Organizations end up managing people as depreciating costs, not appreciating assets, under the pressure of short-term profits and a high-consumption, low-investment society.

Stress is a known biopsychosocial variable that intervenes between workplace factors and individual health. It arises from a mixture of the pressure of demanding work conditions and individual responses to that pressure. Yet, is stress a problem to be managed by the individual or by the organization? Most stress research has looked primarily at individual coping, rather than at the role of the work environment in stress. The concern has been with the particular, not the general, and with the cell, not the whole body. In reality, stress must be managed from both the individual and the organizational perspectives.

The concept of *organizational health* attempts to blend these two perspectives. Organizational health represents far more than the traditional treatment of specific health issues at the workplace, such as the institution of health-promotion programs for individuals, the provision of health benefits, and the application of occupational health and safety policies. Organizational health describes a new way of defining the values, goals, policies, and practices of work organizations. It is necessary both to define fully what this concept means and to understand how it can be applied and tested in the American workplace.

A model of organizational health must integrate and go beyond the prevailing paradigms. This model of work must be based on a new conceptual framework—a fresh way of looking at human beings in organizational settings. The core of this conceptual framework is a new employer—employee relationship: one that is healthy and positive, is mutually reinforcing, and brings together successful healthy adults with healthy, productive organizations.

It is striking how similar the needs of both individuals and organizations are to seek these same goals. There will always be obstacles to organizational health, but there will always be resources as well. What is critical for both individuals and organizations is to pursue health as a desired goal.

Research that supports the concept of organizational health draws on an enormous variety of disciplines: medicine, public health, management, psychology, sociology, anthropology, and political science. From this diversity of disciplines, certain major themes emerge—all of which look at the issue of stress in the larger organizational context: the importance of organizational culture and climate, the nature of job stress and burnout, the issue of performance monitoring, the impact of particular kinds of high-risk occupations, and a clearer understanding of the kind of continuing research that is needed to understand the interaction of the individual and the organization. Such themes and issues are explored in this book.

Fortunately, organizational research is moving in the right direction. A growing body of research is substantiating the value of healthy organizations for healthy people. In addition, the work of a growing number of healthy leaders and their organizations is living testament to the possibility for real-world change. One can find such healthy organizations in the for-profit, nonprofit, and public sectors. They evidence a deeper understanding of human-development issues in the new workplace and a more effective use of their human assets. A new paradigm of work—a new business logic—is also emerging, in which employee development and innovation and customer relationships have become new forms of capital and critical assets for achieving success.

For this movement to continue, a greater understanding about this new model of healthy, high-performance work is needed—a model that simultaneously promotes human development, organizational effectiveness, and economic success. This book represents one step further in that direction.

Robert H. Rosen
President, Healthy Companies

Preface

This book owes its existence to a partnership that began nearly a decade ago to address the problem of stress in the workplace. At that time, the American Psychological Association (APA) joined forces with the National Institute for Occupational Safety and Health (NIOSH) to refine and implement NIOSH-proposed strategies for the prevention of work-related psychological disorders.[1] This initiative was driven by emerging data, such as escalating worker compensation claims for mental disorders, that suggested that stress was becoming a major occupational health problem. Indeed, by the early 1980s, NIOSH had listed psychological disorders among the 10 leading occupational illness and injuries.[2]

The first product of the APA–NIOSH partnership was a jointly sponsored national conference in 1990 titled *Work and Well Being: An Agenda for the 1990s*. This conference attracted a large number of participants from around the globe, and its proceedings were subsequently published in two APA Books. The first book, *Work and Well-Being: An Agenda for the 1990s*, suggested ways of improving the organization of work and described surveillance and mental health delivery systems to help prevent job stress and associated health disorders.[3] The second book, *Stress and Well-Being at Work: Assessments and Interventions for Occupational Mental Health*, presented a series of international reports on occupational mental health risks and interventions.[4] The conference also provided the impetus for the initiation of a graduate fellowship program in occupational health psychology; the start-up of a new journal, the *Journal of Occupational Health Psychology*; and a subsequent conference on job stress in 1992.

The 1992 conference, *Stress in the 90s: A Changing Workforce in a Changing Workplace*, drew over 800 international participants and dealt with a broad range of topics including workforce diversity, the work–family interface and cross-cultural aspects of job stress, emergent organizational risk factors for job stress, and job stress interventions. The present book is the second of three volumes derived from that conference. The first book, *Job Stress in a Changing Workforce: Investigating Gender, Diversity, and Family Issues*, dealt with the shifting demographics of the workforce, work–family dynamics, and implications for job stress.[5] In this second volume, attention turns away from individual factors and workforce characteristics toward organizational factors

---

[1]Sauter, S. L., Murphy, L. R., & Hurrell, J. J., Jr. (1990). Prevention of work-related psychological disorders: A national strategy proposed by the National Institute for Occupational Safety and Health (NIOSH). *American Psychologist, 45*, 1146–1158.

[2]Millar, J. D. (1984). Letters. *Journal of Occupational Medicine, 26*, 340–341.

[3]Keita, G. P., & Sauter, S. L. (Eds.). (1992). *Work and well-being: An agenda for the 1990s*. Washington, DC: American Psychological Association.

[4]Quick, J. C., Murphy, L. R., & Hurrell, J. J., Jr. (Eds.). (1992). *Stress and well-being at work: Assessments and interventions for occupational mental health*. Washington, DC: American Psychological Association.

[5]Keita, G. P., & Hurrell, J. J., Jr. (Eds.). (1994). *Job stress in a changing workforce: Investigating gender, diversity, and family issues*. Washington, DC: American Psychological Association.

and their relationship to job stress. The volume looks at changes in job demands and associated stress risks in the workplace of the 90s, as well as new ways of conceptualizing and assessing organizational risk factors for job stress. We hope that the original studies presented here will lead to improved ways of investigating and understanding stressful working conditions in today's changing work environment. The third volume resulting from the 1992 conference will deal with both individual and organizational interventions to reduce stress at work.

We thank Judy Nemes of the American Psychological Association for her extensive editorial support in the preparation of this volume, Lynn Letourneau for her assistance with administrative details, and several anonymous reviewers for their valuable suggestions for chapter revisions. Special thanks go to Michael J. Colligan, James C. Quick, Julian Barling, and Kevin Kelloway who generously provided assistance and advice to the editors. Finally, we thank each of the chapter authors for their patience and steadfastness during the process of preparing this book for publication.

Steven L. Sauter
Lawrence R. Murphy

1

The Changing Face of Work and Stress

Steven L. Sauter and Lawrence R . Murphy

Two decades ago, the National Institute for Occupational Safety and Health (NIOSH) published a technical report on what has become one of the most well-known studies of job demands, stress, and health. This study, which was conducted under contract by investigators from the University of Michigan Institute for Social Research (Caplan, Cobb, French, Van Harrison, & Pinneau, 1975), made several important contributions to the field of job stress. It provided the first comparative analysis of psychological job demands and health across multiple occupations. It also provided an initial test of the person–environment fit theory of job stress. Perhaps of greatest importance, however, was that the study defined an array of what have been subsequently referred to as *workplace psychosocial factors*, which influenced future investigation and understanding of job-stress risk factors. Included among these factors are now-familiar constructs such as job complexity; workload and workload variability; opportunity for skill utilization; social support from work peers, supervisors, and family; role clarity; and so on.

This taxonomy of psychosocial factors has been extensively incorporated in subsequent stress research and theory (e.g., Hurrell & Murphy, 1992), and there is still concerted study of such factors as work roles, social support, and so on in the etiology of job stress. However, in the 20 years since the seminal research by the Institute for Social Research, there have been important theoretical developments that have influenced the way risk factors for job stress are conceptualized. For example, as illustrated in Robert Rosen's Foreword to this volume, there is an increasing focus on more global aspects of organizational design and function (e.g., organizational climate) as determinants of worker well-being. Additionally, there have been dramatic changes in the structure of work, such as the emergence of the service sector, that have brought new types of stressors to bear on the workforce. The purpose of this volume is to highlight developments in both of these areas (i.e., in the way we look at risk factors for job stress conceptually and in the nature of stressors confronting today's workforce).

The volume begins with a series of chapters that bring a new perspective to occupational-stress research in terms of the way psychosocial risk factors for occupational stress and health are characterized. In contrast to a focus on

1

specific aspects of job design, work roles, and interpersonal relationships at work, which has predominated occupational-stress research (e.g., see International Labour Office, 1986), chapters in Part I address more macroscopic aspects of the organizational environment—its culture and climate—as determinants of both organizational effectiveness and worker well-being. This is an exciting new line of inquiry that is already beginning to pay dividends in occupational health in general. Recent studies by NIOSH, for example, have shown that such organizational climate factors as perceived "safety climate" are significant predictors of exposure to both infectious disease and ergonomic risks in the workplace (Dejoy, Murphy, & Gershon, in press; NIOSH, 1993b). However, work to dimensionalize and operationalize these more global organizational features and to examine their importance and role in the stress process in relation to more micro-organizational factors is only just beginning. Chapters in Part I provide a cross section of developments in this area.

Chapters in Part II address the increasingly familiar demand–control model of job stress (Karasek, 1979; Karasek & Theorell, 1990). Of relevance to the theme of this volume is the way that risk for job stress is conceptualized according to this model. The model posits that job strain (stress) results when job-decision latitude (control) is not commensurate with the psychological demands imposed by the job. Although both the demand and control constructs as operationalized by Karasek would appear to be multidimensional, the simplicity of this two-dimensional formulation stands in contrast to more complex and molecular analyses of organizational risk factors for job stress (Caplan et al., 1975; Cooper & Marshall, 1976; Katz & Kahn, 1978, Matteson & Ivancevich, 1989).

With other data on the effects of control and control-like constructs (e.g., autonomy and participation), accumulated research on the demands–control formulation leaves little room for question regarding the importance of controllability for worker health (see Sauter, Hurrell, & Cooper, 1989, for a review). Indeed, evidence is sufficiently convincing to have influenced safety and health policy. For example, the Swedish Work Environment Act (Ministry of Labor, 1987) mandated that work "be arranged in such a way that the employee himself can influence his work situation" (p. 3). NIOSH (1988) has similarly recommended that workers "should be given the opportunity to have input on decisions or actions that affect their jobs and the performance of their tasks" (p. 105).

Still, research addressing the demand–control model continues at a furious pace. Much of this work is aimed at validity issues (i.e., the ability of the model to predict health outcomes). A related topic of investigation is whether job demands and control combine in an interactive or additive fashion to influence health. A cross-cutting issue of particular relevance is whether the demand–control formulation is too restrictive. Data presented by J. Johnson and Hall (1988) suggest that the predictive capacity of the model is enhanced by adding social support as a third dimension. Relatedly, Kasl (1989) raised concerns regarding the theoretical definition and conceptual boundaries of control—which has been broadly operationalized in extant research—noting the potential for overlap with other concepts and measures, such as job complexity or challenge. Part II provides an overview of current research and perspectives on several of these issues.

Parts III and IV of this book turn toward the changing work environment and emergent stressors in the workplace. A hallmark of this change is the decline in the manufacturing sector and the ascendance of the service and information industries as the predominant forms of work in America and in other postindustrial economies. The service sector now accounts for more jobs than all other sectors combined and will be responsible for virtually all near-term job growth in the U.S. economy through 1995 (Bezold, Carlson, & Peck, 1987; W. Johnson & Packer, 1987; U.S. Department of Labor, 1992).

Both service and information work have fostered risks not envisioned in past years. Violence, resulting in part from increased public exposure in service work, ranks as the third leading cause of death from injury among workers (NIOSH, 1993a), and emergent data now suggest that the threat of violence may be an important contributor to occupational stress among workers (North-western National Life, 1993). As predicted more than a decade ago (Giuliano, 1982), there are now few office jobs that have not been affected by comput-erization and advanced information systems, and this trend continues in the factory environment with the proliferation of advanced manufacturing tech-nologies. However, less clearly foreseen were the potential stressors associated with this technology, such as increasing psychological or cognitive demands of modern work (Ganster, Hurrell, & Thomas, 1987) or the intrusive use of computers for monitoring workers.

Numerous other changes in work life have been witnessed in the past two decades. Notable examples include the expansion of work hours and the evap-oration of leisure time, the emergence of the contingent workforce, and the dramatic growth of such industries as health care, in which worker stress seems to be endemic. Although research lags in many areas, important strides have been made to characterize stressful aspects of some of these developments, such as the emergence of electronic monitoring of work performance.

Monitoring work performance certainly is not new, but advances in com-puter mechanization and automation of work have created the opportunity for detailed and continuous performance monitoring unlike any time in the past. Data on the prevalence of electronic monitoring in the workplace are not readily available. However, a 1987 study by the Congressional Office of Tech-nology Assessment estimated that as many as 6 million workers were eval-uated using data obtained through electronic monitoring (U.S. Congress, Office of Technology Assessment, 1987). It is recognized that, in principle, electronic monitoring can enhance work life; for example, monitoring can improve the accuracy and timeliness of feedback and provide for fairer compensation of performance. However, there is also widespread and growing concern over negative effects of electronic monitoring on work practices and, in turn, on worker stress and health (see Schleifer, 1992). It is feared, for example, that the practice of close monitoring may degrade employee–supervisory relation-ships or result in work overload because of implicit or explicit expectations for increased productivity. Because of this potential and the scope of monitoring in the workplace, all of Part III is devoted to this subject.

The chapters in Part IV of this volume look at the spectrum of emergen
risks for job stress, focusing on the nature of the occupation itself. In this part
special attention is given to the growing number of jobs in the health and
helping professions. Employment in the health care sector was projected to
increase by one third from 1985 to 1995 (Silvestri & Lukasiewicz, 1985). By
the close of the past decade, this type of work represented the third larges
job category in the service sector (W. Johnson & Packer, 1987).

The risk of job stress in health care professions has been the subject of
considerable investigation. More than 30 years ago, Guralnick (1963) produced
evidence of higher than expected rates of suicide among health professional
(physicians, dentists, nurses, and health technologists). Subsequent work has
extended these findings to other stress-related outcomes and health profession
(Hoiberg, 1982; Milham, 1983; Payne & Firth-Cozens, 1987). The nursing
profession has received particular attention in this research. In the United
States, nursing is among the fastest-growing professions (Silvestri & Luka
siewicz, 1985), and evidence suggests that job-stress risks may be especially
pronounced among nurses. In addition to the myriad stressors, ranging from
high responsibility for people to infectious disease exposure, faced by mos
health care professionals, recent studies have indicated that nurses may also
be at high risk for exposure to violence by patients (Lipscomb, 1992; Lusk
1992). In a 1993 survey of working conditions and health in 10,000 nurses
rates of stress-related disease (hypertension, cardiovascular disease, ulcers
and colitis) and affective disturbances (exhaustion–fatigue, tension, depres
sion, and sleep disturbances) were found to be substantially higher among
nurses than in the general population (Service Employees International Union
1993). Not surprising in light of these findings is that two thirds of the surveyed
nurses reported that they were ready to leave their professions or current jobs

Although substantial information has been accumulated on the stress risk
in core health care professions, surprisingly little information exists about
stress and stress-related disorders among many allied health professions o
within specific sectors of health care and helping professions. NIOSH is at
tempting to advance knowledge in this area by, for example, supporting re
search on stress in minority medical residents. In Part IV, the primary air
is to illuminate knowledge of stress risks across a broader array of healt
professions, with an emphasis on emergency-response and critical-care healt
workers. Additionally, this part draws attention to occupational differential
in stress risks in general and provides some focus on potentially risky job
that have received little attention in the stress literature so far.

Any discussion of risk factors for job stress would be incomplete withou
addressing methodological concerns that challenge knowledge in this area
One recurrent critique of research methods in occupational stress relates t
the use of self-report or questionnaire techniques (vs. observation or rating
by others) for the assessment of exposure to suspected stressors. Because in
dividual perceptions of the work environment can be affected by dispositiona
factors, the reliability and validity of self-report measures of the working
conditions may be threatened. (It is worth noting, however, that some aspect
of the environment--such as relationships with supervisors--may be mea

surable only by self-report.) Another major concern relates to the heavy reliance on cross-sectional research designs in stress research, which reduces confidence in causal interpretations.

As attention to psychological stressors in occupational-health research and policy increases, concerns regarding the adequacy of methods to identify job-stress risk factors and their effects take on greater importance. Chapters in fifth and final part of this volume review familiar and not-so-familiar methodological threats to the credibility of job-stress research and discuss a variety of strategies to minimize these problems. Importantly, Part V also raises new research-design issues, such as the importance and method of assessing cumulative or chronic exposures to workplace stressors in defining stress and health risks.

In summary, recent years have witnessed unprecedented changes in the design and demands of work and shifting scientific paradigms for investigating the stresses imposed by the changing work environment. This volume provides a cross section of these developments in an effort to promote the understanding and control of risk factors for job stress and to thus protect the well-being of workers.

References

Bezold, C., Carlson, R., & Peck, J. (1987). *The future of work and health.* Dover, MA: Auburn House.

Caplan, R., Cobb, S., French, J., Van Harrison, R., & Pinneau, S. (1975). *Job demands and worker health: Main effects and occupational differences.* Washington, DC: U.S. Department of Health, Education, and Welfare.

Cooper, C., & Marshall, J. (1976). Occupational sources of stress: A review of the literature relating to coronary heart disease and mental ill health. *Journal of Occupational Psychology, 49,* 11–28.

DeJoy, D., Murphy, L., & Gershon, R. (in press). The influence of employee, job/task, and organizational factors on adherence to universal precautions among nurses. *International Journal of Industrial Ergonomics.*

Ganster, D., Hurrell, J., & Thomas, L. (1987). Development of a scale to assess occupational cognitive demands. In G. Salvendy, S. Sauter, & J. Hurrell (Eds.), *Social, ergonomic and stress aspects of work with computers* (pp. 231–238). Amsterdam: Elsevier.

Giuliano, V. (1982). The mechanization of office work. *Scientific American, 247*(3), 67–75.

Guralnick, L. (1963). *Mortality by occupation and cause of death (No. 3). Mortality by industry and cause of death (No. 4). Mortality by occupation level and cause of death (No. 5) among men 20–64 years of age vs. 1950* (Vital statistics—special reports, Vol. 53). Washington, DC: U.S. Government Printing Office.

Hoiberg, M. (1982). Occupational stress and illness incidence. *Journal of Occupational Medicine, 24,* 351–354.

Hurrell, J., & Murphy, L. (1992). Psychological job stress. In W. Rom (Ed.), *Environmental and occupational medicine* (pp. 675–684). Boston: Little, Brown.

International Labour Office. (1986). *Psychosocial factors at work: Recognition and control* (Report of the Joint International Labour Office/World Health Organization Committee on Occupational Health). Geneva: International Labour Office.

Johnson, J., & Hall, E. (1988). Job strain, workplace social support and cardiovascular disease: A cross-sectional study of a random sample of the Swedish working population. *American Journal of Public Health, 78,* 1336–1342.

Johnson, W., & Packer, A. (1987). *Workforce 2000: Work and workers for the 21st century.* Indianapolis, IN: Hudson Institute.

Karasek, R. (1979). Job demands, job decision latitude, and mental strain: Implications for job redesign. *Administrative Science Quarterly, 24*, 285–307.

Karasek, R., & Theorell, T. (1990). *Healthy work.* New York: Basic Books.

Kasl, S. (1989). An epidemiologic perspective on the role of control in health. In S. Sauter, J. Hurrell, & C. Cooper (Eds.), *Job control and worker health* (pp. 161–190). New York: Wiley.

Katz, D., & Kahn, R. (1978). *The social psychology of organizations* (2nd ed.). New York: Wiley.

Lipscomb, J. (1992). Violence toward health care workers. *American Association of Occupational Health Nursing Journal, 40*, 219–227.

Lusk, S. (1992). Violence experienced by nurses aides in nursing homes: An exploratory study. *American Association of Occupational Health Nursing Journal, 40*, 237–241.

Matteson, M., & Ivancevich, J. (1989). *Controlling work stress: Effective human resource and management strategies.* San Francisco: Jossey-Bass.

Milham, S., Jr. (1983). *Occupational mortality in Washington State, 1950–1979* (DHHS NIOSH Publication No. 83-116). Washington, DC: U.S. Government Printing Office.

Ministry of Labor. (1987). *The Swedish work environment act (with amendments) and the Swedish work environment ordinance (with amendments).* Stockholm: Author.

National Institute for Occupational Safety and Health. (1988). Proposed national strategy for prevention of work-related psychological disorders. In *Proposed national strategies for the prevention of leading work-related diseases and injuries, Pt. 2* (NTIS No. PB89-130348, pp. 95–119). Cincinnati, OH: Author.

National Institute for Occupational Safety and Health. (1993a). *Alert: Request for assistance in preventing homicide in the workplace* (Pub. No. 93-109). Cincinnati, OH: Author.

National Institute for Occupational Safety and Health. (1993b). *Health hazard evaluation report: HETA 90-013-2277, U.S. West Communications, Phoenix, Arizona, Minneapolis, Minnesota, Denver, Colorado.* Cincinnati, OH: Author.

Northwestern National Life. (1993). *Fear and violence in the workplace.* Minneapolis, MN: Author.

Payne, R., & Firth-Cozens, J. (1987). *Stress in health professionals.* New York: Wiley.

Sauter, S., Hurrell, J., & Cooper, C. (1989). *Job control and worker health.* New York: Wiley.

Schleifer, L. (1992). Electronic performance monitoring (EPM). *Applied Ergonomics, 23*, 4–5.

Service Employees International Union. (1993). *The national nurse study.* Washington, DC: Author.

Silvestri, G., & Lukasiewicz, J. (1985, November). Occupational employment projections: The 1984–95 outlook. *Monthly Labor Review*, 42–47.

U.S. Congress, Office of Technology Assessment. (1987). *The electronic supervisor: New technology, new tensions.* Washington, DC: U.S. Government Printing Office.

U.S. Department of Labor, Women's Bureau. (1992). *Women workers outlet to 2005.* Washington, DC: Author.

CONCEPTUALIZING RISK FACTORS FOR JOB STRESS: NEW PARADIGMS

Part I

Organizational Culture and Climate

Introduction

Organizational culture and climate have been subjects of study in social and organizational psychology for several decades. However, investigation of these aspects of work is a relatively new phenomenon in the occupational-stress literature. In the opening chapter of this part, Jaffe brings together knowledge of organizational psychology, motivation, and stress in support of his thesis that the health of the organization and the worker are inseparable and are defined by the organizational culture (which is manifested in the organization's policies). Although this type of thinking is beginning to permeate occupational-health theory, empirical study of this proposition is still in the formative stage. The next three chapters in this part represent efforts to gain an initial understanding of the relationship between organizational culture–climate characteristics and stress at work. It is interesting that the approaches of these studies are at considerable variance with one another, indicating that this is a field of work that is still in the exploratory or preparadigmatic stage. The chapters by Jones, Flynn, and Kelloway, by van der Velde and Class, and by Michela, Lukaszewski, and Allegrante each dimensionalize organizational culture–climate characteristics in qualitatively different ways, and each postulates different types of mechanisms linking culture and climate to stress. With regard to the latter, Jones et al. suggest that perceived organizational support moderates the effects of job stressors, such as role conflict, on job satisfaction. Van der Velde and Class, alternatively, reverse the position of culture and roles in the causal sequence leading to stress, suggesting that organizational culture defines roles and role problems. Finally, Michela et al. propose a direct relationship between organizational climate and stress. Despite their theoretical differences, which will need to be addressed in future work, each study found an association between culture–climate factors and well-being, supporting the significance of these factors in the stress process.

The final chapter in this part by Fisher, Semko, and Wade reports an effort to measure hostile workplace climate. Although further developmental and validation work is needed, this effort is of particular importance because it provides the building blocks for assessing a key organizational stressor in today's increasingly diverse workplace.

2

The Healthy Company: Research Paradigms for Personal and Organizational Health

Dennis T. Jaffe

Health-promotion programs have traditionally focused on individual factors that affect health: personality factors and health behaviors by which the individual could lessen or prevent health risks. Although individual factors are important aspects of organizational health, this chapter examines the *organizational* factors that support individual health and organizational effectiveness.

The very structures, values, cultures, and working relationships inherent in an organization may lead to health problems. Many of the programs and efforts that have been implemented to make organizations more productive may have the unintended effects of causing more personal distress and illness. The question arises of whether the arrangements that companies have developed to increase productivity and manage change are antithetical to personal health. Can personal health and well-being be made consonant with organizational effectiveness?

Organizational health implies an expanded notion of organizational effectiveness. Traditionally, effectiveness was defined as meeting profit, production, service, and continuity goals. Organizational health, as I define it here, adds a further dimension, raising several questions: How well does the organization treat its people? What are the connections between traditional measures of effectiveness and the health and well-being of people working in the organization? Do effective organizations also support the growth and development needs of their employees? Another factor is the morale, level of satisfaction, growth and development, and motivation of employees. This concern can be even broader, if the needs of customers, suppliers, owners, and community members that are touched by the organization are considered as well. A healthy organization, I suggest, will create health for its employees and the people and communities it touches.

In this chapter, I explore four theoretical–research approaches to the

I would like to acknowledge the help and support of Bob Rosen, president of the Healthy Companies Project, Alan Westin, chairman of the Research Council, the other members of the team, and all the researchers and organizational consultants who helped me locate resources, critiqued concepts, and reacted to drafts of this chapter.

healthy organization that have appeared in various traditions of organizational psychology and management literature. I look at four major research–practice paradigms: work stress, organizational redesign, human resource policies, and the psychodynamic study of managers. I review the literature within each tradition and examine how that tradition contributes to the concept of a healthy organization. Finally, I explore the links among organizational productivity and effectiveness; employee commitment, motivation, and growth; and employee health and well-being. These three areas, traditionally studied separately, are in fact highly interdependent. This chapter gathers the evidence for this.

Of course, healthy human relationships are only one factor in determining organizational effectiveness. Positive human relationships alone may be important, even necessary, but they are not sufficient for organizational success. Strategy, technology, information systems, and effective structures, for example, are also critical. Several factors exist that are important in determining organizational success. It is the relative contribution of each factor that must be assessed by researchers.

Perspectives on organizational health need to take into account the current difficult environment for organizations. It is a difficult era for every organization because multiple pressures make accomplishing goals ever more difficult. Although there are many contexts, sizes, cultural concerns, and issues facing organizations, certain societal dynamics affect nearly every organization: an environment of continual, fast change; evolution from physical work to knowledge-based work; globalization of organizational culture and competition; diminishing resources, increasing costs, and pressure to do more with less; and greater diversity of workers and work values.

These external and internal shifts affect how organizations are structured and the pressures and challenges they face. A healthy organization in the current environment may look very different from a healthy organization of a former generation. This chapter explores how organizations are changing to meet contemporary demands and changes in the workplace, without sacrificing the well-being of their employees.

Models for Healthy Organization

Can a healthy organization exist, or does the working environment necessarily create pressure and strain on valuable individuals that lead to physical illness and emotional distress? What are the key workplace factors that support personal health? Does the identification of these factors highlight promising lines of empirical research that lead to theoretical models? Can these models be used to make organizations more effective?

It is difficult for researchers to explore healthy organizations. One problem is that we often look at organizational development by focusing on the new technology or organizational structure and how they are used, not on the human context and organizational climate in which they are used. For the latter task, we must clearly and accurately measure the climate and have ways to look at alternatives. Additionally, workplace diversity makes it hard to generalize without high levels of abstraction. Is there anything to be said about organizations in general, or does every healthy organization need to follow a different drummer? Finally, if the ideal or healthy organization does not yet exist, then the study of current examples will necessarily be incomplete and will not include certain key possible dimensions. This is therefore a look at what can be, not at what is.

These concerns are not entirely new. The study of organizational health as it is currently understood actually began in the 1960s as a concern of humanistically oriented researchers, including McGregor (1960), Argyris (1958, 1964), Schein (1986), and Maslow (1965). They were concerned not only with the effectiveness of organizations themselves, but also with how they use their employees. Each researcher published formulations that included the concept of organizational health.

Argyris (1958, 1964) and McGregor (1960) looked most closely at the topic of concern in this chapter. McGregor presented the traditional, bureaucratic model of organization, which he called *Theory X*, and an emerging humanistic model—in which management practices were more supportive, participative, and engaged people's needs to learn—called *Theory Y*. Argyris asked how organizations could fulfill the most essential human needs and still remain effective: Could an effective organization meet the needs of a great number of its employees? Marxist theory had suggested that the individual and the organization were in perpetual conflict, and the rise of labor unions and government regulation tended to reflect that view (Bluestone & Bluestone, 1992). These classics asserted that when an organization is under pressure and needs to adapt and grow, the ability to tap the creative energy and internal commitment of its people, at all levels, is its most important competitive edge. Subsequent research has confirmed many of these hypotheses (Lawler, 1986; Levering, 1988; Peters & Waterman, 1982).

Motivation theorists such as Maslow have noted that work can fulfill not only basic human needs for security, but also higher needs for creativity, competence, meaning, and participation in human community. The traditional organization viewed humans as wanting only extrinsic rewards for their work: pay, promotion, job security, and status. Newer theorists suggest that an organization that engages a person's higher needs could command more commitment and productivity, benefiting both the employees and the organization. For example, Maccoby (1988), a humanistic motivation theorist and business consultant, used interview data from large companies to posit that a healthy company is one that follows a new set of work values—that allows employees at all levels to experience individuation, creativity, and love. Rather than the perpetual conflict posited by the Marxists (Bluestone & Bluestone, 1992) between person and organization or owner and labor, these new theorists suggested that there is the possibility of a common ground, in which all parties can work cooperatively to get their needs met.

Another perspective on organizational health is to view the organization as a personlike entity and propose what elements are needed for it to act as a healthy organism. The organization can be viewed as having needs, drives, and integration, somewhat like a person. Bennis, for example, proposed a model that applied Marie Jahoda's classic definition of individual health, which related four factors—adaptability, sense of identity, capacity to test reality, and integration—to the organization as a whole (reported in Schein, 1986).

By viewing organizations as humanlike systems, it is intriguing to conceptualize each organization as a growing type of living organism, evolving in its own way. One might see the current free enterprise, each-company-for-itself phase as similar to adolescence. The company is narcissistic and self-absorbed, believing that "I know everything" and "I'm the center of the universe"—not acknowledging its connection with others. This is a parasitic stage, which is based on exploitation. The evolving organization needs help in growing to another stage. The next stage of development, which is fast emerging, is a stage of young adulthood, in which relationship, partnership, and interconnectedness become possible and important. This more grown-up organization is a symbiotic one, seeing its growth and development as connected to others. Itself and others can win. Is there anything to this metaphor?

Like humans, organizations develop in response to both environmental demands and an inner biological clock of stages of growth and development. There have been many lifestyle models of stages of organization development, such as Greiner's (1976) classic formulation. As the environment changes, organizations must adapt and change in response. Lawrence and Lorsch (1967) found evidence that the traditional, hierarchical, bureaucratic organization, as has grown over the past century, may not be effective in environments of continual, fast change. In addition, it has been suggested by many of the researchers discussed in following sections that these traditional organizations have the unintended consequence of diminishing the health and well-being of employees by not allowing them to contribute the full measure of their talents and abilities and by creating work environments that threaten long-term health. Although no study has dealt with all of the factors that create organizational well-being, theorists have begun to suggest that new forms of organizational structure may be more supportive of personal health and effectiveness.

Another perspective on healthy organizations comes from realizing that its valuable assets—its people and their level of skills and knowledge—can leave at any time. People, unlike a factory, cannot be owned. If employees exercise their right to leave, then the company is diminished. Thus, a company must learn how to keep its employees there and positively motivated to perform to the highest level of their abilities. Reich (1990), Kelley (1985), and Handy (1989) have suggested that as we move from a production- and machine-centered society to one in which knowledge is king (even in manufacturing), organizations need to look at how they support and retain their employees. There is a vast market for knowledgeable people outside the organization (Bridges, 1994; Reich, 1990). Also, as employees see how valuable they are to the organization, they get more power and leverage to ask for what they want and need. The organization can no longer get away with giving purely extrinsic, or limited, rewards. Employees with more power demand more varied and personalized rewards as well as a voice in governance. This explains some of the recent dynamics in the organizational world.

Today's healthy company, thus, has many reasons for valuing its employees by attending closely to all of their human needs. The organization that best attends to its employees keeps them and gets the most from them. This means attending not only to their needs for basic survival, but also to the higher needs for learning, participation, and meaning. This trend has emerged at a time when organizations, to cut costs and increase productivity, are forced to let many of their employees go. The smaller core of employees that remain begin to realize that they are the key source of value for the company. They thus ask for more incentives, in the form of financial rewards for success, that increasingly include stock or part ownership, and a voice in governance. Employees need more incentives for "membership," and the idea of sharing ownership is common in top management (along with stock options) and is now moving down the organization.

Although employees realize their newly enhanced value and are getting more power and organizations are finding new ways to sustain commitment, innovative creativity, and effectiveness from fewer employees, there are other stakeholder groups who have power. For the organization to be successful and healthy, employee power must be balanced with support for the needs and values of other shareholder groups. The healthy organization must support shareholder value (or whoever is the relevant group to a public organization, the elected representatives, the board, and the contributors). It must also build supplier and customer support with integrity and by offering good value, keeping its agreements, and doing its job well. Support from the community in which it is based and the society in which it is embedded is also necessary. Recent studies of effective companies by Beer, Eisenstat, and Spector (1990) and by Kotter and Heskett (1993) found that success comes not from paying exclusive attention to employees, but from balancing the needs and demands of all stakeholders. Organizations cannot be exclusively employee focused, just as they cannot be just market or stockholder focused. This balance includes a balance of control, influence, and sharing of rewards among the different constituencies. It begins to look like healthy companies must learn what healthy societies have known: how to balance power between different interest groups.

Thus, the model must be broadened by asking, "A healthy company for whom?"

1. It can be healthy for itself by growing, being efficient, being adaptable, and being coherent—following anthropologist Jahoda's four qualities of health, adapted by Bennis to organizations (reported in Schein, 1986).
2. It can be healthy for stockholders by increasing the value of stock and by offering them a positive image of the company.
3. It can be healthy for employees, offering a healthy place for them to work; meeting their highest needs for growth, meaning, and participation; and offering them a workplace and company that they can have pride in.

    It is also important to ask which employees the organization should be healthy for. Some companies have created a healthy environment for top managers but a stifling one for lower levels. Some companies reward executives disproportionately, which suggests that they are more responsible for organizational success—a traditional notion.

4. It can be healthy for suppliers and customers by offering them good service, high value, dependable goods, honest and helpful interactions, good products, and in all ways a good partnership.

5. It can be healthy for the community by seeing itself as interdependent on other resources, taking responsibility for nonrenewable resources, for the viability of the community, and for the concerns of its environment and its people. It can make a long-term commitment to the economic, social, and community development that protects not just its current profits, but also its long-term future. This issue relates to Senge's (1990) mention (from the work of ecologist Garrett Hardin) of "Who speaks for the commons?" Social responsibility investment groups include this category in their decision to invest in a company and sometimes pressure a company to adapt new policies that respect the community.

These different levels of health are not easily accommodated. For example, many organizations find that stockholders' demand for short-term gains appear antithetical to long-term community needs. Or conflict occurs among investment in the long-term value of employees' value to the company, environmental and community pressures, and stockholder demands for higher returns. Also, meeting the demands of Peters and Waterman's (1982) "passion for the customer" can burn out committed employees. Each of these types of health can easily conflict with the others. Therefore, a healthy company must have a good method of discussing, adjudicating, and resolving conflicts between these different constituencies. Meek, Woodworth, and Dyer (1988) suggested that the most difficult and pernicious area of conflict is the one between absent owners and employees and the other constituencies. Therefore, some form of employee ownership may be critical in a healthy organization.

Key Healthy-Company Paradigms

I contacted organization researchers concerning research having a bearing on organizational health. In addition, a literature survey was done in several management libraries. The most surprising experience was that few, if any, empirical researchers looked at organizations in relation to employee health. Although everyone agreed it was important and worth doing, the study of healthy human growth and development within organizations has not yet begun in earnest.

There is almost no history of the study of the particular issue of concern in this chapter. Therefore, this review had to be abstracted from research, case studies, and theoretical accounts that bear on some aspect of personal and organizational health. In effect, this is a first attempt to stake out a domain for study and to integrate relevant sources to consult.

The other discovery was the variety of different fields relevant to the questions of organizational health. Disciplines ranging from medicine, public health, management, psychology, sociology, and anthropology to political science contain relevant data. In addition, there were different literatures on public and private organizations. Despite this diversity, certain major themes emerged.

Four lines of research seemed most relevant. The first, the study of work stress, is one of the most well developed. But most stress research has focused on individual coping and adaptation to stress rather than on work environments and how they can produce or alleviate stress. The second line of research has been organizational redesign, involving management research and action inquiry, which looks at how to create effective workplaces. Its findings suggest intervention methods that might create healthy organizations. This literature has looked primarily at the connection between human behavior and organization effectiveness and not at how workplaces produce health and wellbeing. Third, there is a large literature on human resource policies and their effects on people and the organization. Changing workplaces, and the changing mix of workers, forced changes in organizational policies. The fourth line of research stems from the psychodynamic study of managers and suggests that only a psychologically healthy leader can produce a healthy organization.

None of these four broad disciplinary areas in itself looks at the totality of issues defined as *organizational health*, but together the four disciplinary perspectives, or paradigms, lead to a comprehensive view of both human and organizational growth and development. Each paradigm includes a theoretical perspective on organization and health, a set of variables and relationships that are the focus, and a preferred style of investigation. I consider each separately because they each have a different disciplinary focus, set of research questions, and style of research and do not reference one another's work.

The Job-Stress—Burnout Paradigm

Stress is the intervening psychophysiological variable between workplace factors and individual physical and emotional health. Stress arises from a mixture of the pressure of demanding work conditions and individual responses to them. Negative stress precedes or influences most physical and emotional ailments. Stress is not an objective phenomenon, because different people experience and perceive organizational conditions differently. In addition, because of personal style and history, people respond differently to organizational pressure. Some people experience more stress, and therefore more stress-related dysfunction, than others. Organizational culture includes values about the style of work and how employees manage stress. Different organizations, and different jobs, demand different styles of stress response. It has been suggested (Jaffe & Scott, 1994) that organizations have to select people whose stress-response style fits into the organizational climate.

Stress research has traditionally focused on skills and aspects of the individual's coping with stressful situations. The study of healthy organizations looks beyond this, at workplace factors that regulate and define relationships and structures that amplify or reduce stress. This paradigm includes works examining environmental–workplace factors that create personal stress, physical symptoms, and emotional distress, which may be linked to physical illness and which certainly in turn diminish work performance.

Control and job stress. Karasek and Theorell (1990) offered the most comprehensive and perhaps the only book that makes the link between the work redesign paradigm and the stress paradigm. Its thesis is that, more important than dysfunctional personal coping responses to stress, it may be the very design of workplaces that create ill health. Their research at the Karolinska Institute of Sweden has suggested that only when a workplace begins to redesign itself to create more opportunities for all workers to exercise control and experience social support will it support personal health. This book thus links sociotechnical variables about the nature of the workplace with individual health variables.

To study the healthy individual at work, one has to study the healthy workplace. In their analysis, based on several studies of their own, Karasek and Theorell (1990) examined relationships among several sets of variables. They focused not on the entire workplace but on the qualities of the worker's job. They looked specifically at three variables in relation to work stress: job demands, which is the pressure for results at work; control, which is the degree of discretion for the worker over using skills and allocating work; and social support, which is the positive personal relationships with supervisor and co-workers.

Their model looks at how these three factors interact on the job. They were especially concerned about the links between high-demand work and high and low control. They found that in high-demand–low-control environments (strain), health and stress problems—especially heart disease—are greater than in what they called *active environments*, which are high demand–high control.

Today's workplaces are almost exclusively high-demand environments. Even Karasek and Theorell's (1990) research—much of the data for which was gathered a decade ago—may have underestimated the degree of work demands in current jobs. When there is fast change, restructuring, or downsizing, work demands increase and resources diminish. As employees are given more responsibility and tasks, they face more pressure at work. This is especially true because many employees, especially at lower levels, have spent their entire lives in organizations that diminish their control and responsibility while incurring the number of demands placed on them. However, work environments that emphasize employee control and support are even more necessary today. This research provides a health justification for the shift from a traditional, hierarchical workplace toward one in which there is more employee participation and active involvement in planning and change.

Karasek and Theorell (1990) made a novel addition to their theory in the form of a feedback loop about learning and personal growth. Under threat and pressure, people get more rigid and less flexible and find their perceptions and judgment blocked by intense emotions. In the strain environment, people are inhibited from learning by increasing demands and therefore cannot master their environments. This leads to low morale, illness, lost productivity, and rigidity of response.

In an active work environment, however, people have more opportunity to experiment, learn new skills, and apply them, which leads to greater mastery over stress and therefore greater satisfaction and health. Thus, the two environments get more extreme and differentiated over time, unless resources aid the mastery and learning of people in the strain environment. A workplace where people have control over demands tends to be a learning environment, whereas the more traditional work style tends to inhibit employee learning. This aspect of Karasek and Theorell's (1990) model again suggests that the participatory workplace is more adaptive in a demanding environment.

Karasek and Theorell (1990) suggested that job redesign to provide people with more control and support is a key element in creating healthy workplaces. Workplace democracy, which includes self-determination and empowerment for people at all levels of the organization, is the vehicle for greater organizational health. Greater self-determination and less division of labor leads to more effective work. Karasek and Theorell cited the extensive sociotechnical redesign efforts and research conducted in Sweden and in the United States and suggested that allowing greater discretion and control and providing workers opportunities for continual learning will lead to greater individual health, employee satisfaction, and organizational effectiveness. Karasek and Thorell (1990) documented the positive links between satisfaction and redesign for greater control and provided evidence for the link between redesign and effectiveness. Their theoretical model attempts to provide the link between health and redesign.

One limitation of their study is that it focuses on "job" design rather than on workplaces as a whole. They assumed that jobs can be specified according to the degree of control that a person has over them and focused on programs that increase the discretion that a worker has on the job. However, increasingly, jobs are fluid, multitask, and in continual flux. Bridges (1994) argued that the job is a social artifact and is fast becoming obsolete. As workers in traditional jobs become involved in work enhancement or participate in quality programs, the degree of control that an employee has in a traditionally highly structured, low-control type of work expands. Karasek and Theorell (1990) looked at the progression from job design, to stress, to health. A healthy company model might be concerned with a further link between organizational design and job design.

A related line of research, which supports Karasek and Theorell (1990), comes from the St. Paul Fire and Insurance Companies (1985), malpractice and liability insurers for organizations and hospitals. Research by Jones, Barge, and Kunz (1985) led to the development of the *Human Factors Inventory*, a heavily validated instrument recently revised by the St. Paul companies that assesses employee attitudes about stress in their workplace. The survey is given to every employee in a company choosing to participate and from the results, specific interventions are designed. Intervention is oriented to the at-risk work groups or factors uncovered by the survey.

A representative example of this research is a survey conducted with the employees of the Armstrong Transfer and Storage Company. This survey (*The Human Factor*, 1985) uncovered several risk factors including high personal stress, employee counterproductivity, low morale, alcohol and drug use, and technostress. As a result, a multilevel intervention was designed that affected every aspect of the company. Although not quite an organizational redesign, many policies and aspects of working relationships and environments were modified. Within 3 years, the number of accident claims was cut by half, and workers' compensation and overexertion injuries were cut even more dramatically. Many of the companies that participated in the program experienced similar dramatic drops in claims.

Ongoing research by St. Paul looks not at the individual or his or her job but to the team as the basic work unit. A number of company surveys, followed by interventions, have suggested that the level of stress, commitment, communication, and satisfaction of the team as a whole relates to its level of health as an aggregate. They selected work groups that are high and low stress, as defined by the inventory, and found that high-stress work groups tend to have higher liability and workers compensation claims, accidents, illness, and other related costs. St. Paul's evaluations of case studies of interventions offer evidence that when stress is reduced by improving communication and work relationships, claims (and therefore costs) go down. A review study by Gustello (1993) made a case that group and organizational interventions are more effective than individual ones.

Effective coping: Burnout or hardiness. The other area of focus for the stress paradigm is on the more and less effective responses of individuals to workplace stressors. Many researchers have used the well-validated *Burnout Inventory* (Maslach & Jackson, 1981) and the related (nearly opposite) *Hardiness Scale* (Maddi & Kobasa, 1984) to explore individual coping and health. Maddi and Kobasa developed a model, similar to that of Antonovsky (1987), that suggests factors that can help preserve an executive's ability to manage stress without endangering health and that builds on the stress–coping models of Lazarus (1966, coping styles), who is one of the few coping theorists to focus their research on coping in the workplace. They study the positive coping style that preserves health. They find that hardy (e.g., healthy, stress resistant) managers were also more satisfied with their work. The researchers are not looking at effectiveness of managers, although their data suggest that the healthy executives are also among the more effective.

One factor in hardiness that the researchers have neglected is the factor of social support, which they feel is not correlated with health. But extensive evidence cited by Karasek and Theorell (1990) on social support leads me to believe that support should be added to the hardiness model as a fourth factor (using their C convention, I suggest that it be termed *connection*).

Maddi and Kobasa (1984) presented some research into programs to develop hardiness in employees and suggested that in times of continual change (and therefore high stress, ambiguity, and loss of control), hardiness is a resource that can be developed, and its skills can be valued, encouraged, and even taught in the organization. Their method, unfortunately, is to offer individual or group therapy to employees. They do not deal with organizational factors.

Burnout is an increasingly common term referring to an extreme response to demanding (especially emotionally demanding) work, where the individual becomes depleted and unable to work. The three hardiness factors—commitment, challenge and control—can be seen as the mirror opposites of the three factors that Maslach and Jackson (1981) associated with burnout (emotional exhaustion, depersonalization, and diminished sense of accomplishment).

Although both burnout and hardiness refer to individual responses, research has begun to look at workplace factors that produce high and low burnout, or hardiness. For example, Golembiewski, Munzenrider, and Stevenson (1986) administered the Burnout Inventory to all employees in several organizations. Supporting the St. Paul Fire and Marine Insurance Companies (1985) findings, they found that burnout was a quality of the work team, rather than the individual. If one person was burned out, then it was likely the rest of the team was as well. Their book proposes a developmental-phase model of the progressive development of burnout in an organization. It suggests that in many workplaces, especially the two public organizations that they studied, that burnout—experienced as diminished commitment, involvement, and satisfaction in work—is very prevalent. Golembiewski et al. then looked at workplace factors that produce burnout, especially work and team relationships, and concluded that the workplace and especially the relationships of a work team, not personal factors, are the key contributors to burnout.

The Work Redesign–Organizational Development Paradigm

This approach looks at the specific organizational forms, processes, and models that influence people's motivation, satisfaction, and effectiveness at work. It presumes that people are motivated by internal desires for meaning, growth, participation, and making a difference, as well as by external needs for reward, status, and security. Research into organizational design and employee response has suggested that workplaces allowing for satisfaction of these intrinsic motivations will be more effective, more fulfilling, and, by implication, more healthy.

The role of employee participation. The field of organizational development—built on the humanistic psychology assumptions of Lewin (1951), Maslow (1965), and McClelland (1975)—has developed into a whole field of study and practice that in the past decade has changed the shape of organizations. A good example of the history and the technology of this approach can be found in Weisbord's (1987) book, which presents the organizational development (now increasingly called *organizational redesign*) perspective that understanding of these existential human concerns leads to effective organizations.

These factors are becoming critical and are making a difference in the workplace. More and more organizations are experimenting with self-management, flattened hierarchy, and participation—not just in the design of individual jobs, but also in the governance and planning for the future of the entire organization. Participants range from team-oriented factories to entire organizations owned by employees in which there are almost no hierarchical relationships. A continuum of levels of participation and intrinsic motivation can thus be envisioned to develop from individual job expansion, to team participation, to employee ownership. Changes in the workplace can then be assessed according to how much self-management they promote.

The first and classic studies of the individual and the organization were conducted by Argyris (1958), who applied the then-new ideas of Maslow (1965) to look at how workplaces frustrate individuals' needs to make a difference and to do meaningful work. In an article in the *Harvard Business Review* (1960), Argyris suggested that organizations that keep employees apathetic, happy, detached, and uninvolved will be successful only so long as the company lacks competition and is not growing. When there is change and stress, such traditional, paternalistic companies will not adapt successfully. This classic formulation seems prophetic today, as do many of the prescriptions in his 1964 book.

Lawler (1986) documented research that was based on evolving workplace practices and suggested that different levels of employee involvement make the workplace more effective and make employees more satisfied. He supported Karasek and Theorell's (1990) model by suggesting that the more employees can be involved in decision making and taking responsibility for work results, the more effective an organization will be. In times of change where there is increased pressure for productivity and an increase in speed to market, participation is a tool for heightening organizational responsiveness. Lawler (1986) and associates surveyed the evidence and types of activity that make up workplaces in which people are treated as adults, are informed, and are involved in making decisions and in accepting responsibility for results. Lawler also showed the variety of approaches to work involvement and participation and some of the research methods that can be used to facilitate and assess its results.

Kanter (1984) studied innovative and financially successful companies through survey, observation, interview, and gathering of indirect data (e.g., financial results and annual reports). She documented the emerging work model that is replacing the traditional hierarchy. Combining sociology and social psychology with a learning model, she suggested that companies that have learned how to allow employees to learn are more able to innovate and develop new ideas. These companies will be the successors and the survivors in the current turbulent business environment. By focusing on innovation as a form of adaptiveness, Kanter showed that companies harnessing the creative energy of employees are more able to meet the new pressures for continual evolution. Her assumption was that work structure determines work relations and that innovation, therefore, has to be embedded in organizational structures, norms, and practices.

One interesting recent offshoot of the organization development school has to do with organizational learning. This approach, more theoretical than empirical, examines the developmental processes that create a self-managing, self-learning system. Research has been initiated by Argyris and Schon (1978) and extended by Senge (1990). Although there is less research to support organizational learning, it offers a powerful theoretical model and extends the organizational-development paradigm into a model that is based on continual learning. Continual learning in an individual represents growth, challenge, creativity, and engagement of higher human needs by the organization. The organizational-learning approach adds a growth dimension to models that is based on satisfaction of basic human needs. These researchers suggested that an organization cannot improve unless it can continually learn and relate organizational learning to processes that support individual learning.

In more recent looks at organizational redesign, Kanter (1989), Beer et al. (1990), and Kotter and Heskett (1993) have noted that successful organizations are not just inwardly focused. The boundary of the organization—as it begins to take on more strategic partnerships, to emphasize customer service, and to collaborate with suppliers and community members—becomes less and less clear. Where does the organization end? Therefore, as I have suggested earlier, employees are only one constituency that participates in governance and control. Newer accounts of organizational redesign include involvement of each of these stakeholders in major decisions. Employees attend stockholders meetings; customers and suppliers work on product development; and employees work with the community on philanthropy, education, and pollution control.

Are healthy companies more profitable and effective? Another way of looking at the success of companies that practice the principles that the above theorists have associated with organizational success and employee well-being is to look at case studies of companies that apply these principles. In the past few years, the *Harvard Business Review* has published several accounts of how complete organizational redesign toward nonhierarchical, supportive, flexible structures—with employee participation, profit sharing, responsibility, empowerment, and authority to make policy—can lead to powerful improvements in both morale and effectiveness. Accounts by Semler (1989), about a large Brazilian company, and Strayer (1990), about Johnsonville Sausage, for example, showed how the model proposed in this paradigm can work. These accounts challenge the traditional Theory X management assumptions that organizations need levels, that people on the top must make policy and decisions, that democracy cannot work in organizations, and that people do not want to work, and they show Theory Y in action.

Works by Levering (1988) and by Lloyd (1990) have looked at the qualities, policies, and values exhibited in the culture of the company and compared them with the outcomes of employee satisfaction and organizational effectiveness. Their surveys have supported this linkage. Levering (1988) abstracted from observations of successful companies that also have positive employee morale to propose a model of a healthy workplace. His inductive model was based on development of trust in the workplace and the key factors that employees reported make up a good workplace. This model links personal satisfaction with one's workplace and with the effectiveness of the organization, and it includes trust, participation, progressive human resource policies, and shared rewards, reflecting the findings of other work redesign researchers. Levering used data gathered from his research on several of the 100 Best Companies in intensive site visits to each of the selected workplaces. He provided evidence that these companies significantly outperform the Standard and Poor Index of financial performance.

Lloyd (1990), a British economist, proposed a well-developed theory of why companies need to, and will, evolve in the direction of altruism, cooperation, and examination of the long-term consequences of their behavior. He used evolutionary theory and research on the game Prisoners' Dilemma, which tests the tendency to cooperate or compete with others, to theorize that companies that adopt a cooperative response to stakeholders will be more successful over time. Applying research from the Prisoners' Dilemma game— which concludes that the strategy of "tit for tat," or responding cooperatively if the other person (organization, customer, employee, competitor, or interest group) does, but standing up for one's interests if the other is competitive or aggressive—Lloyd suggested that such self-protective but cooperative behavior is the best strategy for long-term effectiveness and survival of the organization.

Conducting a study of hostile versus cooperative mergers, Lloyd (1990) found that companies that practiced cooperative mergers far outperformed those that conducted hostile ones by using several measures of financial performance over time. He then categorized British companies as either *nice* or *nasty*, depending on whether they had engaged in any hostile takeovers of other companies. He assumed that the outer behavior of companies was reflected in their internal processes and relationships. The 57 nice companies outperformed the 34 nasty ones by 86%, a figure resulting from a variety of measures of financial success.

Lloyd's (1990) definition of *niceness* was parallel in almost every way to the currently emerging model of a healthy company. He concluded that cooperation as a corporate strategy is more effective for organizations. He explored sharing and cooperation between employees and management, with shareholders, and in the marketplace as adaptive to the organization. Finally, he reported on other studies that revealed similar advantages in financial health for socially responsible companies. One such study reported that between 1974 and 1980 the nice firms grew faster (14% vs. 9%), were more profitable (7% vs. 5% margins), and received higher returns on equity (15% vs. 10%). Lloyd's book represents the most impressive current gathering of data suggesting that the healthy organization is indeed more profitable.

Study of exceptional people and practices. Another research approach (Maccoby, 1988) within the organization-development paradigm selects exceptional managers, leaders, or innovators and explores the personal qualities, skills, and tactics that are key to their effectiveness as well as those such traits that are desired by employees. Many organizations have begun to identify such key competencies. In defining these core skills, researchers (e.g., Maccoby, 1988) use critical incidents—accounts given by exceptional people about what they did in actual key organizational decisions or activities. An analysis of themes in their accounts leads to skill sets that can then be taught, supported, reinforced, and mandated within organizations. This approach goes back to research on self-actualization by Maslow (1965) and humanistic psychology research. Kouzes and Posner (1988) identified leadership skills with critical incidents and survey data. They had leaders write up some of their "personal best leadership experiences." From these responses, they developed their *Leadership Practices Inventory*. This method is an excellent way to research desired practices that might lead to more healthy company practices.

Other recent organizational self-help books, such as Covey's (1989), are long on prescriptions for healthy work relationships that they predict will affect company effectivensss, but, unfortunately, they often contain several weaknesses. They are often very short on empirical evidence (with the exception of the work of Kanter, 1984, and Kouzes & Posner, 1988), and, like research in the stress paradigm, they tend to take the individual perspective that individual coping, rather than work factors, produces organizational success and well-being. A third weakness is that these formulations have relied on what individuals say, rather than on observations or empirical descriptions of what they have done and on how behavior is interpreted by others. This is important because exceptional leaders may unintentionally see their roles as more pivotal than others do.

Corporate Policies That Promote Health

A third perspective on organizational health explores corporate policies and a workplace culture that influence opportunities for employee control and participation, for social support, and for meeting individual needs. These affect individual and organizational health. Corporate human resource policies deeply affect how people experience life in the organization. Policies and structures that provide psychological security, as much as possible within a changing environment, and that provide pathways and outlets for people to contribute to the organization can be expected to influence both personal health and the effectiveness of the organization.

Within this perspective, organizational health can be said to consist of two somewhat overlapping aspects: (a) cultural factors, which are the qualities of the culture, norms, values, relationships, expectations, and leadership of an organization; and (b) policy factors, which are the policies, programs, and initiatives by the company designed as benefits or as aspects of its human resource policy.

From culture to policies. Schein (1985) noted that an organization's culture is very difficult to study. He suggested that single methodological approaches (such as surveys and interviews) can produce only a superficial and limited picture. His anthropological approach involved looking at cultures as wholes and using every possible source of information to interpret and understand the nature of a culture. This approach is the opposite of approaches taken by many management and social science researchers, who look at factors, policies, practices, and qualities in isolation from the whole. The reasons for this is that it is harder, and less clear, to define and observe whole cultures. Exploring culture is an active, interpretive process that involves employees in the process. Cultural factors are much deeper within the fabric of the organization, much more difficult to change, and much less conscious to people within organizations than policies are. However, cultures define the norms about how people are respected and treat each other, how work is defined and structured, and what is valued. These norms certainly are critical to both individual and organizational health and, in turn, lead to specific policies and practices.

Policies are one expression of a culture. They have been more of a focus than culture as a whole because, unlike culture, policies are conscious and unambiguous (in definition, not in practice). They are much easier to change because they are specified and can be modified without necessarily changing the awareness and personal perspectives of a large number of people. They are not as deeply tied to the beliefs of the organization. It may be that a change in policy, as will be outlined below, will influence the culture and values of the organization. Policies have both a formal statement and an informal style by which they are implemented and interpreted. In studying policies, researchers need to move from formal policy statements to examining how an organization actually uses the policy and how the policy affects people.

Although policies (and practices) are critical to organizational health, the exploration of organizational health should not stop with policies but should extend to the cultural style and norms of the organization. Next, however, I present specific areas of focus for organizational policies that promote health.

Healthy policies for the new workforce. Today's workforce increasingly contains diverse cultures, sexes, values, ages, physical capacities, needs, ethnic groups, and family structures. A classic longitudinal study by Bray, Capbell, and Good (1974) of 20 years of development among AT&T managers and a comparison group in the late 1970s, documented the vast changes in the workplace, without exploring their organizational consequences. Enhancing individual health for everyone demands organizational policies that take into account the differing needs of such a multifaceted workforce. In addition, several megafactors pressure organizations to develop policies or responses to these issues, or face extinction. These factors include the following:

1. Increasing health costs, especially in preventable and stress-related areas, such as workers' compensation claims.
2. Projected shortage of employees who have the skills needed in the information-based workplace.
3. Erosion of the traditional, paternalistic job contract—where an employer was expected to "take care" of employees and, in turn, to offer "job security"—because of downsizing, mergers, and restructurings. Loyalty and commitment declines on both sides.
4. New values and expectations among "gold-collar" and other valuable and scarce workers that lead workers to demand greater freedom, autonomy, personal growth, involvement in work, and new work arrangements (i.e., flextime, work at home, and influence on how work is structured).

5.   The differing needs of the many cultural and value groups who demand
     different styles of supervision and different policies from organiza-
     tions. In addition to ethnic differences, there are value, age, and family
     structure differences.

Jamison and O'Mara (1991) looked at human resource policies for this
workforce. They defined a useful model on the basis of observations of the
policies of 133 companies. The encouragement of personal health in an organization, in their model, demands a flex-management model that extends corporate policies, practices, and policies into four key areas: matching people
and jobs, managing and rewarding performance, informing and involving people, and supporting lifestyle and life needs.
     Jamison and O'Mara (1991) suggested that companies need to adopt pol-
icies that support diversity and human growth in each of these areas. The new
policies begin with recruitment and extend to the everyday policies for appraisal and supervision. These policies are so much a part of the fabric of
companies that they are often not reviewed when a company begins to change.
However, if a policy contradicts an organizational value or goal, it can frustrate
or inhibit change, creating further stress. Jamison and O'Mara's book is a
veritable encyclopedia of new work policies and programs, all linked together
by an intriguing, holistic, and easy to apply conceptual framework. Some of
the major focus areas for new policies are described next.

1.   Diversity. Companies are offering training and employment policies
     that help people manage positively the growing diversity of cultures
     and values in the workplace. They are retraining supervisors to take
     into account these differences and to move away from the White-male−
     centric view of employees. In addition to training programs, policies
     of recruitment, supervision, performance evaluation, work rules, ca-
     reer development, and team relations are being reassessed to take into
     account these new realities, leading to broader changes in organiza-
     tional culture.
2.   Work and family. The traditional one-worker−two-parent family is
     almost extinct, as single parent and two-employee families vastly out-
     number the old norm. Organizations that allow flexibility for personal
     and family needs—through providing flexible hours, day care, part-
     time work, home-based work, and by respecting the concerns and needs
     of children and family—are finding that this is a stress reducer that
     increases morale and productivity.
3.   New work arrangements. The traditional nine-to-five day, designed
     for factories, is giving way in the information age to flexible policies
     in all areas. The rise of knowledge work, that is, work that involves
     the gathering, analysis, and creation of information, is allowing people
     to work at home, to set their own hours, and to create new structures
     for coordination and integration of work. Many of these arrangements
     stem from the work redesign movement.
4.   Career planning. Previously, employees planned to move up the pyr-

amid, to work at one or maybe two companies during a career, or to remain in roughly the same job for their entire working lives. This expectation has given way to a whole new procedure. People shift more quickly, and organizations need people with more competencies and more flexibility. People who work in a company want opportunities to learn, develop, and exercise new skills and to know what opportunities they will have in a future, flatter, leaner organization. The new organization values people who have several skills or competencies and who are familiar with several areas of a company. Handy (1989) and others have noted that the traditional career progress of moving up within one company or within a few involves a person following a straight line of development, intensifying his or her skill in a narrow area. The emerging career progression, he noted, is a portfolio, compiled by a person through taking on a series of challenges, learning several skills, and maybe even cycling through vastly different careers and types of organizations. This is true not only for managers but for people at all levels of an organization. To build positive motivation and commitment, these more confusing and more diverse options need to be supported by organizations. Organizations that provide career development, career pathing, and help and support in relocating are viewed by knowledge workers as more humane, challenging, and desirable. Such companies are developing their human assets, rather than continually trying to recruit people with the desired skills who may be less committed or familiar with the organization.

5. Healthy environments for knowledge work. The factory-based workplace is giving way to the service- or knowledge-based workplace, according to Handy (1989), Reich (1990), Zuboff (1988), and Kelley (1985). Although there is less hard physical labor, there are unique and additional stresses and consequences of information work that produce their own unique ailments. Studies of work environments, in terms of ergonomics and the psychological consequences of such work, have revealed that some changes and reforms are needed in the knowledge-based workplace. Howard (1985) wrote a critique of the new workplace, suggesting that it contains many dehumanizing hazards; Zuboff studied the consequences of the new computer-based workplace and suggested that it provides a double-edged sword that can be used for domination or liberation, depending on how its policies are implemented. For example, such workplaces promote democracy, generalized skills, information flow, and teamwork but also deprive people of sensory feedback, personal context, and variety.

6. Ethics and fair treatment policies. The psychological work contract expresses the implicit assumptions that employees and workplaces expect from each other. This contract has been shifting drastically in recent years, as employers limit what they offer to employees. The new contract, assumed by many companies, limits the responsibility of the employer to the employee and reduces paternalism and what can be expected from employment. This has produced anger, confusion,

pain, and uncertainty. Employees perceive, rightly, that the rules have changed in midgame, and often the company is not entirely candid or clear itself about the nature or extent of the shift. Companies have been forced to clarify their norms for treatment of employees as they are changing and reducing their workforces and, sometimes, to defend them in court. Misunderstandings and confusion are common. Companies respond to this by clarifying and codifying their policies, creating ombudspersons and procedures to support and guarantee fair treatment. These provide a legal base for people to understand the nature of the bond between company and employee. See Jaffe, Scott, and Tobe (1994) for a review of the emerging model of the new psychological work contract.

7. Employee ownership. Employee control and satisfaction, as well as health, may lead to pressure for the actual experience of sharing ownership of the organization. Employees may ask, "If I change and become more productive, and deepen my responsibility and commitment, what will I get in return?" They are demanding more control and more resources, which puts them in conflict with another stakeholder group— the owners. One aspect of empowerment and shared responsibility is actual ownership of the organization. Levering (1988) suggested that employee-owned workplaces create greater satisfaction and effectiveness. This suggests that the employee-owned workplace may be similar to the healthy workplace envisioned by Karasek and Theorell (1990). Quarrey and Rosen (1991), in their review article, surveyed the existing research on effects of employee ownership. Their major finding was that employee ownership in itself has no effect on corporate performance, unless it is accompanied by a participation program so that employees experience psychological as well as financial ownership. Among a matched group of companies, they found that when ownership was accompanied by participative management, the growth rate of companies increased significantly. In addition, employees had more positive feelings about the company, stayed longer on the job, and had more information to perform their jobs more effectively. Their findings suggest that employee learning is heightened for a significant group of employee–owners, who therefore are able to contribute more to the fortunes of the company and in turn feel better about their involvement in the company.

The Social–Psychodynamic Paradigm

It has long been noted that the character of strong leaders deeply marks their organizations. Many companies with strong cultures and values reflect the values stamped on them by their founders. In other ways, the personal character of employees is an important factor in how healthy an organization can be. Organizational character can also reflect dysfunctional societal values, for example, when a company embodies a "win at all costs," "competition is like war," or "if you're not exhausted you aren't really working" orientation. A series of researchers has looked at the possibility of a healthy organization arising when enough of the individuals within the organization have reached a life phase of personal health and can, in turn, impart these values to the culture. Instead of looking at how the organization affects the individual, this paradigm looks at how individual and social character affect the organization. Its leading figures include Levinson (1983), Maccoby (1988), Kaplan (1991), and Kets de Vries and Miller (1984). This view is leadership focused, and one of its key insights is that the organization, often very early in its development, takes on the personality characteristics and even the level of maturity of its founder. These qualities outlast the individual leader, but until the leadership grows and develops, the organization is stuck.

In contrast with the redesign and human resource perspectives, this perspective sees organizations as very difficult to change, reflecting its roots in psychodynamic theory, which presupposes a highly intractable character structure. Nonetheless, psychodynamic researchers have looked deeply at the qualities that individuals bring to their work, what motivates them, and the nature of highly pathological organizations. Their perspective complements the other paradigms I have discussed and offers both insights and a methodology for looking at how organizations come to be so unique, at the deepest level of individual–work relationships. Organizations, these researchers remind us, are the primary vehicle through which many people choose to express their life commitment, their personal identity, or their life meaning. Therefore, because organizations mean so much to some individuals, especially those at the top, attempts to get these people to change are much more difficult.

In addition, the conception of the unconscious suggests that there are experiences within organizations that remain hidden from ordinary awareness. Just as in the case of an individual unconscious, if there is an organizational unconscious, then rational or conscious attempts to change or modify organizations will be curiously incomplete or ineffective. Such has been the experience of many interventionists who have tried to change organizations.

This paradigm looks at the psychodynamic issues in development of work relationships, leadership, and career development. Its research is conducted through intensive psychotherapy, interviewing, case studies, and the clinical method—rather than surveys—and tries to apply conceptions of unconscious psychodynamic processes to the organization. Rather than studying many organizations broadly, this paradigm looks deeply at a very few cases for its insights. It also applies psychodynamic formulations of impairment to organizational situations.

Organizations are seen as manifestations of the level of the leader's development. The organization, especially the pathological one, is viewed as a reflection, or re-creation, of the founder's character. In effect, the leader causes the organization to be functional, healthy, or dysfunctional. Healthy organizations arise when healthy people start them and, in turn, select healthy people for healthy reasons to do the tasks needed to grow the organization.

There are two major subparadigms. The first is researchers who fit psychodynamic formulations into a cultural context. They look at the interaction of personal and life cycle development and how the organization is influenced and affected by social values and cultural issues. The work of LaBier (1986), Kaplan (1991), and Maccoby (1988) exemplifies this social–psychoanalytic approach.

A second group consists of researchers who use models of early psychodynamic personality development to explain organizational issues. This group— including Levinson (1983), Kets de Vries and Miller (1984), and Hirschhorn (1988)—sees organizations as reservoirs for projection of intrapsychic issues and as undermined in their work tasks by their capacity to help people fulfill psychic defense operations. They see organizations brought down because people's fears, anxieties, and needs for security are more influential on their behavior than their aspirations and goals. Organizations become unhealthy because people's anxieties divert them from their espoused function. Organizations are not in conflict with people, as in the Marxist perspective but, rather, people are in conflict with organizations. Their research model often suggests that organizational problems stem from the leaders' psyche. In effect, they frequently look at the organization as a projection, or construction, of the leader. Their approach to health is also personalistic: Heal the leader and you heal the organization.

Social psychodynamics. Maccoby's (1988) work has been the most methodologically precise and empirically based. He explored factors that create positive work motivation. He sought out exemplars of effective management in several large companies and used a methodology that combined participative study, open-ended interviews, and surveys of these high achievers. Executives from several public and private organizations were involved in the study as collaborators. They were interviewed at length about their work, values, aspirations, family life, and key formative experiences. After 20 or 30 interviews have been completed the team analyzes them and creates working typologies that will be tested out with further interviews and surveys. This is a much deeper, reflective, and interactive version of the key-competency research method.

Maccoby's (1988) sample represents a criterion of excellence (e.g., high-tech managers and State Department leaders). His project focused on the relation between their values and performance and thus offers a yardstick with which to compare others. Maccoby's research teams included representatives of the group being studied to help with the selection process, which made the research process collaborative. He reported that more and more employees, at all levels, experienced themselves as "knowledge" workers—motivated by meaning, internal commitment, participation, and a desire to shape the future of the organization. Perhaps unlike previous generations, today's workforce demands and desires responsibility and connection to broader organizational issues.

LaBier (1986) suggested that social demands, unrealistic expectations of reward, and the values and character of the modern workplace add to the psychic stress of individuals and make it difficult for successful executives to experience well-being. His research might be considered the dark side of Maccoby's (1988) formulations. Issues such as the underutilization of people's talent; the lack of personally validating career paths; and rewards for bullying and oppressive behavior within traditional, presumably unhealthy organizations all create distrust and conflict in individuals. LaBier looked at how the values that define success generate conflict for the most successful achievers. In addition, these employees may not be consciously aware of the costs of their success or its relation to the structure and values of their workplaces.

Kaplan (1991) and associates studied 40 top managers in depth, looking at the dynamics, origins, and effects of their driven style. Their research model is highly intensive, using deep involvement, assessment instruments, extensive personal feedback, depth interviewing, and organizational development work with their organizations. All of their formulations are shared with the subject and are mutually validated.

Kaplan's (1991) model looks at how leaders can manage to grow personally and also achieve breakthroughs in their leadership. Although not directly concerned with organizational health, his findings suggest that even though there is an intense focus on work in these driven people, the key to health and effectiveness lies in achieving some sort of balance between work and personal life. Kaplan also looked at the generation of self-esteem in cases in which the manager must respond to situations that generate high anxiety. He was especially interested in how managers grow in high-anxiety (e.g., high-stress or high-demand) environments. His concern was to avoid the fate described by LaBier (1986) and to create workplaces that provide learning experiences to develop new managers, without negative personal consequences. Kaplan saw every manager as inevitably confronting costs and trade-offs in adapting to his or her organizational niche. Each of these psychodynamic models suggests pathways for workplaces to redefine motivations, working relationships, and implicit expectations to support psychological health and well-being.

The organizational unconscious. The second subparadigm was best illustrated in a book by Kets de Vries and Miller (1984). Using several case studies, they looked at organizations as having unconscious personalities that can be considered neurotic. These neurotic corporate styles stemmed from the personality dynamics of the leader–founder and became structured into the culture and process of the organization. Adopting psychodynamic practice, they suggested that therapeutic consultation could help correct these difficulties. Viewing the organization as an organism much like a person is revelatory, but it is also limited in that psychotherapeutically based methods of changing an organization or creating organizational health are very costly and time consuming and they deal with changing executive character rather than other aspects of organization.

Smith (1993), a professor at the Wharton School, provided some curious support for the model of organizational unconsciousness. He was struck by the high incidence of cancer in one organization that he worked with. Looking at other organizations, he found that some of them, especially those under stress, produced a prevalence of certain ailments in their employees. He is currently defining the qualities of organizations that tend to produce cancer, heart disease, depression, and some ailments. Meanwhile, he has defined typologies for pathological organizations, such as *runaway companies*, which have inadequate boundaries, and *gridlocked companies*, which repeat patterns that people find it difficult to escape from. In a similar perspective, Shaef and Fassel (1988) have used the addiction paradigm to look at how organizations produce addictive and codependent behavior in employees.

Integrating the Four Paradigms for Action

The four research–action paradigms have largely developed in isolation from one another. Their research is based within different disciplines, and they have not developed a common language or tradition of looking at their common implications. Policies have been created to respond to organizational needs, and the diverse research traditions have been pursued in different academic departments, with researchers of various backgrounds and relationships to the organizations they study. Therefore, when a convergence is found, it should be attended to.

Despite the paucity of research bearing directly on healthy organizations, data from the four paradigms suggest common themes and dimensions that can be combined to inform issues of organizational health. Research today tends to cross the paradigms more and more. For example, Karasek and Theorell's (1990) research within the stress paradigm has led them into the work redesign paradigm. Psychodynamic and work redesign researchers share a common perspective on humanistic motivations—suggesting that a working person has complex values and motivations, which a savvy workplace must address. Organizational policies reflect insights from work redesign researchers.

The core issues that have been presented as arising from the stress paradigm—commitment, control, and social support—are central to the work redesign literature. Both paradigms suggest that a workplace where people are treated with respect, which allows employees freedom to design their jobs and how they work together to achieve results, which provides personal support and sense of community, and which makes allowances for outside family involvement supports employee well-being and organizational effectiveness. Quarrey and Rosen (1991), Levering (1988), Ludeman (1989), and Lloyd (1990) have gone further, suggesting that these workplaces lead to more profitable and productive companies as well. These factors emerge clearly from their research and observations. The research issues for the future appear to be measuring these factors in the workplace, mapping their interaction, and finding interventions that increase their prevalence.

Every company today seems to espouse work values of respect for employees, communication, shared responsibility, empowerment, and teamwork. However some companies have far less of these in evidence than others. In some organizations, a single visionary supervisor, or unit manager, may allow greater employee freedom and support than another, which is in line with the research of the psychodynamic paradigm. Sadly, other managers tend to have blind spots about their own performance and abilities, such that the managers who have the most difficulty in allowing employee freedom and self-expression are often those who feel that they have this in abundance. Dealing with the personal blind spots of leaders and managers is the concern of the psychodynamic researchers, and this seems critical to creating organizational health. If individual managers cannot learn to understand the consequences of their own behavior, then no amount of policies or programs can produce health within an organization. Also, organizations espouse values or institute policies that their actual behavior by organizational representatives may not reflect.

There is a promising convergence among these four paradigms. Each offers important insights into healthy companies. Stress research defines the core factors that individuals need for health and well-being. Work redesign presents a powerful technology for developing the new workplace and a vision of what the nonbureaucratic, shared-control workplace looks like. Employee needs in this paradigm are similar to the needs identified by the stress researchers. Corporate policies seem to reflect and offer data to support the other paradigms. The psychodynamic paradigm explores the blind spots and blockages in individual leaders that prevent them from allowing other people the freedom and self-expression that they need for well-being; it also offers some hints about why leaders continue to pursue self-defeating and even destructive paths in their organizations. The motivational assumptions of all four paradigms that see working people as having complex needs, desiring to make a difference, and searching for meaningful work, are similar. Finally, all the research models point to workplaces that are designed and embody different corporate policies than many organizations have today. The pragmatics of what policies support effective and humane workplaces are suggested in human resource literature, and, happily, these emerging policies are in line with the findings of researchers in the other three paradigms.

Abstracting from research within all four paradigms, there are several values or qualities that appear to promote individual and organizational health and well-being. The more that organizational norms, policies, behaviors, and culture support human needs for security, personal growth, participation and involvement, and meaning, the healthier the organization will be. The research cited here also suggests that such factors will lead to greater productivity and effectiveness.

At a time when the employee–organization work contract is strained by downsizing, cutbacks, lower expectations, and unexpected changes, these factors create a framework by which individual needs can be balanced with organizational imperatives. If the organization must negotiate a different implicit psychological work contract with its employees that is more limited and less entitling and paternalistic than in the past, then the company must take care to create connection with its people that supports all of their human needs.

Conclusion

In this chapter, I have explored the theoretical and research literature that defines the concept of the healthy organization. I have reviewed literature that defines the qualities making up a healthy organization, rather than focusing on particular organizations. I have also presented different perspectives on how such organizations develop and how they can be created with professional intervention.

The literature on organizational health has been separated into several paradigms or discipline—research—action perspectives. Their data and models converge around certain core concepts, and what sparse data that exist seem to support these generalizations. But their themes are very broad generalizations, in need of much more empirical support to define them operationally, to measure their presence, and to detect their dynamics.

The core concept of the healthy organization appears to suggest that the key to health lies in the redefinition of the relationships, expectations, obligations, and interactions between employees and organizations. Currently, and traditionally, organizations have not been responsible for giving employees very much, other than some rudimentary safeguards and competitive wages. The concept of organizational health suggests that organizations might benefit by seeing their relation with the person in far broader terms. Each party — employee and organization — must take on added responsibility and give more, but in return each will also receive more value from one another. This mutually beneficial contract may help the organization derive more value from its human assets, just as it may offer more to the employee.

The model of employee—organization relationship is less like the traditional work contract and more like the social contract of a democracy. Although organizational "citizens" have more responsibility on a daily basis than societal citizens, the concept suggests that they are treated by the organization as full adults, with certain rights, and that the contract implies serious obligations for both parties. The concept of human rights and democracy, which underlies many of the theories promoting health in individuals and organizations, is one that has only recently begun to be explored within organizations. The new social contract in the healthy organization sees its employees as adults who can contribute greatly to the organization, provided they are given outlets for basic security and their higher needs are met — for meaning, learning, information, and participation. On another level, the organization must take seriously its responsibility as a part of its community and the world by entering into ethical, fair, open, and balanced relationships with its owners, customers, families of employees, suppliers, and community. A healthy organization in the community must engage a broader constellation of concerns, just as it must deal with the broader needs of each individual. This is an exciting model — a vision of organizations that help their employees learn and grow and are helpful and responsible to their broader communities. The literature on healthy companies defines such an exciting vision of the employee—organization—community linkage.

References

Antonovsky, A. (1987). *Unraveling the mystery of health.* San Francisco: Jossey-Bass.

Argyris, C. (1958). The organization: What makes it healthy? *Harvard Business Review.*

Argyris, C. (1964). *Integrating the individual and the organization.* New York: Wiley.

Argyris, C., & Schon, D. (1978). *Learning organizations.* Reading, MA: Addison-Wesley.

Beer, M., Eisenstat, R. A., & Spector, B. (1990). *The critical path for corporate renewal*. Cambridge, MA: Harvard Business School Press.

Bluestone, B. J., & Bluestone, I. (1992). *Negotiating the future*. New York: Basic Books.

Bray, D. G., Capbell, R. J., & Good, D. L. (1974). *Formative years in business*. New York: Wiley.

Bridges, W. (1994). *Jobshift*. Reading, MA: Addison-Wesley.

Covey, S. R. (1989). *The seven habits of highly effective people*. New York: Simon & Schuster.

Cox, A. (1982). *The Cox report on the American corporation*. New York: Delacorte.

Golembiewski, R. T., Munzenrider, R. F., & Stevenson, J. G. (1986). *Stress in organizations: Toward a phase model of burnout*. New York: Praeger.

Greiner, L. (1976). Evolution and revolution as organizations grow. *Harvard Business Review*.

Gustello, S. J. (1993). Do we really know how well our occupational accident prevention programs work? *Safety Science, 16*.

Handy, C. (1989). *The age of unreason*. Cambridge, MA: Harvard University Press.

Hirschhorn, L. (1988). *The workplace within*. Cambridge, MA: MIT Press.

Howard, R. (1985). *Brave new workplace*. New York: Penguin Books.

Jaffe, D., & Scott, C. (1994). *Self-renewal*. Los Altos, CA: Crisp.

Jaffe, D., Scott, C., & Tobe, G. (1994). *Rekindling commitment*. San Francisco: Jossey-Bass.

Jamison, D., & O'Mara, J. (1991). *Managing workforce 2000*. San Francisco: Jossey-Bass.

Kanter, R. (1984). *The change masters*. New York: Simon & Schuster.

Kanter, R. (1989). *When giants learn to dance*. New York: Simon & Schuster.

Kaplan, R. (1991). *Beyond ambition: How driven managers can lead better and live better*. San Francisco: Jossey-Bass.

Karasek, R., & Theorell, T. (1990). *Healthy work: Stress, productivity, and the reconstruction of working life*. New York: Basic Books.

Kelley, R. E. (1985). *The gold collar worker*. Reading, MA: Addison-Wesley.

Kets de Vries, M. F. R., & Miller, D. (1984). *The neurotic organization*. San Francisco: Jossey-Bass.

Kotter, J., & Heskett, T. (1993). *Corporate culture and performance*. New York: Free Press.

Kouzes, J., & Posner, B. (1988). *The leadership edge*. San Francisco: Jossey-Bass.

LaBier, D. (1986). *Modern madness: The emotional fallout of success*. Reading, MA: Addison-Wesley.

Lawler, E. E., III. (1986). *High-involvement management*. San Francisco: Jossey-Bass.

Lawrence, P. R., & Lorsch, J. W. (1967). *Organization and environment*. Cambridge, MA: Harvard University Press.

Lazarus, R. S. (1966). *Psychological stress and the coping process*. New York: McGraw-Hill.

Levering, R. (1988). *A great place to work*. New York: Random House.

Levinson, H. (1983). Reciprocation: The relationship between man and the organization. In M. F. R. Kets de Vries (Ed.), *The irrational executive* (pp. 264–285). Madison, CT: International Universities Press.

Lewin, K. (1951). *Field theory in social science*. New York: Harper & Row.

Lloyd, T. (1990). *The nice company*. London: Bloomsbury.

Ludeman, K. (1989). *The worth ethic*. New York: Doubleday.

Maccoby, M. (1988). *Why work? Leading the new generation*. New York: Simon & Schuster.

Maddi, S., & Kobasa, S. (1984). *The hardy executive: Health under stress*. New York: Dow Jones Irwin.

Maslach, C., & Jackson, S. F. (1981). The measurement of experienced burnout. *Journal of Occupational Behavior, 2*, 99–113.

Maslow, A. H. (1965). *Eupsychian management*. Homewood, IL: Irwin/Dorsey Press.

McClelland, D. (1975). *Power: The inner experience*. New York: Wiley.

McGregor, D. (1960). *The human side of enterprise*. New York: McGraw-Hill.

Meek, C., Woodworth, W., & Dyer, W.G. (1988). *Managing by the numbers: Absentee owners and the decline in American industry*. Reading, MA: Addison-Wesley.

Peters, T., & Waterman, R. (1982). *The search for excellence*. New York: Harper & Row.

Quarrey, M., & Rosen, C. (1991). *Employee ownership and corporate performance*. Oakland, CA: National Center for Employee Ownership.

Reich, R. (1990). *The work of nations*. New York: Knopf.

Schein, E. H. (1985). *Corporate culture and leadership*. San Francisco: Jossey-Bass.

Schein, E. H. (1986). *Organizational psychology* (3rd ed.). Englewood Cliffs, NJ: Prentice Hall.

Semler, R. (1989). Managing without managers. *Harvard Business Review*.

Senge, P. (1990). *The fifth discipline*. New York: Doubleday Currency.

Shaef, A., & Fassel, D. (1988). *The addictive organization.* New York: Harper & Row.

Strayer, R. (1990). How I learned to let my workers lead. *Harvard Business Review.*

St. Paul Fire and Marine Insurance Companies. (1985). *The human factor.* St. Paul, MN: Author.

Summers, T., DeNisi, A., & DeCotiis, T. (1989). Attitudinal and behavioral consequences of felt job stress and its antecedent factors. *Journal of Social Behavior and Personality,* 4(5).

Weisbord, M. (1987). *Productive workplaces: Organizing and managing for dignity, meaning and community.* San Francisco: Jossey-Bass.

Zuboff, S. (1988). *In the age of the smart machine: The future of work and power.* New York: Basic Books.

3

Perception of Support From the Organization in Relation to Work Stress, Satisfaction, and Commitment

Bill Jones, Deborah M. Flynn, and E. Kevin Kelloway

In this chapter, we examine, as others have, the relationships between such concepts as work stress, social support, job satisfaction, and organizational commitment. Our aim is to show that employees' "global belief concerning the organization's commitment to them" (Eisenberger, Fasolo, & Davis-Lamastro, 1990, p. 57) is a central factor in moderating the effects of work stress on them and on the organization (cf. Eisenberger et al., 1990; Eisenberger, Huntington, Hutchinson, & Sowa, 1986). First, we provide an introduction to the theoretical basis for our use of such terms as *work stress*, *job satisfaction*, *organizational support*, and so on. Second, we describe some empirical work to demonstrate that perceived support from the organization is strongly and causally linked to work stress. Finally, we discuss the possible organizational consequences, including consequences for corporate effectiveness, of our results.

Stress as Role-Playing in the Workplace

A wide range of detrimental personal and organizational consequences has been popularly ascribed to stress. These include effects on health; personal well-being; and such organizational outcomes as increased turnover of staff, absenteeism, and decreased productivity (see, e.g., Cooper & Marshall, 1976; Spector, Dwyer, & Jex, 1988). Many of these effects have been challenged. For example, the commonly accepted relationship between stress and health—in particular, among those with heart disease (e.g., Cooper & Marshall, 1976)— has been questioned on a number of grounds, including inadequate measurement of health variables (Fried, Rowland, & Ferris, 1984) and a failure to consider other intervening, variables (Costa & McCrea, 1987; Watson & Pennebaker, 1989; see also Frese, 1985).

One reason that it may be difficult to draw conclusions about, say, the nature of the relationship between stress and health is that the notion of stress is in itself difficult to elucidate (see, e.g., Motowidlo, Packard, & Manning, 1986). In this chapter, we rely on social role theory as the conceptual basis for thinking about work stress (see, e.g., House, 1981; Kahn, Wolfe, Quinn, Snoek, & Rosenthal, 1964; Lazarus, 1966; Lazarus & Folkman, 1984). As is well-known, role theory as a social–psychological model of work stress takes into account both the objective conditions of the individual's circumstances in the workplace and his or her subjective perceptions of events. The theory holds that the individual at work enacts a special role in which he or she performs tasks in ways largely, if not entirely, specified by the culture of the organization or by the subculture of the specific work group. Stress of one sort or another is seen as an almost inevitable consequence of playing various roles in any complex organization.

A number of interrelated factors appear to make up the constellation of occupational-role stressors. These include conflict, ambiguity, overload, insufficiency, and responsibility for the welfare of other people (e.g., House & Rizzo, 1972; Jackson & Schuler, 1985; Kirkmeyer & Dougherty, 1988; O'Brien, 1982; Osipow & Spokane, 1983; Van Sell, Brief, & Schuler, 1980). *Role conflict* has been defined as an incongruity in the expectations associated with a role (Van Sell et al., 1980). Conflict may occur when the set of role demands contains contradictory expectations, when the expectations of the organization conflict with some value or principle of the individual, or when there are conflicting demands about allocation of time and attention to job and family (e.g., Cooper & Marshall, 1976).

When individuals lack clear information about the expectations associated with a role, the ways in which they may fulfill the role, or the consequences of role performance (Kahn et al., 1964), the role may be described as *ambiguous*. Experimental and longitudinal studies of the effects of role ambiguity have shown that lack of clarity about behavioral expectations results in a greater concern with one's own performance rather than with the performance of the group, in lower actual and perceived group productivity (Jamal, 1984), in less concern or involvement with the group, in lower job satisfaction, in unfavorable attitudes toward others, and in increased tension and anxiety (e.g., Jackson & Schuler, 1985). Role ambiguity has also been causally linked to turnover (Johnson & Graen, 1973), although turnover obviously will also depend on general economic conditions (see, e.g., Hulin, Roznowski, & Hachiga, 1985).

Role overload refers to the number or the intensity of demands that may be made of employees. For example, an employer may demand more of a worker than he or she can reasonably accomplish in a given time, or simply, the employee may perceive the demands of work as excessive. Overload may affect the health of employees, their general attitude toward work, the ways in which tasks are performed, and the feelings employees have about themselves and their jobs (e.g., Kirkmeyer & Dougherty, 1988). *Role insufficiency* refers to a perceived lack of fit between an individual's abilities and training and the requirements of the job (see, e.g., O'Brien, 1982). The tasks for which the individual is employed are seen to lack challenge. Cobb (1973) hypothesized that responsibility for people may be one of the most important sources of occupational stress. Responsibility for others has to do with the responsibility that the person has, or feels, for the performance and welfare of subordinates, colleagues, or members of the public.

Organizational Consequences of Work Stress

Organizational psychologists have demonstrated that a number of consequences of importance to the employing organization are contingent on role stress. In particular, interest has concentrated on the employee's attitude toward work—operationalized as job satisfaction—and on organizational commitment. Satisfaction and commitment have been taken to represent distinct, if correlated, constructs (e.g., Brooke, Russell, & Price, 1988; Mathieu, 1991; Mathieu & Farr, 1991; Meyer & Allen, 1984; Reichers, 1986), even though the reason for the correlation may not always be clear (e.g., Mathieu, 1991).

Job satisfaction may be defined as a multidimensional positive affective response to one's job (Locke, 1976). Satisfaction relates negatively and quite strongly to role ambiguity (e.g., Jackson & Schuler, 1985), role conflict (e.g., Jackson & Schuler, 1985; Reichers, 1986), and role load (e.g., Kirkmeyer & Dougherty, 1988). Satisfaction has also been reliably related to the individual's perception of the possibility of alternative employment elsewhere (cf. Carsten & Spector, 1987; Hulin et al., 1985).

Brooke et al. (1988) have defined *organizational commitment* as follows:

> the relative strength of an individual's identification with and involvement in a particular organization, which is characterized by belief in and acceptance of organizational goals and values, willingness to exert effort on behalf of the organization, and a desire to maintain membership in the organization. (p. 139)

Mowday, Porter, and Steers (1982) have argued that although job satisfaction focuses on the specific tasks that an individual is required to perform, commitment is fundamentally an attitude of loyalty to the employer. Commitment has been found to be quite strongly related to role stress, particularly to conflict (e.g., Reichers, 1986). The degree to which the individual perceives the organization as providing support is also strongly predictive of commitment (Eisenberger et al., 1986). The available psychometric evidence had indicated that perceived organizational support (POS), as conceptualized by Eisenberger et al., and affective organizational commitment represent distinct constructs (Shore & Tetrick, 1991). As we have noted, relations between these variables are the central focus of this chapter.

A considerable number of studies have documented the correlations between role stress and organizational outcomes (see, e.g., Jackson & Schuler, 1985; Kahn et al., 1964; Motowidlo et al., 1986). In general, work stress is negatively correlated with both satisfaction and commitment. Although it seems reasonable to most researchers to believe that increased stress causes a decrease in satisfaction and commitment, there is a dearth of empirical evidence on this point. The relationships among these variables are likely, in fact, to be reciprocal (cf. L. R. James & Tetrick, 1986). If an increase in job satisfaction causes one's commitment to the employing organization to rise, then it will probably also be the case that increased commitment in turn leads to increased satisfaction.

It should also be emphasized that investigations of organizational commitment have characteristically focused on the affective commitment of the employee to the employer, and little attention (until recently) has been paid to the perception by the employee that the employer may entertain any sense of reciprocal obligation.

Social Support and Organizational Support

A number of researchers have suggested that social support provides the most powerful moderator of stressful working conditions in relation to vocational outcomes. Social support, so it is argued, allows individuals to cope with work stress; those who enjoy such support are better able to master conditions and situations that might otherwise tax their adaptive abilities, presumably because they feel valued and are embedded in a network of communication and mutual obligation (e.g., House, 1981; Lazarus, 1966; Lazarus & Folkman, 1984; although, see also Kaufman & Beehr, 1986). In this sense, support has to do with being a member of a relatively informal social network. The effect of the relatively formal networks integral to organizational culture have received much less attention from researchers. Although support must be relevant and related to work (i.e., received from colleagues at work or from superiors) to be effective in regulating the effects of stress (e.g., Ganster, Fusilier, & Mayes, 1986; Kirkmeyer & Dougherty, 1988), such support functions informally and is distinct from organizational structures.

In our view, the work of Eisenberger and colleagues (1986, 1990) in this regard represents a considerable advance. First, they have studied the consequences of the employee's perception that the organization is supportive and committed and the employing organization provides meaningful psychological support to its employees. Second, they have examined support in terms of how the organization as a whole is seen to value the employee. As we have noted, the measurement of commitment has traditionally involved answering a one-sided question: What is the attitude of the employee toward the employer? The measurement of POS is based on the assumption that commitment to the employing organization on the part of employees would increase if they perceived that the organization valued them as individuals (Eisenberger et al., 1990). Eisenberger and colleagues argued that the perception of support from the organization increases affective commitment and also enhances what has been called "calculative" commitment because the individual feels that the organization can be relied on to meet its reciprocal obligations "of noticing and rewarding efforts made on its behalf" (Eisenberger et al., 1990, p. 52). Moreover, "where the employee feels that the organization is committed to him, the organization's gain is more readily perceived as his gain" (Eisenberger et al., 1990, p. 57). In other words, the notion of POS centers on the perceived attitudes of the employer toward the employee.

Altogether, there is little doubt that the construct identified by Eisenberger et al. (1986, 1990) is associated with variables of enormous organizational importance (see also Shore & Tetrick, 1991). One aim of our research was to begin to understand the precise role of POS in relation to satisfaction and commitment. In particular, we were interested in whether support of this nature plays a role similar to social support (Lazarus, 1966) in mediating the organizational consequences of work stress. Consequently, we examined the causal links among three sets of variables—role stress, POS, and the outcomes in job satisfaction and organizational commitment—in three widely different workforces: private-sector manufacturing, education, and the Canadian Federal Public Service.

POS Mediates Work Stress

We administered standardized pencil-and-paper instruments to groups of volunteer employees in the three workforces. All responses were confidential and anonymous. Role stress in the three groups was evaluated by means of Osipow and Spokane's (1983) Work Environment Scale (WES). This scale has six subscales: Overload, Insufficiency, Conflict, Ambiguity, Responsibility for Others, and the Physical Environment. The measure of job satisfaction was taken from the General subscale of the Job Design Inventory (Smith, Kendall, & Hulin, 1969). Organizational commitment was assessed with Meyer and Allen's (1984) Affective Commitment Scale. Finally, POS was evaluated through the Eisenberger et al. (1990) Scale of Perceived Organizational Support.

The three employment groups were drawn from workers in manufacturing, employees of the Canadian Federal Public Service, and professionals involved in assessing special-educational needs. The manufacturing group was made up of 219 skilled shop-floor workers engaged in customized work process in heavy engineering. The workforce was 98% male, with a minimum level of educational attainment of Grade 10. The sample constituted 75% of the available workforce. The public servants included people from three categories: professional–managerial ($n = 20$), supervisory ($n = 39$), and clerical ($n = 34$). The proportion of women varied from .78 (clerical) through .45 (managerial) to .40 (supervisory). Minimum educational attainment similarly varied from Grade 10 (clerical and supervisory) to a bachelor's degree (managerial). Finally, the "special-education" group was made up of professional psychologists, social workers, and teachers delivering special-educational services to a large school district encompassing both urban and rural areas. The group of 55 consisted of 98% of the available workforce. The level of educational attainment was either a bachelor's degree and teaching certificate or a master's degree in psychology or social work. This group was 90% women.

Results

Correlations between variables are shown for each group separately in Table 1. The stress variable is the composite score across the six subscales of the WES. The pattern of correlations was much the same for the three groups. In all three cases, POS was strongly related to work stress. Having demonstrated strong relationships between the variables of interest, we wished to examine the direction of causality. Two causal models were examined. In the first, POS was taken to be a variable that would mediate the effect of stress on job satisfaction. This model is analogous to the conventional notion (e.g., Lazarus, 1966; Lazarus & Folkman, 1984) of the effects of social support either in buffering or in directly affecting the way in which stressors are perceived. In the second, POS was treated as a variable causally responsible for perceived stress. This model was based on the notion that work stress is caused by organizational factors, principally the feeling of not being valued by the employing organization.

A LISREL 7 analysis (Byrne, 1990) was performed to determine the goodness of fit of the two models. Two latent variables—stress and satisfaction—

Table 1. Correlations Between Variables for the Three Groups

Measure	Manufacturing			Special education			Public service			All groups combined		
	POS	Commit	Satis	POS	Commit	Satis	POS	Commit	Satis	POS	Commit	Satis
Stress	−.56**	−.46**	−.56**	−.51**	−.27*	−.58**	−.70**	−.42**	−.33**	−.59**	−.42**	−.45**
POS		.54**	.37**		.22*	.33*		.46**	.30*		.46**	.30*
Commitment			.95**			.98*			.73**			.73**

Note. Stress = combination of Conflict and Ambiguity subscales from the Work Environment Scale (Osipow & Spokane, 1983); Commitment = Affective Commitment Scale (Meyer & Allen, 1984); Satis = General subscale of the Job Design Inventory (Smith, Kendall, & Hulin, 1969); POS = Perceived Organizational Support Scale (Eisenberger, Huntington, Hutchinson, & Sowa, 1986).

*p < .05. **p < .01.

were constructed as the total of the Conflict and Ambiguity subscales of the WES (these variables were the best correlates of POS in all three cases) in the first place and the total of the job satisfaction and commitment measures in the second. The analysis showed the first model to have the better fit, with a nonsignificant chi-square of 1.42. The second model failed to provide an adequate fit. The successful model showed a relatively simple picture, with direct pathways only from stress to POS (-0.55) and, in turn, from POS to the satisfaction (0.26) latent variable. In other words, we can say that POS functions to mediate the effects of conflict and ambiguity on satisfaction with one's work and one's level of affective commitment to the employer. Contrary to Bedeian and Armenakis (1981), conflict and ambiguity may not directly affect commitment (defined in their model by propensity to leave the organization). Our results supported the position taken by Netemeyer, Johnson, and Burton (1990) that conflict and ambiguity have mediated or indirect effects on variables of organizational significance.

What Does Stress Mean in Organizational Terms?

Our research confirmed and extended the ideas of Eisenberger and colleagues (1986, 1990), who have argued that

> the perception of being valued would encourage the incorporation of organizational membership into the employee's self-identity and thereby increase prosocial acts carried out on behalf of the organization. (Eisenberger et al., 1990, p. 52)

Here, we have shown that the perception that the organization is supportive correlates strongly and negatively with work stress and, in turn, influences the degree to which individuals are willing to express satisfaction with the job and the organization.

Social support is said to depend on information that leads an individual to believe that he or she is valued and is embedded in a network of communication and mutual obligation. Our findings in one sense confirmed this result. We argue, however, that the notion of POS is a much more powerful explanation for differences between groups and organizations in the extent to which working conditions are regarded as stressful.

The content of the Eisenberger scale (Eisenberger et al., 1986) goes considerably beyond the usual measures of social support, which have been concerned with the availability of colleagues and friends as agents of reassurance and understanding. POS explicitly focuses on the individual's perception of the organization's attitude toward him or her rather than on how these feelings are mediated. It is worth emphasizing, by way of distinguishing POS from social support, that the magnitude of the effects we have observed is considerably greater than effects often observed between stress and traditional measures of social support. In work with public servants, for example, we have found (Bhalla, Jones, & Flynn, 1991) correlations between a composite measure of work stress and various social support measures in the range from $-.14$ to

−.22. In other words, social support predicted about 2% to 5% of the variation in work stress in comparison with the approximately 50% that we observed here for POS and work stress in a comparable group. Moreover, the effects of social support are by no means consistent. LaRocco, House, and French (1980) found that social support had no effect on job satisfaction (or dissatisfaction) or boredom at work. Kaufman and Beehr (1986) showed that work-group support in one context actually increased the extent to which circumstances were perceived as stressful. Long (1992) studied the possible moderating effects of perceived interpersonal support and supervisor support on work latitude and on disengagement among female clerical workers. She found that supervisor support weakened the relationship between stress and psychosomatic distress, whereas peer support, in fact, strengthened the relationship. In other words, coworkers may serve to confirm and enhance the fears of the employee about the workplace.

In our view, the POS scale is best viewed as assessing both surface and deep aspects of organizational culture. Theorists of organizational culture, such as Schein (1985), have argued that organizational cultures necessarily have a number of levels. The surface level (sometimes called *climate*) has to do with readily observable features of organizational behavior. Scale items, such as "Help is available from my organization when I have a problem" or "The organization tries to make my job as interesting as possible," are observable features of organizational behavior (what Schein, 1985, has called "artifacts"). Other items get at deeper levels of the culture—the values and assumptions that inform observable behavior. Statements such as "The organization strongly considers my goals and values" or "The organization disregards my best interest when it makes decisions that affect me" relate to a reciprocal consideration for personal values rather than to the customary insistence on organizational values, perhaps as defined by company leadership. Statements such as "If given the opportunity, the organization would take advantage of me" or "Even if I did the best possible job, the organization would fail to notice" speak to a culture in which communications are deficient and one-way, a culture in which individual employees are treated as economic units, not as people. The key purpose of organizational culture is to reduce anxiety through providing structure and meaning (see, e.g., Schein, 1985). An employer who is seen to behave in an arbitrary way by not giving credit where it is due or by implicitly rejecting the values of employees is violating a central cultural imperative.

High values of POS imply a congruence between the goals and values of the individual and those of the organization. A good deal of recent research has focused on the congruence of goals and values between different constituents in an organization (e.g., L. A. James & James, 1989; Moglino, Ravlin, & Adkins, 1989; Reichers, 1986; Vancouver & Schmitt, 1991), perhaps because it is felt that less productive organizations experience greater discongruence of goals between important organizational stakeholders (e.g., Moglino et al., 1989). Research has shown that workers tend to be more satisfied and committed when their values are congruent with those of their supervisors (e.g., Moglino et al., 1989). Our results help explain such findings. Congruence of values is likely to be a feature of organizations that employees perceive as supportive.

It has frequently been noted that support from supervisors is modestly related to both work stress and job satisfaction (e.g., Ganster et al., 1986; Jones, Berwald, Catano, & Hackett, 1992; Kirkmeyer & Dougherty, 1988). Our results allow us to speculate that this effect is itself an example of POS. The supervisor is, for most work groups, the immediate representative of the organization and the most powerful individual when it comes to transmitting the values of organizational culture. Hence, in many working environments the supervisor is the organization. The supervisor's response to appropriate effort on the part of the group or of individuals, as well as behavior in response to their needs and problems, may come to stand for the response of the entire culture.

It is known that the supervisor's behavior is strongly associated with work stress, health consequences, and productive behaviors. The attitude of the supervisor directly influences the propensity of workers to show discretionary, "civic" behaviors, such as courtesy, that may not be formally rewarded by the employer but that clearly influence employees' perceptions of the organizational climate and culture (Moorman, 1991). Specific managerial styles seem to be directly related to employees' reported levels of stress. Styles that permit employees to make decisions and feel in control of their activities appear related to the workers' experience of stress and to motivation and productivity (Baard, 1992). As to health consequences, attitudes and behavior on the part of supervisors that workers see as disrespectful, such as yelling or name calling, appear to be strongly predictive of depressive symptoms (Michela, Flint, & Lynch, 1992; see also Sherry & Weller, 1992). Tetrick and Sinclair (1992) found that emotional exhaustion (usually considered one of the components of burnout) was most strongly related to the attitudes of workers' supervisors, and Haynes (1989) concluded that an unsupportive boss was one of the most significant predictors of heart disease among female clerical workers. Finally, we should note that significant numbers of workers are likely to be unhappy with the level or the type of supervision that they receive. Finally, we should note that significant numbers of workers are likely to be unhappy with the level of supervision that they receive (see Jones et al., 1992). In further work, we will focus on the characteristics of supervisors and others that lead to the perception of the organization as supportive.

POS and the Management of Work Stress

All of this suggests that stress management may not be a matter of piecemeal programs as much as it is a matter of organizational reform and redefinition. The model we have presented is relatively simple. We believe it likely that further work would show reciprocal relations between the variables (i.e., that POS may decrease the likelihood that the working environment is perceived as conflictual or ambiguous as well as mediate the effects of conflict and ambiguity for job satisfaction). Organizational change that genuinely respects the values and goals of the employees is therefore likely to reduce the perception that working conditions are stressful. As Motowidlo et al. (1986) noted, stress management "might be accomplished by treating people with more respect, support, and kindness . . . generally fostering more personal warmth in supervision, administration and organizational climate" (p. 627). For the research community, the message should also be clear. As Baard (1992) has stated, "the profession of psychology would do well to accelerate its efforts in providing empirical support for the bottom-line benefits of a more humane treatment of the American workforce" (p. 6).

POS and Organizational Effectiveness

It is important to note that POS appears to be strongly related to productivity. Eisenberger et al. (1990) found that the performance of hourly workers in manufacturing (as assessed through supervisors' reports) correlated highly with POS, and in our own work (Jones et al., 1992), we have found POS to be the most efficient discriminator of groups within the same manufacturing plant that differed in productivity. Because POS is so strongly related to work stress, it is plausible to argue that high levels of conflict and ambiguity may be the sign of an ineffective, relatively unproductive organization (cf. Jamal, 1984).

Conclusions

POS appears to be conceptually different from social support as the concept is traditionally understood. Social support has to do with the operation of networks within the organization that are interposed between the stress-producing aspects of the organization and the individual. POS refers, as we see it, to the general nature of cultural transactions of the organization as an entity.

We believe that POS is potentially a variable of great importance in understanding the connections between factors central to any coherent theory of organizational behavior. These factors include work stress, attitudes toward work, loyalty to the employing organization, and productivity or more broadly organizational effectiveness. Our views have much in common with those recently expressed by L. A. James and James (1989), who argued that "a general factor of personal benefit versus personal detriment" (p. 750) may provide a unifying theme in organizational research. They contended that the notion of *meaning* provided such a theme. We have suggested that cultural meaning in organizational terms may be strongly reflected in workers' perceptions of the supportiveness of their work environment. Investigating organizational climate or culture from the perspective of employees' feelings that they enjoy relevant support and endorsement from employers may suggest functional and effective approaches to stress management and organizational development.

References

Baard, P. P. (1992, May). *Effects of job stress on the organization: Managerial style, worker motivation and productivity.* Paper presented at the APA/NIOSH Conference, Washington, DC.

Bedeian, A. G., & Armenakis, A. A. (1981). A path-analytic study of the consequences of role conflict and role ambiguity. *Academy of Management Journal, 24*, 417–424.

Bhalla, S., Jones, B., & Flynn, D. M. (1991). Role stress among Canadian white-collar workers. *Work and Stress, 5*, 289–299.

Brooke, P. P., Jr., Russell, D. W., & Price, J. L. (1988). Discriminant validation of measures of job satisfaction, job involvement, and organizational commitment. *Journal of Applied Psychology, 73*, 139–145.

Byrne, B. M. (1990). *A Primer of LISREL*. New York: Springer-Verlag.

Carsten, J. M., & Spector, P. E. (1987). Unemployment, job satisfaction, and employee turnover: A meta-analytic test of the Muchinsky model. *Journal of Applied Psychology, 72*, 374–381.

Cobb, S. (1973). Role responsibility: Differentiation of a concept. In A. McLean (Ed.), *Occupational stress*. Springfield, IL: Charles C. Thomas.

Cooper, C. L., & Marshall, J. (1976). Occupational sources of stress: A review of the literature relating to coronary heart disease and mental ill health. *Journal of Occupational Psychology, 49*, 11–28.

Costa, P. T., Jr., & McCrea, R. R. (1987). Neuroticism, somatic complaints and disease: Is the bark worse than the bite? *Journal of Personality, 55*, 299–316.

Eisenberger, R., Fasolo, P., & Davis-Lamastro, V. (1990). Perceived organizational support and employee diligence, commitment, and innovation. *Journal of Applied Psychology, 75*, 51–59.

Eisenberger, R., Huntington, R., Hutchinson, S., & Sowa, D. (1986). Perceived organizational support. *Journal of Applied Psychology, 71*, 500–507.

Frese, M. (1985). Stress at work and psychosomatic complaints: A causal interpretation. *Journal of Applied Psychology, 70*, 314–328.

Fried, Y., Rowland, K. M., & Ferris, G. R. (1984). Physiological measurement of work stress: A critique. *Personnel Psychology, 37*, 583–615.

Ganster, D. C., Fusilier, M. R., & Mayes, B. T. (1986). Role of social support in the experience of stress at work. *Journal of Applied Psychology, 71*, 102–110.

Haynes, S. G. (1989). Women, work, and coronary heart disease: Prospective findings from the Framingham Heart Study. *American Journal of Public Health, 70*, 133–141.

House, S. J. (1981). *Work stress and social support*. Reading, MA: Addison-Wesley.

House, S. J., & Rizzo, J. R. (1972). Role conflict and ambiguity as critical variables in a model of organizational behavior. *Organizational Behavior and Human Performance, 7*, 476–505.

Hulin, C. L., Roznowski, M., & Hachiga, D. (1985). Alternative opportunities and withdrawal decisions: Empirical and theoretical discrepancies and an integration. *Psychological Bulletin, 97*, 233–250.

Jackson, S. E., & Schuler, R. S. (1985). A meta-analysis and conceptual critique of research on role ambiguity and role conflict in work settings. *Organizational Behavior and Human Performance, 36*, 16–78.

Jamal, M. (1984). Job stress and job performance controversy: An empirical assessment. *Organizational Behavior and Human Performance, 33*, 1–21.

James, L. A., & James, L. R. (1989). Integrating work environment of perceptions: Explorations into the measurement of meaning. *Journal of Applied Psychology, 74*, 739–751.

James, L. R., & Tetrick, L. E. (1986). Confirmatory analytic tests of three causal models relating job perceptions to job satisfaction. *Journal of Applied Psychology, 71*, 77–82.

Johnson, T. W., & Graen, G. (1973). Organizational assimilation and role rejection. *Organizational Behavior and Human Performance, 10*, 72–87.

Jones, B., Berwald, M. C. A., Catano, V. M., & Hackett, R. (1992). *Productivity in Canadian manufacturing*. Report to the Manufacturing Research Corporation of Ontario and the Ministry of Industry Science and Technology, Canada.

Kahn, R. L., Wolfe, D. M., Quinn, R. P., Snoek, J. D., & Rosenthal, R. A. (1964). *Occupational stress: Studies in role conflict and ambiguity*. New York: Wiley.

Kaufman, G. M., & Beehr, T. A. (1986). Interactions between job stressors and social support: Some counter-intuitive results. *Journal of Applied Psychology, 71*, 522–526.

Kirkmeyer, S. L., & Dougherty, T. W. (1988). Work load, tension, and coping: Moderating effects of supervisor support. *Personnel Psychology, 41*, 125–139.

LaRocco, J. M., House, J. S., & French, J. R. P. (1980). Social support, occupational stress, and health. *Journal of Health and Social Behavior, 21*, 202–218.

Lazarus, R. S. (1966). *Psychological stress and the coping process*. New York: McGraw-Hill.

Lazarus, R. S., & Folkman, S. (1984). *Stress appraisal and coping*. New York: Springer.

Locke, E. A. (1976). The nature and causes of job satisfaction. In M. D. Dunnette (Ed.), *Handbook of industrial and organizational psychology*. Chicago: Rand-McNally.

Long, B. (1992, May). *Clerical workers: Work stress, social support and coping strategies*. Poster presented at the APA–NIOSH conference, Washington, DC.

Mathieu, J. E. (1991). A cross-level nonrecursive model of the antecedents of organizational commitment and job satisfaction. *Journal of Applied Psychology, 76*, 127–133.

Mathieu, J. E., & Farr, J. L. (1991). Further evidence for the discriminative validity of organizational commitment, job involvement, and job satisfaction. *Journal of Applied Psychology, 74*, 739–751.

Meyer, J. P., & Allen, N. J. (1984). Testing the "side-bet" theory of organizational commitment: Some methodological considerations. *Journal of Applied Psychology, 69*, 372–378.

Michela, J. L., Flint, D. H., & Lynch, A. M. (1992, May). *Disrespectful behavior as a social–environmental stressor at work*. Poster presented at the APA–NIOSH conference, Washington, DC.

Moglino, B. M., Ravlin, E. C., & Adkins, C. L. (1989). A work values approach to corporate culture: A field test of the value congruence process and its relationship to individual outcomes. *Journal of Applied Psychology, 74*, 429–432.

Moorman, R. H. (1991). Relationships between organizational justice and organizational citizenship behaviors: Do fairness perceptions influence employee citizenship? *Journal of Applied Psychology, 74*, 739–751.

Motowidlo, S. J., Packard, J. S., & Manning, M. R. (1986). Occupational stress: Its causes and consequences for job performance. *Journal of Applied Psychology, 71*, 618–629.

Mowday, R. T., Porter, R. M., & Steers, L. W. (1982). *The measurement of organizational commitment*. San Diego, CA: Academic Press.

Netermeyer, R. G., Johnston, M. W., & Burton, S. (1990). Analysis of role conflict and role ambiguity in a structural equations framework. *Journal of Applied Psychology, 75*, 148–157.

O'Brien, G. E. (1982). The relative contribution of perceived skill-utilization and other perceived job attributes to the prediction of job satisfaction: A cross-validation study. *Human Relations, 35*, 219–237.

Osipow, S. H., & Spokane, A. R. (1983). *A manual for measures of occupational stress, strain, and coping*. Columbus, OH: Marathon Consulting Press.

Reichers, A. (1986). Conflict and organizational commitments. *Journal of Applied Psychology, 71*, 508–514.

Schein, E. H. (1985). *Organizational culture and leadership*. San Francisco: Jossey-Bass.

Sherry, P., & Weller, D. (1992, May). *Role of supervisor support in buffering the stress–strain relationship*. Paper presented at the APA–NIOSH conference, Washington, DC.

Shore, L. M., & Tetrick, L. E. (1991). A construct validity study of the Survey of Perceived Organizational Support. *Journal of Applied Psychology, 76*, 637–643.

Smith, P. C., Kendall, L. M., & Hulin, C. C. (1969). *The measurement of satisfaction in work and retirement*. Chicago: Rand-McNally.

Spector, P. E., Dwyer, D. J., & Jex, S. M. (1988). Relation of job stressors to affective, health, and performance outcomes: A comparison of multiple data sources. *Journal of Applied Psychology, 73*, 11–19.

Tetrick, L. E., & Sinclair, R. R. (1992, November). *Personal and environmental effects on the three dimensions of burnout*. Paper presented at the APA/NIOSH conference, Washington, DC.

Vancouver, J. B., & Schmitt, N. W. (1991). An exploratory analysis of the person–organization fit: Organizational goal congruence. *Personnel Psychology, 44*, 333–356.

Van Sell, M., Brief, A. P., & Schuler, R. S. (1980). Role conflict and role ambiguity: Integration of the literature and directions for future research. *Human Relations, 33*, 243–257.

Watson, D., & Pennebaker, J. W. (1989). Health complaints, stress, and distress: Exploring the central role of negative affectivity. *Psychological Review, 96*, 234–254.

4

The Relationship of Role Conflict and Ambiguity to Organizational Culture

Marjolijn van der Velde and Michael D. Class

Role stress, including role conflict and ambiguity (Kahn, Wolfe, Quinn, Snoek, & Rosenthal, 1964), has been the topic of more than 100 studies over the past 20 years (McGee, Ferguson, & Seers, 1989). Most of the research conducted in this area has focused on individual- or group-level factors as casual variables. Recent studies on role stress have investigated such diverse topics as the supervisor–subordinate dyad (Tsui & O'Reilly, 1989), perceived work competency (Chusmir & Koberg, 1989), female entrepreneurs (Stoner, Hartman, & Arora, 1990), job-attribute preferences (Wiersma, 1990), and job and marital satisfaction (Coverman, 1989).

Although many studies have explored role stress, few have paid heed to the suggestion of Van Sell, Brief, and Schuler (1981) that the theoretical framework for studying role stress be expanded to include such constructs in organizational behavior as leader behavior, task design, and organizational structure. The purpose of this chapter is to extend existing research by analyzing the relationship between role stress and organizational culture operationalized in terms of behavioral norms and expectations. We propose that the cultures of many organizations create stress for workers by communicating expectations for behavior that are inconsistent with workers' preferences, are inherently oriented toward conflict, or are proscriptive and ambiguous.

Hypotheses

The general proposition under consideration concerns organizational culture (measured in terms of behavioral norms and expectations) and role stress (measured in terms of role ambiguity, person–role conflict, and intersender role conflict). The data for this study were collected from employees of diverse organizations from the Organizational Culture Inventory (OCI; Cooke & Lafferty, 1986). The OCI measures organizational norms and expectations for 12 different behavior styles. These 12 styles are associated with three general types of organizational cultures: constructive, passive–defensive, and aggressive–defensive. Prior field research and consulting and training experience

---

We thank Robert A. Cooke for his guidance and support throughout this research project.

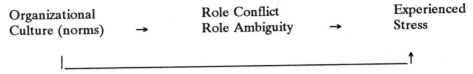

Figure 1. Role conflict and role ambiguity as intervening variables on an organizational culture's relationship to stress.

with the inventory suggest that the constructive styles are positively related to outcomes valued by organizations (e.g., employee satisfaction and motivation) and the defensive styles are negatively related to such outcomes. The specific hypotheses we tested are as follows:

1. The level of role conflict reported by members of organizations is positively related to behavioral norms associated with defensive cultures (both passive and aggressive) and negatively related to norms associated with constructive cultures.
2. The level of role ambiguity reported by members of organizations is positively related to behavioral norms associated with defensive cultures (both passive and aggressive) and negatively related to norms associated with constructive cultures.
3. The level of stress reported by members of organizations is positively related to the level of experienced role conflict and role ambiguity.
4. The level of stress is positively related to behavioral norms associated with defensive cultures and negatively related to norms associated with constructive cultures.

Our proposed theoretical model is shown in Figure 1. As illustrated, behavioral norms are hypothesized to be related to stress both indirectly (through role conflict and role ambiguity) and directly (as proposed in Hypothesis 4). Thus, norms are proposed to have an impact on stress levels above and beyond their indirect effects through role conflict and ambiguity.

Method

Participants

The data for this research were collected by management faculty and students at the University of Illinois at Chicago. The sample consisted of 825 individuals from 162 organizations (approximately 5 respondents per organization or subunit). Respondents represent a broad base of managers and nonmanagers: 52.1% held nonmanagerial positions, women constituted 46.9% of the sample, 49.7% were under 30 years old, and 56.1% had worked with the organization 4 years or less.

Instruments

The data for this study were collected through the OCI (Cooke & Lafferty, 1986). Norms and expectations for the 12 behavioral styles of the OCI are measured by 120 items. The OCI includes sections to collect demographic data on the respondent and his or her position in the organization (reported above). It was administered along with a supplementary survey to measure such outcomes as motivation, job satisfaction, role clarity, cooperation, and role conflict.

Behavioral norms. The 12 behavioral norms measured by the OCI are each measured with a scale made up of responses to 10 items. Respondents are asked to answer in terms of the extent that each behavior helps people (themselves and their coworkers) to "fit in" and "meet expectations" in their organization. Responses are selected from 5-point scale ranging from 1 (*not at all*) to 5 (*to a very great extent*). The responses to the items associated with each style are added to produce a scale score. The higher the style score, the stronger the norms and expectations for behaviors associated with that style.

The internal consistency reliabilities for the 12 scales were acceptable for this sample, with Cronbach alpha coefficients ranging from .72 to .89. The reliability estimates were consistent with those obtained in other samples (e.g., Cooke & Rousseau, 1984; Cooke & Szumal, 1993). To assess agreement among individuals within each organizational subunit, we used the within-group interrater reliability (IRR) method developed by James, Demaree, and Wolf (1984). IRR consists of two components: total variance attributable to random measurement error variance and total variance attributable to common response bias. An IRR estimate was obtained with both the traditional measure of expected variance of 2.0 and the expected variance in the OCI of 1.34. The 12 culture styles were factor analyzed by using principal-components analysis with varimax rotation. The 12 norms factored into three general types of organizational culture in a manner consistent with the conceptual model underlying the inventory:

1. Factor 1: Constructive norms encourage members to behave in ways consistent with higher order needs. The four OCI norms included in this group were humanistic–encouraging, affiliative, achievement, and self-actualizing.
2. Factor 2: Aggressive–defensive norms reflect an organizational culture in which expectations focus on members acting in aggressive ways to protect their security. The four behavioral norms included in this general category were oppositional, power, competitive, and perfectionistic.
3. Factor 3: Passive–defensive norms characterize an organizational culture in which members believe that they must act in defensive ways to protect their security. The four included behavior styles were approval, conventional, dependent, and avoidance.

Role stress. The items measuring role conflict and role ambiguity were adapted from the University of Michigan's Organizational Assessment Package (Survey Research Center, 1975) and Quality of Employment Survey (Quinn & Staines, 1979). Respectively, response options range from 1 (*disagree*) to 5 (*agree*) and from 1 (*not at all*) to 5 (*to a very great extent*). Factor analysis by means of principal-components analysis with varimax rotation confirmed that the items intended to measure role conflict and role ambiguity measures loaded on two different factors. The reliability coefficients for these measures (role conflict, role ambiguity, and stress) were .60, .65, and .63, respectively.

Background data. To control for the possible effects of demographic variables, we included four background measures: age, gender, years with the organization, and organizational level.

Analysis

Role conflict, ambiguity, and experienced stress are individual-level phenomena that are most appropriately measured and analyzed at the level of the respondent. However, shared behavioral norms are unit-level constructs. Therefore, the factor scores obtained through the principal-components analysis of the OCI were aggregated to the unit level. The results of the within-group IRR scores reported earlier justified this aggregation of the OCI scores. The mean score for each respondent's subunit along each general culture style was then assigned to individual members. These aggregated factor scores were used in the regression analyses and carried out at the individual level.

Several regression analyses were conducted. First, role conflict and role ambiguity were independently regressed on the aggregated culture styles. Second, experienced stress was regressed on the role stressors conflict and ambiguity. Finally, to test for the hypothesized direct and indirect relationship of the OCI norms to stress, we used a two-step regression procedure to identify and then control for the intervening effects of stress. In the first step, we regressed the experienced stress measure on role conflict and role ambiguity. We used the resulting standardized residual for stress as the dependent variable in the second equation and regressed this on the aggregated culture styles. We investigated the possible effect of the four background variables (age, gender, years with the organization, and organization level) on experienced role stress by adding these variables to the regression equation.

Results

The results of the role conflict regression supported the first hypothesis: R^2 = .063, $F(3, 795) = 17.9, p \leq .0001$. Role conflict was positively related to both the aggressive–defensive and passive–defensive styles (respectively, β = .11, $p \leq .001$; $\beta = .12, p \leq .001$) and negatively related to the constructive style ($\beta = -.19, p \leq .001$). The results suggest that lower levels of role conflict are reported by employees of organizations with constructive cultures. Simultaneously, organizations that display the characteristics associated with either the aggressive–defensive or passive–defensive styles had employees that reported higher levels of role conflict.

The data did not support the second hypothesis. Results suggest that role ambiguity is related to the constructive culture style ($\beta = .089, p \leq .05$), but in the direction opposite to that predicted. Significant results regarding the defensive styles were not obtained: aggressive–defensive $\beta = -.036 (p = .30)$ and passive–defensive $\beta = .012 (p = .74)$.

The third hypothesis—that role conflict and role ambiguity mediate the impact of the organization's culture style on stress—was supported. The results of this regression are reported in Table 1. Along with two of the demographic variables (age and years in the organization), role conflict and role ambiguity were found to explain a significant amount of the variance in the level of strain reported, $R^2 = .32, F(4, 665) = 77.7, p \leq .001$. Age was negatively related to experienced stress, and number of years with the organization was positively related to stress. Role conflict was positively related to experienced stress, as expected, but role ambiguity was negatively related to stress. Thus, the third hypothesis was supported only with respect to role conflict. With the addition of the three aggregated culture styles, the squared multiple correlation improved to .33, $F(6, 598) = 46.3, p \leq .0001$. The relationship of cultural style to stress was in the direction predicted with the passive–defensive norms (e.g., being positively related to the stress levels reported by individual respondents). However, the increase for the variance explained (.01) was small, suggesting that most of the impact of cultural styles on stress is mediated by role conflict. The apparently weak direct effects of the cultural styles should be interpreted in recognition of the strong common method variance between role conflict and experienced stress. The cultural styles, represented by aggregated scores assigned back to individual respondents, shared less common method variance with the stress measure. This accounts, in part, for results suggesting a stronger indirect than direct impact of behavioral norms on stress.

In summary, these results suggest that the level of stress reported by employees of organizations can be explained by the degree of role conflict and role ambiguity they experience. Role conflict was strongly and positively related to the degree of stress reported, whereas role ambiguity was negatively related. High levels of role conflict were reported by employees whose organizations' defensive norms were strong and constructive norms were weak.

Table 1. Results of Regression of Stress Using Ordered Selection

Variable	β	R^2 (cumulative)
Role conflict	.42	
Role ambiguity	−.23	
Age	−.14	
Years in organization	.11	.32
Constructive style	−.07	
Aggressive–defensive style	.03	
Passive–defensive style	.10	.33

Taken together, these results support the hypothesis that the relationship between cultural norms and stress is mediated by role conflict. The addition of the aggregated culture styles strengthens the regression equation, suggesting that the aggressive–defensive and passive–defensive styles are also directly and positively related to stress, whereas the constructive style is negatively associated with the level of stress reported.

Discussion

The quantitative study of the culture of organizations is a relatively new phenomenon, and researchers are only now beginning to explore the effects that culture has on employees. We have investigated the impact that behavioral norms have on such individual level outcomes as stress and role conflict. Our survey results demonstrate that the culture of an organization does affect the level of stress experienced by individuals within organizations. Although this effect might be primarily indirect, results show that even after adjusting for contributions to stress by role conflict there is still a small, but measurable, direct effect of organizational culture.

There were several limitations to the present study. One limitation was the combining of data for senior- and midlevel managers with data provided by respondents holding nonmanagerial or first-line supervisory positions. Future research focusing exclusively on organizational staff holding middle-management or senior-management positions might produce different results. For example, role ambiguity might be positively related to stress given the high level of uncertainty faced by managers. In addition, we did not consider the industry sector to which an organization belonged. The question of whether role conflict and stress are industry specific (or related to economic cycles or organizational commitments) should be explored. Finally, specific symptoms of strain were not measured in this study. The question of whether behavioral norms, role conflict, or role ambiguity leads to specific physical, psychological, or emotional symptoms remains to be examined.

References

Chusmir, L. H., & Koberg, C. S. (1989). Perceived work conflict and sex role conflict: An empirical study. *Journal of Psychology, 123,* 537–546.

Cooke, R. A., & Lafferty, J. L. (1986). *Organizational Culture Inventory.* Plymouth, MI: Human Synergistics.

Cooke, R. A., & Rousseau, D. M. (1984). Stress and strain from family roles and work-role expectations. *Journal of Applied Psychology, 69,* 252–260.

Cooke, R. A., & Szumal, J. L. (1993). Measuring normative beliefs and shared behavioral expectations in organizations: The reliability and validity of the Organizational Culture Inventory. *Psychological Reports, 72,* 1299–1330.

Coverman, S. (1989). Role overload, role conflict, and stress: Addressing consequences of multiple role demands. *Social Forces, 67,* 965–982.

James, L. R., Demaree, R. G., & Wolf, G. (1984). Estimating within-group reliability with and without response bias. *Journal of Applied Psychology, 69,* 85–98.

Kahn, R. L., Wolfe, D. M., Quinn, R. P., Snoek, J. D., & Rosenthal, R. A. (1964). *Organizational stress: Studies in role conflict and ambiguity*. New York: Wiley.

McGee, G. W., Ferguson, C. E., Jr., & Seers, A. (1989). Role conflict and role ambiguity: Do the scales measure these two constructs? *Journal of Applied Psychology, 74,* 815–818.

Quinn, R. P., & Staines, G. L. (1979). *The Quality of Employment Survey*. Ann Arbor: Institute for Social Research, University of Michigan.

Stoner, C. R., Hartman, R. I., & Arora, R. (1990). Work–home role conflict on female owners of small business: An exploratory study. *Journal of Small Business Management, 28,* 30–38.

Survey Research Center. (1975). *Michigan Organizational Assessment Package: Progress Report II*. Ann Arbor. Institute for Social Research, University of Michigan.

Tsui, A. S., & O'Reilly, C. A., III. (1989). Beyond simple demographic effects: The importance of relational demography in superior–subordinate dyads. *Academy of Management Journal, 32,* 402–423.

Van Sell, M., Brief, A. P., & Schuler, R. S. (1981). Role conflict and role ambiguity: Integration of the literature and directions for future research. *Human Relations, 34,* 43–71.

Wiersma, U. J. (1990). Gender differences in job attribute preferences: Work–home role conflict and job level as mediating variables. *Journal of Occupational Psychology, 63,* 231–243.

5

Organizational Climate and Work Stress: A General Framework Applied to Inner-City Schoolteachers

John L. Michela, Marlene P. Lukaszewski, and John P. Allegrante

Organizational climate is concerned with workers' perceptions and psychologically potent features of the workplace, such as whether workers have autonomy, pride in their work, good working relations with other workers, and many other working conditions (James, 1982). A good deal of controversy exists over the best way to describe the features of the workplace that are encompassed by the concept of organizational climate, and many measurement instruments have been proposed (see Jones & James, 1979; Payne & Pugh, 1976). Nevertheless, as many writers have noted, organizational climate is an essential topic in the social psychology of organizations and has endured for more than 20 years of research in industrial and organizational psychology. For example, it has appeared in Katz and Kahn's (1966) original text on the social psychology of organizations, in recent reviews of the literature on organizational behavior (e.g., Schneider, 1985), and in volumes dedicated to related topics (e.g., Schneider, 1990). It is concerned with the reciprocal interaction of the environment and the person (Schneider & Reichers, 1983) and with psychological mediators of effects of work environment variables on work behavior and satisfaction (e.g., Litwin & Stringer, 1968).

When defined and described in these ways, organizational climate holds promise for theory and research concerning organizational conditions and work stress. In its most general form, stress theory and research locate the origin of stress in the environment, recognizing that characteristics of a person under stress interact with objective features of the situation in the total stress process (e.g., Kasl, 1984). The construct of organizational climate provides an approach

We sincerely thank Saletta Boni, Warner Burke, and Roger Myers for expanding our thinking about organizational climate and person–environment fit; Mollie DeLozier for help collecting the data sets for the present project; and Paul Viboch for facilitating our access to research participants. Dale Griffin, Joanne Wood, and anonymous reviewers provided very helpful comments on a draft of this chapter. This research was partially supported by a University of Waterloo and Social Sciences and Humanities Research Council Award (037-7713) to John L. Michela, who also thanks the Universities of Amsterdam and Waterloo for support during the sabbatical leave in which this chapter was completed.

to capturing the perceptual and experiential components of transactions in the environment, which, in theory, lead to stress.

In this chapter, we present a framework for conceptualizing the link between organizational climate and stress, and we illustrate the use of the framework in a study of stress among public-school teachers. Many theoretical and methodological issues, some familiar and others novel in the stress field, are discussed herein. A pervasive concern, to which we return later in the discussion, is the question of what is added to the study of organizational risk factors by conceptualizing them in terms of organizational climate.

Conceptual Framework for the Study of Climate and Stress

Figure 1 shows how organizational climate was conceived for this investigation as a mediator between organization membership and the symptoms used as indicators of work stress. *Organization membership* refers to the organizational entity or unit to which a worker belongs. The arrow linking organizational membership to climate experience reflects previous research, which has shown that climate experience is significantly affected by working in one versus another corporation or institution, one versus another department, or one or another work group composed of a manager and several subordinates (see James & Sells, 1981, for a review). Under the arrow in Figure 1 connecting organization membership and climate experience, note that a variety of perceptual and evaluational processes probably influence the particular ways that organizational characteristics and events affect the experience of climate. Below climate experience it is indicated that personal psychological factors will cause people to vary from one another in their climate experience, even in the

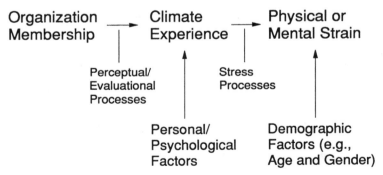

Figure 1. A framework for studying organizational climate and work stress. *Organization membership* refers to the group, department, division, or corporation of which an individual is a member. Various personal–psychological factors, including personal preferences, combine with perceptions of organizational attributes to determine climate experience. Stress is theorized to be manifested in physical or mental strain outcomes when unfavorable climate experience combines with various biopsychosocial factors (operationalized in this study by demographic variables).

same environment. Thus, climate may be construed as a Person × Situation interactionist construct (cf. Stern, 1970).

As a further clarification of what is meant by *organizational climate* in this research, another set of variables might be imagined below organization membership in Figure 1. These are the attributes in which the organizations under investigation vary from one another. Climate varies between organizations to the extent that those organizations vary from one another in terms of attributes that affect the climate. It is these attributes and their effects that are being perceived, evaluated, and otherwise experienced. As James and Sells (1981) put it, organizational climate thus concerns

> the individual's cognitive representations of relatively proximal situational events, expressed in terms that reflect the psychological meaning and significance of the situation to the individual. . . . [Climate dimensions are] interpretive, abstract, generalized, and inferential . . . such as ambiguity, autonomy, challenge, conflict, equity, friendliness, influence, support, trust, and interpersonal warmth. (p. 275)

Because climate is subjective, its measurement usually involves asking workers their perceptions of the work environment in a rather straightforward manner. For example, to measure the social climate conceived in a general way, workers may be asked whether relations among coworkers are warm and friendly or cool and aloof. Equity or fairness may be measured, for example, by questions about whether workers who make the same contributions tend to get the same rewards in the workplace.

The right-hand portion of Figure 1 concerns the hypothesized links between climate experience and *physical or mental strain*, mediated by stress processes. Certainly, there are other factors besides stress processes that influence the symptom experiences or illness measures that researchers use as indicators of strain; these factors are partially represented by the category of demographic factors at the lower right of the figure. Nevertheless, in our investigation, reports of experienced symptoms were interpreted as indicators of physical or mental strain. Contemporary theories hold that such strains are relatively direct consequences of the operation of stress processes (e.g., Harrison, 1978). In accordance with these theories, we predicted that stress processes would lead the strain measures to be associated with climate measures.

The primary focus of this chapter, then, is represented in the middle and right-hand portions of the framework depicted in Figure 1. As mentioned earlier, previous studies have examined what is in the left-hand portion of the model. We are not aware of any prior studies that have examined that shown on the right-hand side of the model as such (i.e., as an organizational climate problem as defined here). Of course, various prior studies of social and organizational conditions at work as stressors are pertinent (e.g., Chesney et al., 1981; Repetti, 1987).

Predicting Stress Outcomes for Teachers From Organizational Climate

The occupational group studied consisted of public-school teachers in elementary through junior high school in a community school district in the northern section of Manhattan in New York City. This group seemed appropriate to the purposes of the study for several reasons. First, the work activities of teachers in various schools seem as similar across schools as the work activities of other occupational groups are across their work organizations. Consequently, occupation was held constant in our design as intended. Second, from the point of view of our design, teachers' employing organizations, namely, schools, have the capacity to vary in the critical respects that are thought to influence organizational climate. Primary among these influences are one's supervisor and peers (Michela et al., 1989), and schools necessarily vary from one another in terms of their administration and faculty group compositions. These variations may have implications for a wide range of organizational climate dimensions, including those concerned with interpersonal relations, task structure, and autonomy.

Third, teachers as an occupational group—and inner-city teachers especially—are exposed to a variety of significant stressors. Evidence on this point comes mainly from research monographs and articles that report teachers' descriptions of conditions that are troubling to them—such as low pay, low prestige, fear of physical assaults from students, lack of respect from administrators or other superiors, and conflicts arising from the role of the teacher and the school in society (e.g., see Cedoline, 1982; D'Arienzo, Moracco, & Krajewski, 1982; Dunham, 1984; Farber, 1984). These writings have suggested that a better understanding of teacher stress and better evidence for specific health consequences of teachers' stress could have considerable significance for public health because teachers are likely to be suffering substantially from detrimental effects of stress.

Hypotheses

The framework shown in Figure 1 does not specify which conditions at work generate stress. Consequently, to generate testable hypotheses, it was necessary to draw on theory and findings from the field of stress research and to try to forge connections between the fields of organizational climate and work stress. We examined the organizational climate survey that we had selected for the study (Litwin & Stringer, 1968) and found three categories of perceived organizational attributes (organizational climate dimensions) for which predictions could be generated from prior stress research. These categories are as follows:

1. We expected dimensions concerning autonomy at work to bear a negative relation to strain on the basis of perceived control on stress and strain (e.g., Karasek et al., 1988).
2. We also expected dimensions concerning warmth, trust, or other favorable qualities of interpersonal relations to be negatively related to strain on the basis of demonstrated effects of social support (Cohen & Wills, 1985).
3. Finally, we expected that dimensions concerning high standards for

work performance would be associated positively with strain, as a work-overload phenomenon (e.g., Karasek, 1979).

Method

Participants

In the primary study, a sample of 266 teachers (Sample 1) from 10 schools in a New York City school district returned by mail a questionnaire they had received at an orientation session for a workplace health-promotion program (see Allegrante & Michela, 1990). The sample size of 266 represented a 35% response rate in relation to the approximate total number of teachers attending the assemblies. In a follow-up study, a sample of 75 teachers (Sample 2) agreed to be interviewed about health, stress, and health promotion and to fill out questionnaires with the interviewer present. The major purpose of the second study was to address concerns raised by primary study's low response rate. In all, 90 teachers had been approached randomly in four schools, yielding a response rate of 83%.

The demographic composition of each sample is described in Table 1. Noteworthy is that gender and racial-group frequencies differed from the U.S. population as a whole. The high number of women in the sample was consistent with the proportion of teachers who were women in the district. The location of the school district in a community with a predominantly minority population probably accounted for the high proportion of non-White teachers in the sample.

Table 1. Demographic Characteristics of Samples

Characteristic	Sample 1 (N = 266)		Sample 2 (N = 75)	
	No.	%	No.	%
Gender				
Male	53	20	18	24
Female	211	80	57	76
No response	2	NA	0	NA
Age (years)				
M	40.8	NA	39.0	NA
SD	9.0	NA	9.4	NA
Race				
White	154	59	38	51
Non-White	105	41	36	49
No response	7	NA	1	NA

Note. NA = not applicable.

Measures

Climate. Organizational climate was measured in both samples with Litwin and Stringer's (1968) questionnaire (Form B), adapted slightly for teachers. One adaptation involved rewording instructions so that they would clearly indicate schools as the organizational context. Specifically, teachers were instructed to

> describe the work climate as it currently exists for the teachers in your school with whom you work most closely—your work "unit," such as a department defined by academic topic, or a grade level. For each statement below . . . please indicate how much you agree or disagree with each statement.

These instructions were followed by 22 statements, such as "In this unit, people are encouraged to initiate projects or approaches that they think are worthwhile." Response alternatives ranged from *definitely disagree* (1) to *definitely agree* (6).

The other minor changes we made from Litwin and Stringer's (1968) questionnaire were in the wording of items, both to be consistent with the concept and term *unit* (as opposed to *organization* in the original form of the questionnaire) and to reflect autonomy, standards, and other dimensions in ways appropriate to the teaching profession. For example, the item quoted in the previous paragraph about taking initiative does not appear in Litwin and Stringer's questionnaire, but a similar item (which might seem odd to teachers and therefore was deleted for this study) is, "Around here management resents your checking everything with them; if you think you've got the right approach you just go ahead." However, most of the changes in items were smaller than this, being confined to reframing questions to in terms of *unit* versus *organization*.

Responses to the climate survey by members of the first sample were analyzed with principal factor analysis. After varimax rotation, 10 of 22 items loaded above .40 on the first three factors, and these 10 items were entered into a second factor analysis. Results of the second analysis are presented in Table 2. Each factor's eigenvalue was above 1.0 before rotation, and 66% of the variance among the 10 items was explained by the three factors.

We labeled the first factor *Achievement* climate when we saw that respondents varied in the extent to which they reported the presence in their work environments of the achievement-facilitating conditions captured by the items with high loadings on Factor 1 (see Table 2). These conditions are high standards for work performance in the work unit, clarity about policies, and group pride. The second factor was labeled *Empowerment* after Burke's (1986) discussion of conditions and processes in work groups that people need to have a sense of autonomy at work. The specific items on the empowerment factor concern perceptions that teachers' opinions are solicited, that teachers influence the actions of the work unit, and that teachers are encouraged to take initiative on their own projects or approaches. The third factor was labeled *Affiliation* climate. We deliberately used the terms *achievement* and *affiliation*

Table 2. Labels, Item Wordings, and Varimax-Rotated Factor Loadings of Items in Climate Composite Variables

Composite variable	Item wording	Factor		
		1	2	3
Achievement	In our unit, we set very high standards for performance.	.84	.09	.09
	The policies of this unit are clearly understood.	.79	.18	.14
	People are proud of belonging to this unit.	.73	.20	.29
Empower-ment	I often have the opportunity to influence the goals or actions of my unit.	.18	.71	.18
	All members of the unit are involved in making important decisions that affect them.	.38	.54	.06
	In this unit, people are encouraged to initiate projects or approaches that they think are worthwhile.	.38	.53	.27
	My thoughts and opinions are rarely asked for. (reverse scored)	.01	−.53	−.08
Affiliation	People in this unit don't really trust each other very much. (reverse scored)	−.16	−.11	−.72
	People in this unit tend to be cool and aloof toward each other. (reverse scored)	−.09	−.09	−.62
	People I work with take a personal interest in me.	.16	.36	.46

in the tradition of Atkinson (1964) and McClelland (1985) with which Litwin and Stringer (1968) identified their work.

Three composite variables were formed in accordance with the factor pattern in Table 2. Items were summed up and weighted equally within each composite. For Sample 1, reliabilities of the composites were .85, .72, and .65 for the achievement, empowerment, and affiliation composites, respectively. The corresponding Sample 2 values were .87, .72, and .52, respectively. Although the lowest of these values lies below conventional standards for reliability, as we show later, this measure was good enough to provide a statistically significant prediction of an outcome in multiple regression analysis. Intercorrelations of these unit-weighted composites were also examined. In both samples, the achievement–empowerment correlation was highest at .47 and achievement–affiliation was lowest at .36 and .07 for Samples 1 and 2, respectively. Affilliation–empowerment yielded correlations of .40 and .35, respectively.

The general plan for the data analysis was to develop and use climate variables as predictors of strain measures in multiple regression analyses. Once we found that the climate variables were substantially intercorrelated, we had to take into account that estimates based on multiple regressions of the association of each climate variable with strain would be unstable if all three variables were included in the equations. Consequently, multiple regression analyses were done separately for each climate variable, with unconditional simultaneous entry in each analysis of a climate measure, age, and gender (in accordance with Figure 1).

Strain. The outcome variable in multiple regression analyses was derived from various analyses, the results of which are presented in Table 3. Data for these analyses were participants' ratings of symptoms on 6-point scales concerning the frequency with which each of 14 symptoms was experienced. The first item, for example, asked "Do you become tired in a very short period of time?" Response alternatives ranged from *once per day or more* (6) to *never* (1). We selected symptoms for inclusion on the basis of their appearance in existing symptom checklists, their associations with stressors in past research, and breadth across mental and physical domains. Principal factor analysis of responses to all 14 symptoms included in the survey for Sample 1 yielded four factors with eigenvalues greater than 1.0, and these factors were rotated to the configuration shown in the middle of the table. The right-hand portion of the table shows the two-factor solution obtained for the six symptoms included in the much briefer survey used with Sample 2. Four symptoms loaded together consistently in both samples, so we added these four (with unit weighting) to form a composite variable interpreted as *mental strain.* Comparison of the wordings of items in this survey with items in prior studies (e.g., Karasek, 1979) suggested that a more specific label for the composite was plausible— namely, *depression.* However, we preferred the more general label of *mental*

Table 3. Varimax-Rotated Factor Loadings of Symptom Reports

Symptom	Sample 1				Sample 2	
	1	2	3	4	1	2
Distracted	.69	.22	.04	.09	.43	.05
Tense	.68	.29	.23	.17	.64	.37
Sad	.60	.23	.17	.15	.80	.12
Overwhelmed	.58	.11	.14	.45	.74	.09
Tired	.55	.10	.19	.03	—	—
Eat for mood	.45	.15	.28	−.25	—	—
Out of breath	.42	.15	.25	−.16	—	—
Can't go to sleep	.19	.88	.10	.14	—	—
Can't stay asleep	.29	.64	.19	.05	—	—
Take sleeping pills	.12	.40	.17	.11	—	—
Lower back pain	.16	.23	.78	.14	—	—
Upper back pain	.19	.14	.44	.01	.08	.85
Loss of appetite	.07	.18	.08	.54	.06	.24
Sweaty palms	.22	.03	.20	.08	—	—

Note. Ns = 266 and 75 for Samples 1 and 2, respectively. Dashes indicate that these symptoms were not included in the survey for Sample 2. Factors with eigenvalues greater than 1.0 were retained for varimax rotation. A composite indicator of mental strain was calculated from the first four symptoms listed (distracted through overwhelmed). The reliability of this composite was .80 in Sample 1 and .74 in Sample 2.

strain because our composite included an item derived from a conception of anxiety (*tense*), and the distracted and overwhelmed items had a good deal of cognitive as well as affective content. (Admittedly, *depression* also has these multiple aspects by some definitions.)

Table 3 shows that additional composites of other strains might have been formed and analyzed or that a more heterogeneous strain composite might have developed. In the rest of this chapter, we focus on four-item mental strain composite, primarily because its availability from both samples allows tests of replication.

Validities of Climate and Strain Measures

Because climate is defined as the way individuals perceive and experience the work environment, any examination of the validity of climate measures is problematic. However, it is known from analyses of large data sets (e.g., $N = 23,096$, in Michela et al., 1989) based on responses to Litwin and Stringer's (1968) questionnaire that statistically significant differences between whole organizations and subunits may be detected with this instrument. This suggested that some validity was to be expected from the questionnaire with a variety of occupational groups and with various composite scoring schemes. We examined validity in the present sample with the present scoring scheme for each of the climate composites by testing for significant differences among schools within each of the two samples. For example, an omnibus F test examining mean differences in achievement climate across the nine schools of Sample 1 with 10 or more identified cases yielded highly significant results, $F(8, 192) = 3, 345, p = .001$. Although we did not obtain differences of this magnitude with all combinations of climate variable and sample, all three climate dimensions were found to differ among schools at the .10 level or better in the first, larger sample. We discounted the nonsignificant results both for reasons of statistical power and because the organizational units themselves (schools) may have been generally similar to one another on some dimensions; this would make it difficult to detect differences even if the measure had this capability (as demonstrated in the analysis of the $N = 23,096$ data set). Also working against obtaining significant differences in tests of differences among schools was the likelihood of heterogeneity within schools (e.g., as a function of one's grade level or department within a school). Thus, we concluded that the three climate composite measures were sufficiently valid.

In a separate set of analyses, we examined the validity, or at least the plausibility, of the symptom reports. We computed partial correlations first between age of respondent and each of the symptoms (controlling for gender) and then between gender of respondent and each of the symptoms (controlling for age). In the first and larger sample, older people reported being out of breath more frequently (partial $r = .20, p = .001$) and having more difficulty staying asleep (partial $r = .25, p < .001$). (Neither of these symptoms was included in the second sample.) These partial correlations with age are in accord with conventional wisdom, if not other data. Data are widely available about the tendency of women to report various symptoms more frequently than men (e.g., McLanahan & Glass, 1985), and the partial correlations with gender of respondent generally conformed to this pattern. For example, in Sample 1, women more frequently reported being tired (partial $r = .14$, $p = .01$) and having upper-back pain (partial $r = .11$, $p = .04$); in Sample 2, women reported being tense more often (partial $r = .27$, $p = .02$) and being marginally more overwhelmed (partial $r = .18$, $p = .07$). Of the few exceptions to the patterns described here, one was readily interpreted as also consistent with the validity of the measures: Men in Sample 1 reported having sweaty palms more often than women (partial $r = .10$, $p = .05$).

Results

We used simultaneous multiple regression analyses to test for associations between each climate dimension and strain. Each analysis contained three predictor variables: age, gender, and one of the three climate dimensions. We were particularly interested to see whether each climate dimension would yield a significant beta weight with age and gender held constant. In fact, age and gender had low correlations with climate dimensions and strain, so their inclusion had relatively little effect.

Empowerment Climate

The first set of multiple regression analyses examined the relation of empowerment climate and mental strain. As predicted, empowerment climate showed a negative relation to mental strain in both samples ($\beta = -.19$ and $-.28$, in Samples 1 and 2, respectively). The variance in mental strain explained uniquely by empowerment was significant in Sample 1, $F(1, 242) = 9.14$, $p < .01$, and in Sample 2, $F(1, 61) = 4.68$, $p < .05$. (Degrees of freedom reflect missing data on various measures.)

These findings provide definite evidence that empowerment climate is associated with mental strain for teachers. The negative direction of the association is consistent with our earlier suggestion that the relation of perceived control and stress may be involved in this association. It may be that teachers who perceive greater control over work activities—in the respects captured by the empowerment climate composite—experience buffering from the primary sources of stress in the school teaching environment. One alternative to this buffering interpretation is that a deficit of the environmental conditions captured by this climate dimension has direct effects on stress and strain.

Affiliation Climate

In the next set of multiple regression analyses, we examined the relation of affiliation climate and mental strain. In both samples, the direction of the association was negative, as predicted, but the association's size and statistical significance depended on exactly how the analysis was carried out. Using our method, established a priori, in which the outcome variable was the average of nonmissing indicators of mental strain (either three or four indicators had to be present) and missing data for either the predictor or outcome variables were handled in pairwise fashion, we found the strength of the association to be statistically significant only in Sample 1: $\beta = -.14$, $F(1, 244) = 4.99$, $p < .05$; Sample 2: $\beta = -.13$. Listwise deletion reduced the effect in Sample 1 to $p < .10$. Additional analyses used results of principal-components analyses of all of the symptom measures available in each sample to form outcome variables. The associations between affiliation climate and an optimally weighted principal-components index of strain were statistically significant both in Sample 1, $\beta = -.13$, $F(1, 226) = 3.91$, $p = .05$, and Sample 2, $\beta = -.33$, $F(1, 55) = 6.17$, $p < .05$. It should be noted that these latter analyses differed from the primary analyses also in the sample composition, because the requirement for no missing data for any of the strain indicator items in the principal-components analyses led to smaller sample sizes. Finally, it should be noted that corresponding results involving the other two climate variables did not show these kinds of differences as a result of how missing data were handled and how strain was indexed.

Achievement Climate

The last set of multiple regression analyses examined the relation of achievement climate and mental strain. In Sample 1 achievement climate was significantly associated with mental strain in a negative direction, $\beta = -.20$, $F(1, 246) = 10.28$, $p < .01$. Results from Sample 2 did not provide a replication of Sample 1 results. Both the simple correlation $(-.06)$ and the beta $(-.08)$ for the association of achievement climate and mental strain were quite small, and their probability levels failed to reach significance.

We are inclined to believe the results from Sample 1 and to discount those of Sample 2 because of the low statistical power resulting from the small sample size of Sample 2. (Sample 2 was drawn not only in an attempt to replicate results but also to demonstrate, as in Table 1, that there was no gross deficiency in sampling in the first study.) Naturally, the lack of a replication requires caution about interpretations of results from the first sample.

The negative direction of the association obtained in the first sample makes it doubtful that work overload is involved in the finding, as we originally predicted in our hypotheses. For this finding there are no obvious counterpart findings outside the climate literature, as there were for the other two climate dimensions, so we do not have as clear a picture of the psychological processes involved. Nevertheless, closer examination of the content of the achievement climate measure—involving high standards, clarity, and group pride—suggested that the measure captured perceptions and experiences of conditions felt to be desirable, which would be expected to bear a negative relation to stress and strain. In the discussion that follows, on underlying processes of organizational climate and stress associations, we develop this line of reasoning further.

Discussion

Our primary objectives in this work were to provide an initial empirical demonstration that organizational climate dimensions are related to work strain and to develop a conceptual framework for understanding these relations. How much progress has been made here toward these aims?

The empirical findings were solid in the case of the empowerment dimension and promising for the affiliation and achievement dimensions. Thus, this study's first objective was met to some degree, with the implication that the aspects of workers' experiences included within the concept of organizational climate are potential stressors.

However, the meanings of the obtained associations with mental strain remain open to interpretation, on both theoretical and methodological grounds. As we focus on these interpretational issues below, we elaborate the conceptual framework in ways intended to illuminate the meanings of climate–stress associations. We then address issues pertaining to generalization to other occupational groups and application of organizational climate theory to stress reduction at work. The thrust of our discussion is to address two broad questions: What is added by framing work-stress research in terms of organizational climate theory and methodology? How should future studies of organizational climate and stress be designed?

Theoretical Issues

Underlying processes of climate–stress associations. Established predictors of work strain, such as work overload and lack of control, have been thought to involve perceptions of threat, wearing effects of sustained arousal, and other relatively familiar and well-understood underlying processes. What might be the corresponding processes by which unfavorable organizational climate conditions generate stress and resultant strain? Previous researchers of climate (e.g., Litwin & Stringer, 1968; Stern, 1970) have suggested that organizational climate is important to other outcomes in part because it captures whether the work environment provides the experiences that workers need or want. This is essentially a question of person–environment (P-E) fit (e.g., Patsfall & Feimer, 1985). A central tenet of P-E fit theory (e.g., Harrison, 1978) is that stress results from not getting what one wants from the environment. Thus, we suspect that many associations between ratings of climate dimensions and strain are to be understood in terms of need or want satisfaction. For example, the association between empowerment climate and strain may, in part, reflect a process in which teachers with relatively low empowerment climate were distressed over not being provided with the kind of working conditions they wanted.

In this vein, organizational climate can serve as a vehicle to broaden the range of variables or conditions at work examined for their stressful effects. For example, experiences of unfair treatment of various kinds at work could be conceptualized and measured as climate dimensions and tested for their effects on stress. A resulting association between unfairness and stress is readily interpretable as involving need or want satisfaction because most people can be assumed to want fairness. With some other climate dimensions it may be necessary to document either that the study sample as a whole wants or needs the conditions captured by the dimension (e.g., challenging work) or that individual variation in the personal need (or want) functions as a moderator of the effect of the working condition on stress.

In future studies, when researchers consider whether a finding is consistent with our theorizing, it is probably not reasonable to require such a moderator effect or other findings that capture P-E fit explicitly as an explanatory variable because the necessary individual-differences variation may not exist in a given sample. Nevertheless, some corroboration may be needed for the suggestion that an association of climate conditions and strain reflect need or want satisfaction processes. For example, we asked members of Sample 1 to rate the extent to which they wanted various conditions at work on an 11-item questionnaire. On the item "I want to influence decisions about what we should try to accomplish in our work unit," 92% of the sample indicated that this was *somewhat, definitely,* or *extremely true of me.* The mean and standard deviations for this item were 3.80 and 0.94, respectively, on a 5-point scale. Clearly these ratings are consistent with the notion that a lack of empowerment would be unsatisfactory. Similarly consistent findings were obtained for personal want items corresponding to the other two climate dimensions. An affiliation-relevant item—"I want to be liked by my colleagues at work"—had a mean and standard deviation of 3.80 and 0.94, respectively, and an achievement-related item—"I want to perform at an 'award-winning' level in my work," yielded 3.70 and 1.14, respectively. This latter finding reconciles the initially unexpected findings for achievement climate if it is assumed that high standards, clarity, and group pride were understood to promote or signify desired high levels of performance.

Multiple facets of climate. Although it is meaningful to examine climate dimensions separately in relation to stress and strain, it is possible that additional information will be gained if future investigators conceptualize climate in a more complex way. After all, in meteorology, *climate* is not temperature, barometric pressure, and other parameters in isolation; it is their configuration. By analogy, one could expect that organizational climate dimensions interact in various ways to magnify or reduce effects on stress and strain. We did not have a priori hypotheses about such interactions and did not conduct tests of interactions for this chapter.

Nevertheless, using data from the larger sample, we did look at climate holistically in a further set of analyses, in which independent and total contributions of the various dimensions were examined. Age, gender, and all three climate dimensions were entered simultaneously as linear predictors of strain in a multiple regression analysis. As noted earlier, we were leery of doing such an analysis because of the correlations among the climate dimensions when dimension scores were calculated as sums of the items that had loaded highly on each of the factors obtained in analysis of the climate questionnaire. (For most purposes, we preferred this scoring because the resulting variables are

most easily interpreted.) Consequently, for the simultaneous analysis we calculated orthogonal principal-components scores from the 22 items on the climate survey. After varimax rotation, these scores showed good correspondence
to the scores on the basis of sums, as evidenced by correlations ranging from
.86 to .92 between corresponding variables of the two kinds (e.g., affiliation
as a sum of the three items identified in Table 2 and as an orthogonal factor
score) and by correlations of .24 or less for noncorresponding variables.

Results of the simultaneous analysis appear in Table 4. The rotated principal components corresponding to empowerment and achievement were seen
to explain statistically significant amounts of variance in strain uniquely,
whereas affiliation provided no additional explanation. The major implication
of this analysis is that there are distinct facets of organizational climate that
exert independent effects on stress and strain. An additional implication is
discussed in the next section.

Methodological Issues

A further set of interpretational issues for this research is common to studies
of work stress that have cross-sectional, self-report designs: Third-variable
causation or reverse causal ordering may underlie the observed associations.
Prominent among third-variable explanations are those concerning rater biases
or negative affectivity (Watson & Clark, 1984). That is, correlations of teachers'
ratings of their work environments (climate) and their physical and emotional
symptoms (strain) may have emanated from individual-differences variation
in tendencies to characterize both variables more or less favorably, depending
on one's affective state. The usual remedy to this possibility is to adopt a
longitudinal design, which has been used effectively in research on workplace
stressors for teachers (Schonfeld, 1992) and other occupational groups. Use of
an organizational-climate framework provides directions for new remedies.
Work in these directions would respond to calls by methodological analysts
(e.g., Frese & Zapf, 1988) for the development of multiple approaches to dealing
with threats to validity in work-stress research.

The first direction toward a remedy is to examine configural or interactive
effects of climate dimensions, as discussed in the preceding section, or to ex-

Table 4. Results of Multiple Regression Analysis Using All Demographic and
Climate Variables as Predictors of Mental Strain in Sample 1

Variable	β	r	sR^2	F	p
Age	.00	.00	.000	0.00	.957
Gender	.06	.05	.003	0.68	.409
Empowerment PC	−.14	−.14	.019	4.34	.038
Affiliation PC	.01	.01	.000	0.02	.893
Achievement PC	−.21	−.21	.044	9.79	.002

Note. PC = principal components. Squared semipartial correlations (sR^2) describe the variance
attributable uniquely to each predictor. Collectively, the predictors yielded a multiple correlation
of .257, $F(5, 210) = 2.98, p = .013$.

amine additive effects of climate dimensions, as demonstrated in Table 4. It is more difficult to dismiss these more complex results by reference to any given rater bias because the rater bias itself would need a corresponding form. Conceivably, a critic could develop an artifactual account by reference to multiple processes. Nevertheless, to the extent that the more complex results are interpretable in terms of organizational climate and stress theory, the burden of proof shifts to the critic to show that a complex artifactual account is equally plausible.

Another remedy involves, in essence, a new basis for characterizing the environment. This basis is the use of average reports about the work environment from groups of workers in the same environment. For example, the various work environments could be conceptualized as the various work groups within an organization, such as academic departments, grade levels within a school, offices at a corporate headquarters (with *offices* defined by a manager and his or her subordinates), or physically separate branches of a bank. In this approach, individuals are maintained as cases in statistical analysis. The strain outcome variable is handled as in other work-stress research, and the objective is to explain variance in strain at the individual level of analysis. The climate or other environmental variable is averaged for each of the environments (departments, etc.), and the average yielded by each person's group is used as the value (for each person in the group) for a predictive variable in multiple regression or similar statistical analysis.

This averaging procedure facilitates causal inference because it dilutes the effects of confounding processes, such as those connected with negative affectivity. This dilution can be pictured by imagining a climate measure or other stress predictor to have three kinds of components: the true score and error components of classical measurement theory, plus one or more bias components influenced by factors common to the predictor and the outcome. As the various group members' predictor scores are averaged, the values of the bias components will tend to go to zero, and thus the biasing factor's influence will be reduced.

Although one could develop an equivalent averaging procedure without approaching it from an organizational-climate framework, the organizational-climate literature (e.g., Payne & Pugh, 1976) has made salient the organizational hierarchy or other structure within which people experience the organization and thus highlights the levels of aggregation or averaging that may be appropriate. An illustration is provided in Figure 2, which depicts the hierarchical structure within which organizational-climate data typically are embedded. For teachers in schools, the hierarchical structure might work up from the individual teacher to a group defined by grade level or academic subject, then to a school, then to a school district, and so forth. When group means are calculated, they must be for a level of aggregation associated with consequential differences in the climate dimension being aggregated and used to predict strain. When the group mean does predict strain, the group differences are ipso facto consequential. When the group mean does not predict strain, further analysis should be done to determine whether there was little opportunity to predict strain as a result of restricted variance among groups

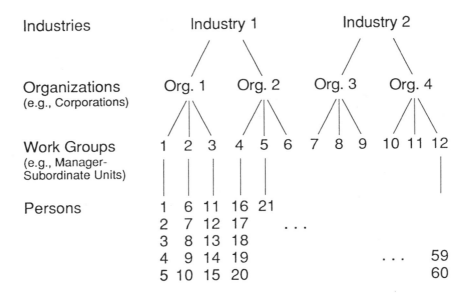

Figure 2. Hierarchical structure of organizational-climate data. In this example, persons are nested in work groups, work groups are nested within organizations (org.), and organizations are nested within industries.

in the climate dimension. This determination may be made by an analysis of variance (ANOVA), which tests differences among groups in individuals' ratings of the climate dimension.

Consistent with the discussion above, we used multiple regression analysis in an attempt to predict teachers' strain from their group mean ratings of climate. However, this attempt failed. As mentioned earlier, we did find evidence of significant and near-significant differences among schools in climate-dimension ratings (by use of n-group ANOVA), so the measures of climate seemed adequate. We suspected that the key problem was in using school as the grouping variable for aggregation. Application of Figure 2 to teachers' circumstances suggested that a consequential level of analysis existed between school and the individual, namely, grade level or academic department (depending on the kind of school). This may be the level of analysis exerting the greatest systematic influence on climate ratings and thus the level at which aggregations should be done to trace causality back to the environment. Unfortunately, in our studies data were not collected on an intermediate level of analysis.

Nevertheless, we are aware of one published study that used this approach successfully. Repetti (1987) was able to predict bank employees' reports of depressive symptoms from the mean ratings given in their bank branches of the social environment (e.g., frequency of conflicts among employees). Concurrent prediction was accomplished in a hierarchical multiple regression analysis. Intuitively, bank branch seemed a good example of the low- to intermediate-level of analysis that we would expect to be consequential.

There are some unsolved complications in this averaging approach, which is why we have called it a *direction* for a new remedy instead of a *solution*. For example, use of a group mean implies the existence of a random-sampling component of variation that is not handled by the fixed-effects models of standard multiple regression analysis. There are also risks of falling prey to versions of the ecological fallacy. Researchers wanting to address these problems should consult pertinent methodological literature in sociology (e.g., Firebaugh, 1980), social psychology (e.g., Kenny & LaVoie, 1985), and organizational psychology (e.g., Dansereau & Alutto, 1990).

Generalizability Issues

An implication of our earlier discussion of P-E fit and need satisfaction processes is that findings relating specific climate dimensions to strain are generalizable among occupational groups only to the extent that personal needs and wishes are shared. For example, there might be an occupational group preferring little personal control, in which case a null or opposite relation of empowerment and strain would be found. There also may be occupational groups with considerable within-group differences in needs and wants, in which case these differences may moderate associations of climate dimensions and strain.

In connection with this point, it seems possible that the replicated findings for empowerment climate also say something about teachers as an occupational group. Empowerment has been debated in education circles for at least a decade. At issue is whether teachers can do their best work with students by being free to "use their own approaches," as our climate survey put it, or whether curriculum designers and others "outside the classroom" have a better perspective on how teaching should be done. The teachers tend to say that they should be empowered. The literature on teacher stress and burnout has offered speculations that empowerment should be good not only for student education but also for reduction of teacher stress and burnout (e.g., Cedoline, 1982). Behind this suggestion, presumably, is the assumption that teachers want to be empowered. Our findings for empowerment were quite consistent with this assumption.

Potential Applications to Workplace Stress Reduction

A final potential contribution of the organizational-climate framework for work-stress research is its facilitation of organizational-level interventions for stress reduction. Most work-stress reduction interventions in the past, such as relaxation and time-management training, have been pitched at the individual level (e.g., McLeroy, Green, Mullen, & Foshee, 1984; Sloan, Gruman, & Allegrante, 1987). Organizational-level interventions may require changes in how people are managed, in work processes, and in other complex matters. Thus, these interventions are difficult, both in technical terms (What to do? Where to begin?) and in political terms (Whose interests will be served?).

The technical contribution of the organizational-climate framework comes from its potential to aid in diagnosing the what and where of the organizational origins of stress. Many relevant aspects of working conditions are readily assessed in an organizational-climate framework for survey research. Data may be analyzed and reported back to managers and their employees in ways consistent with survey-based consultation, thus enabling diagnosis and action planning for organizational-level stress-reduction initiatives (see Israel, Schurman, & House, 1991; Schneider, 1990).

An organizational-climate orientation to work-stress reduction can help with political barriers to organizational change by enhancing the contribution of the stress-reduction initiative to other bottom-line issues in the organization. It is not necessary to argue in favor of stress-reduction activities solely because they are good for the employee or because they are good for the company in ways separate from the core activities of the organization (as when arguing that stress reduction helps to control medical expenses). Current management thinking holds that satisfied employees satisfy customers (e.g., Tornow & Wiley, 1991)—and the customer is "king" today. Thus, if one can argue convincingly that organizational-level stress-reduction interventions will enhance employee satisfaction, managers and executives concerned with customer satisfaction should be motivated to undertake these interventions as well. One way to argue this point is to note the wide range of working conditions that may be assessed in an organizational-climate framework and the likelihood that some of these conditions would be found to require change to maximize employee satisfaction. The difficult part, of course, is to accomplish real change. We know of no better way to do this than to base change initiatives on data including organizational-climate ratings, to involve managers and their employees in change efforts through survey feedback and collaborative-action planning, and to motivate everyone to be committed to the change effort by communicating its benefits for individual employees and for the organization as a whole.

References

Allegrante, J. P., & Michela, J. L. (1990). Impact of a school-based workplace health promotion program on morale of inner-city teachers. *Journal of School Health, 60,* 25–28.

Atkinson, J. W. (1964). *Introduction to motivation.* New York: Van Nostrand.

Burke, W. W. (1986). Leadership as empowering others. In S. Srivastva & Associates (Eds.), *Executive power* (pp. 51–77). San Francisco: Jossey-Bass.

Cedoline, A. J. (1982). *Job burnout in public education: Symptoms, causes, and survival skills.* New York: Teachers College Press.

Chesney, M. A., Sevelius, G., Black, G. W., Ward, M. M., Swan, G. E., & Rosenman, R. H. (1981). Work environment, Type A behavior, and coronary heart disease risk factors. *Journal of Occupational Medicine, 23,* 551–555.

Cohen, S., & Wills, T. A. (1985). Stress, social support, and the buffering hypothesis. *Psychological Bulletin, 98,* 310–357.

D'Arienzo, R. V., Moracco, J. C., & Krajewski, R. J. (1982). *Stress in teaching.* Lanham, MD: University Press of America.

Dansereau, F., & Alutto, J. A. (1990). Level-of-analysis issues in climate and culture research. In B. Schneider (Ed.), *Organizational climate and culture* (pp. 193–236). San Francisco: Jossey-Bass.

Dunham, J. (1984). *Stress in teaching.* New York: Nichols.

Farber, B. (1984). Stress and burnout in suburban teachers. *Journal of Educational Research, 77,* 325–331.

Firebaugh, G. (1980). Assessing group effects: A comparison of two methods. In E. F. Borgatta & D. J. Jackson (Eds.), *Aggregate data: Analysis and interpretation* (pp. 13–24). Newbury Park, CA: Sage.

Frese, M., & Zapf, D. (1988). Methodological issues in the study of work stress: Objective vs. subjective measurement of work stress and the question of longitudinal studies. In C. L. Cooper & R. Payne (Eds.), *Causes, coping, and consequences of stress at work* (pp. 375–411). New York: Wiley.

Harrison, R. V. (1978). Person–environment fit and job stress. In C. L. Cooper & R. Payne (Eds.), *Stress at work* (pp. 175–205). New York: Wiley.

Israel, B. A., Schurman, S. J., & House, J. S. (1991). Action research on occupational stress: Involving workers as researchers. In J. V. Johnson & G. Johansson (Eds.), *The psychosocial work environment: Work organization, democratization, and health* (pp. 257–278). Amityville, NY: Baywood.

James, L. R. (1982). Aggregation bias in estimates of perceptual agreement. *Journal of Applied Psychology, 67,* 219–229.

James, L. R., & Sells, S. B. (1981). Psychological climate: Theoretical perspectives and empirical research. In D. Magnusson (Ed.), *Toward a psychology of situations: An interactional perspective* (pp. 275–295). Hillsdale, NJ: Erlbaum.

Jones, A. P., & James, L. R. (1979). Psychological climate: Dimensions and relationships of individual and aggregated work environment perception. *Organizational Behavior and Human Performance, 23,* 201–250.

Karasek, R. A. (1979). Job demands, job decision latitude, and mental strain: Implications for job redesign. *Administrative Science Quarterly, 24,* 285–308.

Karasek, R. A., Theorell, T., Schwartz, J. E., Schnall, P. L., Pieper, C., & Michela, J. L. (1988). Job characteristics in relation to the prevalence of myocardial infarction in the U.S. Health Examination Survey (HES) and the Health and Nutrition Examination Survey (HANES). *American Journal of Public Health, 78,* 910–918.

Kasl, S. V. (1984). Stress and health. *Annual Review of Public Health, 5,* 319–341.

Katz, D., & Kahn, R. L. (1966). *The social psychology of organizations.* New York: Wiley.

Kenny, D. A., & LaVoie, L. (1985). Separating individual and group effects. *Journal of Personality and Social Psychology, 48,* 339–348.

Litwin, G. H., & Stringer, R. A., Jr. (1968). *Motivation and organizational climate.* Cambridge, MA: Harvard University Press.

McClelland, D. C. (1985). *Human motivation.* Glenview, IL: Scott, Foresman.

McLanahan, S. S., & Glass, J. L. (1985). A note on the trend in sex differences in psychological distress. *Journal of Health and Social Behavior, 26,* 328–336.

McLeroy, K. R., Green, L. W., Mullen, K. D., & Foshee, V. (1984). Assessing the effects of health promotion in worksites: A review of the stress program evaluations. *Health Education Quarterly, 11,* 379–401.

Michela, J. L., Boni, S. M., Manderlink, G., Bernstein, W., O'Malley, M. N., Burke, W. W., & Schechter, C. B. (1989). *A hierarchical model for estimating influences on organizational climate: Theory, review, methods, and demonstration.* Unpublished manuscript, Columbia University Teacher's College, New York.

Patsfall, M. R., & Feimer, N. R. (1985). The role of person–environment fit in job performance and satisfaction. In H. J. Bernardin & D. A. Bownas (Eds.), *Personality assessment in organizations* (pp. 53–81). New York: Praeger.

Payne, R., & Pugh, D. S. (1976). Organizational structure and climate. In M. D. Dunnette (Ed.), *Handbook of industrial and organizational psychology* (pp. 1125–1173). Chicago: Rand-McNally.

Repetti, R. L. (1987). Individual and common components of the social environment at work and psychological well-being. *Journal of Personality and Social Psychology, 52,* 710–720.

Schneider, B. (1985). Organizational behavior. *Annual Review of Psychology, 36,* 573–611.

Schneider, B. (Ed.). (1990). *Organizational climate and culture.* San Francisco: Jossey-Bass.

Schneider, B., & Reichers, A. E. (1983). On the etiology of climates. *Personnel Psychology, 36,* 19–39.

Schonfeld, I. S. (1992). A longitudinal study of occupational stressors and depressive symptoms in first-year female teachers. *Teaching and Teacher Education, 8*, 151–158.

Sloan, R. P., Gruman, J. C., & Allegrante, J. P. (1987). *Investing in employee health.* San Francisco: Jossey-Bass.

Stern, G. G. (1970). *People in context: Measuring person–environment congruence in education and industry.* New York: Wiley.

Tornow, W. W., & Wiley, J. W. (1991). Service quality and management practices: A look at employee attitudes, customer satisfaction, and bottom-line consequences. *Human Resource Planning, 14*, 105–115.

Watson, D., & Clark, L. A. (1984). Negative affectivity: The disposition to experience aversive emotional states. *Psychological Bulletin, 96*, 465–490.

6

Defining and Measuring Hostile Environment: Development of the Hostile Environment Inventory

Gloria Fisher, Elizabeth M. Semko, and F. John Wade

Most organizations of the 1990s are equal-opportunity employers, and many have affirmative action plans. Most advertise themselves as being nondiscriminatory in hiring and other employment practices. It is common for them to encourage women and minorities to apply. However, there still exist subtle, discriminatory behaviors in the workplace. The term *hostile environment* has a particular meaning in legal and business literature and refers to the climate of an organization that is permeated with hostility or abusive conduct arising from discrimination or prejudice. Courts have defined a hostile environment to exist in a workplace when conditions in the setting are so severe and pervasive that they create an abusive working environment such that an individual's employment situation is altered (*Ellison v. Brady*, 1991; *Hall v. Gus Construction Company*, 1988; *Meritor Savings Bank v. Vinson*, 1986). The use of hostile environment as the basis of a discrimination suit does not require that plaintiffs show a specific discriminatory act had tangible employment-related consequences (such as sexual favors in exchange for a promotion), but they must establish that the debilitating impact on their work environment indirectly affected the conditions of their employment.

For the most part, discussion of hostile environment has been related to forms of sexual harassment. In a review of 57 federal sexual harassment cases since the *Meritor Savings Bank v. Vinson* (1986) case, Koen (1989) noted that 25 cases involved claims of hostile environment. However, hostile environment can also stem from bias related to race, age, national origin, or religion. In *Vance v. Southern Bell Telephone and Telegraph Company* (1989), a Black employee filed a discrimination claim based on hostile environment when he found a noose hanging over his desk. Jones (1986) surveyed Blacks with master's of business administration (MBAs) regarding the environment of their current employment setting. Of those surveyed, 90% viewed the climate of support as worse for them than for their White peers; 84% felt that considerations of race had a negative impact on employment decisions. *Wilson v. Monarch Paper Company* (1991) focused on hostile environment related to age, because signs saying "Wilson is old" were posted in view of other employees.

Demille (1989) found that hostile environment exists on college campuses, as well. She noted that, as a 57-year-old looking for a tenure-track position, she was called "a returning older woman" and was told by an administrator that a graduate fellowship would be wasted on someone that age.

In considering if the environment is abusive, the background and experience of the plaintiff, coworkers, supervisor, and the totality of the physical and psychological environment of the plaintiff's work area may be considered. Although courts have not always agreed on what behaviors constitute hostile environment, the following general guidelines are somewhat consistent throughout the cases: The conduct must be severe or pervasive, occurring with some frequency; it must be unwelcome; and it must be offensive. Offensiveness may be taken from the victim's point of view—using a reasonable person standard.

The present study is an exploratory effort to assess hostile environment as an organizational-climate measure. If a reliable, valid measure of hostile environment were developed, it could provide valuable feedback to employers regarding the perceptions of climate by employees. The purpose of this preliminary study is to begin development of a scale to measure employee perceptions of organizational climate, specifically hostile environment. In this initial investigation, we have constructed an inventory to measure faculty members' perceptions of hostile environment in an institution of higher learning. This study is a starting point for the development of a reliable and valid assessment instrument.

Effects of Hostile Environment

A consistent finding in the literature is that climates of organizations do affect employees (Fleishman, 1953; Kackza & Kirk, 1968; Lawler, Hall, & Oldham, 1974; Lewin, Lippitt & White, 1939; Litwin & Stringer, 1968; Schneider, 1975). Satisfaction and climate have been found to be more closely related than climate and performance.

Landis and Fisher (1987) developed an instrument that measured equal-opportunity climate (including items reflecting gender, race, religion, and national origin bias) in the military. They found significant positive relationships among perceptions of equal-opportunity climate and commitment, satisfaction, and effectiveness.

It appears that there may be major stress implications when an employee perceives a hostile organizational environment. For example, researchers of the Working Women's Institute (Crull, 1979) noted that 63% of women subjected to a sexually hostile work environment suffered physical symptoms, and 96% of the women suffered symptoms of emotional stress. In turn, these reactions resulted in loss of motivation, absenteeism, and diminished productivity. A study by the U.S. Merit Systems Protection Board (1980) found that 42% of female federal government workers were exposed to a sexually hostile environment; negative consequences included emotional or physical difficulties, negative feelings about work, and poor job performance.

More than 98% of Black MBAs who were alumni of the top five graduate business schools have reported that corporations have not achieved equal opportunity for Black managers (Jones, 1986). Of these, 90% viewed their climate of support as worse than that of their White peers. As one of Jones's (1986) survey respondents stated, "when you work your way up, try to conform, and even job hop to other companies only to confront the same racial barriers— well, it's debilitating" (p. 85).

Perceptions

One of the most difficult barriers to overcome in defining and measuring hostile environment is differing perceptions among individuals regarding what constitutes *hostility* in a working environment. In many cases, the behaviors are more subtle than telling someone he or she is fired because he or she is too old or refusing a promotion for someone who would not have sex with the boss. Therefore, there is more room for subjectivity in perceptions. These differing perceptions were demonstrated by Till (1980), who ranked sexual harassment into five general categories, covering a wide spectrum of behaviors—from sexist comments to rape. Categories focusing on seductive behavior and sexist remarks and behavior produced the lowest level of consensus about what was offensive to respondents. Ormerod (1987) also noted differences between men's and women's perception of the offensiveness of sexist behavior, pointing out that these differences in perceptions are not solely because of gender. Bowers (1975) noted that minorities, particularly Blacks, felt more discrimination in the navy; however, the better the climate, the less they felt discrimination. In *The Soldiers Report IV* (1986), differences (level of significance was not reported) were reported between minorities and Whites and between enlisted personnel and officers on such items as "race does not influence whether a soldier will get a fair deal." Fisher (1988) has also reported that differences in race and rank affected perceptions of equal-opportunity climate.

Method

In this study, we used two focus groups with expertise in the areas of discrimination and harassment to develop the Hostile Environment Inventory. The focus groups consisted of two industrial–organizational psychologists, two representatives from the area office of the Federal Equal Employment Opportunity Commission, a personnel administrator, a professor of management, and an attorney who specialized in employment-related cases. Men and women, Blacks and Whites, Christians and non-Christians, and various age groups were represented in the focus groups. Because of the demographics in the area where the research was conducted, we were able to enlist only African Americans and Whites to serve as subject-matter experts. A variety of religious philosophies and persuasions were represented in the focus groups.

Both groups were provided with court definitions, examples, and guidelines regarding hostile environment. Group 1 was asked to contribute behaviorally based items that they believed were examples of hostile environment. They were told that the final instrument would contain items related to gender, race, religion, national origin, and age. Additionally, several items from the equal-opportunity climate instrument developed by Landis and Fisher (1987) were reworded to reflect hostile environment in a academic setting. A total of 60 items were generated. Focus Group 2 was asked to rate each of the 60 behaviors for its degree of importance in contributing to hostile environment. Responses were rated on a 3-point Likert-type scale (1 = *not at all important* to 3 = *very important*). Only items with means above 2.0 were retained because this rating indicated that the item was *somewhat important*. In all, 54 final items were retained (see Appendix A). Response dimensions for the instrument were developed on a five-point Likert-type scale ranging from 1 (*virtually no likelihood that the behavior occurred*) to 5 (*very likely that the behavior occurred*).

Participants

Two hundred copies of the inventory were distributed throughout a historically and predominantly Black university. Sixty-five completed forms were returned, giving a response rate of 33%. Forty-five percent of the participants were African Americans, 14% were Asians, 41% were White, 44% were women, 81% were Christians, and 71% were age 40 or older.

Procedure

Respondents were asked to "indicate the likelihood of the following behaviors having occurred during the past year." They were also asked to provide a summary estimate of the overall climate of the organization they worked for. Response dimensions for the summary measure ranged from 1 (*very hostile*) to 5 (*very fair*). Respondents were also asked to complete a demographic section at the end of the inventory.

Data Analysis

To begin determining construct validity, we conducted an exploratory factor analysis. Internal consistency of the factors was assessed using Cronbach's alpha. Also, correlations between each item and the summary measure of climate were determined. These correlations were calculated to examine the internal consistency of the inventory. The degree of homogeneity of the inventory has some relevance to its construct validity. However, the contributions of internal consistency data to test validation is limited. But in the absence of external data, the researchers used these correlations for initial evaluations of the inventory's construct validity.

Table 1. Rotated Factor Matrix (Varimax) for Race and Gender-Related Items

Item	Factor		
	1	2	3
Race			
Criticize faculty of other race	**.79**	.29	.08
Praise same-race faculty	**.86**	.20	−.05
"You people"	−.06	.14	.04
NAACP poster	.19	.07	−.01
Promotion for same race	**.80**	.21	.23
Black calls Black "brother"	**.59**	.36	.04
Unqualified White promoted	−.10	.02	.41
Derogatory racial remarks	.48	**.65**	.11
Reprimands other race	**.79**	−.02	.43
Dining hall sitting	.32	.48	**.53**
Faculty development for same race	**.84**	.19	.33
More attention to same race	**.79**	.19	.23
Better qualified not promoted	.28	.14	**.75**
White not considered	**.69**	**.53**	.19
Racial joke	.18	**.84**	.15
White faculty fired	**.77**	.01	.34
Spouses offered work	**.76**	.45	.18
White "relating" to Black student	**.69**	.33	.34
Extra work from same race	.37	.15	**.72**
Founder's Day speaker	**.54**	.36	.35
Gender			
Man touches female faculty	.15	.29	**.79**
Male faculty says "Honey"	−.03	.39	**.76**
Asks woman to meet off campus	.19	.03	**.82**
Female faculty takes notes	.24	**.75**	.21
Men bring chips, women bring platters	**.54**	**.51**	.32
Unqualified woman tenured	.34	.10	**.74**
"Department better before women"	.33	.38	.25
Man shows *Penthouse*	.36	−.14	**.50**
Female time-consuming tasks	.39	**.62**	.22
Male chair to female secretary	−.00	.48	.17
Woman has less office space	.18	**.76**	.28
Female PhD called *Ms.*	.44	**.62**	−.10
Female faculty ignored	**.74**	.39	.08
All department chairs are men	.26	.22	−.02
Woman called "too sensitive"	**.79**	.16	.30
"I wonder who she slept with"	.27	.49	.43
How to dress to avoid harassment	**.70**	.26	.22
Woman hired at lower salary	**.55**	**.62**	.11
Woman denied tenure	**.71**	**.52**	−.03
After filing complaint, woman denied tenure	**.81**	.09	.22

Note. Factors loading at .50 or higher are shown in boldface. NAACP = National Association for the Advancement of Colored People.

Results

The inventory consisted of 54 items plus a summary item. The items focused on age ($n = 5$), race ($n = 20$), gender ($n = 21$), religion ($n = 4$), or national origin ($n = 3$). Four of these variables (race, gender, religion, and national origin) are addressed in Title VII (the employment section) of the 1964 Civil Rights Act, which is the foundation of U.S. equal employment opportunity legislation. Age is the subject of another important antidiscrimination law, the Age Discrimination in Employment Act (1967).

These 54 items describe behaviors that could be classified as hostile toward members of a particular race, religion, gender, national origin, or age group. They include actions that could be perceived as offensive, abusive, demeaning, degrading, or intimidating. Additionally, a summary statement was added to the inventory: "Overall, I would rate the environment on campus as very fair to very hostile."

We factor analyzed the race-related items and gender-related items by using a principal-components analysis with varimax rotation. The rotated matrixes are shown in Table 1; those with factor loadings of .50 or higher are in boldface. Note that four items had factor loadings of .50 or higher on two factors. These items were included in the interpretation of the meaning of both factors because there was a relatively high correlation between the item and each factor.

On the basis of the factor analysis and the researchers' interpretations, we developed nine different scales from the individual items. These were tested for reliability (Cronbach's alpha). The scales, their alpha scores, eigenvalues, and the percentages of variance explained are shown in Table 2.

As a first step toward validity testing, we measured the correlations between the scale means and the final summary question. These correlations were used for initial evaluation of the inventory's construct validity. The correlations were negative because the rating scale on the final question was reversed from the scale used for all other questions.

Table 2. Reliability of Scales and Correlations With Summary Question

Scale	No. of items	α	Eigenvalue	Variance explained	r with summary
Over the Hill and Out	5	.89			$-.42$**
Religious Sensitivity	4	.72			$-.30$*
Made in the U.S.A.	3	.84			$-.43$**
Racism	14	.95	9.94	49.7	$-.60$**
Social Cliquishness	3	.74	2.42	12.1	$-.35$*
Minority Misbehavior	3	.74	1.18	5.9	$-.10$
Woman as Interloper	7	.92	9.28	46.4	$-.47$**
Woman as Servant	8	.90	2.15	10.8	$-.40$**
Woman as Sex Object	5	.84	1.42	7.1	$-.26$

Note. The scales Over the Hill and Out, Religious Sensitivity, and Made in the U.S.A. were not factor analyzed.
*$p < .05$. **$p < .01$.

Discussion

In this initial effort, we determined that, despite the subjective nature of perception, it is possible to measure employee perception of organizational climate, specifically of hostile environment. Preliminary validity testing indicated that a construct such as hostile environment exists and is recognized by employees. This is an important first step in the validation effort.

A major limitation of the study was the sample size, because it was not sufficient for a stable factor analysis of the inventory's items. The instrument will be administered to more respondents and more information will be gathered on the religious preferences of the respondents. Choices for religious preferences of the respondents were confined to Christian and non-Christian; several respondents found that having only these two choices was too limiting. Additionally, we will conduct statistical analyses to assess the inventory's reliability and construct validity.

This initial research indicated that several factors may actually contribute to a racially hostile environment: *racism* (illegally making work-related decisions on the basis of race), *social cliquishness* (excluding or degrading persons of a different race in non-job-related interactions), and *minority misbehavior* (minority groups engaging in behavior that undermines racial harmony). Racism accounted for the largest percentage of variance. Thus, this research suggests that managing legally is an important step in reducing or eliminating the perception of a hostile environment. The present research shows that illegal behaviors promote a hostile environment. For example, one of the *racism* items is "An administrator does not recommend promotion for a faculty member of another race but does recommend promotion for an equally qualified member of the same race." However, the research also demonstrates that managing within the letter of the law is not sufficient to eliminate a hostile environment. For example, one of the items included in the *social cliquishness* factor is "A racial joke is overheard in the dining hall." Although the joke may not be illegal and, in fact, such behavior may be protected by the First Amendment, it promotes a hostile environment within the organization.

Ultimately, an instrument measuring hostile workplace environment will be important only if a hostile environment is found to influence the employee or the organization. Thus, future investigations into these relationships should be considered. Recent research indicates that a pervasively hostile environment can influence the amount of stress reported by employees. Continued stress can, in turn, lead to many unsatisfactory outcomes both for the employee and the organization, including health problems, sabotage, turnover, and lack of job satisfaction. Therefore, it is critical to examine whether a causal relationship exists between hostile environment and employee stress. The Hostile Environment Inventory, then, could be useful in pinpointing the specific areas of concern.

References

Bowers, D. G. (1975). *Navy manpower: Values, practices and human resources requirements.* University of Michigan, Institute for Social Research.

Crull, P. (1979). The impact of sexual harassment on the job: A profile of the experiences of 92 women. *Working Women's Research Series* (Research Series Report 3). New York: Working Women's Institute.

DeMille, B. (1989, June 7). Age discrimination in higher education is both overt and subtle. *Chronicle of Higher Education,* B2.

Ellison v. Brady, 924 F.2d 872 (9th Cir. 1991).

Fisher, G. (1988). *Construction and preliminary validation of an assessment instrument and its relationship with organizational outcomes.* Unpublished doctoral dissertation, University of Mississippi, University.

Fleishman, E. A. (1953). Leadership climate, human relations training and supervisory behavior. *Personnel Psychology, 6,* 205–222.

Hall v. Gus Construction Company, 842 F.2d 1010 (8th Cir. 1988).

Jones, E. W. (1986). Black managers: The dream deferred. *Harvard Business Review, 84,* 84–93.

Kackza, E., & Kirk, R. (1968). Managerial climate, work groups, and organizational performance. *Administrative Science Quarterly, 12,* 252–271.

Koen, C. (1989). Sexual harassment: Criteria for defining hostile environment. *Employee Responsibilities and Rights Journal, 2,* 289–301.

Landis, D., & Fisher, G. (1987). *Construction and preliminary validation of an instrument to measure equal opportunity climate* (Contract No. F49620-85-C-0013). Washington, DC: U.S. Air Force Office of Scientific Research.

Lawler, E. E., III, Hall, D. T., & Oldham, G. R. (1974). Organizational climate: Relationship to organizational structure, process, and performance. *Organizational Behavior and Human Performance, 11,* 139–155.

Lewin, K., Lippitt, R., & White, R. K. (1939). Patterns of aggressive behavior in experimentally created social climates. *Journal of Social Psychology, 10,* 271–299.

Litwin, G. H., & Stringer, R. A. (1968). *Motivation and organizational climate.* Boston: Harvard University Graduate School of Business Administration.

Meritor Savings Bank FSB v. Vinson, 477 U.S. 57 106 S. Ct. 2399 (91 L. Ed. 2d 49 1986).

Ormerod, A. J. (1987, August–September). *Perceptions of sexual harassment.* Paper presented at the 95th Annual Convention of the American Psychological Association, New York.

Schneider, B. (1975). Organizational climates: An essay. *Personnel Psychology, 28,* 447–479.

Soldiers Report IV. (1986). Washington, DC: Department of the Army, Directorate of Human Resources Development.

Till, F. (1980). *Sexual harassment: A report on the sexual harassment of students.* Washington, DC: National Advisory Council on Women's Educational Programs.

U.S. Merit Systems Protection Board. (1980). *Sexual harassment in the federal workplace: Is it a problem?* Washington, DC: U.S. Government Printing Office.

Vance v. Southern Bell Telephone and Telegraph Company, 863 F.2d 1503 (11th Cir. 1989).

Wilson v. Monarch Paper Company, 939 F.2d 1138 (5th Cir. 1991).

Appendix A

Hostile Environment Inventory

1. An administrator frequently criticizes a faculty member of a different race but rarely criticizes a faculty member of the same race.
2. An administrator often praises faculty members of the same race and seldom praises faculty members of a different race.
3. When a White administrator is conversing with several Black faculty members, the administrator uses the term "you people."
4. An Equal Employment Opportunity (EEO) officer is fired after supporting an employee with an EEO complaint.
5. A male faculty member frequently touches a female faculty member but never touches another male faculty member.
6. An instructor who has an NAACP poster on his office wall is subjected to derogatory remarks by a White administrator.
7. A male faculty member calls a female faculty member "Honey" or "Dear."
8. An administrator does not recommend promotion for a faculty member of a different race, while recommending equally qualified faculty of the same race.
9. A male administrator asks a female faculty member to meet him off campus to discuss her job performance. He always discusses male faculty members' performance during work hours on campus.
10. It is always a female faculty member who is assigned to take notes at a meeting.
11. A Black administrator addresses Black male faculty as "Brother" but addresses White male faculty as "Doctor."
12. Men are asked to bring sodas and chips to department or school functions; women are asked to bring items such as casseroles, sandwich trays, or meat platters.
13. An unqualified woman is tenured because the dean said it would not look good for equal opportunity not to do so.
14. An unqualified White is promoted because the administration feels that it would look discriminatory not to.
15. A male faculty member states "Our department worked together better before the female faculty member was hired."
16. Derogatory racial remarks are heard in the faculty lounge.
17. A male faculty member repeatedly shows copies of *Penthouse* or similar magazines to female faculty members.
18. An administrator reprimands a faculty member of another race for not attending a meeting; another faculty member of the same race as the administrator receives no reprimand for nonattendance.
19. Faculty of different races do not sit together in the dining hall.
20. A dean approves a faculty development opportunity for someone of the same race; a faculty member of a different race is denied the opportunity.

21. A female faculty member receives more time-consuming committee assignments than a male colleague.
22. A committee on campus has a male chairperson and a female secretary.
23. An administrator gives more attention and time to a faculty member of the same race.
24. An administrator is overheard saying, "A White faculty member was promoted, and a better qualified Black was not."
25. A female faculty member is assigned a less desirable office than a man.
26. A female faculty member with a doctorate is addressed as "Ms."; her male colleague with a doctorate is addressed as "Dr."
27. White applicants for clerical or staff positions are not favorably considered.
28. Suggestions of a female faculty member are ignored by the male chair.
29. A racial joke is overheard in the dining hall.
30. All department chairpersons in a school are men. A female faculty member is consistently mistaken for a secretary.
31. A qualified applicant with a "foreign-sounding" name is not considered for a position.
32. A White faculty member is fired for violating policy by making personal telephone calls at work, but Blacks in violation of the policy are not fired.
33. A Christian prayer is used at the graduation exercises.
34. An administrator is overheard saying, "They want too much money for the car, I'll try to Jew them down."
35. Spouses of highly recruited Black applicants are offered campus work, whereas spouses of highly recruited White applicants are not.
36. When a female faculty member complains of sexual harassment to her dean, he tells her, "you're being too sensitive."
37. When a female faculty member is promoted, a male faculty member makes the comment, "I wonder who she slept with to get promoted so fast."
38. A seminar on sexual harassment focuses only on how women should act and dress to avoid sexual harassment.
39. An administrator expresses concern to a White applicant that he will not be able to relate well to Black students. No similar concerns are expressed to a Black applicant.
40. An administrator demands extra work from faculty members of the same race to "enhance" their careers.
41. A chair asks a faculty member, "what church do you belong to?"
42. An administrator tells the chairs, "let's hire younger applicants because they are easier to motivate."
43. A dean denies a chair's request for a week's vacation time to attend a religious convention.
44. A chair is overheard referring to one of the faculty as "the senior citizen."

45. A woman is hired at a significantly lower salary than a similarly qualified man.

46. A woman is denied tenure, and a similarly qualified man is tenured.

47. An administrator is overheard saying, "although Professor Doe is underpaid, it isn't important that we adjust his salary because at his age he isn't going anywhere."

48. An older faculty member is not given faculty development funds because the dean feels the faculty member is too close to retirement to benefit and it would be a waste of money.

49. The recruitment director said that she doesn't want older faculty to participate in the recruitment efforts because she is afraid they will not relate well to high-school students.

50. A foreign-born professor knows the most about computers in the department. However, the chair assigns an American-born professor to go to dinner with representatives from a Fortune 500 company to discuss the department's computer needs.

51. A foreign-born professor is not asked what times he would like to teach; the preferences of his American-born colleagues are given consideration.

52. After filing a sexual-harassment complaint, a qualified professor is not tenured.

53. A female applicant is asked at her employment interview whether she is married.

54. A Founder's Day speaker makes derogatory generalizations about White America.

Part II

The Job Demand–Job Control Model

Introduction

Karasek's job demand–job control model of stress has captured increasing attention for a variety of reasons including its parsimony—making it communicable and comprehensible to a wide audience—and accumulating studies showing its predictive capacity for an array of health outcomes. As illustrated in the first chapter of this part, by Landisbergis, Schnall, Schwartz, Warren, and Pickering, reviewing extant research on the Karasek model, the model predicts a variety of cardiovascular effects in both cross-sectional and prospective studies. Still, the authors point out, there is a need for further work, including validation studies involving effects on health end points other than cardiovascular disease indicators, study of psychophysiological mechanisms and—of particular relevance to the present volume—alternative formulations of the demand–control model and of the demand and control constructs themselves. With regard to the latter issue, Landisbergis et al. raise the idea of broadening further the demand and control dimensions to better predict health outcomes.

The next two chapters—by Meijman, von Dormolen, Herber, Rongen, and Kuiper and by Radmacher and Sheridan, respectively—add to the veracity of the demand–control model. Radmacher and Sheridan used alternative measures (i.e., other than the Karasek demand and control measures) to assess the stress of working conditions across a variety of occupations. Of interest is that jobs classified as high-strain jobs according to the Karasek model tended to also rank as more stressful jobs according to alternative measures—lending support for the model. However, returning to the issue of the way demand and control are (or should be) operationalized, Radmacher and Sheridan suggest that these dimensions are not well specified in the Karasek model and that further breadth or complexity may create confusion regarding the meaning of these factors—ultimately, serving to reduce the practical value of the model.

The study by Meijman and colleagues is of special interest. It responds to the need for validative study of the demand–control model by using alternative health indicators and to the need for the investigation of mechanisms linking high demands and low control to ill health. In this study, job control was observed to moderate effects of job demands on a number of immunologic and neuroendocrine parameters. Of interest, however, was that some of the effects studied appeared to be more reliably associated with job demands than with control, which provides a bridge to the concluding chapter in this section, by Tattersall and Farmer.

In the final contribution to Part II, Tattersall and Farmer look at the relationship between workload or work demands, control and coping, and worker well-being, reviewing previous literature and providing new data. However, rather than strictly testing the demand–control model per se, Tattersall and Farmer's analysis gives primacy to the effects of work demands on health. Decision latitude (Karasek's control measure), perceived locus of control, coping style (problem vs. emotion focused), and other factors are then discussed as variables that can intervene to affect the regulation of work demands.

7

Job Strain, Hypertension, and Cardiovascular Disease: Empirical Evidence, Methodological Issues, and Recommendations for Future Research

Paul A. Landsbergis, Peter L. Schnall,
Joseph E. Schwartz, Katherine Warren, and
Thomas G. Pickering

Cardiovascular disease (CVD) is the leading cause of death in the United States and accounted for 43% of all deaths in 1991. *Essential* hypertension (those cases in which there is no recognized cause, such as an adrenal gland disorder or kidney disease) affects more than 50 million Americans (American Heart Association, 1993). Some risk factors for CVD have been identified (e.g., cigarette smoking, high serum cholesterol, hypertension, physical inactivity, obesity, and diabetes). Although the causes of essential hypertension are less well-known, increased sodium intake and excess weight are believed to play a role.

During the past decade, attention has focused on the possible role of work-related stress in the etiology of CVD and high blood pressure. A model of occupational stress (see Figure 1) developed by Karasek and colleagues (Karasek, 1979; Karasek & Theorell, 1990) has gained increasing support. Karasek argued that the greatest risk to mental and physical health from stress (including risk of CVD and high blood pressure) occurs in workers facing high psychological workload demands or pressures who also have low control or low decision latitude for meeting those demands.

The Karasek model is valuable because it hypothesizes, in a parsimonious manner, effects of job strain on both health (increasing risk of illness as demands exceed decision latitude [Arrow A in Figure 1]) and behavior patterns. Increases in active learning, participation, and job involvement are predicted to occur more often when the challenges in a situation are matched by the person's control over alternatives or skill in dealing with the challenge (Arrow B in Figure 1), for example, in "active" jobs (Landsbergis, Schnall, Dietz, Friedman, & Pickering, 1992).[1]

---

[1]Although an advantage of Karasek's (1979) model is its simplicity, it does not replace other, more complex and valuable models of occupational stress, such as the person–environment fit

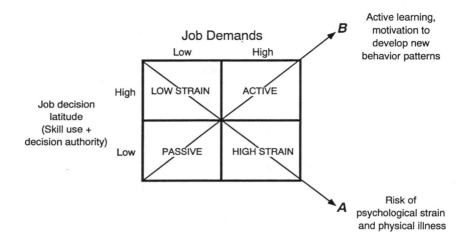

Figure 1.   Karasek job-strain model.

Although significant positive associations between job strain, hypertension, and CVD have been repeatedly observed, important methodological and theoretical issues remain. These include the measurement of blood pressure with ambulatory monitors, the measurement of cumulative exposure to job strain, the objectivity of measures of exposure, formulations of the job-strain model, the scope of the constructs of job demands and job-decision latitude, and assessment and control of potential confounders. We begin with a brief review of job-strain studies, followed with a summary of results from the Cornell work-site study and a discussion of methodological and theoretical issues; we then conclude with suggestions for further research.

Studies of Job Strain and CVD

Over the past 13 years, 36 studies on job strain and all-cause mortality, CVD, or CVD risk factors have been published. These studies—conducted in Sweden, the United States, Finland, Denmark, Australia, and Japan—provide strong evidence that job strain is a risk factor for CVD (Schnall, Landsbergis, & Baker, 1994). Of the 15 studies of CVD (including 2 of all-cause mortality), 13 showed clear associations between job strain and outcome. More important, 7 of the 8 cohort studies showed strong positive associations.

In the 21 studies of CVD risk factors, the following patterns were seen.

---

model originating from the University of Michigan (Caplan, 1983; Caplan, Cobb, French, Van Harrison, & Pinneau, 1975) or the recent refinement of the Michigan model by researchers for the National Institute for Occupational Safety and Health (Hurrell & McLaney, 1988). These models incorporate a variety of perceived and objective stressors; feedback loops; and the potential moderating effects of personality factors, nonwork factors, and demographic measures. However, the job-strain model seeks to identify objective features of the work environment that can be categorized as demands or constraints on control and examines the effects of their co-occurrence (i.e., interaction). It thus emphasizes the stress-producing properties of these objective factors over subjective perceptions or the fit between person characteristics and job characteristics.

Three studies found no association between job strain and serum cholesterol. Two studies found a link between job strain and smoking, whereas 2 did not. (One of the negative studies, however, did show higher rates of smoking at lower levels of job-decision latitude.) Of 8 studies of blood pressure measured in a clinical setting, only 1 found a significant association. However, of the 9 studies where an ambulatory (portable) blood pressure monitor was worn during a workday, 5 showed strong positive associations between job strain and blood pressure, whereas the remaining 4 yielded a mixture of positive and null results. Because ambulatory blood pressure measurement is more reliable (because there is no observer bias and the number of readings is increased) and is a more valid measure of average blood pressure (because blood pressure is measured during a person's normal daily activities) than casual measures of blood pressure, we feel confident in placing more emphasis on the ambulatory blood pressure results. Two of the 5 positive ambulatory blood pressure studies are described in more detail below.

Results From the Cornell Work-Site Study

Case-Control Study

An ongoing prospective cohort study of healthy employed men and women in New York City, aged 30 to 60 years, was begun in 1985 at Cornell University Medical College. A nested case-control study design, which included 262 men from eight worksites in a wide variety of white-collar and blue-collar jobs, was implemented as part of the first wave of data collection. Eligible cases ($n = 85$) had diastolic blood pressure (DBP) above 85 mm Hg at both screening and recruitment or were taking antihypertensive medication, whereas controls ($n = 177$) had DBPs less than or equal to 85 mm Hg at both screening and recruitment. Each participant wore a 24-hour ambulatory blood pressure monitor, completed detailed psychosocial and health questionnaires (including the Karasek Job Content Questionnaire [JCQ]; Karasek et al., 1985), received a medical examination, and provided blood and urine samples. Other known risk factors for hypertension were evaluated. In the first wave of the study, participants exposed to job strain (21% of the sample) were at significantly increased risk of hypertension (being a case; see Table 1) with other possible risk factors controlled for (e.g., age, race, education, body mass index, Type A behavior, alcohol use, smoking, 24-hour urine sodium, and physical exertion level of the job) along with a potential confounder of this association (work site; Schnall et al., 1990).

Cross-Sectional Study

The same sample was analyzed with mean ambulatory blood pressure as the outcome rather than case-control status (Schnall, Schwartz, Landsbergis, Warren, & Pickering, 1992). Using an analysis of covariance, we found that job

Table 1.   Risk Factors for Hypertension: New York City Work-Site Blood Pressure
Study (N = 262)

Risk factor	Adjusted odds ratio (95% confidence interval)		p
Age 51–60 (vs. 30–40)	11.4	4.3–30.4	<.0001
Age 41–50 (vs. 30–40)	6.4	2.6–15.7	<.0001
Alcohol	3.0	1.4–6.3	.005
Job strain	2.9	1.3–6.6	.011
Body mass index	1.3	1.1–1.5	.0009
Race (Other than White)	1.7	0.6–5.3	ns
Smoking	1.5	0.7–3.3	ns
Physical exertion	1.1	0.7–1.8	ns
Type A behavior	1.1	0.5–2.2	ns
Education	1.0	0.8–1.2	ns
Urine sodium	1.0	1.0–1.0	ns

Note.   Risk estimates reflect the independent effect of each variable, controlling for all other
variables in the model. The full model was computed by unconditional logistic regression.
Worksite was also controlled for and was coded as seven dummy variables. *ns* = Not significant.

strain was associated with an elevation in work systolic blood pressure (SBP)
of 6.8 mm Hg (p = .002) and in work DBP of 2.8 mm Hg (p = .03), after
adjusting for the same risk factors and potential confounders. This effect per-
sisted in home and sleep blood pressures, indicating that job strain is associated
with a generalized and persistent arousal beyond the immediate work situation. Job strain was also associated with an increase in left ventricular mass
index (LVMI) of 9.7 g/m^2 (p = .001).

Prospective Cohort Study

The original 262 participants and 22 additional men eligible for the cohort
study were followed for 3 years. Of the 284 eligible men, 195 completed the
protocol. Analysis of cohort data displayed a pattern of blood pressure change
consistent with the initial case-control and cross-sectional findings. Workers
exposed to job strain at both waves of data collection (n = 15) had a greater
increase in work DBP (+4.0 mm Hg, p = .015), controlling for the covariates
listed above, than the reference group (no exposure at either wave, n = 138),
whose DBP barely changed. The DBP of the group that moved from job strain
to no job strain (n = 25, DBP = −1.6) decreased over time, whereas, con-
versely, the adjusted DBP of the group that moved from no strain to job strain
(n = 17, DBP = +0.9) increased. Differences in blood pressure across the four
exposure groups were significant (p = .031). A similar pattern emerged for
work SBP (Schnall, Landsbergis, Schwartz, Warren, & Pickering, 1992).

   These results were consistent with a study of 3-year change in casual blood
pressure at one of the cohort study work sites—a major New York City bro-
kerage firm undergoing mass layoffs (Schnall, Landsbergis, Pieper, et al.,
1992). Increases in blood pressure over 3 years were associated with having a

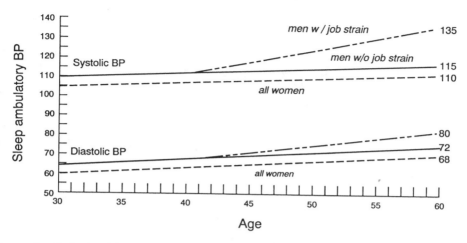

Figure 2.   Relationship of mean sleep ambulatory blood pressure to age, by gender and job strain. Work site, race, and body mass were controlled for.

clerical job title (a proxy measure for job strain) but were not associated with anticipation of job loss.

Demographic Variables

In other analyses (Schwartz, Schnall, Warren, & Pickering, 1992), first-wave data for all eligible participants have been examined. This included a ninth work site and women from three of the first eight work sites. Of the total sample (N = 373), 22% were women, 18% were African American, and 6% were Hispanic. Regression models of six dependent variables (SBP and DBP— at work, home, and during sleep) included, as independent variables, four demographic measures (age, body mass index, race, and gender), whereas job strain, other control variables, all two-way, and various three-way interaction terms were eligible for entry in a stepwise procedure.

Across all six blood pressure measures, each of the four demographic variables were significantly associated with outcome. African Americans had significantly higher SBP (ranging from 5.7 to 8.5 mm Hg) and DBP (4.0–6.0 mm Hg) than other groups. Men had significantly higher SBP (5.5–7.5 mm Hg) and DBP (2.9–4.2 mm Hg) than women. The most significant term[2] in all six equations and the only consistent result (aside from the four demographic measures) was a three-way interaction (Gender × Job Strain × Number of Years Over Age 40). Job strain affected blood pressure only for men (not women), and this effect began at age 40 and increased steadily thereafter (see Figure 2). This is consistent with the hypothesis that it is the cumulative exposure to job strain (rather than current exposure) that affects blood pressure. With this three-way interaction term in the model, the coefficient for the main effect of age was substantially smaller. This indicates that the relation-

---

[2]The significance of the three-way interaction term was $p < .0001$. No other variable in the stepwise regression was significant beyond the .01 level.

ship of age to blood pressure may be relatively weak for those not in high-strain jobs. Although one other study (Light, Turner, & Hinderliter, 1992) also failed to find an association between job strain and ambulatory blood pressure for women, two studies have observed this association among women (Theorell et al., 1993; Van Egeren, 1992).

Future Research Directions

Biological Mechanisms

So that the biological mechanisms by which job strain may affect blood pressure can be assessed, several new tests have been added to the Cornell work-site study. One was for urinary catecholamines and cortisol, and another was an ultrasound procedure to measure the extent of atherosclerosis in the carotid artery. In addition to associations between job strain and standard coronary risk factors (e.g., blood pressure), other hypothesized pathways by which job strain might affect CVD are an increase in the mass of the heart's left ventricle (measured by LVMI); an increase in the speed of coronary atherosclerosis, through such mechanisms as coagulation; and the precipitation of myocardial infarction or arrhythmias among vulnerable people with underlying heart disease.

Cumulative Exposure

To date, the Cornell work-site study has assessed only current exposure to job strain, which cannot adequately reflect interpersonal differences in cumulative exposure. For example, 22% of its participants changed job-strain status over the first 3 years of the study. Some older participants with high blood pressure may have worked for years in high-strain jobs, but were eventually promoted (to a job with more authority or skills) and were therefore classified as not exposed in this analysis. In theory, a measure of cumulative exposure should provide a more rigorous test of the job-strain hypothesis.

Although the cross-sectional Age × Strain interaction (the apparent lack of effect among the 30- to 40-year-olds in the study) suggested an induction period of at least one decade. Cohort findings, stratified by age group, suggested that blood pressure increases occurred over 3 years, even in the youngest (30- to 40-year-old) group (Schnall, Landsbergis, Schwartz, et al., 1992). Therefore, complete work histories are now being collected from study participants. From these, we will be able to estimate whether cumulative exposure (e.g., number of years in high-strain work) is a better predictor of CVD risk than only current exposure. In addition, we will be able to estimate the induction period for hypertension due to job strain, whether exposures early in life or later in life are more consequential, and whether the negative effect of job strain on blood pressure can be reversed by a certain number of years working in a nonstrain job (Landsbergis, Schnall, Schwartz, Warren, & Pickering, 1995).

More Objective Measures of Job Strain

Self-report bias is a potential problem in many job-strain studies because exposure has often been assessed through questionnaires completed by study participants. Self-reports may be inaccurate descriptions of job characteristics or may be biased by personality characteristics. However, although self-reports of work characteristics may be affected by perceptions, this does not make them primarily subjective. In addition, they are not measures of perceived stress, because someone can work in a job with high demands and low decision latitude and not report feelings of stress.

Concerns about the subjectivity of perceptions in self-report data have been substantially addressed by 11 job-strain studies in which national averages of job characteristics for a particular job title are assigned to individuals having that job title, thereby effectively excluding the subjective component of reported job-characteristics data (Schwartz, Pieper, & Karasek, 1988). This procedure, designed to establish a consensus of workplace observers, results in more objective measures of stressors because "they are independent of a person's cognitive and emotional processing" (Frese & Zapf, 1988, p. 378). The imputation technique may also be effectively applied within a workplace, by averaging people's ratings of job demands, job-decision latitude, and other job characteristics within a job title. A person's self-reported job-characteristics score can be removed from the average score for his or her job title, and the resulting adjusted job title average can then be assigned to the person. This would ensure the goal of independence when predicting outcomes for individuals.

However, this strategy can result in substantial misclassification because of within-occupation heterogeneity of job characteristics and a loss of statistical power for detecting job-strain effects. Despite these limitations, 7 of 11 CVD and CVD risk-factor studies using the imputation method have yielded significant positive findings (Schnall et al., 1994), providing strong support for Karasek's model. Yet, use of this method is becoming increasingly problematic in the United States because U.S. national averages have been based on the 1969, 1972, and 1977 Quality of Employment Surveys (Karasek et al., 1985) conducted by the U.S. Department of Labor. National occupational averages may have changed substantially over the intervening period. Although we believe that the imputation methodology has wide applicability in this and other areas of research, it requires that large nationally representative surveys such as the Quality of Employment Surveys be conducted periodically.

To assess more objective cumulative exposure, Johnson and Stewart (1993) constructed a job exposure matrix in Sweden (with job title-specific, age-group, and gender-specific scores) in a study population that included information about previous job titles. Job characteristics were then imputed to study participants on the basis of length of employment in a particular job. A similar matrix could be created in the United States, but, again, it would have to be based on updated national job-characteristics surveys. Ideally, a research study would use the imputed data as well as self-reported data.

Other strategies need to be developed for obtaining more objective measures of job strain and of job stress in general. One strategy has been to use outside expert observers. In one of the few studies in which expert ratings were available (of education "expected of a particular occupation"), those ratings were highly correlated (rs = .64–.69) with self-reports of "intellectual discretion" (Karasek, Baker, Marxer, Ahlbom, & Theorell, 1981). (Lower correlations would be expected between expert observers and self-reports for "psychological workload demands," which are more subjective and have less between-occupation variance than measures of decision latitude [Schwartz et al., 1988].) Another strategy, being used in the Cornell work-site study, is to examine other features of the work environment that may be correlated with job strain (e.g., involuntary overtime, low educational requirements of the job, assembly-line work, electronic monitoring, and short-cycle-time work).

Although these techniques for obtaining more objective measures of job strain are valuable for internal validity, they are of limited value for the goal of understanding the social context of stress in a particular workplace because they are inherently reductionist and exclude from analysis the meaning that events have for participants. To accomplish the goals of understanding context or conducting and evaluating interventions, standardized scales (such as those from Karasek's JCQ) need to be used in combination with qualitative data collection techniques and questions specific to a particular job and workplace. Qualitative data collection and analysis methods (e.g., focus groups, interviews, and ethnographic observation; Neale, Singer, & Schwartz, 1987; Patton, 1987) are among the techniques that overcome the limitations of quantitative instruments and analysis.

Formulations of the Job-Strain Model

Job strain has been defined as an interaction between job demands and job-decision latitude (Karasek, 1979). However, a variety of mathematical forms of job strain have been used in CVD research studies. Only three of six studies (Haratani, Kowakami, & Araki, 1992; Johnson & Hall, 1988; Landsbergis, Schnall, Schwartz, Warren, & Pickering, 1994) found a significant interaction effect with the traditional partialed product-interaction term for Latitude × Demands, after controlling for the main effects of latitude and demands. More frequently, a dichotomous, trichotomous, or four-level exposure variable was constructed (high demands plus low latitude), with typically significant positive effects. In addition, in all six studies that used a quotient term (demands divided by latitude) to operationalize job strain, significant associations were found (Schnall et al., 1994). Main effects were often not reported in the studies using dichotomous or quotient terms. Therefore, it remains to be seen whether a strict interaction formulation (with no main effects) or a model including some main effects of job demands and job-decision latitude as well as an interaction term best describes the effect of job strain on cardiovascular health. Karasek (1989) suggested that true interaction effects are frequently difficult to detect because of a lack of statistical power. With respect to the job-strain model in particular, he argued that the exact form of an interaction term is not the main issue because "the primary 'interaction' claimed for the model is that two separate sets of outcomes (e.g., risk of illness and activity level) are jointly predicted by two different combinations of psychological demands and decision latitude—an interaction of significant practical importance" (p. 143).

The possible existence and location of a threshold of effect for job strain remains to be determined. Data from the Cornell work-site study suggest a significant effect of job strain (using the quotient term) on work and home ambulatory blood pressure at cutpoints beginning at about the upper third of the distribution of job strain and increasing in magnitude at narrower cut-points. The group defined by the lowest third of decision latitude and the highest third of demands (6.5% of the sample) had work SBPs that were about 9 to 12 mm Hg higher than those in low-demand or high-latitude groups. (Patterns for DBP were less clear.) The use of national means for decision latitude and demands to define the high-strain group (8% of the sample) increased effect sizes to 11.5 mm Hg SBP and 4.1 mm Hg DBP. Therefore, in this sample, effects were observed for a range of formulations of job strain. Job strain appeared to have a threshold of effect and increasing effects at higher levels (or doses) of job strain (Landsbergis et al., 1994).

Components of the Job-Strain Model

Associations between job strain, hypertension, and CVD have been reported with varied (and often rather narrow) operationalizations of demands and control. One of the next stages in research is to assess whether broader operationalizations of these concepts will hinder or improve the ability to predict ill health and whether certain dimensions of demands and control may be more strongly associated with hypertension and CVD. For example, levels of workers' influence—not just on the individual's task, but higher level influence at the group, department, or company level, either individually by workers or collectively—also need to be examined (DiMartino, 1992; Israel, Schurman, & House, 1989; Johnson, 1989). In the Cornell work-site study, adding a measure of organizational influence to the task-level decision-latitude variable produced a greater risk of hypertension because of job strain (odds ratio [OR] = 3.7, 95% confidence interval [CI] 1.6–8.5; Landsbergis et al., 1994).

The Job Demands scale in the JCQ (Karasek et al., 1985) primarily contains measures of workload demands, along with one item on role conflict. However, it has been suggested that a broader formulation of job demands may be appropriate. For example, both the JCQ and the generic job-stress instrument developed by the National Institute for Occupational Safety and Health (NIOSH) (Hurrell & McLaney, 1988) from the Michigan job-stress model (Caplan et al., 1975) have items measuring cognitive demands. In addition, the Michigan model and the NIOSH instrument each contain items on job demands, such as role ambiguity, responsibility for people, and threat of violence or injury.

Workplace social support was added to the job-strain model as a third major psychosocial job characteristic in four CVD studies as well as to a number of studies of psychological strain outcomes. The combined hazard has been referred to as *iso-strain*, or socially isolated high-strain work. Three of the four CVD studies have provided evidence of interaction—a buffering of the effects of job strain by social support (Astrand, Hanson, & Isacson, 1989; Johnson & Hall, 1988; Johnson, Hall, & Theorell, 1989). Therefore, we recommend that future job-strain studies examine the potential main and moderating effects of social support.

Potential Confounding Variables

Related job characteristics. Physical activity is protective of CVD, and overall self-reported physical activity at work has been controlled for in many of the job strain–CVD studies (Schnall et al., 1994). However, variations in physical position and activity during a workday have been shown to affect ambulatory blood pressure readings (Pickering, 1991). Therefore, participants in the Cornell work-site study record their position for each blood pressure reading and now wear a small device—known as an *actigraph*—along with their ambulatory blood pressure monitor to measure changes in physical activity throughout the day. Future analyses will include these measures as independent and control variables.

Other workplace characteristics (e.g., job insecurity, and chemical and physical work hazards) also need to be assessed and controlled for. Modest elevations of blood pressure have been associated with noise (Talbott et al., 1985), presence of lead (Pirkle, Schwartz, Landis, & Harlan, 1985), and job insecurity (Kasl & Cobb, 1983). CVD has been associated with exposure to carbon monoxide, solvents, other chemicals, and shift work (Kristensen, 1989). Blood lead levels of some participants in the Cornell work-site study will be measured to examine whether lead is possibly a confounder or effect modifier of the job strain–blood pressure relationship.

Nonwork sources of stress. The research on job strain and both CVD and psychological distress has made an important contribution to the understanding of a major environmental source of stress. Of course, important sources of stress exist outside the work environment, and these have been carefully examined in major bodies of research, including those on stressful life events and on work–family role conflict. The concept of control as a critical moderator of demands has influenced recent work in those research traditions. For example, controllability of stressful life events has been considered an important variable in modifying the effects of events (Kasl, 1983, p. 95). Measures of control, demands, support, and conflict (and their interaction) in home and family settings have also provided valuable insights (Hall, 1992). Person–environment fit researchers as well have emphasized control as a significant variable in their model (Caplan, 1983). Such nonwork sources need to be incorporated into any complete model of stress and health.

Personality. Most job-strain researchers recognize that characteristics of the individual play a role in the development of stress symptoms and illness. We believe it is unlikely, however, that such characteristics explain the reported associations between job strain and hypertension or CVD. Type A behavior, for example, is primarily associated with higher status, success-oriented jobs, making it an unlikely confounder of job strain and CVD. In the Cornell work-site study, Type A behavior was most prevalent in active jobs (Landsbergis et al., 1992) and was not associated with hypertension. (In addition, in this study the Type A scale was controlled for.) In fact, hypertensive participants did not differ significantly from normotensive control participants on anger, anxiety, hostility, Type A behavior, or other psychological measures in the Cornell work-site study (Schnall et al., 1990). Although some research has suggested associations between some personality characteristics and hypertension and CVD (Friedman et al., 1994), in most positive studies participants with hypertension have been aware of their blood pressure and, thus, these associations could result from diagnosis and labeling rather than represent a cause of the illness (Rostrup & Ekeberg, 1992).

Research on the effects of personality measures also needs to consider the potential influence of job characteristics in shaping personality. For example, Kohn and Schooler (1982) demonstrated that the substantive complexity of work (closely related to decision latitude) predicted increased intellectual flexibility, nonauthoritarianism, and intellectually demanding leisure time activities 10 years later. In Sweden, workers whose jobs became more passive (low demand–low latitude) over 6 years reported less participation in political and leisure activities. In contrast, workers in jobs that became more active participated more in these activities (Karasek & Theorell, 1990).

Intervention Studies

In the United States, efforts to reduce occupational stress continue to focus primarily on changing the individual behavior of employees (e.g., relaxation techniques, exercise, diet, and cognitive–behavioral skills; Ivancevich, Matteson, Freedman, & Phillips, 1990). However, the accumulation of evidence linking job stress (including job strain) to CVD risk (and other negative health outcomes) has resulted in a variety of job-redesign and public-education programs (DiMartino, 1992; Karasek & Theorell, 1990), the joint conference between the American Psychological Association and NIOSH that gave rise to this volume, and several intervention studies designed to alter the work environment to reduce job stressors (e.g., Cahill & Feldman, 1993; Israel et al., 1989). It is important that such programs and studies be promoted and flourish. It is also critical that work-environment reform efforts and new work systems such as Total Quality Management, whether or not part of a formal intervention study, be carefully evaluated.

Interventions to reduce job strain will differ in character from traditional heart disease risk-factor interventions (e.g., changes in diet, smoking cessation, exercise, weight loss) that are based on individual lifestyle changes. They will be guided by methods developed in social psychology and sociology, primarily participatory action research. This process involves having researchers and organization members (usually management and employee representatives) participate jointly in all aspects of the intervention—including needs assessment, developing targets for change, feedback, planning, intervention, and evaluation (Israel et al., 1989). The goals of such a process are both evaluation and workplace change. This will necessitate the use of both quantitative and qualitative research methods; multiple levels of intervention (e.g., individual, work group, and organizational); longitudinal designs; as well as the measurement of process, impact, and outcome (thus requiring multidisciplinary teams skilled in these techniques; Israel, Schurman, Hugentobler, & House, 1992). Although changes in risk factors and resulting impacts on health will be more difficult to isolate than in a clinical-intervention trial, such methods provide a key to both changing structural aspects of the workplace that cause stress and understanding the change process.

Conclusion

The evidence supporting the existence of a relationship between job strain and CVD is quite strong.[3] Prior to the Cornell work-site study and several other recent studies, however, evidence for a relationship between job strain and CVD risk factors was mixed. Results from the Cornell work-site study have indicated a relationship of job strain (a) to hypertension (defined from casual blood pressure readings taken on two separate occasions); (b) to ambulatory blood pressure at work, at home, and during sleep; (c) to enlargement of the heart; and (d) to 3-year changes in ambulatory blood pressure.

All of this suggests several important directions for future research in this area. First, we would like to learn whether job strain is related to any of a variety of structural characteristics of the cardiovascular system (e.g., left ventricular mass, arterial wall thickness, or the presence of atherosclerotic plaques). Second, there is a need to investigate alternative biophysiological mechanisms by which job strain may elevate blood pressure, both acutely and chronically (e.g., activation of the sympathetic nervous system).

Much work also needs to be done on refining the job-strain concept and its measurement. At the conceptual level, it remains to be seen whether job strain would predict CVD outcomes better if the two underlying dimensions—

---

[3] The possible association between job-strain and health outcomes other than cardiovascular disease and hypertension also needs further investigation. Some evidence exists linking job strain with psychological-distress outcomes (Sauter, Murphy, & Hurrell, 1990), such as exhaustion or depression (Karasek, 1979) or job dissatisfaction (e.g., Karasek, Triantis, & Chaudhry, 1982; Landsbergis, Schnall, Dietz, Friedman, & Pickering, 1992). In addition, several recent studies have suggested that job strain may play a role in the development of adverse pregnancy outcomes, such as low birth weight (Brandt & Nielson, 1992; Homer, James, & Siegel, 1990) or pregnancy-induced hypertension (Landsbergis, Hatch, & Zhang, 1993). A recent review suggested that musculoskeletal disorders may be associated with psychosocial job stressors similar in concept to job strain, such as monotonous work, high perceived workload, time pressure, low job control, and lack of social support (Bongers, deWinter, Kompier, & Hildebrandt, 1993). Another job stressor, electronic performance monitoring, may also be associated with the development of cumulative trauma disorders (Smith, Carayon, Sanders, Lim, & LeGrande, 1992). Finally, several studies have suggested that psychosocial job factors (although not job strain, specifically) may be associated with "sick building syndrome" (National Institute for Occupational Safety and Health, 1991) and alterations of the immune system (Henningsen et al., 1992).

job demands and decision latitude—were broadened to include such factors as role conflict, responsibility for people, job insecurity, supervisory authority, or influence on organizational decision making. Most existing operationalizations of job strain have used narrower definitions. A major measurement issue in research on psychosocial risk factors for CVD is the potentially subjective quality of the predictors. Most of the job-strain research has been based on self-report data. Therefore, it is important to determine whether it is mostly the objective characteristics of jobs or an individual's subjective perception and evaluation of them that is most closely associated with changes in blood pressure or the development of CVD. We have suggested several possible approaches that might be used for assessing job characteristics more objectively.

In addition, people change jobs, and jobs change their characteristics. Most of the empirical analyses of job strain, blood pressure, and CVD have relied on cross-sectional assessments of job strain. Yet, most of the hypotheses implicitly assume a putative effect of long-term (chronic) job strain, analogous to that of smoking. We have described attempts by Johnson and Stewart (1993) and Landsbergis et al. (1995) to retrospectively estimate cumulative exposure to job strain.

Although refinements in the measurement of job strain and the assessment of additional intermediate outcomes are likely to improve understanding of job strain's relationship to CVD, the most stringent tests of the job-strain hypothesis are likely to come from intervention studies that have yet to be conducted. Successful intervention studies should be able to demonstrate that manipulation of job demands or decision latitude can result in clinically meaningful changes in blood pressure, other structural characteristics of the cardiovascular system, or CVD risk. The considerable literature on organizational interventions and change strategies provides a useful guide to efforts to reduce the CVD risk that results from job strain.

In summary, although existing research leads us to be fairly confident that a relationship exists among CVD, hypertension, and job strain, much work needs to be done before researchers fully understand this relationship so that they can test and refine methods for modifying job design and work organization to reduce the risk of these diseases.

References

American Heart Association. (1993). *1994 heart and stroke facts*. Dallas, TX: Author.

Astrand, N. E., Hanson, B. S., & Isacson, S. O. (1989). Job demands, job decision latitude, job support, and social network factors as predictors of mortality in a Swedish pulp and paper company. *British Journal of Industrial Medicine, 46*, 334–340.

Bongers, P. M., deWinter, R. R., Kompier, M. A. J., & Hildebrandt, V. H. (1993). Psychosocial factors at work and musculoskeletal disease: A review of the literature. *Scandinavian Journal of Work Environment and Health, 19*, 297–312.

Brandt, L. P. A., & Nielson, C. V. (1992). Job stress and adverse outcome of pregnancy: A causal link or recall bias? *American Journal of Epidemiology, 135*, 302–311.

Cahill, J., & Feldman, L. H. (1993). Computers in child welfare: Planning for a more serviceable work environment. *Child Welfare, 72*, 3–12.

Caplan, R. D. (1983). Person-environment fit: Past, present and future. In C. L. Cooper (Ed.), *Stress research* (pp. 35–78). New York: Wiley.

Caplan, R. D., Cobb, S., French, J. R. P., Jr., Van Harrison, R., & Pinneau, S. R., Jr. (1975). *Job demands and worker health* (Publication No. 75-168). Cincinnati, OH: National Institute for Occupational Safety and Health.

DiMartino, V. (1992). *Conditions of work digest: Anti-stress programs.* Geneva, Switzerland: International Labor Office.

Frese, M., & Zapf, D. (1988). Methodological issues in the study of work stress: Objective vs. subjective measurement of work stress and the question of longitudinal studies. In C. L. Cooper & R. Payne (Eds.), *Causes, coping and consequences of stress at work* (pp. 375–411). New York: Wiley.

Friedman, R., Schnall, P. L., Pieper, C. F., Gerin, W., Landsbergis, P. A., & Pickering, T. G. (1994). *Psychological variables in hypertension: The "hypertensive personality" revisited.* Manuscript submitted for publication.

Hall, E. M. (1992). Double exposure: The combined impact of the home and work environments on psychosomatic strain in Swedish men and women. *International Journal of Health Services, 22,* 239–260.

Haratani, T., Kawakami, N., & Araki, S. (1992). *Job stress and cardiovascular risk factors in a Japanese working population.* Paper presented at the Ninth International Symposium on Epidemiology in Occupational Health, Cincinnati, OH.

Henningsen, G. M., Hurrell, J. J., Baker, F., Douglas, C., MacKenzie, B. A., Robertson, S. K., & Phipps, F. C. (1992). Measurement of salivary immunoglobulin A as an immunologic biomarker of job stress. *Scandinavian Journal of Work Environment and Health, 18*(Suppl. 2), 133–136.

Homer, C. J., James, S. A., & Siegel, E. (1990). Work-related psychosocial stress and risk of preterm, low birthweight delivery. *American Journal of Public Health, 80,* 173–177.

Hurrell, J. J., & McLaney, M. A. (1988). Exposure to job stress: A new psychometric instrument. *Scandinavian Journal of Work Environment and Health, 14*(Suppl. 1), 27–28.

Israel, B. A., Schurman, S. J., & House, J. S. (1989). Action research on occupational stress: Involving workers as researchers. *International Journal of Health Services, 19,* 135–155.

Israel, B. A., Schurman, S. J., Hugentobler, M. K., & House, J. (1992). A participatory action research approach to reducing occupational stress: Phases of implementation and evaluation. In V. DiMartino (Ed.), *Conditions of work digest: Anti-stress programs* (pp. 152–163). Geneva, Switzerland: International Labor Office.

Ivancevich, J. M., Matteson, M. T., Freedman, S. M., & Phillips, J. S. (1990). Worksite stress management interventions. *American Psychologist, 45,* 252–261.

Johnson, J. V. (1989). Collective control: Strategies for survival in the workplace. *International Journal of Health Services, 19,* 469–480.

Johnson, J. V., & Hall, E. M. (1988). Job strain, work place social support, and cardiovascular disease: A cross-sectional study of a random sample of the Swedish working population. *American Journal of Public Health, 78,* 1336–1342.

Johnson, J. V., Hall, E. M., & Theorell, T. (1989). Combined effects of job strain and social isolation on cardiovascular disease morbidity and mortality in a random sample of the Swedish male working population. *Scandinavian Journal of Work, Environment and Health, 15,* 271–279.

Johnson, J. V., & Stewart, W. (1993). Measuring work organization exposure over the life course with a job-exposure matrix. *Scandinavian Journal of Work, Environment and Health, 19,* 21–28.

Karasek, R. A. (1979). Job demands, job decision latitude, and mental strain: Implications for job redesign. *Administrative Science Quarterly, 24,* 285–308.

Karasek, R. A. (1989). Control in the workplace and its health-related aspects. In S. L. Sauter, J. J. Hurrell, & C. L. Cooper (Eds.), *Job control and work health* (pp. 129–159). New York: Wiley.

Karasek, R. A., Baker, D., Marxer, F., Ahlbom, A., & Theorell, T. (1981). Job decision latitude, job demands, and cardiovascular disease: A prospective study of Swedish men. *American Journal of Public Health, 71,* 694–705.

Karasek, R. A., Gordon, G., Pietrokovsky, C., Frese, M., Pieper, C., Schwartz, J., Fry, L., & Schirer, D. (1985). *Job Content Instrument: Questionnaire and users' guide.* Lowell: University of Massachusetts.

Karasek, R. A., & Theorell, T. (1990). *Healthy work.* New York: Basic Books.

Karasek, R. A., Triantis, K. P., & Chaudhry, S. S. (1982). Coworker and supervisor support as moderators of associations between task characteristics and mental strain. *Journal of Occupational Behavior, 3*, 181–200.

Kasl, S. (1983). Pursuing the link between stressful life experiences and disease: A time for reappraisal. In C. L. Cooper (Ed.), *Stress research* (pp. 79–102). New York: Wiley.

Kasl, S. V., & Cobb, S. (1983). Variability of stress effects among men experiencing job loss. In L. Goldberger & S. Breznitz (Eds.), *Handbook of stress* (pp. 45–65). New York: Free Press.

Kohn, M. L., & Schooler, C. (1982). Job conditions and personality: A longitudinal assessment of their reciprocal effects. *American Journal of Sociology, 87*, 1257–1286.

Kristensen, T. S. (1989). Cardiovascular diseases and the work environment: A critical review of the epidemiologic literature on chemical factors. *Scandinavian Journal of Work Environment and Health, 15*, 245–264.

Landsbergis, P. A., Hatch, M., & Zhang, H. (1993). Psychosocial workplace risk factors for pregnancy-induced hypertension (abstract). *American Journal of Epidemiology, 138*, 606.

Landsbergis, P. A., Schnall, P. L., Dietz, D., Friedman, R., & Pickering, T. G. (1992). The patterning of psychological attributes and distress by job strain and social support in a sample of working men. *Journal of Behavioral Medicine, 15*, 379–405.

Landsbergis, P. A., Schnall, P. L., Schwartz, J. E., Warren, K., & Pickering, T. G. (1994). The association between ambulatory blood pressure and alternative formulations of job strain. *Scandinavian Journal of Work, Environment and Health, 20*, 349–363.

Landsbergis, P. A., Schnall, P. L., Schwartz, J. E., Warren, K., & Pickering, T. G. (1995, May). *Association between cumulative exposure to job strain and ambulatory blood pressure.* Paper presented at the First International Symposium on Work Environment and Cardiovascular Diseases, Copenhagen, Denmark.

Light, K. C., Turner, J. R., & Hinderliter, A. L. (1992). Job strain and ambulatory work blood pressure in healthy young men and women. *Hypertension, 20*, 214–218.

National Institute for Occupational Safety and Health. (1991). *Indoor air quality and work environment study* (HETA 88-364-2102). Cincinnati, OH: Author.

Neale, M. S., Singer, J. A., & Schwartz, G. E. (1987). A systems assessment of occupational stress: Evaluating a hotel during contract negotiations. In A. W. Riley & S. J. Zaccaro (Eds.), *Occupational stress and organizational effectiveness* (pp. 167–203). New York: Praeger.

Patton, M. Q. (1987). *How to use qualitative methods in evaluation.* Newbury Park, CA: Sage.

Pickering, T. G. (1991). *Ambulatory monitoring and blood presure variability.* London: Science Press.

Pirkle, J. L., Schwartz, J., Landis, J. R., & Harlan, W. R. (1985). The relationship between blood lead levels and blood pressure and its cardiovascular risk implications. *American Journal of Epidemiology, 121*, 246–258.

Rostrup, M., & Ekeberg, O. (1992). Awareness of high blood pressure influences on psychological and sympathetic responses. *Journal of Psychosomatic Research, 36*, 117–123.

Sauter, S. L., Murphy, L. R., & Hurrell, J. J. (1990). Prevention of work-related psychological disorders. *American Psychologist, 45*, 1146–1158.

Schnall, P. L., Landsbergis, P. A., & Baker, D. (1994). Job strain and cardiovascular disease. *Annual Review of Public Health, 15*, 381–411.

Schnall, P. L., Landsbergis, P. A., Pieper, C. F., Schwartz, J., Dietz, D., Gerin, W., Schlussel, Y., Warren, K., & Pickering, T. G. (1992). The impact of anticipation of job loss on psychological distress and worksite blood pressure. *American Journal of Industrial Medicine, 21*, 417–432.

Schnall, P. L., Landsbergis, P. A., Schwartz, J. E., Warren, K., & Pickering, T. G. (1992, September). *The relationship between job strain, ambulatory blood pressure and hypertension.* Paper presented at the Ninth International Symposium on Epidemiology in Occupational Health, Cincinnati, OH.

Schnall, P. L., Pieper, C., Schwartz, J. E., Karasek, R. A., Schlussel, Y., Devereux, R. B., Ganau, A., Alderman, M., Warren, K., & Pickering, T. G. (1990). The relationship between "job strain," workplace diastolic blood pressure, and left ventricular mass index. *Journal of the American Medical Association, 263*, 1929–1935.

Schnall, P. L., Schwartz, J. E., Landsbergis, P. A., Warren, K., & Pickering, T. (1992). The relationship between job strain, alcohol and ambulatory blood pressure. *Hypertension, 19*, 488–494.

Schwartz, J. E., Pieper, C. F., & Karasek, R. A. (1988). A procedure for linking psychosocial job characteristics data to health surveys. *American Journal of Public Health, 78*, 904–909.

Schwartz, J. E., Schnall, P. L., Warren, K., & Pickering, T. G. (1992, November). *The role of demographic factors in the job strain model: Independent or non-independent risk factors.* Paper presented at the APA–NIOSH Conference on Occupational Stress, Washington, DC.

Smith, M. J., Carayon, P., Sanders, K. J., Lim, S-Y., & LeGrande, D. (1992). Employee stress and health complaints in jobs with and without electronic performance monitoring. *Applied Ergonomics, 23*, 17–27.

Talbott, E., Helkamp, J., Matthews, K., Kuller, L., Cottington, E., & Redmond, G. (1985). Occupational noise exposure, noise-induced hearing loss, and the epidemiology of high blood pressure. *American Journal of Epidemiology, 121*, 501–514.

Theorell, T. G., Ahlberg-Hulten, G., Jodko, M., Sigala, F., Soderholm, M., & de la Torre, B. (1993). Influence of job strain and emotion on blood pressure in female hospital personnel during work hours. *Scandinavian Journal of Work Environment and Health, 19*, 313–318.

Van Egeren, L. F. (1992). The relationship between job strain and blood pressure at work, at home, and during sleep. *Psychosomatic Medicine, 54*, 337–343.

8

Job Strain, Neuroendocrine Activation, and Immune Status

Theo F. Meijman, Max van Dormolen,
Robert F. M. Herber, Herman Rongen, and
Symen Kuiper

Evidence on the influence of psychosocial stress factors on immune functioning is growing (Ader, Felten, & Cohen, 1991). Most of the research with humans has been directed to distressing life events and affective states, such as bereavement, unemployment, marital disruption, and depression, or to such acute stressors as academic examinations or short electric shocks (for overviews, see Jemmott & Locke, 1984; Kaplan, 1991; O'Leary, 1990). Work-related factors have been addressed in a series of interrelated studies by Ursin and colleagues (Endresen, Ellertsen, et al., 1991; Endresen, Relling, et al., 1991; Endresen, Vaernes, Ursin, & Tonder, 1987; Ursin et al., 1983, 1984; Vaernes et al., 1988, 1991). Various immune system parameters have been used in these studies. Among these were plasma (immunoglobulin G [IgG] and immunoglobulin M [IgM]) and salivary (immunoglobulin A) concentrations of immunoglobulins. Other parameters were counts of lymphocyte cells and natural killer (NK) cells and such functional parameters as antigen- and mitogen-induced lymphoproliferative responses and NK cell activity. All this research has revealed mixed effects. In general, negative relations between the stress factor and the assessed immune system parameter have been found, pointing in the direction of immunosuppressive effects.

Opposite results have also been reported. Several processes have been identified that could mediate the relationships between stress factors and immune functioning. Among these are the nature and duration of the emotional stimulus and the role of neuroendocrine mediators. In human studies, control beliefs have turned out to be another possible mediating variable. Brosschot (1991) and Brosschot et al. (1994) presented evidence on how the relations of stress from unpleasant minor events and daily hassles with various immune system parameters can depend on one's personal control beliefs. As far as the belief that one's life is not under one's control but, instead, is mainly controlled by (powerful) others is related to lower counts of several important immune cells in peripheral blood, the stress measures were hardly directly related to the immune parameters. However, the interaction of the stress measures and the control measure added to the variance explained by the main effect of the control measure. The more reported stress and the less the belief in control over one's own life, the lower the numbers of several cell types (among others, leucocytes, lymphocytes, B cells, T cells, T-helper [TH] cells, T-suppressor [TS] cells, and NK cells; $rs = -.25$ to $-.42$).

The results concerning the interactive effect of beliefs of control over one's own life and the stress from minor life events and daily hassles on immune status are of interest to researchers of stress in working life. In the job-strain theory by Karasek (Karasek, 1979; Karasek & Theorell, 1990), the interaction between *job demands*—defined as the psychological stress involved in accomplishing the workload—and *decision latitude*—the worker's potential control over his or her task and his or her conduct during the working day—plays a key role. Both job characteristics supposedly influence aspects of employee well-being and physical health, but employees in jobs perceived to have both low decision latitude and high job demands are particularly at risk. The two job characteristics, job demands and decision latitude, from this job-strain model are conceptually related to the stress and control variables used in studies of general life stress by Brosschot (1991) and by Brosschot et al. (1994). Thus, it might be expected that similar relations of the variables from the domain of work stress would be observed, with several parameters indicating the immune status of workers. Karasek's model has mainly been investigated in epidemiological studies that used data on well-being or self-reported health and general cardiovascular outcomes. We expand this frame of reference in our study, including neuroendocrine and immunological outcomes to gain more insight into the mechanisms that may mediate the poorly understood process between the exposure to the job-strain factors and the complicated outcome measures on well-being and health.

Purpose

Because the study had an exploratory character, we formulated two general expectations (outlined below).

1. Following the general theories of psychoimmunology, we expected both job characteristics to be related in a particular direction, in accordance with the counts of the most important immune cells in peripheral blood. That is, there should be two specific main effects: the higher the level of (perceived) job demands, the lower the values of the cell counts; and the lower the level of (perceived) decision latitude, the lower the values of the cell counts.

2. We expected that the interaction of the two job characteristics would add to these main effects. In particular, we thought that the higher levels of (perceived) job demands, combined with the lower levels of (perceived) decision latitude, should correlate with the lower values of cell counts.

Our first expectation was stronger than was justified from results of Brosschot's

(1991; Brosschot et al., 1994) studies. However, the main hypothesis of psychoimmunology is that stress factors have general immunosuppressive effects, particularly when these factors have a more chronic character. Although counts of immune cells are not the strongest indicators of such effects, the lower cell-count values are generally interpreted as such. The second expectation follows the main results from Brosschot's studies. Testing it could be conceived as a replication of these studies, using stress and control variables from another domain of human life. It is also a test of the main hypothesis of Karasek's (1979; Karasek & Theorell, 1990) model of job strain.

Because psychoimmunological effects may be mediated by neuroendocrine processes, the two catecholamines—adrenaline and noradrenaline—were taken into account in our study.

Methods

Participants

The participants were 37 cargo handlers: White, male shift workers with a mean age of 33.4 years ($SD = 6.5$, range = 22–53 years). They worked in the same company, and they participated voluntarily. All were studied during a day off after an evening shift. Each worker responded to a questionnaire with items concerning the perceived level of demands and decision latitude in his job. Samples of urine were collected at 1 p.m. for the period from 9:00 a.m. to 1 p.m. Peripheral blood samples were also taken at 1 p.m.

The participants were studied in two groups on different occasions: 19 participants, during a period of 4 weeks in the spring; and 18 participants 8 months afterward, also during a period of 4 weeks. Moreover, from a subsample of 27 participants—18 from the first group and 9 from the second group—blood samples were taken twice, during a day off after an evening shift and during another day off separated at least 1 week from the first sampling day. In both cases the samples were taken at 1 p.m. This procedure was followed to control for the stability of the immune parameters under study.

Analytical Procedures

We determined excretion levels of adrenaline and noradrenaline in the urine samples by means of an automated high-performance liquid chromatography method for biological fluids, used according to Boos, Wilmers, Sauerbrey, and Schlimme (1987) and modified to permit determination in urine. The method consists of a static premixer, followed by precleaning and clean up on a precolumn, and subsequent separation on the analytical column. Detection takes place by postcolumn derivation and fluorescence detection. Quality control was performed by running three control urine tests with three different levels periodically among the samples. Excretion rates of the catecholamines were expressed as nanograms per minute.

The lymphocyte subset analyses were performed on whole blood. For this procedure, 3.5 ml of blood were collected in a tube containing the anticlotting agent ethylenediaminetetraacetic acid (EDTA). A 100-ml sample was used for each subset test. The cells were stained using simultests with monoclonal antibodies conjugated directly with the substances fluorescein isothiocyanate and phenylethylamine against CD3(leu4)/CD19(leu12), CD4(leu3)/CD8(leu2A), and as control antibodies IgG_1/IgG_2 — all monoclonal antibodies from Becton–Dickinson USA. The whole blood samples were incubated with the different monoclonal antibodies for 30 min at 4° C. Most erythrocytes were removed by using an excess of a lysis medium, containing 150 µl NH_4CL, 10 µl $KHCO_3$, and 0.1 µl EDTA. This mixture was incubated for about 10 min. Cells were washed twice with the chemical substance phosphate-buffered saline (PBS), fixated with 1 ml 0.5% paraformaldehyde in PBS, and kept at 4° C until analyzed. Before flowcytometric analysis (FACScan, Becton–Dickinson USA), the cells were washed again and resuspended in PBS. The immune parameters used in this study were the count of lymphocytes and cell counts of CD3 (T cell), CD4 (TH cell), CD8 (TS cell), CD4/CD8 (T-helper–T-suppressor [THTS] ratio), and CD19 (B cell). Table 1 shows the information on the stability of the immune parameters.

Intercorrelations of the lymphocytes and CD3, computed on the original sample of 27 participants, were low. After we removed the 3 participants with the largest deviations between the two lymphocyte values, the intercorrelations increased to an acceptable level. In Table 1, the results of the multivariate analysis of variance (MANOVA) on the values of the various immune parameters are also presented (MANOVA, $N = 24$; between factor: the two subgroups of participants studied separately with an 8-month interval; within factor: the two blood samples of the same participant gathered with 1-week interval. No differences in mean values of the immune parameters were found between the two subgroups of participants or between the two blood samples taken from the same participant. We decided to disregard the 3 participants with the deviating lymphocyte values for further analysis. Thus, the total number of participants used in the analyses was 34, and only the values of the immune parameters on the basis of blood samples taken on the day off after the evening shift were used, because this provided the largest number of participants from a comparable condition.

Scales Measuring Job Demands and Decision Latitude

Two scales were used to measure the job characteristics. They were derived from Johnson, Hall, and Theorell (1989). The Job Demands Scale had eight items with four response categories (*strongly agree*, *agree*, *disagree*, and *strongly disagree*). Examples of the items are "I have to work very hard" or "My job is hectic." The Decision Latitude Scale also had eight items with the same four response categories. Examples of the items are "I have influence on the planning of my work activities" or "I can choose my own rest pauses." In earlier research (Hogervorst, 1992; van Vliet-Kroon, 1992) with various Dutch populations of industrial and health-service workers, the items of the two scales

Table 1. Stability of the Immune Parameters Under Study

| Parameter | Original sample[a] ($N = 27$) | After removal of 3 participants | MANOVA ($N = 24$) | | | | | |
| | | | Subgroup[b] | | Sampling day[c] | | Interaction | |
			$F(1, 22)$	p	$F(1, 22)$	p	$F(1, 22)$	p
Lymphocytes	0.27	0.73	2.70	.11	0.18	.67	0.01	.98
CD3 (T cell)	0.61	0.74	4.56	.05	0.01	.91	1.02	.32
CD4 (TH cell)	0.85	0.90	1.73	.21	0.24	.63	2.04	.17
CD8 (TS cell)	0.88	0.89	1.54	.23	0.01	.98	0.15	.70
CD4/CD8 (THTS ratio)	0.79	0.83	1.43	.25	0.11	.74	0.16	.69
CD19 (B cell)	0.81	0.82	0.90	.35	1.27	.27	0.15	.71

Note. MANOVA = multivariate analysis of variance; THTS = T-helper–T-suppressor.
[a] Intercorrelation (r_{pm}) of immune parameters assessed at 2 days with 1-week interval.
[b] Between-factor subgroup, with 8-month time period between groups.
[c] Within-factor sampling day, with 1 week between samples.

fit well in the unidimensional cumulative scaling models of Mokken (Mokken & Lewis, 1982) and Rasch (Molenaar, 1983). Alpha coefficients of internal reliability were above .85 for the two scales in these studies, and the two variables were intercorrelated below .25 in these studies.

Statistical Analyses

We studied the direct relations of the job characteristics and their interactions with each catecholamine and with each immune parameter first, using hierarchical multiple regression analyses (SPSS), entering the two variables of job demands and decision latitude together in the first step and their cross product— both variables in z scores—in the second step. This procedure has been recommended by Cohen and Cohen (1983). The critical test for an interaction is the increment in squared multiple correlation when a cross product is added to a regression equation already containing main effects. A statistically significant increase in squared multiple correlation provides evidence for an interaction effect over and above the joint, additive combination of the variables themselves. Because the intercorrelation of the two job characteristic scales in the present study was $-.12$, no problems of collinearity were expected.

Second, we studied the contribution of the catecholamines. Because the intercorrelation of the catecholamines was expected to be high, and this could create problems of collinearity, we separately analyzed each catecholamine. Either adrenaline or noradrenaline was entered in the first step, and then the two variables—job demands and decision latitude—were entered together in the second step, and their cross product was entered in the third step.

Results

Intercorrelations

In Table 2 the intercorrelations (r_{pm}) of the variables are shown, together with the means and the standard deviations.

The intercorrelation of the catecholamines was high at .68, $p < .01$. The intercorrelations of the catecholamines and the immune parameters were low, with the exception of noradrenaline and lymphocytes, which reached a moderate level: .32, $p < .05$. The catecholamines correlated differentially with the job characteristics: Job demands correlated .34 ($p < .05$) with adrenaline, and decision latitude correlated .25 ($p < .10$) with noradrenaline. The intercorrelations of the two job characteristics and the immune parameters reached a moderate level with respect to CD4: $-.44$ and $-.57$ ($p < .01$), and with respect to CD4–CD8: -0.23 ($p < .10$) and $-.38$ ($p < .05$). Decision latitude, but not job demands, correlated with CD8: .27 ($p < .10$), and with CD19: -0.37 ($p < .05$). The Job Demands $\times$ Decision Latitude cross product correlated .29 ($p < .05$) with adrenaline, .26 ($p < .10$) with noradrenaline, and .44 ($p < .01$) with lymphocytes.

Table 2. Means, Standard Deviations, and Intercorrelations of Variables

Variable	M	SD	Adrena-line	Nora-drenaline	Job demands (JD)	Decision latitude (DL)	JD × DL
Adrenaline	9.30	6.70	—	.68	.34	.10	.29**
Noradrenaline	43.20	21.90	.68***	—	.07	.25*	.26*
Lymphocytes	43.00	11.10	.12	.32**	.13	.12	.44***
CD3 T cell	67.00	8.40	−.07	.10	−.21	−.07	−.13
CD4 TH cell	41.00	7.40	−.14	.02	−.44***	−.57***	−.16
CD8 TS cell	32.00	7.00	−.10	−.06	.07	.27*	
CD4−CD8 THTS ratio	1.46	0.47	−.04	−.03	−.23*	−.38**	−.15
CD19 B cell	13.00	5.00	−.03	−.17	−.09	−.37**	−.17

Note. For intercorrelation of JD with all other variables, $M = .06$ ($SD = .99$). For intercorrelation of DL with all other variables, $M = .04$ ($SD = .85$).
*$p < .10$. **$p < .05$. ***$p < .01$.

Regressions

In Table 3, the results of the regression analyses are presented. The equation of the regression of the job characteristics and their cross product on nora-drenaline was not significant. It reached a marginally significant level ($p < .09$) in the case of adrenaline. The contribution of the two job characteristics to the variance was 14% ($p < .10$), which could be mainly ascribed to job demands ($\beta = .37$, $p < .09$). The cross product of the job characteristics did not add to the equation.

The final equations (i.e., after Step 2) with respect to CD3, CD8, and CD19 were not significant. However, the regression of the two job characteristics on CD19 reached a marginally significant level ($p < .07$). After the first step, 16% of the variance of CD19 was explained, which could be ascribed mainly to decision latitude ($\beta -.39$, $p < .05$).

The two job characteristics did not contribute to the equation of the regression on lymphocytes. Their cross product, however, added 22% ($p < .01$) to the variance, and the total equation after Step 2 was significant, $R = .50$; $F(3, 30) = 3.3$, $p < .04$. In Figure 1 this interaction effect is presented.

To show this interaction effect graphically, we divided the participants into two groups according to their scores on the Decision Latitude Scale. The cutting score was the median that was computed on the populations originally used in the construction of the scale (Hogervorst, 1992; van Vliet-Kroon, 1992). Nineteen participants belonged to the low decision latitude group (LDL), and 15 participants belonged to the high decision latitude group (HDL). The correlation of job demands and lymphocytes in the LDL group was −.40 ($p < .05$), and in the HDL group it was .62 ($p < .01$).

The regression on CD4 was highly significant after Step 2, $R = .77$; $F(3, 30) = 15$, $p < .01$ (see Table 3). Both job characteristics added to the equation: 60% of the variance, $p < .01$. Their cross product did not contribute.

The regression equation with respect to CD4 and CD8 was highly significant after Step 2, $R = .56$; $F(3, 30) = 4.6$, $p < .01$. The two job characteristics

Table 3. Hierarchical Regression of Job Demands and Decision Latitude and Their Cross Products on the Neuroendocrine and Immune Parameters

Step	Noradrenaline		Adrenaline		Lymphocytes		CD3 T cell		CD4 TH cell		CD8 TS cell		CD4–CD8 THTS ratio		CD19 B cell	
	1	2	1	2	1	2	1	2	1	2	1	2	1	2	1	2
Step 1																
Job demands (JD)	**.11**	**.07**	**.37**	**.33***	**.12**	**.03**	**-.22**	**-.21**	**-.53**	**-.54***	**.10**	**.14**	**-.29**	**-.34**	**-.14**	**-.13**
Decision latitude (DL)	**.26**	**.21**	**.16**	**.10**	**-.11**	**-.22**	**-.10**	**-.08**	**-.64**	**-.65***	**-.29**	**-.34***	**-.42**	**-.50***	**-.39**	**-.37***
ΔR²	.07		.14		.02		.05		.60		.08		.23		.16	
p<	.31		.10		.64		.43		.01		.25		.02		.07	
Step 2																
JD × DL		**.21**		**.22**		**.49***		**.08**		**.04**		**-.19**		**.31***		**-.08**
ΔR²		.04		.05		.22		.01		.01		.03		.09		.01
p<		.25		.20		.01		.65		.69		.29		.07		.64
Total equation																
R		.34		.43		.50		.25		.77		.35		.56		.41
R² (adjusted)		.02		.11		.17		—		.56		.03		.25		.08
F(3, 30)		1.3		2.4		3.3		0.6		15.0		1.4		4.6		1.9
p<		.31		.09		.04		.59		.01		.27		.01		.15

Note. Beta weights are in boldface. THTS = T-helper–T-suppressor.
p < .10.   **p < .05.   ***p < .01.

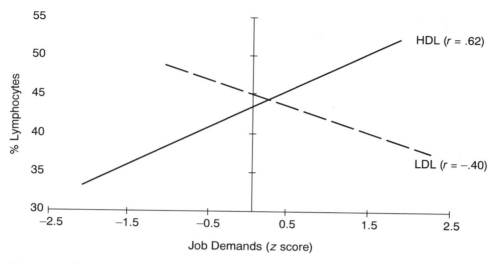

Figure 1. Regression lines showing count of lymphocytes on job demands. Nineteen participants had low decision latitude (LDL), and 15 participants had high decision latitude (HDL).

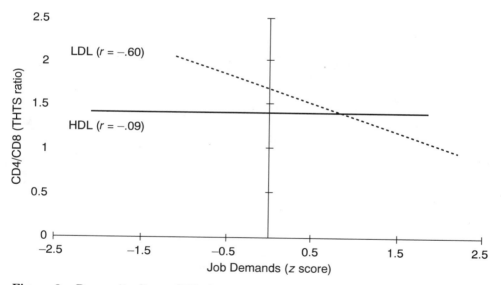

Figure 2. Regression lines of T-helper–T-suppressor ratio on job demands. Nineteen participants had low decision latitude (LDL), and 15 participants had high decision latitude (HDL).

contributed 23% ($p < .02$) to the variance. Their cross product added 9% ($p < .07$). This interaction effect is presented in Figure 2. The correlation of job demands and CD4 and CD8 in the LDL group was $-.60$ ($p < .01$), and in the HDL group it was $-.09$ ($p < .40$).

Table 4. Hierarchical Regression of Noradrenaline, Job Demands, and Decision Latitude on the Immune Parameters

Step	Lymphocytes			CD4 (TH cell)		
	1	2	3	1	2	3
Noradrenaline	**.31***	**.35***	**.27***	.02	**.21***	**.21***
R^2-change	.10			.00		
$p <$	.07			.94		
Job demands (JD)		.08	.02		**−.55***	**−.55***
Decision latitude (DL)		−.20	−.29*		**−.71***	**−.72***
ΔR^2		.04			.66	
$p <$		.44			.01	
JD × DL			**.44****			.01
ΔR^2			.17			.00
$p <$			.02			.92
Total equation						
R			.56			.82
R^2 (adjusted)			.22			.62
$F(4, 29)$			3.40			14.40
$p <$			.03			.01

Note. Beta weights are in boldface.
*$p < .10$.   **$p < .05$.   ***$p < .01$.

Contribution of the Catecholamines

The job characteristics and their cross product correlated moderately with the catecholamines, and noradrenaline correlated with lymphocytes (see Table 2). To assess their contribution to the regression on the immune parameters over and above the job characteristics, we conducted separate analyses for each catecholamine by entering either adrenaline or noradrenaline in Step 1, the job characteristics in Step 2, and their cross product in Step 3. No substantial differences with the results reported in Table 3 were found. Adrenaline never added to the equations. Noradrenaline did have a contribution in the regression on lymphocytes and on CD4. It did not contribute to the equation in the other cases. These results are summarized in Table 4.

Discussion

The results of our study need to be interpreted with great care, considering its small sample size and the number of analyses that have been performed with the same sample. In this section, we first address some methodological issues to appreciate the limitations of our study and then discuss some theoretical aspects of the results.

Methodological Considerations

Statistical power analysis (Cohen, 1992) suggests that at a power level of .80, with an alpha of .5 and a medium population effect size (ES), a multiple regression analysis with three independent variables requires at least 76 participants—and at least 34 participants when a large ES is expected. Thus, it might be concluded that the risk of a Type II error is acceptable when a significance level below .05 was reached in the present study. However, a caveat remains warranted, and replication of our study is certainly needed to reach more definite conclusions. Another objection to our results might be the influence of outliers. Statistical analyses with the standard SPSS procedures revealed no serious problems in two analyses that yielded significant final equations: the regressions on lymphocytes and CD4. However, one participant could be considered as an outlier. Removal of this participant from the analysis did not change the effects that were reported in Table 3 in a significant way. A final objection pertains to the interdependence of the statistical analyses. It might be argued that, according to Bonferroni rules, with eight analyses significance at .01 (in fact, $p = .006$) is needed to minimize Type I errors at alpha $= .05$. In two of our analyses, this criterion was reached.

Theoretical Considerations

Employees have different evaluations of the demands in their jobs, their workload, and their possibilities for control, even when they work in similar jobs. Such interindividual differences in the perception of workload and control over work activities turned out to be related to some immune parameters in the present study, in particular to the percentage of lymphocytes: the count of the TH cells and the related parameter, the THTS ratio. A weak relation was found with the urinary excretion rate of adrenaline.

With respect to the lymphocytes, the results followed our expectations. Perceived control moderated the relationship between the experienced workload and this immune parameter. A higher perceived workload in combination with a lower perceived control did go together with a lower value of the immune parameter. However, when perceived control was relatively high, the perception of one's job as more demanding was related to higher values of this immune parameter. Brosschot (1991) and Brosschot et al. (1994) reported relations between daily hassles or unpleasant minor life events and the number of lymphocytes that were moderated by control beliefs, which was similar to the results in our study. In the Brosschot (1991) study, a correlation of the interaction of unpleasant life events and lack of own control of $-.40$ was reported, after removal of their main effects in the regression on the cell-count values of lymphocytes. In our study, the same statistic was .44 (the opposite sign was due to differences in scaling of the control variable between the two studies). The results with respect to the main effect of perceived workload and CD4 (TH cell) were also in concordance with the expectations. The higher load levels did go together with the lower values of this immune parameter. However, this relationship was not moderated by the control variable. In fact, the relationship of the control variable with CD4 conflicted with the expectations. Instead of a positive correlation, a negative correlation was found. Thus, we are left with the unexpected negative correlation between the variable that was used to measure perceived control in the present study and CD4. In the

Brosschot (1991) study, a nonsignificant correlation $(-.14)$ in the expected direction was found between the relevant control measure (lack of control over one's own life) and CD4. Although several animal studies suggested at least a nonnegative relationship between controllability and immune parameters, there have been reports in the literature on immunosuppressive effects after controllable shocks in humans (Weisse et al., 1990) and in animal studies (for an overview, see Bohus & Koolhaas, 1991). It may be concluded, therefore, that the evidence on the relation between controllability and immune parameters is more complex. Bohus and Koolhaas, for example, pointed to the complication that the impact of control behavior may be very different depending on the individual styles of coping with stressors. In the Brosschot study, some evidence with respect to this complication was reported. Although both the belief that one is in control of one's own life (measured by an internal locus of control scale) and the desire for control were correlated positively with various immune parameters, their interactions with life stress were in opposite directions. Participants with a strong belief that they can determine the outcomes of events (*internals*) may be positively challenged by life stressors. An opposite effect may occur for participants who highly desire control. It seems quite plausible that confronting many stressors is more taxing if one badly wants to control each one of them.

With respect to CD4–CD8 (THTS ratio), the results of the present study followed our expectations. Perceived control moderated the relationship of the experienced job demands and CD4–CD8. In the group of participants with high perceived control, the evaluation of job demands was not related to the immune parameter. In the other group, with low perceived control, this relation was negative: The higher the level of job demands, the lower the value of CD4–CD8. The main effect of job demands followed expectations: The higher score on job demands, the lower value of CD4–CD8. However, the main effect of decision latitude turned out to be opposite to our expectation. This might have been due to the strong negative relation that was found in the present study of decision latitude with CD4.

Several studies have been reported on the relationship between catecholamines and immunological parameters in humans (Crary et al., 1983; Jabaaij, 1992; Landmann et al., 1984). The results were inconclusive. None of these studies used urinary excretion rates of the catecholamines, as we did in our study. Only in the regression on lymphocytes was a small contribution to the equation found with respect to noradrenaline (urinary excretion rate). Up until now, the evidence from the psychoimmunological research is still conflicting, but it warrants the hypothesis that control might have a key role in possible relationships between stress variables and immune parameters. The results of the present study on job-strain variables are no exception. Although they certainly need to be confirmed, they still justify the conclusion that it might be a fruitful research endeavor to study the role of controllability in more detail in the study of job strain and immune functioning. Karasek's theory on the impact of the interaction of (high) job demands and (low) decision latitude on outcomes of health and well-being provides an interesting framework in this respect.

References

Ader, R., Felten, D. L., & Cohen, N. (Eds.). (1991). *Psychoneuroimmunology* (2nd ed.). San Diego, CA: Academic Press.

Bohus, B., & Koolhaas, J. M. (1991). Psychoimmunology of social factors in rodents and other subprimate vertebrates. In R. Ader, D. L. Felten, & N. Cohen (Eds.), *Psychoneuroimmunology* (2nd ed., pp. 807–830). San Diego, CA: Academic Press.

Boos, K. S., Wilmers, B., Sauerbrey, R., & Schlimme, E. (1987). Development and performance of an automated HPLC-analyzer for catecholamines. *Chromatographia, 24,* 363–370.

Brosschot, J. F. (1991). *Stress, perceived control and immune response in man.* Unpublished doctoral dissertation, University of Utrecht, The Netherlands.

Brosschot, J. F., Benschop, R. J., Godaert, G. L. R., Olff, M., De Smet, M., Heijnen, C. J., & Ballieux, R. E. (1994). Influence of life stress on immunological reactivity to mild psychological stress. *Psychosomatic Medicine, 56,* 216–224.

Cohen, J. (1992). A power primer. *Psychological Bulletin, 112,* 155–159.

Cohen, J., & Cohen, P. (1983). *Applied multiple regression/correlation analysis for the behavioral sciences.* Hillsdale, NJ: Erlbaum.

Crary, B., Hauser, S. L., Borysenko, M., Kutz, I., Moban, C., Aults, K. A., Weiner, M. L., & Benson, M. (1983). Epinephrine-induced changes in the distribution of lymphocyte subsets in peripheral blood of humans. *Journal of Immunology, 131,* 1178–1181.

Endresen, I. M., Ellertsen, B., Endresen, C., Hjelmen, A. M., Matre, R., & Ursin, H. (1991). Stress at work and psychological and immunological parameters in a group of Norwegian female bank employees. *Work and Stress, 5,* 217–227.

Endresen, I. M., Relling, G. B., Tonder, O., Myking, O., Walther, B. T., & Ursin, H. (1991, Winter). Brief uncontrollable stress and psychological parameters influence human plasma concentrations of IgM and complement component C3. *Behavioral Medicine,* 1991/1992, 167–176.

Endresen, I. M., Vaernes, R., Ursin, H., & Tonder, O. (1987). Psychological stress factors and concentration of immunoglobulins and complement components in Norwegian nurses. *Work and Stress, 4,* 365–375.

Hogervorst, P. A. M. (1992). *Arbeid en gezondheid: relaties met taakeisen en autonomie* [Work and well-being: The relationship between job demands and task autonomy] (Report A&G-92-11). Amsterdam, The Netherlands: University of Amsterdam Faculty of Medicine, Study Centre on Work and Health.

Jabaaij, L. (1992). *Stress-related immune modulation in humans.* Unpublished doctoral dissertation, University of Utrecht, The Netherlands.

Jemmott, J. B., III, & Locke, S. E. (1984). Psychosocial factors, immunologic mediation and human susceptibility to infectious diseases: How much do we know? *Psychological Bulletin, 95,* 78–108.

Johnson, J. V., Hall, E. M., & Theorell, T. (1989). Combined effects of job strain and social isolation on cardiovascular disease morbidity and mortality in a random sample of the Swedish male working population. *Scandinavian Journal of Work and Environmental Health, 15,* 271–279.

Kaplan, H. B. (1991). Social psychology of the immune system: A conceptual framework and review of the literature. *Social Science and Medicine, 33,* 909–923.

Karasek, R. A. (1979). Job demands, job decision latitude and mental strain: Implications for job redesign. *Administrative Science Quarterly, 24,* 285–308.

Karasek, R., & Theorell, T. (1990). *Healthy work: Stress, productivity and the reconstruction of working life.* New York: Basic Books.

Landmann, R. M. A., Muller, F. B., Perini, C., Wesp, M., Erne, P., & Buhler, F. R. (1984). Changes of immunoregulatory cells induced by psychological and physical stress: Relationship to plasma catecholamines. *Clinical and Experimental Immunology, 58,* 127–135.

Mokken, R. J., & Lewis, C. (1982). A nonparametric approach to the analysis of dichotomous item responses. *Applied Psychological Measurement, 6,* 417–430.

Molenaar, I. W. (1983). Some improved diagnostics for the failure of the Rasch model. *Psychometrika, 48,* 49–72.

O'Leary, A. (1990). Stress, emotions and human immune function. *Psychological Bulletin, 108,* 363–382.

Ursin, H., Mykletun, R., Isaksen, E., Murison, R., Vaernes, R., & Tonder, O. (1983). Immuno-globulins as stress markers. In R. J. E. Ballieux, J. F. Fielding, & A. L'Abbate (Eds.), *Break-down in human adaptations to stress* (pp. 681–690). Dordrecht, The Netherlands: Martinus Nijhoff.

Ursin, H., Mykletun, R., Tonder, O., Vaernes, R., Relling, G., Isaksen, E., & Murison, R. (1984). Psychological stress-factors and concentrations of immunoglobulins and complement components in humans. *Scandinavian Journal of Psychology, 25,* 340–347.

Vaernes, R. J., Knardahl, S., Romsing, J., Aakvaag, A., Tonder, O., Walther, B., & Ursin, H. (1988). Relations between environmental problems, psychology and health among shiftworkers in the Norwegian process industry. *Work and Stress, 2,* 7–15.

Vaernes, R. J., Myhre, G., Aas, H., Homnes, T., Hansen, I., & Tonder, O. (1991). Relationships between stress, psychological factors, and immune levels among military aviators. *Work and Stress, 5,* 5–16.

van Vliet-Kroon, N. (1992). *Leeftijd en arbeidscapaciteit* [Age and the capacity to work] (Report A&G-92-24). Amsterdam, The Netherlands: University of Amsterdam Faculty of Medicine, Study Centre on Work and Health.

Weisse, C. S., Pato, C. S., McAllister, C. G., Littman, R., Breier, A., Paul, S. M., & Baum, A. (1990). Differential effects of controllable and uncontrollable acute stress on lymphocyte proliferation and leucocyte percentages in humans. *Brain Behavioral Immunity, 4,* 339–351.

9

An Investigation of the Demand–Control Model of Job Strain

Sally A. Radmacher and Charles L. Sheridan

Karasek and Theorell (1990) have proposed a set of interacting psychosocial factors associated with work that has a profound influence on a host of variables ranging from the productivity to the health of workers. The primary factors are psychological demand and decision latitude (control). Control and demand interact in the model, resulting in four job-strain categories: *low strain* (low demand and high control), *active* (high demand and high control), *passive* (low demand and low control), and *high strain* (high demand and low control). High-strain jobs have the most negative consequences for workers and have been associated with increased blood pressure (Theorell, 1990; Theorell et al., 1991), increased risk for cardiovascular disease morbidity (Johnson, Hall, & Theorell, 1989), and increased risk for both hypertension and structural changes of the hearts in working men (Schnall et al., 1990).

Although this and other research have strongly supported the job-strain model, not all studies have. For example, although Hurrell and McLaney (1989) found main effects for job control and job demand on job satisfaction, they did not find an interaction between the two variables. Ganster (1989) analyzed other nonsupportive studies and noted that they used measures that were more narrowly defined than those used by Karasek and Theorell (1990), especially in the area of control. This suggests that research on the demand–control model may require methodological scrutiny, particularly with respect to the measurement of job strain.

This issue of narrow versus broad definitions of job strain is only one of many that should be considered. There is a wide range of operational definitions of job strain in the literature. For example, one important issue has to do with the use of employee reports (usually termed *subjective*) versus standardized job classifications (*objective*). There has been strong support for the use of objective rather than subjective measures. For example, Theorell et al. (1991) found occupational classifications more useful in predicting variations in blood pressure because of the tendency of participants with hypertension to underreport problems. In addition, Netterstrom and Sjol (1991) found coronary risk factors significantly related to objective measures of job strain (job classifications), but there was not a significant correlation with subjective measures. Furthermore, they found poor agreement between the subjective and the objective measures of job strain. They suggested that the obvious underreporting of job strain may be due to acceptance of working conditions and the tendency of hypertensives to suppress problems. Murphy, Hurrell, and Quick (1992) argued that subjective assessments of job strain should be augmented by objective measures by citing research that shows these two types of measures can differentially predict subjective (affect) versus objective (physiological measures) outcome variables.

There is a certain ambiguity in subjective measurement of strain. Subjective measures differ considerably depending on whether they are *proximal* or *distal* measures. There may be a difference between self-reports of individuals' feelings about their working conditions (proximal) and self-reports of individuals' observations of their working conditions that could possibly be verified by others (distal). An example of a proximal self-report item might be "Never time to do the job as well as one would like to." A distal self-report item would be "Does your job require that you do the same thing again and again?" These two types of subjective measure might relate quite differently to standardized (objective) job measures. We deal in more detail with differences between operational definitions of objective and subjective strain in the discussion section.

Although the evidence supporting the job-strain model is compelling, it is still relatively early in its development and needs further refinement. Karasek and Theorell (1990) acknowledged criticisms that the model tends to be simplistic and may omit some important dimensions related to job strain. The practice of using broad occupational classifications to assign workers to job-strain categories has been supported by the research cited above. However, there should still be concern about the extent to which jobs change over time and the recognition that the variation of regional and organizational environments within any one occupation may influence the psychosocial characteristics of work.

Our study directly compared employee self-reports of job stress with occupational classifications. In addition, it attempted to determine whether the dimensions of demand and control would emerge empirically from data collected in assessments of job stress gathered independently of that model. Participants were assigned to groups on the basis of objective job classifications to determine whether their self-reported stress patterns would correspond to those predicted by the model.

Method

Participants

Measures were obtained on 1,010 participants during two different time periods. The first set of data was collected in 1981 and involved 439 participants (44% men and 56% women) from 20 different occupational classifications. The mean age of these participants was 37 years, with ages ranging between 18 and 68 years. The second set of data was collected in 1992 and involved 562 participants (53% men and 47% women) from 20 different occupational classifications. The mean age of this group was 40 years, with ages ranging between 18 and 76 years.

Measures

Stress levels were measured with the Quick-Scan Stress Test, a 27-item checklist of stressors that is a short form of the Comprehensive Scale of Stress Assessment (CSSA), Part I (Sheridan & Smith, 1987), with items selected specifically for a large-scale community intervention on work stress. Many of the Quick-Scan items are shown in the factor analysis of the items (see Table 1). The CSSA was developed in the 1970s from a large pool of items reflecting

Table 1. Factor Loadings for Quick-Scan Stress Test Items ($N = 1,010$)

Factor and item	Factor loading
Factor 1—Demand	
Having too much to do	.70
Working against a tight schedule	.68
Working long hours	.68
Being bombarded by questions and requests	.62
Not having enough leisure time	.61
Being overburdened with responsibility	.52
Factor 2—Control of Access to Positions and Rewards	
Suffering a loss of status	.67
Losing your job	.62
Not getting the rewards you had hoped for	.54
Having little control over what happens to you	.51
Working or living in situations where things are disorganized	.32
Factor 3—Family Conflicts	
Experiencing a great deal of family friction	.75
Finding yourself in a position in your primary relationship (e.g., with spouse or mate) in which anything you say or do will be wrong	.70
Not having friends or relatives who will help you when you need help	.53
Factor 4—Lack of Skill Discretion and Task Identity	
Having to do jobs you cannot cope with	.63
Having to do jobs you have no interest in	.63
Not knowing the end product of your work	.54
Factor 5—Lack of Environmental Control	
Experiencing high-level noise at work or home	.75
Spending time in work areas or rooms that are drab, uncomfortable, and depressing	.75
Working at a task that requires constant attention and that leaves little room for initiative	.37
Factor 6—Job Strain Outcomes	
Not having the opportunity to see friends socially	.61
Not having enough money to meet expenses	.57

stressors derived from an analysis of the massive literature on stress in work, home, and other environments. It has well-established validity and reliability. The Quick-Scan coefficient alphas for this study were .79 for the 1981 data and .81 for the 1992 data, indicating a respectable degree of internal consistency for the measure.

Design and Procedure

Both data sets are convenience samples. The 1981 data were collected with the cooperation of various business and labor organizations during a communitywide campaign to ameliorate work stress. With some minor exceptions, the 1992 data were collected at several workplaces in the same general metropolitan area, but from a suburban area that is generally considered to be a less stressful environment (i.e., it is more homogeneous, has less population and traffic, and lower crime rates).

Many of the occupations were collapsed according to the Equal Employment Opportunity Commission's (EEOC's) "Description of Occupational Classifications." The EEOC descriptions seemed particularly suitable for this purpose because they include descriptions of the skill levels for each classification. For example, *laborers* are described as unskilled workers who "perform elementary duties that may be learned in a few days and require the application of little or no independent judgement." In addition, each description gives several examples of specific occupations (e.g., carwashers, farm workers, and stevedores are classified as laborers). Specific occupational titles were used when there was a sufficient number of people holding a specific title (e.g., secretary or college faculty).

Occupational classifications were assigned to the job-strain categories on the basis of survey data set forth by Karasek and Theorell (1990). Although the use of job classifications is considered objective, it is acknowledged that it was necessary to make some subjective decisions in the assignment process. For example, college professor was not listed in the Karasek and Theorell tables, but it seemed reasonable to classify that occupation as high demand and high control (active). Homemakers and students from both data sets were omitted from the job-strain categories analyses because these positions are not described as occupations by Karasek and Theorell or the EEOC occupational classifications. All data that were omitted from the job-strain categories analyses were included in the factor analysis.

Results

Job-Strain Model Dimensions

Principal factors extraction with varimax rotation was performed on the combined data from 1981 and 1992. Because our interest was in the categorization of stressors, three items on the scale that related to symptoms were not included in this analysis. Six factors with eigenvalues greater than 1.0 were extracted and accounted for 46.3% of the variance. As shown in Table 1, the first factor represents the demand dimension of the job-strain model, especially as it relates to time pressures and excessive work. All of the items on Factor 1 had loadings above .50, and the factor accounted for 17.6% of the variance.

The second, fourth, and fifth factors all seem to reflect various aspects of the control dimension. Together, these three control factors account for 18.6% of the variance. The third factor reflects family conflict, which may be one of the critical dimensions that has been omitted from the job-strain model (e.g., Barnett, Davidson, & Marshall, 1991). This single factor accounts for 5.8% of the variance. The sixth factor does not appear to be related directly to job strain; however, it is included in the table because of the exploratory nature of this study. It may be that Factor 6 reflects an outcome of job strain. Factor 6 accounts for 4.4% of the variance.

Job-Strain Categories

The 1981 means for the four job-strain categories were in the direction predicted by the demand–control model, except for the low-strain-jobs category (see Table 2). The differences between job-strain categories were statistically significant, $F(3, 386) = 17.47, p < .0000, \eta^2 = .12$. Ad hoc comparisons revealed a statistically significant difference between high-strain jobs and the other three categories ($p < .05$); however, the differences between those categories were not statistically significant.

The 1992 means for the four job-strain categories were also in the predicted direction, except the means for passive jobs and active jobs were the same (see Table 3). The differences between the 1992 job-strain categories were statistically significant, $F(3, 518) = 5.42, p < .001, \eta^2 = .03$. Ad hoc comparisons revealed a statistically significant difference between passive jobs and the active jobs and low-strain jobs. Statistically significant differences were also found between high-strain jobs and the active jobs and low-strain jobs ($p < .05$). Statistically significant differences were not found between passive jobs and high-strain jobs or between active jobs and low-strain jobs.

Discussion

Job-Strain Model Dimensions

Given that this stress measurement was created independently of the demand–control model, the degree to which the factors correspond to that model is striking. The items loading on the first factor clearly reflect the dimension of demand as described by Karasek and Theorell (1990). Four of the items that loaded on this factor related to time pressures. The other two items loading on this factor, "Being bombarded by questions and requests" and "Being overburdened with responsibility," reflect excessive workload.

Table 2. Means and Standard Deviations of Stress Scale Responses by 1981 Occupations Within Job-Strain Categories

Job-strain categories	M	SD
Total sample ($N = 390$)	8.4	4.7
Low-strain jobs ($n = 16$)	7.2	6.4
Craft workers ($n = 11$)	8.3	7.2
Technicians ($n = 5$)	5.0	3.7
Active jobs ($n = 142$)	7.0	4.0
Nurses ($n = 35$)	6.7	4.0
Psychologists ($n = 34$)	6.6	3.4
Teachers ($n = 26$)	8.8	4.5
Television production ($n = 19$)	7.3	4.1
Managers ($n = 16$)	7.1	3.1
Business owners ($n = 16$)	6.7	4.1
Counselors ($n = 8$)	7.4	4.1
Professionals ($n = 7$)	4.3	2.8
Passive jobs ($n = 91$)	8.0	3.7
Operatives ($n = 29$)	8.4	4.0
Clerical ($n = 9$)	8.4	3.6
Secretary ($n = 31$)	7.3	3.6
Sales clerks ($n = 17$)	9.2	2.7
Laborers ($n = 5$)	5.0	4.3
High-strain jobs ($n = 122$)	10.8	5.3
Air-traffic controllers ($n = 48$)	12.5	4.5
Firefighters ($n = 28$)	11.1	7.0
Data processing ($n = 17$)	10.1	3.9
Computer operators ($n = 21$)	8.1	4.1
Service employees ($n = 8$)	8.9	6.2

Three of the factors reflected various aspects of the control dimension of the job-strain model. The second factor is not emphasized by the job-strain model but seems to encompass items that relate to control of access to positions and rewards described by Landy (1992). He viewed these aspects of control as being influenced by cultural or societal influences that limit access not only to advancement but to employment itself. Although the items in Factor 2 are not as clearly related as they are in Factor 1, a certain pattern does emerge. "Suffering a loss of status," "Losing your job," and "Not getting the rewards you had hoped for" are items that are linked to position and reward. Certainly, the psychological effects of unemployment have been well documented and obviously constitute an important control variable (O'Brien, 1986). Factors 4 and 5 relate to aspects of control dealing with lack of skill discretion and task identity and lack of environmental control, respectively. Both factors confirm recognized dimensions of control in the job-strain model.

The degree of correspondence between standard job classifications and employee reports suggests that there is considerable redundancy in the two types of measures. Because others have found differences in the way objective and subjective measures of stress relate to various outcome measures, our finding is somewhat puzzling. Because many of the items in the Quick-Scan

Table 3. Means and Standard Deviations of Stress Scale Responses by 1992 Occupations Within Job-Strain Categories

Job-strain categories	M	SD
Total sample ($N = 522$)	7.3	4.6
Low-strain jobs ($n = 25$)	5.8	4.9
Technicians ($n = 15$)	6.0	4.7
Craft ($n = 10$)	5.4	5.4
Active jobs ($n = 245$)	6.5	4.1
Nurses ($n = 16$)	8.2	4.4
Television production ($n = 14$)	7.3	3.4
Managers ($n = 48$)	7.3	4.4
Teachers ($n = 29$)	6.9	3.9
Police ($n = 11$)	6.8	4.8
Professionals ($n = 17$)	6.4	3.9
College faculty ($n = 82$)	6.2	3.8
Counselors ($n = 8$)	7.1	6.5
Executives ($n = 25$)	3.0	2.2
Passive jobs ($n = 102$)	8.0	5.1
Sales clerks ($n = 32$)	9.5	4.4
Clerical ($n = 15$)	7.5	5.1
Secretary ($n = 22$)	7.3	4.4
Laborers ($n = 25$)	7.2	6.5
Operatives ($n = 8$)	7.8	4.5
High-strain jobs ($n = 150$)	8.0	4.7
Service employees ($n = 59$)	9.6	4.3
Printers ($n = 30$)	8.5	4.8
Air-traffic controllers ($n = 35$)	6.8	4.3
Firefighters ($n = 26$)	5.4	5.5

inventory ask for reports of environmental circumstance rather than inner states, it would be worthwhile in future research to distinguish between employee self-reports of outer (distal) versus inner events (proximal), thereby resolving some of the ambiguity in the term *subjective*.

Because the Quick-Scan Inventory was not designed to focus exclusively on the workplace, it included relevant items external to the work situation. Inclusion of these external items revealed a family-conflict factor that is not reflected in the dimensions of the job-strain model. There is a growing awareness that balancing work and family roles is becoming a major stressor to many of today's workers. As Millar (1992) noted, "What the worker brings to the job may be as important as what the job brings to the worker" (p. 6). He suggested that stress outside the work environment may interact with work stress to affect health, just as cigarette smoking multiplies the effects of asbestos and radon exposures. Landy (1992) also raised the issue of interaction between work and nonwork roles and suggested that work strain may spill over to nonwork environments and vice versa. It seems clear that evaluations of worker stress should not be limited to assessments of workplace stress and that a more comprehensive approach to worker stress might well account for more of the variance in outcome measures.

The factor analysis of these data tends to support the importance of the dimensions of demand and control, but it also suggests that an expansion of these dimensions would be appropriate. Karasek and Theorell (1990) have argued that the simplicity of the model is essential for practical interdisciplinary applications, and we support this parsimonious approach. However, rather than expanding the model by including the work dimensions of support and physical demand, the contribution of nonwork (family and social) variables should be thoroughly investigated. Inclusion of a family–social dimension may be a more fruitful strategy because work-related support and physical demand may already be reflected to a large extent in the demand–control dimensions. Several of the scales of the Comprehensive Scale of Stress Assessment from which the Quick-Scan Inventory is derived (Sheridan & Smith, 1987) cover major dimensions of workplace stress, including demand and control, but also assess such things as primary relationship stress and the stress of nonprimary social relationships (Radmacher & Sheridan, 1989).

Job-Strain Model Categories

From the perspective of statistical significance, the results of this research tend to provide support for the use of job classifications in occupational-stress research. With few exceptions, the means of the self-report stress measures for the job strain categories were in the direction predicted by the job-strain model. However, the findings that may be of the most interest are the differences and inconsistencies within the categories and between the two decades. These differences and inconsistencies suggest that the zeitgeist and the locations of the workplaces may be sources of great variation in the psychosocial characteristics of any given occupation.

One of the most striking inconsistencies within groups is the mean stress level for executives, which is the lowest for all categories in both data sets. Karasek and Theorell (1990) classified being an executive as an active job (high demand and high control). Although the notion of executive stress is a popular one, it does not seem reasonable to place executives in the same job-strain category as middle managers, nurses, and teachers. Because the most salient demand on executives is decision making, which is considered an important element of control, it may be that the low-strain category would be a more appropriate classification. This is a population that obviously warrants further study.

There are some interesting differences between the 1981 and 1992 data within occupational classifications. (However, it should be noted that the means for 1981 and 1992 were essentially the same for the only occupation, television production, that involved the same workplace and essentially the same people.) We are not suggesting that statistical comparisons between decades would be appropriate because of the obvious threats to external validity. However, we do think an examination of the threats themselves has some practical significance. If occupational classifications are to be used to investigate occupational stress, researchers need to be aware that the differences between environments and changes over time may alter the psychosocial characteristics of any job.

A notable example is the obvious difference in the reported stress levels of air-traffic controllers between 1981 and 1992. Both sets of data were collected in the same region; however, there were dramatic differences in the zeitgeist between the two decades. The 1981 data were collected just prior to the 1981 air-traffic controllers strike and subsequent dissolution of their union. The controllers were very dissatisfied with supervisory policies and their workloads at that time (Karasek & Theorell, 1990). Because of the dissolution of the union, it is doubtful that any of the 1981 controllers participated in the 1992 data collection. In conversations with air-traffic controllers, we learned that management had adopted new practices that encourage more employee involvement in air-traffic control procedures. Evidently, management has implemented a committee approach that allows controllers to share in work-related decisions. There have also been improvements in the equipment since 1981, and in this particular region, the traffic appears to be down because of airline bankruptcies. It is interesting that our awareness of these changes in air-traffic controller stress came from informal employee reports of external work conditions. Such reports should be formalized and used to offset the limitations of standard job classifications.

Other informal observations suggest that such quasi-objective employee reports are of value. For example, there are several examples of the important role that the location of an occupation may have on stress levels. The controllers we interviewed wanted us to clearly understand that there were great differences in job stress between locations. They suggested that we would obtain very different results if we investigated the stress levels of controllers at Chicago or Atlanta, two major airline hubs. A similar situation accounts for the differences in the self-report of stress between the 1981 data for firefighters and the 1992 data. The 1981 data fit the high-strain category nicely. However, the 1992 mean for firefighters is less than the mean for the low-strain category. The 1992 data were collected from firefighters in a suburban area that is known for its low crime and arson rates. The firefighters we interviewed, like the air-traffic controllers, were quick to emphasize that our results would be quite different if we investigated firefighters who worked in the inner city. The location of the occupation is also the likely reason why teachers in the 1981 sample reported more stress than the 1992 sample. The teachers who participated in 1992 were from the same suburban location as the 1992 firefighters. The teachers who participated in 1981 data collection were from the inner city.

Each data set contained a job-strain category whose mean was not in the direction predicted by the job-strain model. In the 1981 data, the mean for the low-strain category was higher than the mean for the active jobs. This finding may be due to the small sample size ($n = 16$) for that group. In the 1992 data, the means for the passive jobs and high-strain jobs were the same. That is due in part to the low mean for firefighters.

The job-strain model predicts similar stress levels for active and passive jobs; however, passive jobs means are significantly higher than means for active jobs in both data sets. Karasek and Theorell (1990) have identified passive jobs as the second major psychosocial work problem. Landsbergis (1988) suggested that low demand–low control jobs may lead to something similar to learned helplessness, which involves the loss of problem-solving abilities and the willingness to make decisions and face challenges. Considering that both sets of data were convenience samples and that the assignment of participants to groups was far from exact, the fit between data and model appears to strengthen the case for using occupational classifications. However, the inconsistencies and differences discussed suggest that the location of the job and the zeitgeist do have an impact on the psychosocial dimensions of an occupation.

Conclusions

Overall, it is remarkable that this independent set of stress assessments yielded data with underlying patterns so consistent with the job-strain model and that it is supportive of the use of broad occupational classifications to assign workers to job-strain categories. The Quick-Scan Stress Scale used in this study was not developed with any awareness of the job-strain model. The 1981 data were gathered before the job-strain model was known to us, and the 1992 data were gathered with the same scale. The convergences between the patterns revealed in the present data and those predicted by the job-strain model suggest that we are dealing with some very real underlying dimensions of job stress.

On the other hand, the present data suggest strongly that the job-strain model is an oversimplification and some aspects of it may even have a degree of logical incoherence. The term *control* seems intuitively clear, especially as delineated by Karasek and Theorell (1990). However, as Ganster (1989) has noted, the job-strain model's construct of control is difficult to interpret because it is combined with aspects of job complexity and challenge. This study's factor analysis also suggests that, empirically, control is composed of several orthogonal dimensions, providing further support that the seemingly unitary construct may not really be unitary at all but merely a heading that covers a number of independent dimensions. Obviously, there is an advantage to keeping the model simple; however, for research purposes, the long-range effect of having one of the main categories essentially incoherent may be to create confusion. More research should be conducted within the framework of the more complex model uncovered here to learn whether others can replicate these patterns and whether these dimensions have some pragmatic value. Ultimately, a second-generation model might be developed from the original.

Our data provide an external validation of the use of broad occupational classifications to measure work stress. Again, it is striking that data gathered independently of the model correspond so well to its categories. There have been several compelling criticisms of subjective assessments of stress on the grounds that certain people (e.g., hypertensives) tend to underreport stress. At the other polarity is recent work suggesting that negative affectivity leads to overreporting of stress (e.g., Watson & Pennebaker, 1989). In the sense of involving employee self-reports, the Quick-Scan Scale is a subjective measure, yet it corresponds very closely in this study to the more objective occupational classifications.

It will not be easy to resolve the apparent discrepancies across studies regarding the usefulness of objective versus subjective assessments of strain because the terms *objective* and *subjective* are operationally defined in a variety of ways. Although we, and many other investigators, have used job classifications as an objective measure of strain, some investigators have labeled site-specific categorizations by supervisors as objective. For example, Fox, Dwyer, and Ganster (1991) used head nurses' assessments of patient load, patient-contact hours as a percentage of total work time, and number of deaths as an objective measure of strain. This kind of objective measure may provide different results from those obtained with occupational classifications.

There are a number of aspects of objective rating that may be of significance. Are they broad occupational classifications, or are they site-specific? Do they involve assessment of many events at a micro level or an assessment of a few clear dimensions? Are ratings merely of the presence or absence of events or of their frequency or likelihood? Are the events easily subject to external verification? For example, the head nurses in the Fox et al. (1991) study may well have been able to check their ratings against specific documentation of workload.

The structure of subjective ratings can also vary in many ways besides being employee self-reports. As we suggested earlier, employees can be asked to assess their personal feelings about working conditions, their observations of the work environment, or do both at once. The cognitive demands of the ratings may vary depending on whether the employee is asked to state whether or not an event occurred versus estimating its frequency (e.g., "Were you required to work overtime?" vs. "How many hours of overtime did you work in the last month?"). One might reasonably expect the latter to be a more "noisy" measure. There may also be variations in the range of dimensions rated (i.e., specific details of job stressors versus ratings of a few major features).

All these types of variation in objective and subjective ratings may differ, while being termed mere variations on a single dimension of objectivity versus subjectivity. For example, Fox et al. (1991) treated site-specific ratings of three externally verifiable, readily countable dimensions on the part of head nurses as their objective rating of job strain. The self-ratings of the nurses were multifacted but were generally much more detailed and specific than those of the head nurses. The nurses' ratings sometimes included both proximal and distal assessments and generally required that they make estimates of the frequencies of events.

Clearly, it would be best not to treat variations so complex as mere variations of objectivity versus subjectivity. Future work should be done to determine whether the subcategories of subjective report do indeed correlate differentially with different types of standard job classifications and whether they relate differently to outcome variables.

The close correspondence between objective measures and subjective measures of the type used here indicates that, on a large scale, either measure could be used. Alternatively, a combination of objective classifications and employee (or, perhaps, supervisor) reports of site-specific, external work stress might be the most fruitful approach. Researchers in this field need to come to some kind of consensus on the operational definition of strain. It would also be productive to conduct an investigation to determine the optimal weighting of subjective and objective classifications in predicting outcomes (e.g., multiple regression with objective measures of physiological status as the outcome variables).

References

Barnett, R. C., Davidson, H., & Marshall, N. L. (1991). Physical symptoms and the interplay of work and family roles. *Health Psychology, 10,* 94–101.

Fox, M. L., Dwyer, D. J., & Ganster, D. C. (1991). Stress and control among nurses: Effects on physiological outcomes. In *Best papers proceedings, National Academy of Management* (pp. 267–271). Miami, FL: National Academy of Management.

Ganster, D. C. (1989). Worker control and well-being: A review of research in the workplace. In S. L. Sauter, J. J. Hurrell Jr., & C. L. Cooper (Eds.), *Job control and worker health* (pp. 3–24). New York: Wiley.

Hurrell, J. J., Jr., & McLaney, M. A. (1989). Control, job demands, and job satisfaction. In S. L. Sauter, J. J. Hurrell Jr., & C. L. Cooper (Eds.), *Job control and worker health* (pp. 97–103). New York: Wiley.

Johnson, J. V., Hall, E. M., & Theorell, T. (1989). Combined effects of job strain and social isolation on cardiovascular disease morbidity and mortality in a random sample of Swedish males working population. *Scandinavian Journal of Work, Environment & Health, 15,* 271–279.

Karasek, R., & Theorell, T. (1990). *Healthy work: Stress, productivity, and the reconstruction of working life.* New York: Basic Books.

Landsbergis, P. A. (1988). Occupational stress among health care workers: A test of the job demands-control model. *Journal of Organizational Behavior, 9,* 217–239.

Landy, F. J. (1992). Work design and stress. In G. P. Keita & S. L. Sauter (Eds.), *Work and well-being: An agenda for the 1990s* (pp. 119–158). Washington, DC: American Psychological Association.

Millar, J. D. (1992). Public enlightenment and mental health in the workplace. In G. P. Keita & S. L. Sauter (Eds.), *Work and well-being: An agenda for the 1990s* (pp. 5–8). Washington, DC: American Psychological Association.

Murphy, L. R., Hurrell, J. J., Jr., & Quick, J. C. (1992). Work and well-being: Where do we go from here? In G. P. Keita & S. L. Sauter (Eds.), *Work and well-being: An agenda for the 1990s* (pp. 331–347). Washington, DC: American Psychological Association.

Netterstrom, B., & Sjol, A. (1991). Glycated haemoglobin (HbA1C) as an indicator of job strain. *Stress Medicine, 7,* 113–118.

O'Brien, G. E. (1986). *Psychology of work and unemployment.* New York: Wiley.

Radmacher, S. A., & Sheridan, C. L. (1989). The global inventory of stress: A comprehensive approach to stress assessment. *Medical Psychotherapy: An International Journal, 2,* 183–188.

Schnall, P. L., Pieper, C., Schwartz, J. E., Karasek, R. A., Schlussei, Y., Devereux, R. B., Ganau, A., Alderman, M., Warren, K., & Pickering, T. G. (1990). The relationship between job strain, workplace diastolic blood pressure, and left ventricular mass index. *Journal of the American Medical Association, 263,* 1929–1935.

Sheridan, C. L., & Smith, L. K. (1987). Toward a comprehensive scale of stress assessment: Development, norms, and reliability. *International Journal of Psychosomatics, 34,* 48–54.

Theorell, T. (1990). Family history of hypertension: An individual trait interacting with spontaneously occurring job stressors. *Scandinavian Journal of Work, Environment & Health, 16,* 74–79.

Theorell, T., deFaire, U., Johnson, J., Hall, E., Perski, A., & Stewart, W. (1991). Job strain and ambulatory blood pressure profiles. *Scandinavian Journal of Work, Environment & Health, 17,* 380–385.

Watson, D., & Pennebaker, J. W. (1989). Health complaints, stress, and distress: Exploring the central role of negative affectivity. *Psychological Review, 96,* 224–254.

10

The Regulation of Work Demands and Strain

Andrew J. Tattersall and Eric W. Farmer

The theme of this chapter is stress and workload regulation and the relationships among work demands, well-being, and performance. The task and personal factors, such as controllability and coping, that may influence those relationships are discussed. It is argued that a multimeasurement approach is necessary to understand fully the nature of stress and its effects in terms of performance and safety in cognitively demanding work such as air-traffic control, process control, and medical monitoring. Some preliminary data are presented from a two-part study of air-traffic controllers that investigated the influence of naturally occurring workload on performance and psychological and physiological state.

Lazarus (1991), among others, has suggested that to understand stress in the workplace individual patterns of response to various working conditions need to be studied, rather than simply attempting to identify adverse conditions of work. In other words, even if it were possible to identify all potential sources of stress in the workplace, this would not allow the confident prediction of the effects of these stressors on individual performance and well-being. A more detailed understanding is needed of the cognitive control processes that govern individual responses to different work demands. It is argued that individuals in many jobs, particularly those involving high levels of cognitive demands, may be able to exert some degree of control over their work to deal with perceived demands. Furthermore, individuals may differ in the extent to which they use different strategies in applying control activity. They may be used to prevent either negative psychological states or decrements in work performance in difficult or demanding situations (Hockey, 1986; Hockey, Briner, Tattersall, & Wiethoff, 1989; Hockey & Tattersall, 1989). General patterns of response—in terms of costs or benefits to the individual and organization related to performance, well-being, and health—are therefore likely to be difficult to predict. This is especially so, given the evidence that strain may be manifested in a number of different ways depending on the nature of the task and the individual (e.g., Broadbent, 1985; Frankenhaeuser, 1986; Hockey, 1986). In other words, differences in preferred styles of behavior and use of short-term strategies to deal with work demands may result in a variety of changes in performance, affective state, and psychophysiological activity.

Workload and Occupational Stress

A well-accepted definition of occupational stress is that stress results from a failure of an individual to adjust satisfactorily to the constant changes (or demands) in the work environment (e.g., Appley & Trumbull, 1986). In transactional models of human stress (e.g., Harrison, 1978; Lazarus, 1966), appraisal and coping are central features, and stress is seen not simply as a dimension of the physical or social environment, in terms of demands or events, or simply as the responses associated with the consequences of stress. Rather, it is the interactive nature of the relationship between demands and the perception of and response to the demands that is important. An individual's response to stress (or demand) may be mediated through a process of cognitive appraisal of the nature and extent to which the situation is considered to be threatening and appraisal of the range of actions that may be available to deal with the stress or demands (Lazarus & Folkman, 1984). There may be a mismatch between the demands perceived by individuals and the resources available to deal with those demands. This mismatch is associated with job strain, for example in the person–environment fit model of occupational stress, where excessive demands or opportunity to satisfy personal needs may not be met by the skills of an individual or the opportunities in the job (e.g., Harrison, 1978).

Controllability and Coping

An important implication of this view of the process of stress and coping is that individuals do not generally respond passively to work demands. The extent to which individuals are able to control the work environment may determine the effectiveness of particular coping strategies and, thus, the extent to which personal and organizational goals are met. Karasek (1979, 1981) has highlighted the importance of controllability over the working environment in his model of job demands and job-decision latitude. Job-decision latitude refers to the potential for control or discretion over work activities (e.g., opportunities to make decisions about the work, the use of a variety of skills, and the organization of work activities). Karasek (1979) reported that highly demanding jobs were more likely to result in psychological and physical ill-health if they were also associated with low levels of control over the work. However, active jobs with high levels of job demands and decision latitude allow workers to develop appropriate skills and behavior at work. Despite the high demands, these jobs are associated with greater satisfaction and lower levels of depression. There appears to be an interactive relationship between demand and control. The exact nature of the relationships among work demands, control, and job strain, however, may be more complex, first in terms of the relationships among demand, discretion, and well-being (Warr, 1990), and second in the light of possible interactions with locus of control (Parkes, 1991). Nevertheless, the beneficial implications concerning control over work are clear, as are the effects of efficient coping processes.

Coping is generally considered to be the process of executing a response when a situation is appraised as stressful by an individual (Latack & Havlovic, 1992). The manner in which an individual deals with or reacts to the working environment is acknowledged to be an extremely important mediator, or possible moderator, in the work-stress process. Lazarus and Folkman (1984) distinguished between problem-focused coping (concern with task goals) and emotion-focused coping (concern with one's own state). Problem-focused strategies are aimed at the situation, and the management of a stressor might involve direct action and the use of effort and planning, whereas emotion-focused coping is concerned primarily with the emotional discomfort associated with the situation and its regulation.

Schonpflug (1986), however, suggested that coping behavior, effective or otherwise, may not always result in positive consequences. He argued that stress states may be aggravated or prolonged by both maladaptive (e.g., drinking and smoking, suppression or avoidance of demands) and adaptive coping efforts. Active coping, or taking direct action to meet increased work demands, for example, may involve increased effort expenditure over long periods. This may result in performance decrements and an impaired psychological and physiological state as a result of depletion of energetic resources such as biochemical agents needed to activate the system. An active coper, using problem-focused strategies to deal directly with the stressor, may accept fatigue, for example, as a short-term cost to maintain performance and to avoid the development of more major problems in the task. Disengagement from the task may occur either as a result of giving up or in a more strategic manner when the costs of coping are calculated to exceed the benefits, in which case help or external services may be sought by an individual. Therefore, to a large extent the effects of work on well-being and performance depend on the way in which individuals manage or regulate their internal and external resources. These issues are discussed further in the next section.

The Management of Workload

Workload, although a difficult concept to define, is often identified as an important potential stressor in many occupations. Work overload has been described as quantitative, if the amount of work exceeds the ability of an individual to meet the demands over a given period of time, or qualitative, if the requirements of the work exceed the skills, knowledge, and abilities of an individual. Underload has also been investigated as a source of stress, whereby the demands of the job fail to meet the needs of the individual (Frankenhaeuser & Johansson, 1981). As the nature of the tasks in many jobs has changed markedly in recent years toward more cognitively demanding work, the focus on mental workload rather than physical workload has been increasingly apparent. It is especially relevant in relation to complex industrial and medical situations—such as process control, air-traffic control (ATC), and medical monitoring—where safety and health are critically dependent on human performance.

Operators who are able to exercise control over aspects of their task—such as work scheduling, planning, and effort regulation—may have much more control over performance and strain outcomes. However, although performance may be maintained at a desirable level (determined by personal and perceived organizational goals), the effort required to deal with the demands is observed as costs in other systems (e.g., Frankenhaeuser, 1986; Mulder, 1986). Steptoe (1983) discussed a number of studies that show how the effort required to exert control over situations may result in more pronounced physiological responses. Increased physiological activation, indicated by higher levels of blood pressure and heart rate, was observed when participants were engaged in effortful problem solving or activity in a controllable situation. Hockey and Wiethoff (1990) reported a longitudinal study of doctors in which high and low workload conditions were found to result in different patterns of affective state. Although anxiety increased with workload, only those identified as active copers showed significant effects of workload on fatigue. They also found that particular patterns of endocrine activity were associated with different aspects of performance following extended work shifts. This is consistent with numerous studies by Frankenhaeuser and her colleagues, which have demonstrated that changes in catecholamine and cortisol excretion are associated with increased work demands. The patterning of these changes reflects active management of work and opportunity for control over work. Generally, it has been found that increased catecholamine excretion and lower levels of cortisol excretion and anxiety are associated with active processing strategies that are linked with increased control and effort investment. Distress and an increase of both catecholamines and cortisol levels are associated with passive conditions or strategies (Frankenhaeuser, 1979, 1986).

Factors affecting workload regulation include differences in behavioral style, as well as the long- and short-term health and well-being of individuals. Relationships have been found, for example, between locus of control and problem-oriented coping (Parkes, 1984), suggesting that it is possible to identify styles of behavior that may influence workload-management processes. Fatigue, other suboptimal internal states, or particular environmental conditions could also affect the particular regulatory mode chosen to deal with a particular situation. Prolonged active management of the resources required to meet task demands may lead ultimately to a deterioration in performance, but there may also be implications for short-term well-being and longer term health. The experience of workload is thus unlikely to depend simply on task load but on the interaction of task demands, how these demands are dealt with by an operator, and the level of performance achieved. Task demands are clearly important but are mediated by effort and the priority placed on the particular tasks by an individual.

Umbers (1979) has reported that even experienced process-control operators resort to a closed-loop mode of performance when under high levels of workload or when unfamiliar situations or problems occur. Closed-loop strategies are seen by operators as being less skilled and efficient than open-loop strategies, which involve more planning and a broader understanding of the system as a whole. Closed-loop strategies may result in operators taking action only in response to a situation or problem once a fault or emergency has occurred. Impending catastrophic events are more likely to be identified and predicted following the use of more general problem-solving (open-loop) strat-egies. Sperandio (1978) observed that air-traffic controllers vary their strat-egies according to task demand, and, furthermore, they take fewer variables into account as the traffic load increases. Similarly, in a study of process control, Bainbridge (1974) found that participants under pressure used quicker, less accurate methods of finding data values. Although discretion to use open-loop control may normally be preferred by operators and lead to enhanced performance and safety, this discretion could be seen as a demand in itself imposed by the structure of the task or job.

The methodological implications are that to understand the relationship between demanding situations and changes in well-being and health, it is necessary to investigate changes in different domains. This will involve the short-term and long-term assessment of individual physiological and affective states, as well as cognitive activity as implicated in performance.

Workload Assessment

Many different measures of workload have been developed, but their effective use in particular situations is likely to depend on their sensitivity to changes in demand, their ability to distinguish different kinds of demand, and their suitability or relevance to that situation. See Damos (1991) for detailed reviews of these techniques and the criteria that may govern their use and applicability in different situations.

It is abundantly clear that it is not possible to measure an operator's workload simply by using measures of objective task demands or primary task performance. Task strategies may differ between skilled and inexperienced operators, and the health and state of the operator may determine the perceived difficulty of a task. Primary task measures might indicate that the current task is being performed successfully, and one might conclude, therefore, that levels of workload are appropriate. The safety record in ATC, for example, is currently very impressive. However, if workload increases, the effects may only be detected once performance suffers or errors are made. Secondary task measures may be more sensitive to changes in demand or working procedures, but unless the allocation of resources to the two tasks is controlled, it can be difficult to interpret the secondary task performance decrements. Norman and Bobrow (1975) introduced the important concepts of resource-limited processes, which are limited by the effort invested in a task and the priority placed on task performance, and data-limited processes, which are constrained by the quality of information rather than by increases in effort. In work situations, operators may compensate for any increase in task demands by increasing the amount of effort invested in the task. Therefore, observed performance levels may remain constant, but the operator experiences increased workload. Con-versely, a reduction in the level of performance may result either because operators cannot maintain the level of effort expenditure required or because they lower their criteria for adequate performance. Therefore, task perfor-mance in resource-limited tasks may be limited by the effort put into the task (related to the priority that an individual places on performance and on the difficulty of the task).

Other than performance measures, both physiological and subjective measures for assessing workload have been developed. Some physiological measures—of cortisol, adrenaline and noradrenaline, for example—involve the analysis of body fluids. Urine analysis allows measures of longer term changes in state through assessment of cortisol and catecholamine concentration. Sustained stress states show increased levels of these hormones. Blood or saliva samples may provide shorter term measures of fluctuations in state. Other physiological measures of workload and effort are related to cardiac function. A number of studies now suggest that the power in the midfrequency band of the heart rate variability (HRV) spectrum (0.07–0.14 Hz) is related to the level of mental effort invested in a task by an individual (Aasman, Mulder, & Mulder, 1987; Tattersall & Hockey, 1990; Vicente, Thornton, & Moray, 1987). Such variability has been found to decrease as a function of task difficulty in a number of laboratory tasks such as tracking, memory search, and classification (Mulder, 1980). It is argued that bursts of suppressed vagal control correspond to periods of momentary effort or controlled processing. The assessment of pupil dilation and brain function has also been used, but the advantage of measures of cardiac function are that they can be continuously and independently applied without intrusion to the primary task.

Subjective measures are also relatively easy to use. Asking workers to rate the levels of demand they experience and their state of well-being and health has face validity at least. There are a number of validated scales to assess workload (e.g., Hart & Staveland, 1988; Reid & Nygren, 1988), mood (e.g., Mackay, Cox, Burrows, & Lazzerini, 1978; Warr, 1989), and longer term health. Importantly, significant relationships have been found between subjective responses and specific physiological responses, such as that between cortisol and subjective distress (Frankenhaeuser & Johansson, 1986) and effort and heart rate variability (Aasman et al., 1987; Vicente et al., 1987).

Stress and Workload in Air-Traffic Control

ATC operations have been the focus of a great deal of research and popular interest for a number of years. One reason for concern is that air-traffic loads are increasing around the world. The nature of the traffic is also changing, and a number of technological advances in equipment have also affected the nature of the job. The ATC safety record is good, but if staffing levels do not match the increase in air traffic, then it can be argued that the objective workload of controllers is increasing. Automation, or the introduction of equipment to reduce controller and pilot workload and to augment performance, has not always led to a reduction of errors in ATC systems (Danaher, 1980). Operators often report a sense of disengagement from the task in highly automated situations, and there are problems of boredom and distraction when the skilled components of tasks are removed. The "out-of-the-loop" role that may be forced on an operator in a highly automated system may thus impair performance and increase frustration and anxiety (Bainbridge, 1987; Wiener, 1985). There is a need to understand the nature of the management of those demands by controllers with regard to their health and well-being and the quality of overall system performance.

Studies of air-traffic controllers are equivocal in their findings with respect to health changes as a consequence of the work. Some reviews of stress and ATC suggest that controllers' health is not unduly affected by the job (e.g., Melton, 1982), and a number of studies reviewed by Smith (1980) failed to find clear evidence of health problems associated with ATC. Cobb and Rose (1973), alternatively, reported that the incidence of hypertension, diabetes, and ulcers was significantly higher in a sample of more than 4,000 American air-traffic controllers than in a comparison group of more than 8,000 other aviation workers. They also found that air-traffic controllers suffered from a higher incidence of hypertension and peptic ulcers when working in high-density traffic areas. Rose, Jenkins, and Hurst (1978) carried out a 3-year study of controllers taking repeated blood pressure measures and confirmed that hypertension was the most frequent chronic illness among controllers and occurred more often than in comparison groups.

Air-Traffic Control Questionnaire Study

The first part of this study was a survey carried out among the population of air-traffic controllers in the United Kingdom. Only a very brief summary of the results is given here (see Farmer, Belyavin, Berry, Tattersall, & Hockey, 1990, for full details). The aims were to identify sources of stress in ATC work, to assess the impact of these factors on health and well-being, and to evaluate the role of mediating factors such as coping strategies. The first section of the questionnaire included the Occupational Stress Indicator (Cooper, Sloan, & Williams, 1988), which comprises a series of questionnaires relating to general sources of occupational stress, individual characteristics such as locus of control, coping strategies, and the consequences of stress for the individual and the organization in terms of mental and physical health and job satisfaction. The second section was devised to complement the other information collected by requesting information specifically related to ATC work. This included biographical information such as sex, age, domestic circumstances, ATC unit, and job functions. It also addressed potential sources of stress in ATC, including items concerning duty hours, ergonomic factors concerned with equipment reliability and the design of workplaces, workload, and other factors relevant to ATC duties. Questionnaires were sent to all operational controllers in the United Kingdom; 618 controllers from 25 different units in Great Britain returned completed questionnaires (55.1% response rate). The respondents had a mean age of 40 years and a mean length of operational service of 17 years.

The general sources of stress causing most concern to air-traffic controllers were related to organizational rather than task factors, although peak traffic loads and extraneous traffic were major sources of stress. The organizational structure and climate were rated significantly greater than factors intrinsic to the job, organizational role, problems at home, and relationships at work. Of the more specific ATC-related sources of stress, three factors were identified with a principal-components analysis that accounted for the major sources of variation. These factors related to equipment (e.g., reliability and layout), workload (e.g., length of shifts and duty periods; traffic levels; and unpredictable, extraneous traffic), and external factors (e.g., housing problems and public comment). The major sources of stress were associated with peak traffic loads, extraneous traffic, length of time at peak load, and unbroken duty periods with difficulties in finding extra help. The relationships between the sources of stress and outcome variables were investigated with multiple regression techniques. Subjectively rated workload was found to be related to the workload and external factors rather than factors relating to equipment. Sleep quality was directly influenced by workload, but workload also affected adversely the perception of organizational structure and climate, which also influenced sleep quality. Satisfaction with the job itself was related to workload but was more strongly associated with the intermediate effect of workload on the stress of the managerial role. Overall job satisfaction was negatively associated with the stress associated with the equipment and workload, both directly and through the effects of these variables on the perception of organizational climate.

Of the outcome measures, controllers were very satisfied with the type and scope of job tasks, but they were less satisfied with the organizational design and structure, organizational processes, relationships at work, and the value placed on their efforts. Ratings of these other dimensions of job satisfaction were found to be lower than the other occupational groups for whom norms are available (Cooper et al., 1988). The job offers a lack of opportunities for consultation, and there are problems of low staff morale, staff shortages, and lack of training. Controllers also appeared to perceive their work activities as more open to external control than other occupational groups, apart from blue-collar workers (Cooper et al., 1988). Mental and physical health were not reliably different from the other occupational groups, although controllers tended to report more psychosomatic complaints than other groups. Mental health was affected adversely by workload, and physical health was associated with the stress created by both workload and external factors.

On the basis of these results, a number of recommendations were made about the effective design and management of ATC operations. A number of problems could be alleviated by relatively minor changes to work organization and design. The design of shift work and the length of duty periods were considerable concerns at busy units. Other ergonomic design issues, particularly relating to workstations and radio and telephone communications, can be identified, and problems specific to individual units can be solved. Some of the major problems, however, were seen to be associated with the structure of the organization. Job satisfaction was found to be generally low among the controllers sampled, although they were satisfied with the job tasks themselves. The perception of organizational structure and climate was unfavorable, indicating problems with management structure and prospects for promotion. Interventions at the organizational level might improve the sense of personal control of individuals through increasing their participation in decision making. There are also implications for selection, in terms of individual placement in specific jobs, and training, which may include training in stress management and effective planning and scheduling of work. It is known that knowledge, skill, and effective effort regulation may play a moderating role in meeting work demands. It is certainly possible to develop potentially efficient strategies for coping with work demands, even if it is not possible to remove all potential sources of stress from the workplace.

Air-Traffic Control Workload Study

The questionnaire study is typical of many cross-sectional studies of occupational stress and health and provides interesting background information about possible sources of stress and the coping strategies and behavioral styles that might be generally effective in moderating job strain. But even if the job were changed in the light of these recommendations, the argument that there is a need to investigate the manner in which individual controllers interact with the task under different levels of demand is a powerful one. The main interest of the second part of the study is the trade-off between task demands and the costs of regulatory activity. A more focused study of a sample of 66 controllers was carried out in which data were collected for whole working shifts on two occasions (during busy and quiet periods in the year) in four different sites varying in traffic load around the United Kingdom (Farmer, Belyavin, Tattersall, Berry, & Hockey, 1991). Subjective ratings of mood and workload were collected throughout each day, together with saliva and urine samples from which measures of cortisol and catecholamines were derived. Electrocardiogram (ECG) measures of heart rate and HRV were collected throughout the shift. The controllers also completed a set of cognitive tasks (verbal reasoning and paced visual monitoring) at the beginning and the end of each day. Data concerning coping behavior and locus of control had been collected previously in the survey phase of the study.

Method

Participants. The participants were 66 operational air traffic controllers (57 men and 9 women) who volunteered to take part in the study. They were employed at four different ATC centers (two in the southeast of England, one in Wales, and one in Scotland). The participants were representative of the ATC centers with regard to variables such as age and experience.

Design. Data were collected during the morning shift (approximately 7 a.m. to 2 p.m.) on two occasions. One shift was during the summer period (June, July, and August) and one in the spring (March, April, and May, but avoiding the Easter period) or autumn (September, October, and November). The summer period is known to be busier than the other two periods in terms of traffic load. The order in which participants were tested on the two shifts was counterbalanced. At the time of the study, controllers worked a maximum of two hours before being required to take a break for half an hour. On each shift data were collected before and after the shift, as well as at the start of each break period.

Measures

Subjective measures: The NASA Task Load Index (TLX; Hart & Staveland, 1988) was used to assess perceived workload. Ratings were obtained after each duty period and at the end of the shift. The TLX is made up of six dimensions of workload (mental demand, physical demand, temporal demand, performance, effort, and frustration). Participants rated their workload in terms of each of these dimensions on a 20-point scale. At the beginning of the shift they were asked to rank the six dimensions in order of importance as determinants of workload. These rank orderings were used to assign weights to the ratings.

The Sheffield Mood Adjective Checklist (Warr, 1989) was used to assess three major dimensions of mood (anxiety–tension, depression, and fatigue). Participants rated each of 20 adjectives on a 20-point scale to represent their mood at the start and the end of the shift and after each duty period during the shift.

Physiological measures: Urine was collected during the two halves of the shift and was later analyzed for cortisol, adrenaline, and nonadrenaline. A small sample of saliva (maximum of 5 ml) was collected at the beginning and the end of the shift and at the start of each rest break following a duty period. These samples were analyzed per volume for cortisol concentration. Urinary and salivary cortisol concentrations were determined by radioimmunossay techniques. Rates of excretion of urinary catecholamines were determined by a trihydroxyindole fluorometric method (Crout, 1961).

Heart rate data were collected using a portable ECG amplifier–trigger connected to an event data collector. Three pregelled, silver–silver chloride electrodes were applied to three sites on the participants' chests and connected to the ECG, which was carried on a belt and did not restrict movement or normal work performance. Data were collected continuously for the whole of the shift and during the preshift and postshift testing periods. The data were analyzed using a cardiovascular spectral analysis program (CARSPAN; Van der Meulen & Mulder, 1987). Mean heart rate and HRV (the amplitude of the midfrequency band, 0.07 Hz–0.14 Hz, of the HRV spectrum were derived for each 4-min period during the session.

Performance tests: Two short cognitive tasks were performed by the participants at the beginning and at the end of each of the two shifts. The visual vigilance task involved the detection of weak signals in noise (Neuchterlein, Parasuramn, & Jiang, 1983). A series of 500 single digits was presented at a rate of one per second. A button-press response was required each time a signal (the digit 0) appeared. Stimuli were degraded by the addition of a pattern mask. The digits subtended a visual angle of 1.2° vertically and 0.6°

horizontally at a viewing distance of approximately 0.75 m. Signals were presented on 25% of trials; the nontargets (digits 1–9) appeared with equal probability. Reaction times were recorded for correct and incorrect responses.

The second task was a version of the verbal-reasoning task described by Baddeley (1968), which required participants to indicate whether statements correctly or incorrectly described the order of two letters. On each trial a letter pair, AB or BA, was presented visually together with a verbal statement of the relationship. "A is not followed by B-BA," for example, required the response *true*. At each testing time, 32 problems were presented. These tasks were used because of the difficulty in measuring overall performance in complex work systems such as ATC. Errors in performance may be infrequent and minor slips difficult to detect (e.g., Empson, 1991). Therefore, tasks were chosen that were thought to simulate different aspects of ATC work and to be sensitive to fatigue and levels of workload over the working day, for example, in vigilance performance after prolonged periods of monitoring.

Results

The analyses undertaken to date have investigated differences between and within objectively and subjectively determined high- and low-workload shifts. The summer shift is referred to as the high-workload shift and the spring or autumn shift as the low-workload shift. Further analyses of the trade-offs between the different measures in relation to individual styles of behavior are currently being carried out.

Subjective ratings of workload were higher during the summer months, $F(1, 37) = 8.40, p < .01$. The total TLX score was obtained by summing the scores on each of the six dimensions following weighting of the scores with importance rankings. Mental demand was ranked as the most important dimension, followed by temporal demand, performance, effort, frustration, and physical demand. A simple measure of traffic count, however, did not appear to be an adequate predictor of subjective workload. Communications load was more clearly associated with mental demand and effort and traffic load with frustration.

Analyses of variance (ANOVAs) were carried out on each of the three dimensions of mood (depression, fatigue, and anxiety) to investigate changes during the shift (before or during shift) and high–low workload effects. Depression ratings were elevated during high-workload conditions, $F(1, 55) = 4.35$, $p < .05$, and were higher before than during the shift, $F(1, 55) = 13.66, p < .001$. There was no interaction between the two variables. Fatigue was also elevated during high-workload conditions, $F(1, 55) = 6.11, p < .05$, and higher ratings were found before the shift compared with during the shift, $F(1, 55) = 29.43, p < .001$. There was a significant interaction indicating that fatigue was rated significantly higher before, but not during, the high-workload shift, $F(1, 55) = 4.53, p < .05$. Ratings of state anxiety were also higher under high-workload conditions, $F(1, 38) = 4.60, p < .05$, but lower before than during the shifts, $F(1, 38) = 6.12, p < .05$. Although there was no interaction at the

5% level, planned comparisons indicated a significant difference between high-and low-workload conditions during the shift. There were clearly effects of high-workload conditions on each of the three dimensions of mood, but fatigue and depression showed a different pattern of effects to anxiety. Fatigue and depression levels were raised at the start of high-workload shifts, perhaps as a result of the sustained effects of the busy summer months. However, the ratings on these two dimensions dropped particularly during the high-workload shifts. This may reflect active involvement in the task during the day, but the impact of this increased activity may only be measurable in terms of aftereffects rather than during the shift itself. In this study the aftereffects were observed as elevated levels of fatigue and depression at the start of the shift. Anxiety, alternatively, appeared to be affected more transiently and increased particularly during high-workload shifts. These findings are somewhat consistent with the results of Hockey and Wiethoff (1990). To confirm these tentative conclusions, however, data need to be collected on off-duty days in addition to workdays over a longer period of time.

ANOVAs were also carried out on the biochemical data. See Table 1 for a summary of the excretion rates during the two halves of high- and low-workload shifts. The standard errors of estimates of the mean that are presented in Table 1 were derived from the ANOVAs, satisfying the requirement for homogeneity of variance. Salivary cortisol concentration was greater during high-workload than low-workload shifts, $F(1, 56) = 5.35, p < .05$, and greater before the shifts than during, $F(4, 56) = 37.99, p < .001$. It declined during the shift but not as clearly in the latter half of the shift under high workload. There were no reliable effects of workload in the analyses of urinary cortisol or urinary adrenaline, but there was a significant interaction between workload and the two halves of the shift for urinary noradrenaline, $F(1, 20) = 5.63, p < .05$. Noradrenaline excretion decreased over the low-workload shift but increased in the second half of the high-workload shift (see Table 1). These findings perhaps reflect active coping with the quantity of demands during high-workload shifts.

Mean heart rate and the mean amplitude of the midfrequency (0.10 Hz) component of the HRV spectrum were calculated for each successive 4-min period during the shift. Mean values were compared for working periods, rest breaks, and preshift and postshift performance-testing periods. Heart rate did not reliably differ between high- and low-workload shifts, but differences be-

Table 1. Excretion Rate (ng/min) of Cortisol, Adrenaline, and Noradrenaline During the First and Second Half of High- and Low-Workload Shifts

	Shift				Standard error of estimates of the mean
	Low workload		High workload		
Excretion	First half	Second half	First half	Second half	
Urinary cortisol	94.15	125.29	109.21	95.14	10.40
Urinary adrenaline	9.81	10.28	11.95	10.02	1.22
Urinary noradrenaline	44.40	36.45	43.40	51.00	3.77

tween the four types of activity were found, $F(3, 45) = 42.00, p < .001$. See Table 2 for mean heart rate and HRV levels during different activities. The overall standard error estimate is presented following a test for homogeneity of variance.

There were significant differences between each type of activity ($p < .01$) with postshift testing giving the lowest mean heart rate, then preshift testing, then during working periods, with the highest heart rate observed during work breaks. This pattern of results may reflect differences in physical activity during the different periods. Increased heart rates were also found in the busier units (Heathrow Airport Control Centre and London Air Traffic Control Centre), but it is difficult to associate levels of workload or task variables with these differences as the factor of work location failed to interact with any of the other variables. The HRV measure did not show a difference between high- and low-workload conditions, although there was a significant effect of activity, $F(3, 45) = 152.05, p < .001$ (see Table 2). HRV was suppressed, indicating increased mental effort, during the performance-testing periods, compared with the working periods and rest breaks ($p < .05$).

Visual vigilance performance was affected by workload, but verbal-reasoning performance appeared to be insensitive to the effects of work between testing times or between high- and low-workload shifts. For visual vigilance performance, signal detection measures of d' (sensitivity) and beta (criterion) were calculated and subjected to ANOVAs. Sensitivity was lower before the shift than after the shift, $F(1, 54) = 6.64, p < .01$, and there was a significant interaction between workload and time of testing, $F(1, 46) = 7.46, p < .01$, revealing improved sensitivity over low-workload days but not during high-workload days ($p < .01$). No significant effects of workload or time of testing were found for the criterion measure. Verbal-reasoning performance was superior at the end of the shift compared with preshift performance. Speed of response did not differ significantly between high- and low-workload shifts

Table 2.   Heart Rate (Beats per Minute) and Heart Rate Variability (Log Transformed Values of Power [Hz⁻¹] in the Midfrequency Band of the Heart Rate Variability Spectrum) for Each Activity During High- and Low-Workload Shifts

	Shift	
Measure	Low workload	High workload
Heart rate[a]		
Preshift tests	79.3	78.7
Work periods	81.8	80.7
Break periods	83.8	83.4
Postshift tests	76.0	74.5
Heart rate variability[b]		
Preshift tests	6.39	6.40
Work periods	7.29	7.35
Break periods	7.20	7.17
Postshift tests	6.60	6.57

[a]Standard error of estimates of the mean = 1.36.
[b]Standard error of estimates of the mean = 0.097.

(4.56 s and 4.57 s) but was faster after the shift, $F(1, 50) = 41.14, p < .001$. A comparable analysis of errors showed no differences between high and low workload, but errors were less frequent after the shift than before, $F(1, 50) = 19.34, p < .001$. There appear to be effects of familiarity or practice that make interpretation of these data difficult; however, there is evidence that the speed of unpaced work seems to increase later in the day (Broadbent, 1971).

Discussion

This study investigated the effects of naturally varying workload in ATC on performance and physiological and affective state. Several measures were sensitive to the increased workload during the summer months and indicate the negative consequences of dealing with those demands. The overall pattern of the mean results across the sample can be interpreted as indicating active, problem-focused coping. The demands of the work appear to be manageable in the short-term at least, in that no major errors or problems were reported by the controllers, but there are certain costs associated with the increased effort expenditure during the high-workload days.

Dimensions of mood were affected in different ways by increased workload. Anxiety increased during high-workload days, but preshift levels were not affected by workload. In contrast, depression and fatigue were both higher at the start of the day and during the high-workload period. Although fatigue decreased to a greater extent during high-workload than low-workload days, the levels were still higher at the end of the the high-workload day. There may, therefore, be chronic aftereffects associated with the management of high levels of demand, but confirmation of this possibility would require repeated measurements at different times of day. The performance-test results support the notion that controllers become more actively engaged in the task during the shift. They tend to show an improvement in performance over the day, with the important exception of visual vigilance sensitivity, the ability to detect signals in noise. This measure showed an improvement on low-workload days but not on high-workload days and suggests that heavy work demands in ATC may have a detrimental effect on monitoring performance.

The pattern of hormone excretion during high workload is consistent with the findings of Frankenhaeuser (1986; e.g., cortisol and noradrenaline excretions are greater under conditions associated with lowered control and increased distress). This pattern may have long-term consequences for the health and well-being of controllers if sustained over long periods. The subjective ratings of workload were sensitive to differences in objective load on the two days, with mental demand and effort being predicted by the number of outgoing calls to aircraft. Hurst and Rose (1978) identified peak traffic and the duration of radio communications as the two major factors influencing behavioral responses (subjectively rated task pacing–demand) in ATC. Unlike their findings, the traffic count was related only to frustration in this study, although peak levels of traffic were rated as being highly stressful in the survey. At the level of analysis carried out to date, the heart rate results are not very clear, but they confirm earlier results that HRV is sensitive to effort expenditure in laboratory tasks (e.g., Mulder, 1980). However, this measure may show different patterns of effort expenditure for different individuals, and the gross level of analysis of group data could be obscuring the more complex effects of workload.

The analyses linking the individual-differences data from the survey and the workload data are yet to be completed. These will investigate the role of individual differences in workload management by examining the differences in the trade-offs between performance, affective state, and physiological state as a function of style of coping and locus of control. It is hypothesised that more active copers will be more likely to maintain performance under high-workload conditions but will show greater physiological and psychological effects of this activity. It would be desirable for further research to focus on the effects of sustained demands over longer periods of time than was possible in this study because there are indications that there may be chronic effects of sustained exposure to high workload. The survey suggested that the morning shifts investigated in this study were not associated with the highest ratings of workload and fatigue, and therefore, the reported effects may actually be an underestimate of the potential impact of workload on well-being and performance.

These preliminary results suggest that multilevel measurement techniques can provide a broad assessment of the impact of different work demands. Further studies, both controlled laboratory-based studies and field-based studies, are necessary to refine the techniques, but a model of stress and workload management based on findings from such studies should allow the more accurate prediction of states or situations in which a breakdown in skills might occur. Such a breakdown is referred to by air-traffic controllers as "losing the picture," when they experience difficulties in attending to and remembering accurately relevant information about aircraft under their control. It is precisely this kind of situation that should be avoided in work in which safety is critically dependent on performance.

Conclusions

It has been argued that, although it is possible to identify potential sources of stress at work, there is still a pressing need to evaluate the impact of these stressors, particularly those related to task demands. A methodological framework has been outlined that may offer an effective way to understand the relationships between work demands and strain. Preliminary data were presented from a story of workload and stress in ATC, and later analyses will investigate the way in which control processes are applied by individuals depending on individual differences in long-term styles and short-term strategies. When applied effectively, they may be used to prevent decrements in work performance under difficult conditions, but there may be costs as well as benefits associated with particular patterns of adaptation in terms of changes in affective state and physiological activity. Work strain may therefore only be measurable in the form of trade-offs between performance and other domains of individual activity. This involves the identification of patterns of adjustment to workload variations with repeated measures of performance and subjective and physiological state.

References

Aasman, J., Mulder, G., & Mulder, L. J. M. (1987). Operator effort and the measurement of heart-rate variability. *Human Factors, 29*, 161–170.

Appley, M. H., & Trumbull, R. (1986). *Dynamics of stress.* New York: Plenum.

Baddeley, A. D. (1968). A 3-minute reasoning test based on grammatical transformations. *Psychonomic Science, 10*, 341–342.

Bainbridge, L. (1974). Analysis of verbal protocols from a process control task. In E. Edwards & F. P. Lees (Eds.), *The human operator in process control* (pp. 146–158). London: Taylor & Francis.

Bainbridge, L. (1987). Ironies of automation. In J. Rasmussen, K. Duncan, & J. Leplat (Eds.), *New technology and human error* (pp. 271–283). New York: Wiley.

Broadbent, D. E. (1971). *Decision and stress.* San Diego, CA: Academic Press.

Broadbent, D. E. (1985). The clinical impact of job design. *British Journal of Clinical Psychology, 24*, 33–44.

Cobb, S., & Rose, R. M. (1973). Hypertension, peptic ulcer, and diabetes in air traffic controllers. *Journal of the American Medical Association, 224*, 489–492.

Cooper, C. L., Sloan, S. J., & Williams, S. (1988). *Occupational stress indicator.* Windsor, England: NFER-Nelson.

Crout, J. R. (1961). Catecholamines in urine. *Standard Methods in Clinical Chemistry, 3*, 62–80.

Damos, D. L. (Ed.). (1991). *Multiple-task performance.* London: Taylor & Francis.

Danaher, J. W. (1980). Human error in ATC system operations. *Human Factors, 22*, 535–545.

Empson, J. (1991). Cognitive failure in military air traffic control. In J. A. Wise, V. D. Hopkin, & M. L. Smith (Eds.), *Automation and systems issues in air traffic control* (pp. 339–348). Berlin: Springer-Verlag.

Farmer, E. W., Belyavin, A. J., Berry, A., Tattersall, A. J., & Hockey, G. R. J. (1990). *Stress in air traffic control: I. Survey of NATS controllers* (Rep. No. 689). Farnborough Hauts, England: Royal Air Force, Institute of Aviation Medicine.

Farmer, E. W., Belyavin, A. J., Tatersall, A. J., Berry, A., & Hockey, G. R. J. (1991). *Stress in air traffic control II: Effects of increased workload* (Rep. No. 701). Farnborough Hauts, England: Royal Air Force, Institue of Aviation Medicine.

Frankenhaeuser, M. (1979). Psychoneuroendocrine approaches to the study of emotion as related to stress and coping. In H. E. Howe & R. A. Dienstbier (Eds.), *Nebraska Symposium on Motivation* (pp. 123–161). Lincoln: University of Nebraska Press.

Frankenhaeuser, M. (1986). A psychobiological framework for research on human stress and coping. In M. H. Appley & R. Trumbull (Eds.), *Dynamics of stress* (pp. 101–116). New York: Plenum.

Frankenhaeuser, M., & Johansson, G. (1981). On the psychophysiological consequences of under-stimulation and overstimulation. In L. Levi (Ed.), *Society, stress and disease: Vol. 4. Working life* (pp. 291–210). Oxford, England: Oxford University Press.

Frankenhaeuser, M., & Johansson, G. (1986). Stress at work: Psychobiological and psychosocial aspects. *International Review of Applied Psychology, 35*, 287–299.

Harrison, R. V. (1978). Person-environment fit and job stress. In C. Cooper & R. Payne (Eds.), *Stress at work* (pp. 175–205). New York: Wiley.

Hart, S. G., & Staveland, L. E. (1988). Development of a NASA TLX (Task Load Index): Results of empirical and theoretical research. In P. Hancock & N. Meshkati (Eds.), *Human mental workload* (pp. 139–183). Amsterdam: Elsevier.

Hockey, G. R. J. (1986). A state control theory of adaptation and individual differences in stress management. In G. R. J. Hockey, A. W. K. Gaillard, & M. G. H. Coles (Eds.), *Energetics and human information processing* (pp. 285–298). Dordrecht, The Netherlands: Martinus Nijhoff.

Hockey, G. R. J., Briner, R. B., Tattersall, A. J., & Wiethoff, M. (1989). Assessing the impact of computer workload onoperator stress: The role of system controllability. *Ergonomics, 32,* 1401–1418.

Hockey, G. R. J., & Tattersall, A. J. (1989). The maintenance of vigilance in automated monitoring. In A. Coblentz (Ed.), *Vigilance and performance in automatized systems* (pp. 13–22). Dordrecht, The Netherlands: Kluwer.

Hockey, G. R. J., & Wiethoff, M. (1990). Assessing patterns of adjustment to the demands of work. In S. Puglisi-Allegra & A. Oliverio (Eds.), *Psychobiology of stress* (pp. 231–239). Dordrecht, The Netherlands: Kluwer.

Hurst, M. W., & Rose, R. M. (1978). Objective job difficulty, behavioural response, and sector characteristics in air route traffic control centers. *Ergonomics, 21,* 697–708.

Karasek, R. A. (1979). Job demands, job decision latitude, and mental strain: Implications for job redesign. *Administrative Science Quaterly, 24,* 285–308.

Karasek, R. A. (1981). Job design latitude, job design, and coronary heart disease. In G. Salvendy & M. J. Smith (Eds.), *Machine pacing and occupational stress* (pp. 45–55). London: Taylor & Francis.

Latack, J. C., & Havlovic, S. J. (1992). Coping with job stress: A conceptual evaluation framework for coping measures. *Journal of Organizational Behavior, 13,* 479–508.

Lazarus, R. S. (1966). *Psychological stress and the coping process.* New York: McGraw-Hill.

Lazarus, R. S. (1991). Psychological stress in the workplace. *Journal of Social Behavior and Personality, 6,* 1–13.

Lazarus, R. S., & Folkman, S. (1984). *Stress, appraisal and coping.* New York: Springer.

Mackay, C., Cox, T., Burrows, G., & Lazzerini, T. (1978). An inventory for the measurement of self-reported stress and arousal. *British Journal of Clinical Psychology, 17,* 283–284.

Melton, C. E. (1982). *Physiological stress in air traffic controllers: A review* (Rep. No. FAA-AM-82-17). Washington, DC: Federal Aviation Administration.

Mulder, G. (1980). *The heart of mental effort.* Groningen, The Netherlands: University of Groningen.

Mulder, G. (1986). The concept and measurement of mental effort. In G. R. J. Hockey, A. W. K. Gaillard, & M. H. G. Coles (Eds.), *Energetics and human information processing* (pp. 175–198). Dordrecht, The Netherlands: Martinus Nijhoff.

Neuchterlein, K., Parasuraman, R., & Jiang, W. (1983). Visual sustained attention: Image degradation produces rapid sensitivity decrement over time. *Science, 220,* 327–329.

Norman, D. A., & Bobrow, D. G. (1975). On data-limited and resource-limited processes. *Cognitive Psychology, 7,* 44–64.

Parkes, K. R. (1984). Locus of control, cognitive appraisal and coping in stressful episodes. *Journal of Personality and Social Psychology, 46,* 655–668.

Parkes, K. R. (1991). Locus of control as moderator: An explanation for additive versus interactive findings in the demand-discretion model of work stress? *British Journal of Psychology, 82,* 291–312.

Reid, G. B., & Nygren, T. E. (1988). The subjective workload assessment technique: A scaling procedure for measuring mental workload. In P. A. Hancock & N. Meshkati (Eds.), *Human mental workload* (pp. 185–218). Amsterdam: North-Holland.

Rose, R. M., Jenkins, C. D., & Hurst, M. W. (1978). *Air traffic controller health change study* (Federal Aviation Administration Report No. FAA-AM-78-39). Washington, DC: U. S. Department of Transportation, Office of Aviation Medicine.

Schonpflug, W. (1986). Effort regulation and individual differences in effort expenditure. In G. R. J. Hockey, A. W. K. Gaillard, & M. H. G. Coles (Eds.), *Energetics and human information processing* (pp. 271–284). Dordrecht, The Netherlands: Martinus Nijhoff.

Smith, R. C. (1980). *Stress, anxiety and the air traffic control specialist* (Federal Aviation Administration Report No. FAA-AM-80-14). Washington, DC: U.S. Department of Transportation, Office of Aviation Medicine.

Sperandio, J. (1978). The regulation of working methods as a function of workload among air traffic controllers. *Ergonomics, 21,* 195–202.

Steptoe, A. (1983). Stress, helplessness and control: The implications of laboratory studies. *Journal of Psychosomatic Research, 27,* 361–367.

Tattersall, A. J., & Hockey, G. R. J. (1990). The assessment of workload in a complex monitoring and fault diagnosis task. In D. Brogan (Ed.), *Visual search* (pp. 383–390). London: Taylor & Francis.

Umbers, I. G. (1979). Models of the process operator. *International Journal of Man–Machine Studies, 11*, 263–284.

Van der Meulen, P., & Mulder, L. J. M. (1987). *CARSPAN user's guide.* Groningen, The Netherlands: Institute for Experimental Psychology, University of Groningen.

Vicente, K. J., Thornton, D. C., & Moray, N. (1987). Spectral analysis of sinus arrhythmia: A measure of mental effort. *Human Factors, 29*, 171–182.

Warr, P. B. (1989). The measurement of well-being and other aspects of mental health. *Journal of Occupational Psychology, 63*, 193–210.

Warr, P. B. (1990). Decision latitude, job demands, and employee well-being. *Work and Stress, 4*, 285–294.

Wiener, E. L. (1985). Beyond the sterile cockpit. *Human Factors, 27*, 75–90.

EMERGENT RISKS IN TODAY'S WORKPLACE

Part III

A Risky Management Practice: Electronic Performance Monitoring

Introduction

In 1987, the Congressional Office of Technology Assessment authored a report that equated the recent increase in workplace computerization with increased potential for electronic monitoring of workers. This report, which addressed monitoring of both work performance and worker behavior in general, suggests that electronic monitoring may threaten privacy, fairness, and quality of work life and may contribute to stress and stress-related illness. Although there has been extensive, subsequent discussion of these concerns (see, for example, *Applied Ergonomics*, Vol. 23, No. 1), the possible risks of electronic monitoring of workers have received surprisingly little formal study. These chapters focus specifically on electronic performance monitoring (EPM) in the workplace, beginning with a comprehensive update by Aiello and Kolb of EPM practices and suspected health and performance effects. The two following chapters describe empirical studies of EPM but ask slightly different types of questions. The chapter by Silverman and Smith is of particular interest because it addresses the fundamental issue of whether it is close monitoring of performance per se that is stressful or whether the presumed stress effect is specific to the use of computers (versus, for example, monitoring by supervisors) for performance monitoring. Furthermore, the study investigates not only self-reports of distress but also collateral psychophysiological reactions. The chapter by Schleifer, Galinsky, and Pan poses the issue somewhat differently. In this study, it was assumed that EPM is stressful only to the extent that EPM alters basic task dimensions by affecting, for example, perceived workload or job control. Although suffering the limitations of all laboratory research, the results of these two studies are impressive, if not somewhat surprising. Together, the studies would seem to suggest that the risks of EPM lie less in the practice of close monitoring or the use of computer technology for monitoring than in the secondary effects of EPM on job design.

11

Electronic Performance Monitoring: A Risk Factor for Workplace Stress

John R. Aiello and Kathryn J. Kolb

Recent advances in office automation have led to profound changes in the manner in which many employees are supervised in the workplace. Electronic performance monitoring (EPM) has made it possible for managers to obtain detailed records about the moment-to-moment performance of their employees, without employees knowing when, or even that, their work is being observed (cf. Aiello, 1993). Although employees expect to have their performance examined and evaluated, EPM magnifies the pervasiveness of observation and the degree of concealment used to obtain performance measures. Substantial controversy has surrounded the use of these systems, as workers complain about loss of privacy, increased stress, and declining job satisfaction. Alternatively, advocates contend that EPM facilitates goal setting and the provision of objective feedback, and as such is associated with higher productivity.

Use of EPM systems in the workplace is increasing at a dramatic rate. In 1987, the Office of Technology Assessment of the U.S. Congress estimated that 6 million American workers were evaluated with measures derived from electronic monitoring systems. By 1990, that number grew to include more than 10 million employees nationwide (9 to 5, Working Women Education Fund, 1990). Between 1990 and 1992, some 70,000 U.S. companies spent more than $500 million on employee-surveillance software, and by 1996, experts predict that the expenditure will exceed $1 billion (Bylinsky, 1991; Halpern, 1992). Workers who perform service or clerical functions—such as preparing travel reservations, processing insurance claims, or performing data-entry functions—are most likely to be targeted by their employers for electronic observation. Nevertheless, computer systems have also been designed that permit the monitoring of work generated by professional, technical, and managerial personnel (Bylinsky, 1991; Garson, 1988; U.S. Congress, Office of Technology Assessment, 1987).

The body of empirical research that examines the effects of EPM on employees and their supervisors is growing, yet is still far from substantial. This chapter reviews the data that have been collected to date and explores the relationships that studies have found between EPM, stress, and productivity in the workplace. First, we describe the many variants of EPM systems and discuss the advantages and disadvantages associated with their use. We then focus on studies that have examined EPM and stress and explore potential mediators and moderators involved in the monitoring–stress connection. The influence of electronic observation on productivity is examined next. Finally, recommendations are offered to those who are considering introducing EPM in the workplace.

Dimensions of Electronic Performance Monitoring

EPM involves an assortment of technology-facilitated practices that allow managers to record and evaluate the work performed by employees. EPM systems vary along a number of important dimensions that appear to influence the impact monitoring has on workers. More research needs to be conducted to document the frequency with which each of these practices is used and to clarify their differential impact on workers.

Means of Observation

EPM may involve the use of telephone technology such as private branch exchanges (PBXs) to observe and record employee telephone activity or the use of computer software and local-area network (LAN) technology to evaluate the work employees perform on their computers (U.S. Congress, Office of Technology Assessment, 1987). Both telephone and computer monitoring systems permit managers to observe the real-time performance of workers (e.g., when managers listen in on telephone conversations conducted between employees and customers) and allow performance statistics to be accumulated without real-time observation by a manager (e.g., when length of telephone conversations and number of calls handled are recorded).

Target of Observation

Monitoring systems may be used to record work products, such as the number and accuracy of keystrokes, or employee behaviors, such as the amount of time spent on bathroom breaks and in other nonproductive activities. Additionally, monitoring systems may be used to observe and evaluate the performance of individual employees or may be used to produce aggregated statistics that reflect only the performance of the larger work group.

Pervasiveness

Companies vary in the degree to which they use continuous or intermittent monitoring. In continuous monitoring, a second-by-second accounting is made of every keystroke and telephone conversation executed by a worker, whereas in intermittent monitoring, periodically obtained work samples are analyzed.

Recipient

Companies vary in the degree to which they communicate the products of monitoring to employees and their supervisors. Individual performance statistics may be available only to the worker and may not be communicated to his or her supervisor, may be discussed privately between a worker and his or her manager, may be posted for all employees to review, or may not be shared with employees at all.

Purpose

In some cases, EPM is introduced into organizations to facilitate the achievement of positive objectives. For example, information obtained from computer monitoring systems has been used to help employees set realistic goals and obtain immediate and objective feedback (Smith, 1988). These same performance measures also allow managers to identify and reward high-achieving employees (Sherizen, 1986). In other organizations, EPM has been implemented as a punitive device that is designed to catch employees when they stray, even momentarily, from meeting specified standards (9 to 5, Working Women Education Fund, 1990).

Concomitant Practices

Companies combine EPM with a variety of other managerial practices that influence how employees respond to electronic observation. For example, some companies use EPM in conjunction with goal setting, quota systems, high-stakes reward systems, or machine pacing of work (Bylinsky, 1991; Griffith, 1993; Laabs, 1992; 9 to 5, Working Women Education Fund, 1990).

Advantages and Disadvantages

Companies and workers report numerous benefits and costs associated with EPM. A summary of these advantages and disadvantages can be found in the Appendix.

Advantages

EPM systems furnish managers with detailed, objective information about employee productivity, data that can help managers provide workers with immediate feedback and with more meaningful and less subjective performance evaluations (Grant, Higgins, & Irving, 1988). This information can be used to identify training needs and to facilitate goal setting (Sherizen, 1986) and as such may lead to gains in productivity (Irving, Higgins, & Safayeni, 1986). Additionally, EPM affords employees more flexibility in work location and work hours because it provides a means for managers to monitor employees who telecommute or work "flex hours." Finally, monitoring systems provide managers with useful information they can use when allocating resources, developing budgets, and conducting other planning activities.

Disadvantages

However, these benefits are not cost-free. Many workers complain that EPM represents an invasion of privacy and refer to the systems as "Big Brother" (e.g., Carey, 1985; Hershman & Rozen, 1984). Likewise, monitored workers often report feeling more stressed and less satisfied than nonmonitored workers who perform comparable jobs (Irving et al., 1986). Monitoring can lead to a reduction in contact between employees and their supervisors and coworkers (Aiello, 1993; Amick & Smith, 1992). Productivity can be affected as well because workers complain that monitoring systems reward attention to quantity, causing them to sacrifice the quality of their work (Grant et al., 1988; Irving et al., 1986). Some organizations have used EPM to facilitate work speedups (9 to 5, Working Women Education Fund, 1990), leading monitored employees to assert that they work in "electronic sweatshops" (Garson, 1988). Finally, feelings of stress can increase among supervisors because they become overwhelmed by the need to review the vast quantity of data that EPM systems generate and by demands to provide more feedback to employees (Aiello, 1993).

EPM and Stress

A number of studies have reported a link between EPM and increased stress. One investigation compared survey responses of 50 clerical employees whose work was monitored by computer with the responses of 94 nonmonitored employees who performed comparable jobs. Self-reported stress was higher among the monitored workers (Irving et al., 1986). In another study in which 762 telecommunications workers completed surveys, monitored employees reported feeling significantly higher levels of tension, anxiety, depression, anger, and fatigue than nonmonitored employees (Smith, Carayon, Sanders, Lim, & LeGrande, 1992). These results have been replicated in the laboratory, where computer-monitored participants obtained significantly higher scores on Spielberger's State Anxiety Scale (Aiello & Shao, 1992, 1993). One laboratory experiment demonstrated that regardless of whether participants received positive or negative feedback about their performances, they felt more pressured by their supervisor when their work was electronically observed (Aiello et al., 1991).

Stress Mediators

Why do so many electronically monitored workers feel stressed? One possibility is that monitoring may reduce opportunities for employees to receive social support from their peers and supervisors in the workplace (Amick & Smith, 1992). Social support has been shown to protect individuals from stress by providing an additional resource to help cope with stressors (such as a helping hand to accomplish a difficult task) and an outlet for expressing tension (Cobb, 1976; Cohen & Wills, 1985).

In one study, monitored workers reported feeling lonely at work because all of the information they needed to do their jobs was provided at their workstations or through their terminals, eliminating the potential for contact with coworkers during a walk across the office to retrieve a file or to consult a manual (Aiello, 1993). Although lack of physical mobility is a common complaint among video display terminal workers, EPM may motivate workers to move around the office even less frequently. In one case study, airline reservationists, directory-assistance operators, and other workers reported feeling more physically and socially isolated from their coworkers when they were monitored. They explained that they were more reluctant to leave their terminals because even brief absences would be recorded by computer (Cahill & Landsbergis, 1989).

Increased competition among monitored coworkers may reduce the quality of support provided by work peers, even when the amount of interaction remains constant. One study found that monitored employees focused on enhancing individual productivity at the expense of meeting group goals (Grant & Higgins, 1989). In another study, monitored workers revealed that they adopted strategies that transferred more time-consuming work to their peers in an effort to keep their own production numbers at or above standard. Almost 25% of monitored directory-assistance operators admitted to disconnecting customers who may have needed more than the 22 s allocated to provide assistance, assuming that when the customer called back they would reach another operator (Aiello, 1993).

Monitoring may reduce the amount of social support workers receive from their supervisors because either the quantity or the quality of the interaction is reduced. Although monitored workers report receiving more feedback than nonmonitored workers (Irving et al., 1986), the monitoring system itself may replace the supervisor as the source of feedback, thereby limiting the amount of face-to-face contact employees have with their managers. EPM systems allow supervisors to transmit feedback messages to employees rather than providing evaluative information in person. The need for supervisor intervention may be displaced all together by computer-generated feedback messages that automatically display when performance varies from some preset standard. In the extreme, feedback may even be provided subliminally by monitoring systems, as messages flash on workers' screens informing them to work faster (9 to 5, Working Women Education Fund, 1990). Research needs to examine the degree to which these practices are actually being used in the workplace.

Monitoring may erode the quality of interaction between supervisors and their employees, as employees become nothing more than "a faceless stream of information" (Amick & Smith, 1992, p. 10). One study found that, in a monitoring environment, supervisors were more likely to adopt an authoritarian, coercive, quantity-oriented management style, where interaction with employees was limited to addressing workers' failure to satisfy production standards (Amick & Smith, 1992).

Job design changes that are associated with increased stress may accompany the introduction of EPM in an organization. A number of studies have found that monitored employees report having heavier workloads and less control over their work (e.g., Irving et al., 1986; Smith et al., 1992), a combination that has been shown to produce high levels of strain among workers (Karasek & Theorell, 1990). Because the jobs that are typically monitored (i.e., repetitive clerical tasks; U.S. Congress, Office of Technology Assessment, 1987) usually demand high levels of output while providing little employee control (Karasek & Theorell, 1990), monitoring may transform positions that are already characterized by high job strain into even more stressful positions.

Psychological demands may increase among monitored workers as productivity reports reflecting each workers' output are posted for all to see. Likewise, monitoring systems can be used as a means to privately coerce employees to produce at higher levels (9 to 5, Working Women Education Fund, 1990). Feelings of control may be lost when employees are urged to perform at some uniform rate, eliminating their ability to set their own work pace. For example, micromanaged employees who are more productive in the morning may be punished when their performance slows in the afternoon. One worker revealed, "I once had to blow my nose, and the supervisor saw the 'make busy' signal flashing and immediately came over to my position" (9 to 5, Working Women Education Fund, 1990, p. 12). Control also may be lost when individual variation in work style is discouraged. For example, one monitored airline reservationist was reprimanded for furnishing "superfluous information" when she made a supportive comment to a customer who complained about the difficulties of constant travel (9 to 5, National Association of Working Women, 1991).

Even when opportunities for social support, demands for productivity, and perceptions of control are held constant, as was done in two laboratory studies, monitored respondents have reported feeling more stress than nonmonitored respondents (Aiello & Shao, 1992, 1993; Chomiak, Kolb, & Aiello, 1993). If field studies replicate these results, we may find that monitoring influences an employee's perceptions of the workplace, even though objective conditions have not changed. Monitoring may encourage workers not to take advantage of existing opportunities for social support. For example, a monitored worker may choose not to make a brief comment to a coworker for fear that her productivity may be momentarily reduced. Also, although objective demands for productivity may not have changed, monitored workers may perceive that they are supposed to be more productive, merely because their output is being continuously recorded.

Stress Moderators

Are there any ways to limit the amount of stress felt by electronically monitored workers? Fortunately, research conducted to date suggests that a number of variables may moderate the EPM—stress relationship. These variables include contextual, methodological, and individual factors.

Monitoring Context

EPM may be used in an organization to facilitate training, to provide objective feedback, and to reward high-achieving employees (Sherizen, 1986) or to coerce employees to perform at unreasonably high rates of speed and to punish employees who deviate from these standards (9 to 5, Working Women Education Fund, 1990). To determine if task-climate variables influence the amount of stress experienced by monitored workers, an experiment was conducted in which some participants were told that they would be monitored to prevent them from "fooling around," whereas others were told that the supervisor expected them to perform well and would monitor their work to help document their successful task accomplishment (Aiello & Shao, 1992). A third group of participants who were not monitored at all scored the lowest of the three groups on Spielberger's State Anxiety Scale; however, participants who were monitored in a positive task climate (i.e., who were told that monitoring would document their success) experienced less stress than did those who were monitored in a negative task climate (i.e., who were told that monitoring would catch them fooling around). A reasonable explanation for these results is that a supportive supervisory relationship limited the amount of stress monitored participants felt in the positive task climate, whereas those in the negative task climate experienced a more coercive relationship with their supervisor and thus felt more stressed.

Composition of the work group also may influence the degree of stress felt among monitored workers. A laboratory experiment was conducted in which electronically monitored participants either worked alone, worked as a member of a noninteracting aggregate, or worked as a member of a cohesive work group (Kolb & Aiello, 1993b). Group members reported feeling the least amount of stress, individuals working alone reported feeling most stressed, and aggregate members reported stress levels that were intermediate. If these results generalize to the workplace, we may find that maintaining cohesiveness among monitored workers provides employees with more social support, thereby limiting the degree to which they experience stress.

Monitoring Methodology

Researchers have proposed that variation in perceptions of procedural justice influences satisfaction with EPM (Kidwell & Bennett, 1994) and may influence the degree to which stress is experienced as well. That is, employees who feel that monitoring is fair should feel more satisfied and less stressed. In contrast, employees who feel that monitoring is unfair should feel less satisfied and more stressed.

What methodological factors influence the degree to which monitoring systems are perceived as fair? Few empirical studies have examined this question; however, some plausible answers have been proposed. Systems that measure the most important and appropriate tasks are likely to be considered more fair than systems that focus on irrelevant or less important criteria. For example, many monitoring systems measure performance quantity while failing to capture information related to performance quality. Monitored workers report that although such systems may be objective, they are hardly fair because they do not adequately measure an important component of their jobs (Grant & Higgins, 1989). General Electric implemented a customer-service monitoring system that emphasized operator quality and deemphasized call quantity and found that customer and employee satisfaction improved (Bylinsky, 1991). Similarly, Toyota focused its monitoring efforts on the quality of service provided to customers and found that employee morale rose. A number of customer-service representatives actually asked to be monitored more frequently (Laabs, 1992).

Monitoring systems that maximize employee control, participation, and ownership are likely to be perceived as being more fair and less stressful than systems that limit employee control. For example, at AT&T, self-managed call centers were established in which more experienced telephone operators monitored, coached, and counseled their less experienced coworkers. Employee response has been favorable (Bylinsky, 1991; Laabs, 1992).

Employee control also may be enhanced or restricted depending on how monitoring outputs are used. When performance statistics are not shared with employees or when individual performance data are posted for all employees to review, workers may feel less control over their own products. Alternatively, when performance data are discussed privately between an employee and his or her supervisor, employees may feel less coerced and dominated.

Systems that are flexible enough to permit correction of errors provide employees with more control over monitoring and thus should be less stressful. However, some systems punish employees for system downtimes because they do not allow unrecorded entries to be manually updated (Aiello, 1993). Two studies found that when aggregated work-group statistics, rather than individual performance data, were electronically accumulated and reported, participants felt less stressed (Aiello et al., 1991; Kolb & Aiello, 1993b). Perhaps this was because group-level monitoring provided shared performance goals that strengthened the cohesiveness of the work team, whereas individual monitoring broke down cohesiveness when group members competed with one another. To protect both the privacy and health of monitored workers, laws have been enacted in some countries (e.g., Norway and Sweden) that limit the degree to which individual performance may be electronically monitored, although work-group–level monitoring is permitted (U.S. Congress, Office of Technology Assessment, 1987).

Monitoring salience may influence the degree to which workers feel stressed. In one laboratory study, some respondents were told only once that their work would be monitored by computer, other respondents were frequently reminded that their work was being monitored by computer, and a third group of respondents was told that its work would not be monitored at all (Chomiak et al., 1993). Self-reported stress levels were higher among those assigned to the highly salient monitoring condition (i.e., the condition in which respondents were frequently reminded about monitoring), whereas those who were only told once about monitoring did not score significantly higher than nonmonitored respondents.

Studies need to be conducted to assess the degree to which continuous versus intermittent monitoring influences perceptions of stress. On the one hand, knowledge that every keystroke and conversation is being counted, timed, and analyzed may overwhelm workers and may prevent them from taking even momentary breaks. On the other hand, employees whose work is monitored only intermittently may experience concern over whether the obtained work sample accurately reflects their total performance. Likewise, studies need to be conducted to examine whether employees ever adapt to monitoring and perhaps consider monitoring less stressful over time. In contrast, studies may find that the effects of monitoring accumulate over time, until the stress imposed on workers becomes unbearable. One experiment examined respondents who were monitored for 2 1/2 hours and found no signs of adaptation (Chomiak et al., 1993); however, studies that explore the effects of monitoring over months and years should prove to be more informative.

Individual Differences

Little attention has been directed toward studying individual differences in responses to EPM. Aiello and Svec (1993) did find that monitored participants with an external locus of control experienced more stress than those with an internal locus of control, supporting the notion that perceptions of control over monitoring and the work environment limits the degree to which stress is perceived. Chalykoff and Kochan (1989) proposed that various management practices influence the degree to which employees are satisfied with EPM; however, they acknowledged that some employees so object to EPM that they will never be satisfied.

Who are these dissatisfied workers likely to be? We can speculate that people who highly value personal privacy and individual control may never accept the outside regulation imposed by EPM. In contrast, people who are highly oriented toward authoritarianism may feel that EPM is appropriate. People who are computer-phobic may feel anxious when a technology that they do not understand encroaches on yet another component of their life. In contrast, technophiles may respect the technology and welcome the challenge that EPM represents, even eagerly exploring ways to "beat the system."

Differences in task ability are likely to produce differences in perceptions of monitoring. Research needs to be conducted to explore this possibility. For example, when EPM is coupled with a high-stakes reward system or the public posting of performance statistics, strong performers may benefit and therefore view the practice more positively than weaker performers who fear for their paychecks and their jobs. In one study, high levels of physical and psychological distress were reported by monitored workers who were unable to perform at or above standard (Schleifer, Galinsky, & Pan, 1992). It also is possible that high performers may feel more stressed and less satisfied under group-monitoring conditions where their individual contributions are not recognized. In contrast, low performers may feel less stressed under group monitoring.

Supervisor Responses

Only a few studies have examined how supervisors are responding to and using information collected from EPM systems (e.g., DeNisi & Aiello, 1993; Fenner, Lerch, & Kulik, 1993; Kulik & Ambrose, 1993). One study reported that supervisors felt that their workloads increased dramatically when computer monitoring was introduced (Chalykoff & Kochan, 1989). Without EPM, effective supervisors have been found to spend only 2.9% of their time monitoring employee performance (50% more than ineffective supervisors; Komaki, 1986). Given the vast quantities of data that EPM systems generate, it is conceivable that supervisors must devote a larger portion of their workday to reviewing and responding to that data. Supervisors have reported that their employees expect to get more feedback after monitoring systems have been instituted, placing supervisors under more pressure to provide employees with information about their performance (Aiello, 1993). Employee-oriented supervisors may also feel concerned that the monitoring technology has disrupted their relationships with their employees, placing a computer between human beings who used to enjoy positive interactions. As such, supervisors may find that EPM makes their jobs more stressful.

EPM and Productivity

Although the available research is limited in scope, there does appear to be a connection between EPM and stress. Monitored workers tend to report feeling more stressed than nonmonitored workers. This relationship appears to be moderated by various contextual, methodological, and individual factors. The relationship between EPM and productivity is less well established. In the sections that follow, we review studies that have examined the influence of monitoring on productivity and consider possible mediators and moderators of that relationship.

Anecdotal reports indicate that electronically monitored workers increase the quantity of their output while sacrificing performance quality (Grant et al., 1988; Irving et al., 1986). This is often explained by the fact that EPM systems typically accumulate and report quantitative measures such as record counts and adherence to time standards but rarely capture and analyze subjective information such as the quality of interactions with customers.

Several studies bring into question, however, the premise that EPM invariably leads to productivity improvements. Two recent experiments (Aiello & Shao, 1992; Aiello & Svec, 1993) found that participants who worked on tasks that require considerable thought and skill performed significantly worse when their performance was monitored by computer than when their performance was not electronically observed. Yet, other studies (Aiello et al., 1991; Chomiak et al., 1993) found that participants working on easy assignments, such as repetitive data-entry tasks, showed significant performance gains with computer monitoring.

Mediators of Productivity Change

How can these apparent discrepancies be resolved? The pattern of declining productivity when complex tasks are monitored and increasing productivity when simple tasks are monitored fits nicely with the predictions offered by research examining the phenomena of social facilitation. Social facilitation research examines how individuals respond when performing in the presence of others (e.g., in the presence of a monitoring supervisor) and predicts that complex task performance will suffer and simple task performance will improve when others are present (Zajonc, 1965). Social facilitation effects have been thought to derive from the mere presence of an audience or coactors (Zajonc, 1965), evaluation apprehension (Cottrell, 1972), self-presentation concerns (Duval & Wicklund, 1972), and attentional conflict (Baron, 1986).

The mere-presence hypothesis (Zajonc, 1965) posits that individuals have an arousal-inducing influence on one another and that arousal facilitates people's ability to work on simple tasks but impairs their ability to successfully complete difficult assignments. The evaluation-apprehension model (Cottrell, 1972) asserts that concern over outcomes and negative evaluations produces arousal that influences performance in either a positive or a negative direction, depending on task difficulty. The self-presentation model (Duval & Wicklund, 1972) asserts that the presence of an audience leads individuals to focus more attention on themselves, whereby they notice discrepancies between ideal and actual performance. Efforts to repair those discrepancies are expected to facilitate performance under simple task conditions; however, the model is less clear about why performance declines under complex task conditions. Finally, the attentional–conflict model (Baron, 1986) proposes that monitoring produces a distraction that motivates workers to narrow their focus onto central task cues. Because successful execution of a simple task typically requires the processing of only a limited range of stimuli, focusing on central cues actually facilitates performance. In contrast, because attending to a wider range of cues is often required for successful execution of a complex task, monitoring difficult assignments leads to productivity impairment.

None of these models has been tested explicitly in conjunction with EPM; however, one study (Kolb & Aiello, 1993a) did find that participants monitored by computer felt more highly evaluated than those who were not monitored, lending support to the evaluation-apprehension explanation. Another study

(Chomiak et al., 1993) simultaneously manipulated exposure to computer monitoring and a secondary distraction (noisy interruptions) and found that performance on a simple task improved under both the monitoring and noisy distraction conditions, providing support to the attentional–conflict model. Further support for the attentional–conflict hypothesis is obtained from a study that used regression techniques to partial out the effects of arousal, evaluation apprehension, distraction, and feedback and found that distraction mediated the process whereby monitoring affected performance (Stein & Aiello, 1992).

If the results of these laboratory studies generalize to the workplace, we should expect EPM to be associated with productivity improvements (at least with respect to performance quantity) when repetitive tasks are monitored and productivity impairment when more intellectually demanding tasks are observed. The preponderance of the workers subject to EPM perform repetitive, clerical tasks (U.S. Congress, Office of Technology Assessment, 1987). Productivity should be enhanced among these workers. Still, trends indicate that the work performed by technical, professional, and managerial personnel may be electronically observed in the near future (Bylinsky, 1991; Garson, 1988; U.S. Congress, Office of Technology Assessment, 1987). On the basis of the research cited above, this practice may be unwise.

Moderators of Productivity Change

Just as contextual and methodological variables moderate the degree to which monitored workers experience stress, recent research suggests that contextual and methodological factors moderate the degree to which EPM influences productivity. These limiting factors are reviewed next.

Monitoring Context

Work climate appears to moderate the relationship between EPM and productivity. In one study (Aiello & Shao, 1992), subjects worked in either a negative task climate, in which the supervisor used a Theory X style of management (McGregor, 1960), or a positive task climate, in which the supervisor used a Theory Y management style. In addition, some participants were told that their work on a complex, anagram-solving task would be monitored by computer, whereas others were told that their work would not be observed. As predicted, monitored participants performed more poorly on the difficult task than nonmonitored participants; however, performance loss was reduced among monitored participants who worked in the positive task climate.

Employees' perceptions of control might influence their productivity in a monitoring environment. In a laboratory experiment, some respondents were provided with a means to shut off monitoring while they worked on a complex task, whereas other respondents were not afforded this option (Aiello & Svec, 1993). Monitored respondents who were provided with a means to turn the monitoring off produced significantly less than monitored respondents who were able to shut off monitoring, even though no one elected to exercise this option.

Relationship with work peers also appears to influence productivity. A study that examined the influence of social context on simple task performance (Kolb & Aiello, 1993b) found that members of cohesive work groups were more productive than members of noninteracting aggregates, who were more productive than individuals who worked alone. When the presence or absence of monitoring was manipulated orthogonally to social context, these researchers found that individually monitored cohesive group members were most productive, whereas nonmonitored individuals working alone were least productive. Kolb and Aiello explained that the presence of both an audience (a monitoring supervisor) and coactors (work peers), combined with the facilitative influence of group cohesiveness (cf. Tziner, 1982), enhanced simple task performance among monitored members of cohesive groups. In contrast, nonmonitored participants who worked alone lacked the motivating influence of an audience, coactors, and cohesiveness.

Methodological Factors

One might expect that workers who are monitored individually will be more productive than group-monitored workers where performance statistics are aggregated with data from their work peers. This hypothesis is based on social-loafing theory (cf. Harkins, 1987), which predicts that people exert more effort when they believe that they are working alone than when they believe that their work is being combined with that of others. Researchers (e.g., Harkins, 1987) have demonstrated that evaluation and identifiability of individual contributions are required if group performance losses are to be prevented.

This hypothesized pattern of results has not been found (at least in the laboratory) when EPM is used. In one study (Aiello & Svec, 1993), respondents who worked on a difficult task were more productive when their work was monitored at the group level than when individual efforts were observed. Two other experiments examined monitoring and productivity on simple tasks (Aiello et al., 1991; Kolb & Aiello, 1993b) and found that the performance of individually monitored participants and group-monitored participants did not differ significantly; however, individually monitored participants did feel more stressed than group-monitored participants. It would seem that monitoring at the work-group level may be used as an effective strategy to achieve managerial monitoring goals while limiting the degree of stress imposed on employees. Further research is needed to identify which work conditions, if any, lead to loafing when group-level monitoring is used.

EPM is often used in conjunction with the provision of feedback and goal setting (Sherizen, 1986). Feedback and goal setting without EPM have been used effectively in organizations as a means of enhancing productivity (e.g., Erez, 1977). A recent study (Aiello & Shao, 1992) found that productivity loss may be reduced among monitored workers who perform complex tasks, when feedback and goal setting are combined with EPM. The same study found that monitored workers who performed simple tasks increased their productivity even further when feedback and goal setting were used in conjunction with electronic observation (Aiello & Shao, 1992).

Recommendations to Employers

EPM may be used to identify training needs within an organization, to facilitate goal setting, to make performance evaluations more objective, and to assist in managerial planning. Workers who perform well-learned, repetitive tasks also may be more productive (at least with respect to output quantity) when their work is electronically observed. However, several disadvantages that demand serious attention appear to accompany these benefits. A number of studies have found that electronically monitored workers experience more stress than their nonmonitored counterparts (cf. Aiello & Shao, 1993). Monitored workers also may be more likely to focus on performance quantity while sacrificing performance quality, a problem that no organization can tolerate in an increasingly competitive global marketplace. Finally, studies suggest that employees who perform tasks that require considerable skill and intellectual involvement perform worse, even quantitatively, when their work is electronically observed.

These findings are based on a limited number of studies, some of which were conducted in the laboratory and demand replication in the field. Nevertheless, within this research, provisional advice can be found for employers who want to obtain the benefits of EPM while avoiding its costs. The studies reviewed in this chapter indicate that a number of factors appear to moderate the degree to which employees feel stressed or produce at a diminished level when monitoring is used. Many of these moderators influence stress and productivity by varying the amount of social support and individual control provided to monitored employees.

For example, when supervisors maintain positive interactions with their employees, both stress and productivity loss are likely to be reduced. Similarly, when monitored employees work in cohesive work groups, they may feel less anxious and become more productive. EPM can lead to deteriorated relationships among employees, their supervisors, and their work peers; however, this loss of social support need not be inevitable.

When monitoring systems are implemented, efforts should be directed toward maintaining positive interactions between supervisors and employees. This can be accomplished by introducing monitoring as a means by which supervisors and employees in partnership set goals and work toward enhancing productivity. By using the products of EPM to supplement, rather than replace, "management-by-walking-around," face-to-face personal interactions between supervisors and their monitored employees may be maintained.

Similar efforts need to be directed toward developing and maintaining cohesiveness among work-group members. This may be accomplished by monitoring at the work-group level, rather than at the individual level. Work-group level monitoring may limit negative in-group competition and may facilitate the development of work-group goals while reducing the stress that derives from electronic observation. Likewise, other formal and information interventions that foster cohesiveness and supportive interactions among co-workers should be encouraged.

Negative consequences associated with EPM may be reduced by implementing practices that enhance the degree of control employees exercise over monitoring and their larger work environment. Involving employees in the planning of EPM systems and the negotiation of reasonable work standards should help increase their sense of ownership and satisfaction. Providing means by which workers can review, and when necessary correct, the outputs of monitoring systems should enhance their feelings of control. Monitoring work products, such as keystrokes, rather than employee behaviors, such as time spent on breaks, should help reduce perceptions of being spied on and dominated. Finally, sharing performance data privately between individual employees and their supervisors, rather than posting production statistics or not sharing monitoring outputs at all, should help enhance the sense of control workers have over their own productivity.

Implemented properly, EPM may provide substantial benefits to companies and their employees. EPM can be used as a means by which supervisors and employees in partnership set goals and work toward enhancing productivity. Under these productive conditions, workers have responded favorably to the practice. For example, one employee at Hughes Aircraft indicated, "I think it's great. A way to find out where you are" (Griffith, 1993). In contrast, inappropriate use of EPM may produce nothing more than increased stress and disgruntled workers. Employees who feel spied on and dominated by monitoring are likely to echo the sentiments of one airline reservationist in Texas: "This is America. We don't have to live like this" (9 to 5, Working Women Education Fund, 1990, p. 1).

References

Aiello, J. R. (1993). Computer-based work monitoring: Electronic surveillance and its effects. *Journal of Applied Social Psychology, 23,* 499–507.

Aiello, J. R., DeNisi, A. S., Kirkhoff, K., Shao, Y., Lund, M. A., & Chomiak, A. A. (1991, June). *The impact of feedback and individual/group computer monitoring on work effort.* Paper presented at the meeting of the American Psychological Society, Washington, DC.

Aiello, J. R., & Shao, Y. (1992, May). *Effects of computer monitoring on task performance.* Paper presented at the meeting of the Society for Industrial and Organizational Psychology, Montreal.

Aiello, J. R., & Shao, Y. (1993). Electronic performance monitoring and stress: The role of feedback and goal setting. In G. Salvendy & M. Smith (Eds.), *Human computer interaction: Software and hardware interfaces.* Amsterdam: Elsevier.

Aiello, J. R., & Svec, C. M. (1993). Computer monitoring and work performance: Extending the social facilitation framework to electronic presence. *Journal of Applied Social Psychology, 23,* 537–548.

Amick, B. C., III, & Smith, M. J. (1992). Stress, computer-based work monitoring and measurement systems: A conceptual overview. *Applied Ergonomics, 23,* 6–16.

Baron, R. S. (1986). Distraction-conflict theory: Progress and problems. *Advances in Experimental Social Psychology, 19,* 1–40.

Bylinsky, G. (1991, November). How companies spy on employees. *Fortune,* pp. 131–140.

Cahill, J., & Landsbergis, P. A. (1989, November). *Electronic monitoring: Analysis of current practices and implications for occupational stress.* Paper presented at the meeting of the American Public Health Association, Chicago.

Carey, E. (1985, October, 7). Big Brother is watching you work. *Toronto Star,* p. A1.

Chalykoff, J., & Kochan, T. A. (1989). Computer-aided monitoring: Its influence on employee satisfaction and turnover. *Personnel Psychology, 40,* 807–834.

Chomiak, A. A., Kolb, K. J., & Aiello, J. R. (1993, April). *Effect of computer monitoring and distraction on task performance.* Paper presented at the meeting of the Eastern Psychological Association, Washington, DC.

Cobb, S. (1976). Social support as a moderator of life stress. *Psychosomatic Medicine, 38,* 300–314.

Cohen, S., & Wills, T. A. (1985). Stress, social support, and the buffering hypothesis. *Psychological Bulletin, 98,* 310–357.

Cottrell, N. B. (1972). Social facilitation. In C. G. McClintock (Ed.), *Experimental social psychology.* New York: Holt, Rinehart & Winston.

DeNisi, A. S., & Aiello, J. R. (1993). *Computer monitoring and patterns of performance: Effects on performance ratings and recommendations.* Unpublished manuscript.

Duval, S., & Wicklund, R. A. (1972). *A theory of objective self-awareness.* San Diego, CA: Academic Press.

Erez, M. (1977). Feedback: A necessary condition for the goal setting-performance relationship. *Journal of Applied Psychology, 62,* 624–627.

Fenner, D. B., Lerch, F. J., & Kulik, C. T. (1993). The impact of computerized performance monitoring and prior performance knowledge on performance evaluation. *Journal of Applied Social Psychology, 23,* 573–601.

Garson, B. (1988). *The electronic sweatshop.* New York: Simon & Schuster.

Grant, R., & Higgins, C. (1989). Monitoring service workers via computer: The effect on employees, productivity, and service. *National Productivity Review, 8,* 101–112.

Grant, R. A., Higgins, C. A., & Irving, R. H. (1988). Computer performance monitors: Are they costing you customers? *Sloan Management Review, 29,* 39–45.

Griffith, T. L. (1993). Teaching Big Brother to be a team player: Computer monitoring and quality. *Academy of Management Executive, 7,* 73–80.

Halpern, S. (1992, May). Big boss is watching you. *Details,* pp. 18–23.

Harkins, S. G. (1987). Social loafing and social facilitation. *Journal of Experimental Social Psychology, 23,* 1–18.

Hershman, A., & Rozen, M. (1984, January). Corporate Big Brother is watching you. *Dun's Business Month,* pp. 36–39.

Irving, R. H., Higgins, C. A., & Safayeni, F. R. (1986). Computerized performance monitoring systems: Use and abuse. *Communications of the ACM, 29,* 794–801.

Karasek, R., & Theorell, T. (1990). *Healthy work: Stress, productivity, and the reconstruction of working life.* New York: Basic Books.

Kidwell, R. E., Jr., & Bennett, N. (1994). Electronic surveillance as employee control: A procedural justice interpretation. *Journal of High Technology Management Research, 5,* 39–58.

Kolb, K. J., & Aiello, J. R. (1993a). *The effects of computer monitoring in a multiple task environment.* Paper presented at the meeting of the Eastern Psychological Association, Washington, DC.

Kolb, K. J., & Aiello, J. R. (1993b). *Computer monitoring and social context: Impact on productivity and stress.* Paper presented at the meeting of the Society of Industrial and Organizational Psychology, San Francisco.

Komaki, J. L. (1986). Toward effective supervision: An operant analysis and comparison of managers at work. *Journal of Applied Psychology, 71,* 270–279.

Kulik, C. T., & Ambrose, M. L. (1993). Category-based and feature-based processes in performance appraisal: Integrating visual and computerized sources of performance data. *Journal of Applied Psychology, 78,* 821–830.

Laabs, J. J. (1992, June). Surveillance: Tool or trap. *Personnel Journal,* pp. 96–104.

McGregor, D. (1960). *The human side of enterprise.* New York: McGraw-Hill.

9 to 5, Working Women Education Fund. (1990). *Stories of mistrust and manipulation: The electronic monitoring of the American workforce.* Cleveland, OH: Author.

Schleifer, L. M., Galinsky, T. L., & Pan, C. S. (1992, November). *Mood disturbance and musculoskeletal discomfort: Effects of electronic performance monitoring in a VDT data entry task.* Paper presented at the meeting of the American Psychological Association/National Institute of Occupational Safety and Health, Washington, DC.

Sherizen, S. (1986). Work monitoring: Productivity gains: at what cost to privacy? *Computerworld, 20,* 55.

Smith, M. J. (1988). Electronic performance monitoring at the workplace: Part of a new industrial revolution. *Bulletin of Human Factors in Society, 31,* 1–3.

Smith, M. J., Carayon, P., Sanders, K. J., Lim, S.-Y., & LeGrande, D. (1992). Employee stress and health complaints in jobs with and without electronic performance monitoring. *Applied Ergonomics, 23,* 17–28.

Stein, M. B., & Aiello, J. R. (1992, April). *A test of mediating variables in socially facilitated individual task performance.* Paper presented at the meeting of the Eastern Psychological Association, Boston.

Tziner, A. (1982). Differential effects of group cohesiveness types: A clarifying overview. *Society for Personality Research, 10,* 227–239.

U.S. Congress, Office of Technology Assessment. (1987). *The electronic supervisor: New technology, new tensions.* Washington, DC: U.S. Government Printing Office.

Zajonc, R. B. (1965). Social facilitation. *Science, 149,* 269–274.

Appendix

Advantages Associated With Electronic Performance Monitoring

- Can provide immediate, objective feedback
- Reduces bias in performance evaluations
- Helps identify training needs
- Facilitates goal setting
- Can lead to productivity gains
- Facilitates telecommuting and "flex hours"
- Assists in resource planning
- Enhances value of investment in computer systems

Disadvantages Associated With Electronic Performance Monitoring

- Invasion of privacy
- Increases stress and possible negative long-term health outcomes
- Can lower satisfaction and morale
- May reduce contact between employees and supervisor
- May reduce contact between employees and coworkers
- Can lead to focus on work quantity while sacrificing quality
- Can transform work climate into "electronic sweatshop"
- May overwhelm supervisor with data and feedback expectations

12

The Effects of Human Versus Computer Monitoring of Performance on Physiological Reactions and Perceptions of Stress

Marian K. Silverman and Carlla S. Smith

Direct monitoring of work performance is an inescapable part of most people's lives. With a few exceptions, most jobs include an element of being monitored. Many industrial jobs, particularly assembly-line jobs, are closely monitored. Increasingly, the monitoring is done by computer. In addition to assembly work, computerized accounting of performance is used in such service industries as sales, health care delivery, and car rental agencies (e.g., Beardsley, 1987; Booth, 1987). For example, a computer can be programmed to record the number of sales in a predetermined time period.

As a programmable recorder, the computer is an aid in some job settings for managers to keep a continuous account of the performance of their subordinates. Not only can a computer gather and store an unbiased and accurate record of productivity, but it can also log work errors, illegal breaks, and inventory losses for a better estimate of productivity. Therefore, in some job settings, the task of direct surveillance by a biased and inexact human supervisor becomes unnecessary (Beardsley, 1987). From a managerial standpoint, computerized accounting of performance is economically justified because it frees the supervisor from directly monitoring worker performance and allows the supervisor to perform other important organizational tasks, such as training, correcting, rewarding, and evaluating workers.

Generally, the types of jobs that lend themselves to monitoring by computer tend to be those that are unskilled or semiskilled, routine, and not prestigious. These include assembly jobs, typing (word processing), telephone sales, and jobs in service-related industries. Many of these classes of jobs offer lower wages, require less education, are unionized, and are often staffed by women (Beardsley, 1987).

Unions view the introduction of computerized accounting of performance with some apprehension. Union representatives argue that continuous monitoring affects workers in a variety of detrimental ways. Included in the adverse affects are decreases in job satisfaction, privacy, and health (Booth, 1987). Previous research indicates that unskilled workers report less job satisfaction

181

than workers in either professional or management positions (Katz & Kahn, 1978). Whether continuous computer monitoring contributes to further decreases in job satisfaction needs to be researched. In addition, continuous supervision, regardless of the source, results in a loss of privacy and the possibility of abuse (e.g., monitoring nonwork behavior during legal break times). Union representatives also argue that continuous computer monitoring is stressful and results in a number of stress-related ailments, such as cardiovascular and gastrointestinal illness (Beardsley, 1987).

In certain segments of the work world, computer monitoring has the potential to become commonplace. However, as widespread as this potential might be, the extent to which monitoring by a computer (compared with monitoring by a human) might directly affect the physiological responses of the workers is indeterminate. Indeed, despite the large numbers of studies related to stress and health, limited evidence for a causal relationship between monitoring and stress-related illness exists (see the review by Kiecolt-Glaser & Glaser, 1987). Consequently, the information on the health effects of computer monitoring as a stressor has been correlational in nature (Beardsley, 1987). In addition, although job stress and its relation to worker health has been documented (e.g., Frankenhaeuser, 1975; Frankenhaeuser & Gardell, 1976), monitoring, specifically the difference between human and computer monitors, as a stressor has not been investigated in job-stress research. The evidence we do have of a possible effect of computer monitors is inferential, coming from the general work-stress literature.

The primary purpose of this study was to assess the effects of source of monitoring (human or computer) on human physiological reactions and to test whether continuous monitoring by computer is a stressor. Specifically, this research examined whether the source of monitoring (human or computer) affects the arousal level of a worker to such an extent that it can be labeled a stressor.

We attempted to compare physiological reactions of participants being monitored by either a computer or a human. Electronic monitoring has been alleged to cause some stress-related ailments. Although the effects of computer monitoring have been examined for psychological variables such as job satisfaction, the effects of electronic monitoring on physiological reactions have not been examined (Amick & Jacobs, 1986; Chalykoff & Kochan, 1989).

We used arousal measures (urinary cortisol, heart rate, and subjective questionnaire) to assess the effects of monitoring (computer and human). We obtained the measures from participants after continuous computer or human monitoring and compared them with participants performing the task with no monitoring. Therefore, performing a task in a situation that is highly monitored by either human or computer should be more arousing than performing a task in a nonmonitored situation. This hypothesis is consistent with research on evaluation apprehension (Zajonc, 1980), reviewed earlier.

We hypothesized that being monitored during the performance of a task is arousing. In addition, it was hypothesized that there would be a difference in degree of arousal depending on the source of monitoring. Arousal in participants performing while being monitored by a computer were compared with participants performing while being monitored by a person. The direction of the predicted difference was unknown at this point. On the basis of correlational studies provided by the National Institute for Occupational Safety and Health (NIOSH), it was expected that continuous computer supervision would be more stressful than continuous human supervision (Amick & Jacobs, 1986). However, the presence of an evaluative human may be perceived as more salient, and therefore more stressful, than a computer monitor. The effect of mere presence of others (human) as suggested by Zajonc (1980) would predict that human monitoring is more stressful than computer monitoring. We also hypothesized that there is a difference in degree of arousal depending on the source of monitoring.

Method

Participants

Forty female White students enrolled in an introductory psychology class at a medium-size Midwestern university voluntarily participated in this study for course credit. Participants with a history of steroid use were excluded from the study because steroid supplements may decrease the normal levels of cortisol secretion through adrenal suppression. We excluded all men, rather than cause embarrassment by asking about possible illegal anabolic steroid use, commonly used to build muscle mass in adolescent and college-age men. In addition, women are more able to provide two urine samples within a short time than are men.

Experimental Task

Participants performed a mail-sorting task, in which the participant was seated before the visual display terminal of a personal computer. A hypothetical person's name and address appears on the screen. The object is to correctly place the address by zip code into one of nine "slots" using the numeric keypad of a desktop computer. The pacing speed for this monotonous task was set at 4 s per address. A 4-s cycle falls within the bound of monotonous work as defined by Nilsson (1975).

A pretask urine sample was collected and electrodes were attached to record heart rate continuously. After a 10-min learning phase, the participant sorted addresses for one hour. At the completion of the task session, the post-task sample of urine was collected and the participant debriefed.

Experimental Conditions

Respondents were randomly assigned to one of four experimental conditions in a 2 (monitoring source) $\times$ 2 (monitoring level) factorial design. In all four conditions, the computerized mail-sorting task was performed in a soundproof room. In the computer-monitored condition, the respondent was told that the computer would record all responses and was left unattended to perform the task. In the setting where the respondent performed the task alone, she was told that neither the researcher nor the computer would be recording performance and was left unattended to perform the task. In the human-monitored condition, the respondent was told that all responses would be recorded on a clipboard by the researcher (sitting to the left and slightly behind the respondent). In the mere-presence condition, the respondent was told that her performance would not be recorded, and she performed the task in the company of a nonevaluative other. The nonevaluative other served as the control for the effects of evaluation versus the mere presence of another person (Zajonc, 1965) and sat to the left and slightly behind the respondent, quietly reading a book. At no time did the nonevaluative other acknowledge the respondent during task performance. This experimental design resulted in two sources of monitoring (human and computer) and two monitoring levels (constant and none).

Measures

There are two approaches to measuring arousal or reactions to stressful stimuli in human respondents. One general method is the use of self-report questionnaires, and the other is the use of direct physiological measures of arousal. We used a stress questionnaire to assess differences in subjective appraisals of physiological arousal in response to the different monitoring settings. In addition, perceived monitoring was assessed by means of a manipulation check to determine if the settings provided the participants with different perceptions of being monitored. Measures of urinary cortisol and heart rate were used to assess physiological arousal.

Urinary cortisol. Operationally, physiological arousal is measured by the change in pretask and posttask urine levels of cortisol. Many endocrine responses are affected by psychological factors. For example, an animal's appraisal of a situation as threatening results in a cascade of neurohormone release that increases the animal's ability to deal effectively with the threat. Hormones included in one of the branches of this cascade are related through the hypothalamic–anterior pituitary link and include adrenocorticotropic hormone (ACTH) and cortisol. Therefore, we used control as a biochemical indicant of chronic arousal.

In general, cortisol has not been the dependent measure of choice in stress studies because of technical obstacles and because adrenocortical steroids (e.g., cortisol) are tonic—slow to develop and slow to dissipate. However, cortisol has some general characteristics that make it deserving of attention in a short-term arousal situation. First, although the secretion of cortisol is phasic and relatively slower than catecholamines, it is surprisingly sensitive to psychological events. Mason (1972) noted that a variety of psychological stimuli is associated with significant changes in cortisol levels measured over a period of days. Among the psychological stimuli that elicit changes in serum or urinary cortisol levels are novelty, uncertainty, and unpredictability.

Recently, the development and use of sensitive and relatively simple laboratory techniques such as radioimmunoassay have made it possible to detect changes in cortisol levels before and after exposure to short-term psychological stressors. For example, musicians giving public performances had higher urinary cortisol levels than when giving private performances (Fredrikson & Gunnarsson, 1992). Furthermore, the stress of public lecturing significantly elevated urinary cortisol levels in bank employees (Bassett, Marshall, & Spillane, 1987) and student teachers (Houtman & Bakker, 1991). Although there is a time lag compared with serum cortisol levels, measurement of urinary cortisol is a simple, noninvasive collection procedure that provides evidence of physiological arousal.

Heart rate. Heart rate was assessed as the second physiological dependent measure. Of the different measures of physiological arousal, cardiovascular function has been frequently associated with stress and tension. In particular, heart rate generally increases when a participant is placed in a setting requiring preparation for action, as one might find in the alarm stage of the general adaptation syndrome (Selye, 1976). Furthermore, changes in heart rate and blood pressure occur independently of any conscious awareness of emotion, as if the body is anticipating the need to increase metabolic demands (Cacioppo, 1982).

Stress questionnaire. A 10-item stress questionnaire was constructed to assess perceived stress because of the experimental situation. Two items were based on the Anxiety and Stress Questionnaire, developed by House and Rizzo (1972; compiled and reviewed in Cook, Hepworth, Wall, & Warr, 1981), and described the extent to which the respondents felt agitated during the task. Five items were based on a measure of depressed mood at work, developed by Quinn and Shepard (1974; compiled and reviewed by Cook et al., 1981), and described the extent to which the respondents felt tired, irritable, anxious, worried, or preoccupied during the task. The remaining items were constructed specifically for this study to assess subjective appraisal of physical changes, such as cold hands (because of peripheral vasoconstriction), muscle tension, and dry mouth (inhibition of salivary secretion by adrenaline).

Using a 7-point Likert-type response format, scores for the 10 items were summed for a total perceived-stress score. If the respondent disagreed with all the stress items (i.e., did not report any perceived stress), the total score would be 10, with 1 point per item. If the respondent agreed with all the stress items, the total score would be 70, with 7 points per item. A moderate amount of perceived stress would result in a total score of 40, with 4 points per item (coefficient alpha = .55).

Manipulation check. A 5-item manipulation check was constructed to determine whether the participants perceived any group differences in the actual monitored settings and correctly appraised the extent of monitoring imposed on them. Three of the items were created for this study and described the extent to which they felt watched, constrained, and physically confined. One item was based on a psychological constraint item in the measure of higher order need strength, developed by Hackman and Lawler (1971; compiled and reviewed in Cook et al. 1981). The last item is based on a measure of autonomy, developed by Beehr (1976; compiled and reviewed by Cook et al., 1981), and described the extent to which the participants felt free to choose the method of performing the task (coefficient alpha = .49).

In addition, the participants had the opportunity to report the extent to which they felt bothered by being monitored, by the boring nature of the task, and by the act of providing urine specimens. These items were not included in the analysis of the stress items but were used to provide insight into data interpretation.

Apparatus

A No Spin 125-I Cortisol Coated Tube Radioimmunoassay Kit (Cambridge Medical Diagnostics) was used to assay urinary cortisol. Radioimmunoassay uses a fixed amount of radiolabeled protein (125-I cortisol) to compete with unlabeled antigen (sample cortisol) in the respondent's urine for sites on the antibody (cortisol antiserum)–coated tubes. The cortisol (labeled and unlabeled) becomes bound and immobilized onto the antibody sites. The quality of unlabeled cortisol (from the respondent's urine sample) is determined by comparing it with known standards.

Procedure

Participants were introduced to the researcher, the experimental condition, and the sorting task. They were asked to remove their watches to keep them unaware of the duration of the experiment. A baseline urine sample (for cortisol) was collected after informed consent was given and prior to task performance. In all settings, each participant had her heart rate monitored, and the second urine specimen was collected after task performance. The task was performed in a soundproof room to minimize distractions and in the late afternoon and evening to minimize the effect of the circadian cortisol peak that occurs in the morning for most people.

After the task-performance session, each participant completed the two questionnaires described earlier: a manipulation check on the degree of perceived monitoring and a dependent measure of perceived arousal. Finally, the participant was debriefed regarding the purpose of the study.

Results

Manipulation Check

Respondents who participated in the study indicated the degree of perceived monitoring by completing the 5-item manipulation check. A two-way analysis of variance (ANOVA) showed that there was a significant main effect for source of monitoring, $F(1) = 3.47, p = 0.258$. Means and standard deviations indicated that the groups with a human element (in the monitored or mere-presence conditions) reported a higher degree of perceived monitoring than groups that were left alone. Mean scores on the manipulation check in descending order by condition were human monitored (19.4), mere presence (15.4), computer monitored (13.6), and alone (12.8).

Thus, a human presence seemed to be perceived as more salient than a computer presence in relation to degree of perceived monitoring, regardless of actual monitoring. Likewise, participants did not report significant differences in monitoring when left alone to perform the task with or without computer monitoring. It appears that the mere presence of another person is associated with a perception of being monitoring.

Cortisol

There were no significant differences between groups in urinary cortisol for the level of monitoring, $F(1) = 0.68, p = .4148$, the source of monitoring, $F(1) = 0.12, p = .7332$, or the Source $\times$ Level interaction, $F(1) = 0.04, p = .8344$. Cortisol levels collected before the experimental manipulation were significantly higher than levels collected after the experiment, $F(1) = 44.63, p = .00$, probably because of the expected circadian decline of cortisol secretion in the afternoon and evening.

Gain scores (differences between preexperimental and postexperimental manipulation) were used to analyze cortisol differences between groups and to control for circadian variation (see Table 1). Using the gain score of cortisol, we found no significant differences between groups because of the level of monitoring $F(1) = 0.43, p = .5164$, the source of monitoring, $F(1) = 1.47, p = .2325$, or the interaction of source by level, $F(1) = 0.02, p = .8804$. The mean square error for urinary cortisol levels (25.228) was high, indicating a large amount of within-group variability in cortisol levels and possibly masking any differences among groups.

Heart Rate

Heart rate was collected in five 5-min blocks of time: at baseline (after 15 min of rest), from Minute 10 to 15 into the task, from Minute 25 to 30, from Minute

Table 1.   Means and Standard Deviations for Cortisol Gain Scores[a]

Level	Source of Monitoring	
	Computer	Human
Constant	$M = 4.02$	$M = 6.19$
	$SD = 5.14$	$SD = 6.84$
	Min, max $= 0.28, 16.3$	Min, max $= 0.08, 19.5$
None	$M = 3.32$	$M = 4.91$
	$SD = 2.97$	$SD = 4.34$
	Min, max $= 0.64, 9.09$	Min, max $= 1.25, 16.5$

[a]Predifferences and postdifferences in ratio of cortisol (μg/dl)/creatinine (μg/dl).

40 to 45, and from Minute 55 to 60. Each 5-min interval was summed for each group to provide five block totals: baseline, 15, 30, 45, and 60. With these 5-min time blocks, there appeared to be significant differences in heart rate among the groups, $F(4) = 10.90$, $p = .00$. However, these differences were present at the baseline reading before the experimental manipulation. There was no minute effect, $F(4) = 1.15$, $p = .3323$. That is, there were no group differences in heart rate, for either source or level of monitoring (or Source × Level interaction), at the minute-to-minute level of analysis.

To neutralize the differences among groups because of initial variation in baseline heart rates, heart rate gain scores were used. Block means at 15, 30, 45, and 60 min were subtracted from the baseline block mean to provide differences or gain scores. Again, there were no significant differences among groups because of either the level of monitoring, $F(4) = 0.40$, $p = .8087$, the source of monitoring, $F(4) = 1.29$, $p = .2756$, or the interaction between level and source, $F(4) = 19$, $p = .9424$. The mean square error was high (9.88), indicating a large amount of within-group variability in heart rate, possibly masking any differences between groups.

Subjective Report of Arousal and Stress

A two-way ANOVA revealed a main effect for source of monitoring on arousal on the basis of the subjective report of arousal, $F(1) = 5.00$, $p < .03$. Again, a human presence (perhaps being more salient) seemed to be a greater source of perceived stress than a computer presence. However, it should be noted that all groups did report a moderate amount of perceived stress (see Table 2). The mean scores on the perceived stress questionnaires ranged from 29.6 (the computer-monitored group) to 37.8 (the human-monitored group).

Miscellaneous

In addition to the 10 items pertaining to perceived physiological arousal, the stress questionnaire included three items that examined the extent to which

Table 2. Means and Standard Deviations for Stress Questionnaire Scores as a Function of Source and Level of Monitoring[a]

	Source	
	Computer	Human
Level		
Constant	$M = 29.60$ $SD = 7.92$ Min, max = 16, 43	$M = 37.80$ $SD = 7.66$ Min, max = 29, 52
None	$M = 35.10$ $SD = 8.32$ Min, max = 18, 46	$M = 37.50$ $SD = 7.23$ Min, max = 22, 46

[a]Scores on the stress questionnaire could range from 10 (*no perceived stress*) to 70 (*maximally perceived stress*).

the respondent felt bothered by three aspects of the experiment: being monitored, performing a boring task, and giving urine specimens. On the average, respondents did not feel bothered about being monitored ($M = 2.13$, $SD = 1.65$) or about giving urine specimens ($M = 2.38$, $SD = 1.60$). However, respondents on the average did feel bothered by the boring nature of the task ($M = 5.33$, $SD = 1.94$).

Discussion

Many industrial jobs, particularly assembly-line jobs, are closely supervised. Increasingly, the monitoring is done by a computer. Although there are anecdotal reports from labor unions of stress-related illnesses because of electronic monitoring, very few studies have actually investigated a possible link between electronic monitoring, stress, and illness (Smith & Amick, 1989). The present study attempted to investigate the relationship between the source of monitoring (computer or human) and physiological arousal.

We found no significant physiological differences between monitored groups, as measured by urinary cortisol excretion and heart rate. These results did not support the study hypotheses that being monitored causes physiological arousal and that computer monitoring is more arousing than human monitoring. However, there were significant main effects among the groups as measured by subjective reports of stress and perceived monitoring. This may indicate that, although the physiological measures used in this study were not sufficiently sensitive to detect differences, differences did exist. Alternatively, lack of significant results suggests that cortisol might not be a good dependent measure, as other researchers have noted in the past (e.g., Mason, 1972). A significant change in levels of cortisol may not have been expected because of the relatively short exposure time to the stressor. Additional methodological problems associated with cortisol are the wide individual, circadian, and seasonal variations in serum and urinary levels. However, outright dismissal of cortisol as a measure of short-term physiological arousal may be premature.

Limitations of the Present Study

Data interpretation of our research should be made with caution for two reasons, however. The participants tested in this study were undergraduate women. Research suggests that women may be less physiologically reactive than men (see the review by Stoney, Davis, & Matthews, 1987). This may affect the results and interpretation and limit the external validity of this study. In addition, the experimental manipulation for the four monitoring conditions may have been only partially achieved. Post hoc tests indicated that participants did not clearly perceive differences in being monitored by the computer and being left entirely alone to perform the task.

In the real world, monitoring deals with more than short-term performance evaluation. For example, the organization may have severe sanctions for poor performance or there may be managerial and political power issues regarding the use of the information obtained by monitoring. Obviously, there were no sanctions given for poor performance in this experiment. In an organizational setting, there are negative consequences for poor performance that cannot be achieved in a laboratory setting. These real-world issues affect the external validity of this study insofar as any effect obtained in this study should be magnified in the real world. That is, if an effect were noted in this relatively nonthreatening situation where there was no punishment for poor performance, one can easily imagine a heightened reaction to a monitoring situation if the consequences of performance are meaningful.

In addition to the external validity issue, there were sources of error variance because of the experimental methodology. Some participants felt sufficiently bothered by the boring nature of the repetitive mail-sorting task to label the task as a stressor. The task was not expected to be perceived as so tedious after (only) one hour. However, on the average, respondents reported that they felt moderately bothered by the boring nature of the task.

Another potentially stressful characteristic of this particular task involved the use of a computer. Approximately 30% of the participants stated, without prompting, that they had little to no experience with a computer keyboard and expressed some anxiety about being able to perform the task. After the task was explained and the practice session performed, none of the inexperienced participants had any hesitancy about task performance. Nevertheless, the initial hesitancy and anxiety about performing the task on a computer had the potential to add stress to an already-stressful situation.

These potential sources of added stress (boredom and computer anxiety) may explain the large variation in scores on all the dependent measures, particularly the physiological measures. If nothing else, the results dramatize the importance of individual differences in interpretations of an event as stressful and in levels of physiological reactivity.

Physiological Versus Psychological Measures

The lack of agreement between physiological and self-report measures is consistent with previous research that has attempted to correlate the two kinds of measures. Although it appears reasonable to assume that physiological measures and self-reports of arousal should provide converging evidence of stress, people seem to be very poor readers of their bodies' physiological states (Pennebaker, 1982). Self-reports of stress consistently do not correlate well with specific physiological activity. For example, Zillmann (1984) found that, after exercising, people reported that their arousal subsided much quicker than monitored decreases in heart rate and blood pressure. Zillmann concluded that, even with converging evidence of physiological arousal from two sources, people are not accurate estimators of their own arousal states. This conclusion was based on lack of agreement between self-reports and two measures of physiological arousal, heart rate and blood pressure.

Mackay (1980), however, argued that self-reports of stress might be indicators of overall physiological arousal (e.g., a composite score of arousal based on heart rate, respiration, blood pressure, and skin resistance), rather than indicators of any individual physiological response. Hence, a composite physiological score theoretically should correlate with perceptions of stress, even though a single physiological response may not.

A physiological measure that has convergent validity with other measures of sympathetic or adrenocortical arousal would be useful in determining the relationship between job-related stress and physiological arousal. Self-reports of arousal may be good indicators of a composite arousal score, but they are still subject to the usual arguments regarding that lack of reliability and validity of any self-report data. Further research needs to be done to differentiate between the lack of agreement caused by the selection of the wrong set of physiological measures versus the lack of a real relationship between physiological measures and self-reports of stress. This information would be useful in determining the relationship between job-related stress and illness.

Conclusions and Directions for Future Research

To critics, computer monitoring is viewed as an invasion of privacy and another source of work stress and should be banished from the workplace. Critics cite correlational evidence that computer monitoring is associated with increased levels of cardiovascular disease and gastrointestinal illness in workers. Considering the wide variation in reactions to the experimental conditions in the present study as measured by cortisol differences over a relatively short period of time, more research needs to be conducted with physiological responses. In particular, more research is needed to relate physiological data to psychological constructs, such as monitoring.

Differences in level and source of monitoring may result in substantial changes in physiology that extend far beyond what was examined and measured in a one-hour manipulation in a laboratory setting. The experimental human monitor in this study had no organizational sanctions at her disposal. This may partially explain the nonsignificant findings for the physiological measures. Not only was the monitoring nonthreatening, but it was also of very short duration when compared with work experiences. In spite of these relatively innocuous characteristics of the laboratory monitoring, respondents reported significant differences in perceived monitoring and perceived arousal because of the experimental manipulations. Further research with actual employees working on computer-assisted tasks and on shifts longer than a one-hour laboratory allotment of time may be enlightening.

Recently, Chalykoff and Kochan (1989) suggested that employee attitudes toward computer monitoring might influence job satisfaction and turnover. The information gathered from electronic surveillance was viewed more favorably if it were used to improve performance rather than set performance rates. A favorable rating for monitoring may translate into a less aversive situation with correspondingly lower levels of autonomic arousal. Thus, if an employee feels that computer monitoring is necessary and therefore provides unbiased information about performance, it should not be perceived as objectionable. Alternatively, if information gathered from computer monitoring were used to set minimal acceptable performance rates, then it would be viewed by employees as another method of unwelcome organizational control.

Even in the absence of measurable physiological changes, the perception of computer-induced stress might still be important. It may be that physiological measures alone are inadequate to detect actual changes that have negative health consequences. Also, the perception of stress might be an important determinant in a person's level of job satisfaction and affect his or her intent to leave a job, even in the absence of actual physiological stress. Clearly, the use of computers to electronically monitor work performance has substantial potential to improve efficiency in the workplace, but questions regarding long-term health effects remain.

References

Amick, B. C., & Jacobs, J. H. (1986). Assessing the impact of office automation on employee productivity. *Employee Assistance Quarterly, 2*, 31–46.

Bassett, J. R., Marshall, P. M., & Spillane, R. (1987). The physiological measurement of acute stress (public speaking) in bank employees. *International Journal of Psychophysiology, 5*, 265–273.

Beardsley, T. M. (1987). Electronic taskmasters: Does monitoring degrade the quality of working life? *Scientific American, 257*, 32–34.

Booth, W. (1987). Big Brother is counting your key strokes. *Science, 238*, 17–18.

Cacioppo, J. T. (1982). Social psychophysiology: A classic perspective and contemporary approach. *Psychophysiology, 19*, 241–251.

Chalykoff, J., & Kochan, T. A. (1989). Computer-aided monitoring: Its influence on employee job satisfaction and turnover. *Personnel Psychology, 42*, 807–827.

Cook, J. D., Hepworth, S. J., Wall, T. D., & Warr, P. B. (1981). *The experience of work: A compendium and review of 249 measures and their use.* San Diego, CA: Academic Press.

Frankenhaeuser, M. (1975). Experimental approaches to the study of catecholamines and emotion. In L. Levi (Ed.), *Emotions: Their parameters and measurements* (pp. 209–234). New York: Raven Press.

Frankenhaeuser, M., & Gardell, B. (1976). Underload and overload in working life: Outline of a multidisciplinary approach. *Journal of Human Stress, 2*, 35–46.

Fredrikson, M., & Gunnarsson, R. (1992). Psychobiology of stage fright: The effect of public performance on neuroendocrine, cardiovascular and subjective reactions. *Biological Psychology, 33*, 51–61.

Houtman, I. L., & Bakker, F. C. (1991). Stress and coping in lecturing and the stability of responses across practice. *Journal of Psychosomatic Research, 35*, 323–333.

Katz, D., & Kahn, R. L. (1978). *The social psychology of organizations* (2nd ed.). New York: Wiley.

Kiecolt-Glaser, J. K., & Glaser, R. (1987). Psychosocial moderators of immune function. *Annals of Behavioral Medicine, 9*, 16–20.

Mackay, C. J. (1980). The measurement of mood and psychophysiological activity using self-report techniques. In I. Martin & P. H. Venables (Eds.), *Techniques in psychophysiology* (pp. 501–562). New York: Wiley.

Mason, J. W. (1972). Organization of psychoendocrine systems. In N. S. Greenfield & R. A. Sternbach (Eds.), *Handbook of psychophysiology* (pp. 3–91). New York: Holt, Rinehart & Winston.

Nilsson, C. (1975). Working conditions in the sawmill industry: A sociological approach based on subjective data. In B. Thunell & B. Ager (Eds.), *Ergonomics in sawmills and woodworking industries* (pp. 249–260). Stockholm: National Board of Occupation Safety and Health.

Pennebaker, J. W. (1982). Accuracy of symptom perception. In A. Baum, J. Singer, & S. E. Taylor (Eds.), *Handbook of psychology in health* (Vol. 4). Hillsdale, NJ: Erlbaum.

Selye, H. (1976). *The stress of life.* New York: McGraw-Hill.

Smith, M. J., & Amick, B. C. (1989). Electronic monitoring at the workplace: Implications for employee control and job stress. In S. L. Sauter, J. J. Hurrell, & C. L. Cooper (Eds.), *Job control and worker health*. New York: Wiley.

Stoney, C. M., Davis, M. C., & Matthews, K. C. (1987). Sex differences in physiological response to stress and in coronary heart disease: A causal link? *Psychophysiology, 24,* 127–131.

Zajonc, R. B. (1965). Social facilitation. *Science, 149,* 269–274.

Zajonc, R. B. (1980). Compresence. In P. B. Paulus (Ed.), *Psychology of group influence* (pp. 35–60). Hillsdale, NJ: Erlbaum.

Zillmann, D. (1984). *Connections between sex and aggression*. Hillsdale, NJ: Erlbaum.

13

Mood Disturbance and Musculoskeletal Discomfort Effects of Electronic Performance Monitoring in a VDT Data-Entry Task

Lawrence M. Schleifer, Traci L. Galinski,
and Christopher S. Pan

Electronic performance monitoring (EPM) has been defined by the Office of Technology Assessment (OTA) as the "computerized collection, storage, analysis, and reporting of information about employees' activities" (OTA, 1987, p. 3). EPM is used to oversee the productivity of millions of office workers, and its use is expected to expand rapidly throughout the global economy during this decade (Schleifer, 1992). EPM is used in word processing, data entry, insurance claims processing, customer service operations, and telemarketing to monitor and provide feedback for worker performance, enforce performance standards, and administer incentive pay programs. EPM work management provides for the electronic supervision of computer-based work on a second-by-second, keystroke-by-keystroke basis (Smith, 1988).

There is a theoretical basis (Amick & Smith, 1992; Schleifer & Shell, 1992; Smith, Carayon, & Miezio, 1986) and increasing empirical evidence (DiTecco, Cwitco, Arsenault, & Andre, 1992; Schleifer, Sauter, Hales, & Peterson, 1992; Smith et al., 1986; Smith, Carayon, Sanders, Lim, & LeGrande, 1992) suggesting that EPM work management is associated with psychological and musculoskeletal strain. EPM can alter basic job dimensions (e.g., workload and task control) and produce an imbalance between task demands and the worker's resources to adapt. In particular, EPM is likely to be stressful when it is used to enforce compliance with performance standards that workers have difficulty meeting (Schleifer & Shell, 1992). Under such conditions, workers may experience stress through work overload, negative computer–supervisor feedback, and threat of job loss.

This study evaluated mood disturbance and musculoskeletal discomfort effects of the use of EPM to enforce compliance with performance standards

This research was initiated by Lawrence M. Schleifer during his tenure as a research psychologist in the Division of Biomedical and Behavioral Science, National Institute for Occupational Safety and Health, Cincinnati, OH.

for a numeric data-entry task. The study focused on workers who had difficulty maintaining data-entry performance standards of greater than 200 keystrokes per minute and less than six errors per minute; that is, workers who were most likely to experience work overload and negative performance feedback under EPM work-management conditions.

Method

Participants

Forty-seven female data-entry operators (mean age = 24 years, range = 19–38 years) were recruited from a temporary employment agency and paid $7.55 per hour for their participation in the study. The participants were in good general health, with normal or corrected-to-normal visual acuity and no musculoskeletal complaints.

To generate high workload demands under EPM conditions, participation in the study was restricted to those who did not meet performance standards of greater than 200 keystrokes per minute and less than six errors per minute for a numeric data-entry task.

Apparatus

The study was conducted in the Work Stress Laboratory of the National Institute for Occupational Safety and Health (NIOSH). Two IBM PCAT 5170s were used at each workstation to deliver the data-entry task and collect experimental data. Each workstation was also equipped with an IBM 3163 video-display terminal (VDT), an ergonomic table and chair, wrist supports, contrast enhancement filters, and a copyholder. Overhead fluorescent lighting fixtures were fitted with parabolic lenses. The ambient illumination level at each workstation was held constant at 500 lx. Ergonomic adjustments to the workstations were made on an individual basis to maximize physical comfort for each participant.

Task

The data-entry task required participants to enter numbers from bogus Internal Revenue Service (IRS) 1040-EZ tax forms using the numeric keypad of an IBM 3163 VDT. Each form contained 11 fields of numeric data. Participants entered the appropriate numeric information from each field on the printed tax form in a continuous sequence, pressing the *enter* key after each field was completed. All participants performed the numeric data-entry task exclusively with the right hand.

Task Conditions

Participants performed the numeric data-entry task under EPM work-management or no EPM work-management conditions.

EPM work management. In this condition, keystroke and error rates were monitored electronically and performance feedback was provided through each participant's VDT to enforce compliance with a performance standard. The performance standard was designated as a "fair day's work pace"; that is, "the work pace at which an average, well-trained employee can work without undue fatigue while producing an acceptable quality of work" (Nolan, 1983, p. 119).

Through the use of the methods–time measurement procedures (Maynard, Stegemerten, & Schwab, 1948), the fair day's work-pace standard for the data-entry task was determined to be 200 keystrokes per minute.[1] For the purposes of this study, an acceptable level of work quality was set at an accuracy standard of no more than six errors per minute. Following each work period, performance feedback was presented on the video screens of participants in the EPM group. Those who did not meet either the speed or the accuracy performance standard received a negative performance feedback message: "You have not met the minimum performance standard; your performance for this work period is unsatisfactory." Those who met or exceeded both the speed and accuracy criteria received a positive feedback message: "You have met the minimum performance standard; your performance for this work period is satisfactory." Regardless of whether participants in this condition met the minimum performance standard, they received $7.55 per hour for performing the data-entry task.

No EPM work management. In this condition, no work standards were imposed, and no performance feedback was provided to participants. They were instructed to perform the data-entry task at their usual work pace and level of accuracy. All participants received $7.55 per hour for performing the data-entry task.

Stress Measures

Self-reported mood disturbance and musculoskeletal discomfort data were obtained through the use of rating scales administered to respondents through their VDTs. Mood-disturbance measures included *irritation, perceived time pressure, tension, workload dissatisfaction, boredom,* and *fatigue* (for detailed descriptions of these scales, see Caplan, Cobb, French, Van Harrison, & Pinneau, 1975; Schleifer & Amick, 1989). Musculoskeletal discomfort measures included ratings of discomfort, pain, stiffness, or soreness in the *lower back, neck, left shoulder, right shoulder, left elbow, right elbow, left hand,* and *right hand.*

---

[1]Richard Shell, an expert in methods–time measurement, computed the work-pace standard for the data-entry task.

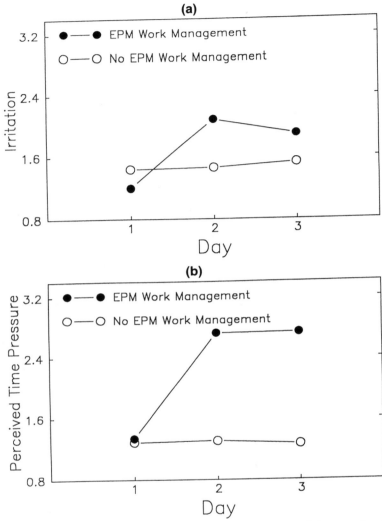

Figure 1. Mean ratings of mood disturbances across the workdays under EPM and no EPM conditions: (a) mean ratings of irritation, (b) mean ratings of perceived time pressure, (c) mean ratings of tension, and (d) mean ratings of workload dissatisfaction. EPM = electronic performance monitoring.

Respondents indicated the degree to which they were experiencing mood disturbances and musculoskeletal discomfort with a category rating scale comprising the whole numbers 1 through 5, with the verbal anchors *hardly at all* and *a great deal* at these two extremes, respectively.

Procedures

Participants assigned to the same condition were tested simultaneously in groups of three or less. Testing occurred over the course of three consecutive

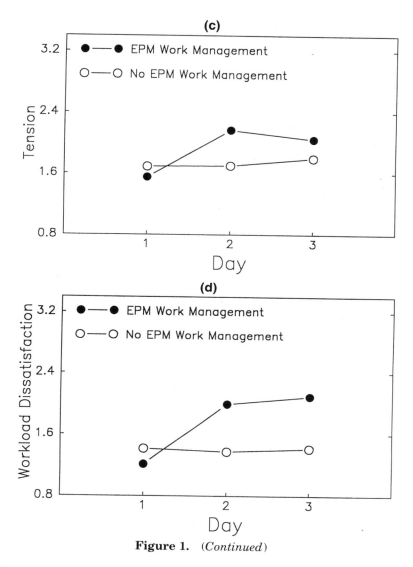

Figure 1. *(Continued)*

days. Each day included six 40-min work periods (three in the morning and three in the afternoon). Mood disturbance and musculoskeletal discomfort ratings were obtained from participants at the end of each work period. They had a 45-min lunch break, a 10-min break in the morning (prior to the third work period), and a 10-min break in the afternoon (prior to the sixth work period).

On the first (baseline) day, no EPM work management (i.e., no work standard or performance feedback) was invoked for either group of participants. Individuals in both groups were simply instructed to perform the data-entry task at their usual work pace and level of accuracy. On the second and third days, EPM work management was in effect only for the experimental group; those in the control group were instructed to continue working at their usual pace and level of accuracy.

Results

Because EPM was not implemented until the second day of testing, it was necessary to examine the mood and musculoskeletal data for significant Task Condition × Day interactions. Such interactions would indicate an EPM effect that was greater than no EPM following, but not during, the first (baseline) day of testing. To this end, planned contrasts were performed across the workdays for the EPM and no EPM task conditions (i.e., Day 1 vs. Day 2 and Day 1 vs. Day 3) with F ratios (SAS Institute, 1987).

Mood Disturbances

Figure 1 presents the mean ratings of irritation, perceived time pressure, tension, and workload dissatisfaction across the three workdays for the EPM work-management and no EPM work-management conditions. Planned contrasts indicated that the increase in mood disturbances from Day 1 to Day 2 were higher for EPM work management than for no EPM work management: irritation, $F(1, 45) = 12.44, p < .01$; perceived time pressure, $F(1, 45) = 27.71$, $p < .001$; tension, $F(1, 45) = 10.27, p < .01$; workload dissatisfaction, $F(1, 45) = 18.57, p < .001$. In addition, the increases in mood disturbances from Day 1 to Day 3 were higher for EPM than for no EPM: irritation, $F(1, 45) = 8.83$, $p < .01$; perceived time pressure, $F(1, 45) = 26.09, p < .001$; tension, $F(1, 45) = 4.07, p < .05$; workload dissatisfaction, $F(1, 45) = 15.88, p < .001$. Ratings of boredom and fatigue increased significantly across the workdays but were not differentially affected by task condition. Boredom ratings, in comparison with Day 1, were higher on Day 2, $F(1, 45) = 6.50, p < .05$, and Day 3, $F(1, 45) = 17.29, p < .001$. Fatigue ratings, in comparison with Day 1, were higher on only Day 3, $F(1, 45) = 6.19, p < .05$.

Musculoskeletal Discomfort

Figure 2 presents the mean ratings of right-hand discomfort across the three workdays under EPM work management and no EPM work management. Planned contrasts indicated that, in comparison with Day 1, right-hand discomfort was significantly higher for EPM than no EPM on Day 3, $F(1, 45) = 5.58, p < .05$.

Regardless of task condition, musculoskeletal discomfort ratings, in comparison with Day 1, were significantly higher on Day 2: neck, $F(1, 45) = 4.23$, $p < .05$; right shoulder, $F(1, 45) = 11.62, p < .01$; right elbow, $F(1, 45) = 7.50$, $p < .01$; and right hand, $F(1, 45) = 14.34, p < .001$; and on Day 3: lower back, $F(1, 45) = 8.74, p < .01$; neck, $F(1, 45) = 5.79, p < .05$; left shoulder, $F(1, 45) = 5.10, p < .05$; right shoulder, $F(1, 45) = 20.60, p < .001$; and right elbow, $F(1, 45) = 14.32, p < .001$.

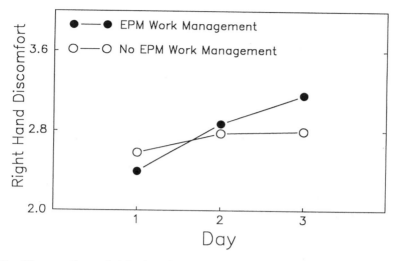

Figure 2.   Mean ratings of right-hand discomfort across the workdays under the EPM and no EPM conditions. EPM = electronic performance monitoring.

Discussion

The results show that the use of EPM work management to enforce compliance with performance standards for a numeric data-entry task promotes psychological strain. Several of the mood disturbance indicators (i.e., irritation, tension, perceived time pressure, and workload dissatisfaction) increased significantly across the workdays under EPM work management.

Right-hand discomfort was the only musculoskeletal symptom that increased under EPM work management across the workdays. This finding is of particular concern because of the increasing reports of hand–wrist disorders among workers engaged in repetitive keyboard tasks (Bernard, Sauter, Peterson, & Hales, 1992; Hales, Sauter, Peterson, & Bernard, 1992; Hocking, 1987; National Institute for Occupational Safety and Health, 1990; Smith et al., 1992).

With respect to several mood disturbance and musculoskeletal discomfort indicators (i.e., fatigue, boredom, lower back, neck, left shoulder, right shoulder, and right elbow), there was a pattern of increased psychological and physical strain across the workdays that was the same under the EPM and no EPM conditions. Apparently, the strain of performing a repetitive data-entry task for sustained periods of time was more pronounced than the strain of EPM for these indicators of mood disturbance and musculoskeletal discomfort. These results are consistent with the premise that data-entry work is intrinsically stressful (Floru, Cail, & Elias, 1985; Gao et al., 1990; Weber, Fussler, O'Hanlon, Gierer, & Grandjean, 1980).

Overall, our results indicate that EPM work management is a source of psychological and physical strain, particularly among data-entry workers who have difficulty maintaining a fair day's work pace. Because performance standards are often fixed in relation to the average performance of a work group

(Schleifer & Shell, 1992), a large segment of workers falling below average may experience mood disturbances and musculoskeletal discomfort under EPM conditions.

The findings of this study extend those of previous studies regarding the apparent relationship between EPM work management and worker stress (DiTecco et al., 1992; Gallatin, 1989; Irving, Higgins, & Safayeri, 1986; Smith et al., 1986; Smith et al., 1992). Moreover, the controlled conditions under which the study was conducted suggest that extraneous job content–climate factors were not responsible for changes in participants' mood and comfort states under EPM conditions. Rather, these changes occurred in direct response to the high workload demands associated with the use of EPM work management to enforce compliance with work standards. Given the short duration of the experiment and the fact that substandard performance had no adverse pay consequences, the EPM stress effects observed in this study may underestimate those produced under actual workplace conditions.

References

Amick, B. C. III, & Smith, M. J. (1992). Stress, computer-based work monitoring and measurement systems: A conceptual overview. *Applied Ergonomics, 23*, 6–16.

Bernard, B., Sauter, S. L., Peterson, M., & Hales, T. (1992, September). *Upper extremity musculoskeletal outcomes among newspapers employees.* Paper presented at the 3rd International Scientific Conference on Work With Display Units, Berlin.

Caplan, R., Cobb, S., French, J. R. P., Van Harrison, R., & Pinneau, R. (1975). *Job demands and worker health* (Publication No. 75-160). Washington, DC: National Institute for Occupational Safety and Health.

DiTecco, D., Cwitco, G., Arsenault, A., & Andre, M. (1992). Operator stress and monitoring practices. *Applied Ergonomics, 23*, 29–34.

Floru, R., Cail, F., & Elias, R. (1985). Psychophysiological changes during a VDU repetitive task. *Ergonomics, 28*, 1455–1468.

Gallatin, L. (1989). *Electronic monitoring in the workplace: Supervision or surveillance.* Boston: Massachusetts Coalition on New Office Technology.

Gao, C., Lu, D., She, Q., Cai, R., Yang, L., & Zhang, G. (1990). The effects of VDT data entry work on operators. *Ergonomics, 33*, 917–924.

Hales, T., Sauter, S. L., Peterson, M., & Bernard, B. (1992, September). *Upper extremity musculoskeletal conditions among VDT users in a telecommunications company* [Abstract Book]. Third International Scientific Conference on Work With Display Units, Berlin.

Hocking, B. (1987). Epidemiological aspects of "repetition strain injury" in Telecom Australia. *Medical Journal of Australia, 147*, 218–222.

Irving, R. H., Higgins, C. A., & Safayeri, F. R. (1986, August). Computerized performance monitoring systems: Use and abuse. *Communications of the ACM, 29*, 794–801.

Maynard, H. B., Stegemerten, G. J., & Schwab, J. L. (1948). *Methods-time measurement.* New York: McGraw-Hill.

National Institute for Occupational Safety and Health. (1990). *Newsday, Inc.* (HETA 89-250-2046). Cincinnati, OH: Author.

Nolan, R. (1983). Work measurement. In R. Lehrer (Ed.), *White collar productivity* (pp. 111–158). New York: McGraw-Hill.

Office of Technology Assessment. (1987). *The electronic supervisor: New technology, new tensions.* Washington, DC: U.S. Congress.

SAS Institute. (1987). *SAS user's guide: Statistics (ver. 6).* Cary, NC: Author.

Schleifer, L. M. (1992). Electronic performance monitoring (EPM). *Applied Ergonomics, 23*, 4–5.

Schleifer, L. M., & Amick, B. C. (1989). System response time and method of pay: Stress effects in computer-based tasks. *International Journal of Human-Computer Interaction, 1*, 23–39.

Schleifer, L. M., Sauter, S. L., Hales, T., & Peterson, T. (1992, September). *Work monitoring, performance standards, and musculoskeletal outcomes* [Abstract Book]. Third International Scientific Conference on Work With Display Units, Berlin.

Schleifer, L. M., & Shell, R. L. (1992). A review and reappraisal of electronic performance monitoring, performance standards, and stress allowances. *Applied Ergonomics, 23*, 49–53.

Smith, M. J. (1988). Electronic performance monitoring at the workplace: Part of a new industrial revolution. *Human Factors Society Bulletin, 31*, 1–3.

Smith, M. J., Carayon, P., & Miezio, K. (1986). *Motivational, behavioral, and psychological implications of electronic monitoring of worker performance* (NTIS PB88-156369). Washington, DC: National Technical Information Service.

Smith, M. J., Carayon, P., Sanders, K., Lim, S. Y., & LeGrande, D. (1992). Employee stress and health complaints in jobs with and without electronic performance monitoring. *Applied Ergonomics, 23*, 17–27.

Weber, A., Fussler, C., O'Hanlon, J., Gierer, R., & Grandjean, E. (1980). Psychophysiological effects of repetitive tasks. *Ergonomics, 23*, 1033–1046.

Part IV

High-Risk Occupations

Introduction

Questions about risk of job stress commonly focus on the level of the job itself (job characteristics), asking, for example, which occupations are most stressful. Unfortunately, surveillance systems that enable collection of data on the prevalence of stress-related disorders of job-stress risk factors across occupations—and thus enable the ordering of occupations according to risk for job stress—are absent or insufficient in the United States. In contrast, the European Community and some member states have recently initiated surveys of work conditions that permit conclusions regarding relative, occupation-specific risk for job stress and changes in risk over time. The first chapter in Part IV, by Houtman and Kompier, describes a national survey of living and working conditions by The Netherlands Central Bureau of Statistics and the analyses of certain risk factors for job stress and health measures across the 20 largest professional groups and the 19 largest branches of industry in The Netherlands from 1977 to 1989. Among the many interesting findings presented are results that support the predictions of social scientists; specifically, psychosocial demands in the workplace, in contrast to physical stressors, seem to have increased markedly over the past two decades. Of particular relevance to this part of the volume, the increase in certain psychosocial demands such as work pace are especially pronounced among health-care workers, presumably adding to stress risk in this type of occupation.

The next four chapters of this part specifically address stress risks in health care jobs, focusing on crisis workers such as emergency response personnel (firefighters and paramedics), hospital emergency-room and critical-care staff, and mental health workers. It could be surmised that these professions would place workers at high risk for stress, given the combination of psychosocial demands that cut across these types of jobs. In addition to time urgency or intense work pace that, as discussed by Houtman and Kompier, is common to these jobs, they also frequently involve a high degree of exposure to life and death situations including violence and extremes in human emotions. But surprisingly, there has been relatively little study of either salient stressors or stress-related outcomes among health workers providing emergency response or critical care.

These chapters begin to clarify stress problems in health care crisis work and to suggest intervention strategies. The chapter by Beaton, Murphy, Pike, and Jarrett indicates, for example, that only a fairly small proportion of firefighters and paramedics may be highly reactive to the stresses of emergency response work, but for this group, fairly intensive psychoeducational interventions that go beyond critical-incident debriefings may be necessary. The prospective study by Revicki and Whitely shows the importance of social support in moderating stress-related depression among emergency-room residents. The chapter by Schaufeli, Keijsers, and Miranda suggests that medical benefits of sophisticated technology in intensive care units (ICUs) is offset both by increased burnout of nurses resulting from the pressures of using this technology and by an adverse effect of technology on the overall performance effectiveness of the ICU. Finally, the chapter by Fong suggests that exposure to violence, which represents a escalating concern in occupational health in general, may be a special and growing risk for mental health providers. Importantly, the chapter discusses attributes of the provider, patient, and therapeutic situation that may promote risk and suggests a series of practical measures that might be used by providers to ensure their personal safety.

Part IV concludes with chapters by Sternbach on stress risks among professional musicians and by McIntosh on exhilarating work. Although the Sternbach chapter does not fit neatly with the emphasis on health care work in this part—except to say, perhaps, that music provides therapy for the soul—it draws attention to a profession possibly at high risk for job stress that has been completely overlooked in prior literature on job stress. For this reason, the editors believed it was important to include this chapter in the volume.

The final chapter addresses an intriguing issue of relevance to the entire part; specifically, what is it about risky or dangerous jobs that often makes them attractive? In her study of nurses, McIntosh argues that exhilaration is a separate dimension of work that goes hand in hand with the objective danger in many jobs and that exhilaration has a salutary influence on well-being that buffers the effects of job stressors. This insight may be of theoretical importance in explaining other related phenomena of interest in occupational safety and health and possibly offering, for example, a fuller understanding of risk-taking behavior.

14

Risk Factors and Occupational Risk Groups for Work Stress in The Netherlands

Irene L. D. Houtman and Michiel A. J. Kompier

In The Netherlands, a causal relation is assumed between work stress and high levels of absenteeism due to sickness and permanent work disability because of psychologically dysfunctioning and depressive symptoms. This hypothesis is supported by Gründemann, Nijboer, and Schellart (1991). Gründemann and associates demonstrated that 58% of employees who experienced psychological dysfunctioning held mental workload responsible for this disablement. Moreover, 35% of the disabled employees reported that they would still be working if preventive measures had been taken at an early stage. Hence, work disablement is to a large extent not only work-stress related but also avoidable.

To take preventive action, insight into the main risk factors for work stress and the occupational groups that are at high risk is a prerequisite. The central issues in this study, therefore, are the identification of risk factors and risk groups for work stress in the working population in The Netherlands and a description of the ways these risks have developed during the past decade.

These issues are addressed by performing secondary analyses on data of a National Work and Living Survey, which provides a representative sample of the working population in The Netherlands and was held in 1977, 1983, 1986, and 1989 by The Netherlands Central Bureau of Statistics. This survey provides information on individual employees, their work, and their health and allows analyses of the 20 largest professional groups and the 19 largest branches of industry in The Netherlands. Before the analyses are discussed, some theoretical notions on work stress are discussed.

Stress is considered to be a state of individuals that arises when they cannot or feel unable to cope with the psychological load imposed on them. When this state arises at work, it is called *work stress*. When recovery does not take place or is insufficient, this state—indicated by emotional, behavioral, and physiological responses—can result in health problems. Risk factors that

This study was supported by a grant from the Dutch Ministries of Social Affairs and Employment and of Health.

give rise to this state are called *stressors*, and groups of employees who are exposed to stressors at work are called *risk groups* for work stress.

One of the most popular models of work stress is the job demands–decision latitude model by Karasek (1979; Karasek & Theorell, 1990). In this model, two main dimensions of stressors are discerned: demands of the job such as work pace and amount of work and the availability of possibilities for control with respect to these demands, called *decision latitude*. The latter comprises two aspects: autonomy in the job and skill or intellectual discretion. The higher the demands or the lower the decision latitude imposed on the employee, the greater the stress-related health risk. The combination of both multiple or high demands and low decision latitude is most detrimental for the employee's health and will, according to the model, result in even more health damage than would be predicted by the sum of both simple effects. The model has been shown to have predictive value for psychological dysfunctioning and depressive disorders, as well as for absenteeism, use of medication, other health behaviors (Karasek & Theorell, 1990), cardiovascular disease (e.g., Siegrist, Peter, Junge, Cremer, & Seidel, 1990), and even musculoskeletal problems (e.g., Bongers, Winter, de Kompier, & Hildebrandt, 1993). Critiques on the model have, however, been directed to the inconsistent finding of interactive effects and to the lack of attention paid to testing the hypothesis that the relations between stressors and health outcomes might not be linear but curvilinear (Furda & Meijman, 1992; Warr, 1990).

Apart from the dimensions of job demands and decision latitude, other dimensions are reported in the literature. The social dimension of work has been proven to be important. Conflicts with colleagues or with supervisors at work may act as potent stressors, whereas social support may buffer stress resulting from other sources (e.g., House, 1983; Karasek & Theorell, 1990). Physical stressors, such as noise, may induce or exacerbate stress effects as well (e.g., Cohen, Evans, Krantz, & Stokols, 1980; Levi, 1983; Van Kamp, 1990).

The National Work and Living Condition Survey does not allow the identification of all types of stressors as mentioned above. Although this survey does contain aspects of job demands, decision latitude (especially intellectual discretion), and physical stressors, it lacks information on social relationships at work. This means that the stress risk of professional groups or branches of industry, for whom this type of stressor is present, will be underestimated.

Methods

The National Work and Living Condition Survey was administered by the Central Bureau of Statistics (CBS) to a representative sample of the working population in The Netherlands every 3 years from 1977 to 1986. The data from 1980 are not used in our analyses because, for that year, no information was available on profession or industrial populations. Information gathered in 1989 will also be used. Because this information was not available at the individual level, but only as sum sources and at the group level, the data gathered in

1989 will be used only for the description of time trends and not for the analyses to identify risk groups.

The numbers of employees in the age range of 18 to 65 years who contributed to the survey are shown in Table 1. The nonresponse was considerable (in 1977, 1983, and 1986, it was 30%, 42%, and 41%, respectively; for 1989, it was 56%). Despite this considerable nonresponse, the sample was found to be representative (Bloemhoff & Smulders, 1991). To improve the reliability of the results, the different samples across time were pooled together. This was considered to be justified because the interrelations of the variables used in this study were found to be stable over the years (Bloemhoff & Smulders, 1994; Houtman, Bloemhoff, Kompier, & Marcelissen, 1991).

In Table 2, the variables indicating psychosocial and physical stressors at work (independent variables) are shown. Data on two health indicators and several personal characteristics that are assumed to act as confounding variables, and will be used in this study, are also shown. One of the health indicators is a short, 13-item questionnaire measuring psychosomatic complaints (Vragenlijst Onderzoek Ervaren Gezondheid-13; Joosten & Drop, 1987). The other health indicator is the percentage of employees who consider their health to be good or quite good. The interrelation between these two health indicators is moderate ($r = .47$; Houtman et al., 1991).

With regard to the personal characteristics, social group is a characteristic that is allocated to a person in relation to his or her profession and position. There are six categories: higher, middle, and lower employees; self-employed persons; blue-collar workers; and unemployed persons.

Identification of Occupational Stressors, Risk Dimensions, and Risk Groups for Work Stress

Risk groups for work stress were identified with a *relative comparison* of either occupational groups or industrial branches with a reference group. The number of occupational groups or industrial branches identified in the sample consisted of the total of groups that had a minimum number of 100 employees. Because the sample was representative of the Dutch working population, the reference group consisted of all employees in the sample. The mean score of this population can be denoted as the average Dutch employee score.

A risk group for work stress was considered to be an occupational group

Table 1. The Size of the Database in 1977, 1983, 1986, and 1989

Year	Total sample	Sample analyzed (age: 18 to 65 years, working)	Sample analyzed as a percentage of total sample
1977	4,159	1,973	47
1983	3,987	1,995	50
1986	4,040	1,897	47
1989	3,100	1,516	49
Total 1977–1986	12,186	5,865	48

Table 2. Variables in the Study: Psychosocial and Physical Stressors at Work, Two
Health Indicators, and Several Personal Characteristics

Work	
High work pace	1 = yes, 2 = no
Monotonous work	1 = yes, 2 = no
Poor opportunities for personal development	1 = yes, 2 = no
Poor fit between work and education or experience	1 = yes, 2 = no
Poor promotional prospects	1 = yes, 2 = no
Dangerous work	1 = yes, 2 = no
Heavy work	1 = yes, 2 = no
Noise at work	1 = yes, 2 = no
Dirty work	1 = yes, 2 = no
Bad smell at work	1 = yes, 2 = no
Health	
Psychosomatic complaints (VOEG-13)	range: 0–13
In (quite) good health (%)	%
Personal characteristics	
Age	1: 18–34
	2: 35–54
	3: 55–
Gender	1 = male, 2 = female
Full-time/part-time work	1: <15 hours
	2: 15–24
	3: 25–34
	4: 35–44
	5: 45–55
	6: >55
Social group	1: lower employees
	2: middle employees
	3: higher employees
	4: self-employed
	5: blue collar
	6: rest category

or an industrial branch that was significantly more frequently confronted with
a specific stressor when compared with the reference group (Student's t test).
For reasons of theoretical importance and simplicity, the stressors were tested
on their independency first. When stressor dimensions were discerned, especially when they had theoretical significance, risk groups were discerned on
the level of stressor dimensions and not on the level of individual stress risks.

If we restrict ourselves to a relative comparison, the number of risk groups
could be underestimated when either the range in stressor levels is relatively
small or when the level of stress risks is high for the entire working population.
When the latter situation occurs, it may indicate that the entire working
population may be considered a risk group with respect to that particular
stressor (dimension). When one third of an occupational group is confronted
with a stressor to which 40% or 50% of the whole working population is confronted, this group is considered favorable with respect to that specific stressor.
However, one third of the employees in that occupation or industrial branch

Table 3.   The 19 Largest Industrial Branches and the
Number of Employees in Each of the Branches

Reference group	5,865
Agriculture and fishing	292
Food industry	150
Printing industry	108
Metal industry	110
Machine industry	100
Electrical industry	102
Construction industry	388
Wholesale trade	294
Retail trade	436
Road transport	111
Communication	112
Banking	123
Professional services	259
Public management	468
Education	475
Health and veterinary services	458
Social services	273
Cultural services	100
Other services	103

are still at risk for problems resulting from that stressor. When the deviation from the average score is small, the relative comparison may even lead to the conclusion that, independent of the percentage of employees confronted with that stressor, no specific risk groups can be discerned for that stressor. Because of this problem, associated with the identification of risk groups by way of a relative comparison, we present absolute percentages as well. Although the choice of a threshold level is arbitrary, we draw special attention to those occupational groups and industrial branches of which 30% or more of the employees report to be confronted with a specific stressor (dimension).

Results

Risk Dimensions for Work Stress

The factor analysis (varimax rotation) resulted in three independent factors with an eigenvalue greater than 1. Together, these three factors explain 45% of the total variance in the questions on work-related risks. These dimensions are (a) Work Pace (eigenvalue = 1.02; explains 9.3% of the variance); (b) Intellectual Discretion, constituted by monotonous work, poor opportunities for personal development, poor fit between work and education or experience, poor promotional prospects (eigenvalue = 1.62; explains 14.7% of the variance; Cronbach's α = .55; factor loadings range from .56 to .77); and (c) Physical

Table 4. The 20 Largest Occupational Groups and the Number of Employees in Each of the Groups

Reference group	5,865
Architects, (technical) draughtsmen, other technicians	218
Physicians, nurses, and related professions	266
Teaching personnel	356
Other professional specialty occupations	159
Managers	222
Secretaries, typists, etc.	153
Bookkeepers, cashiers, and related professions	273
Clerical staff	511
Shop assistants and sellers	267
Waiters, cooks, barkeepers, etc.	109
Housekeeping and caring personnel	228
Cleaning personnel, housekeepers, etc.	145
Agrarians	163
Farm laborers	122
Engineers	178
Electricians	107
Plumbers and related professions	111
Construction laborers	217
Cargo personnel	161
Drivers and related professions	157

Stressors, constituted by heavy work, noise at work, dirty work, bad smell at work, dangerous work (eigenvalue = 2.27; explains 20.6% of the variance; Cronbach's α = .63; factor loadings range from .59 to .71).

The dimension that is mentioned first is, in terms of Karasek's (1979; Karasek & Theorell, 1990) job demands–decision latitude model, a central aspect of job demands. The second dimension makes up Karasek's decision-latitude component, together with decision authority.

Risk Factors and Risk Groups in the Dutch Working Population

The Z scores of the percentage of employees that are confronted with the three dimensions of risk factors, discriminated by way of the factor analysis, and the Z score on health problems are presented for the 19 largest industrial branches (Table 3) and the 20 largest occupational groups (Table 4) in Figures 1 and 2, respectively. The raw percentages for the occupational groups and industrial branches are presented elsewhere (Houtman et al., 1991).

Student's t tests show that a high work pace is significantly more frequent for employees in professional services (accountancy, advisory agencies, journalists, etc.); health and veterinary services; managers; secretaries; physicians, nurses, and other health professionals; and waiters, cooks, and so on. Intellectual discretion is significantly lower for employees in "other services" (mainly cleaning personnel), industry (metal, printing, and food), road transport (cargo

Table 5. Percentage Answering Yes on the Questions About the Presence of Risk Factors at Work in the Years 1977, 1983, 1986, and 1989

Variable	Year			
	1977	1983	1986	1989
Job demands				
High work pace	38	42	47	51
Skill discretion				
Monotonous work	14	13	12	9
Poor possibilities for personal development	33	36	34	34
Poor fit between actual work and education−experience	21	33	34	32
Poor promotion prospects	54	74	70	74
Physical stressors				
Dangerous work	11	9	8	7
Heavy work	20	22	24	23
Noise	29	23	22	28
Dirty work	22	26	25	27
Bad−nasty smell	12	9	9	12
Health				
Psychosomatic complaints	2.2	2.0	1.9	2.2
% General health (very) good	84	86	88	88

handlers, drivers, etc.), communication personnel (e.g., telephone companies), and retail (e.g., shop assistants). Physical stressors are significantly more frequent for employees in industry (mainly metal, construction, machine, and food industry), agriculture, and road transport. Health problems, in this study operationalized as the standardized sum score of psychosomatic symptoms and general health, were most prominent for "other services" (mainly cleaning personnel), social services, road transport, housekeeping and caring professions, farm laborers, and waiters and cooks. Direct standardization with respect to sex, age, full-time−part-time work, and social group does not change the risk profiles for the different occupational groups or industrial branches to a significant extent.

Work-Stress Risks and Health of the Dutch Working Population From 1977 to 1989

Table 5 presents the mean percentages of employees who report to be confronted with the specific risk factors and risk dimensions for the different samples from 1977 to 1989. The percentage of employees who report to be in good or quite good health and the average psychosomatic complaints score are also presented in Table 5.

Table 5 shows that the percentage of employees who report to work in a high work pace has steadily increased about 13% across a period of 12 years. In 1989 half of the employees reported to work in a high work pace.

The overall score on intellectual discretion has not changed much across

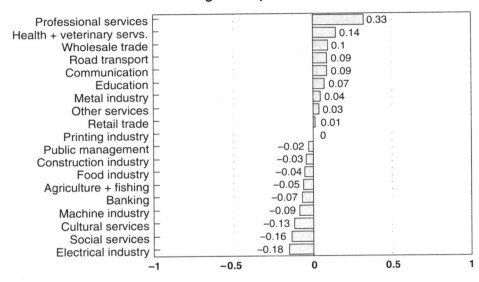

Industrial Branches
High work pace

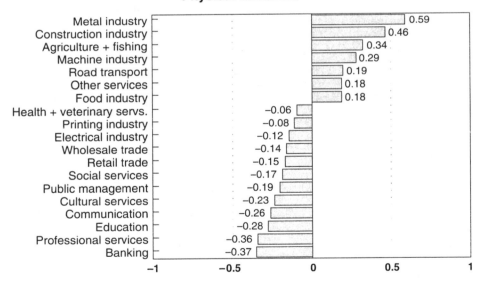

Industrial Branches
Physical stressors

Figure 1. Graphical presentation of the rank order in risk dimensions and health problems for industrial branches. The reference group (the average Dutch employee) constitutes the zero line. Z scores to the right of this zero line indicate that the risk is greater compared with the reference group, whereas Z scores to the left of the zero line

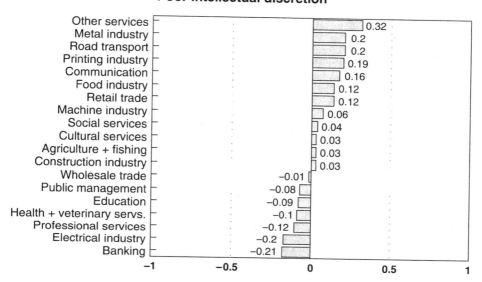

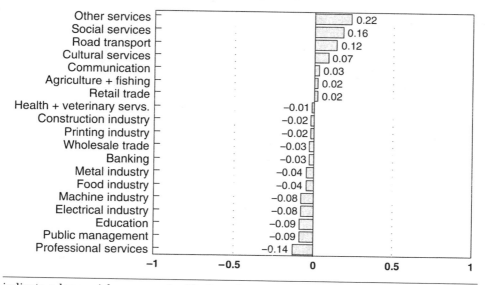

indicate a lower risk compared with the reference group. For high work pace, Z scores $> .13$, $p < .05$; for poor intellectual discretion, Z scores $> .10$, $p < .05$; for physical stressors, Z scores $> .10$, $p < .05$; for health complaints, Z scores $> .10$, $p < .05$.

**Occupational Sector
High work pace**

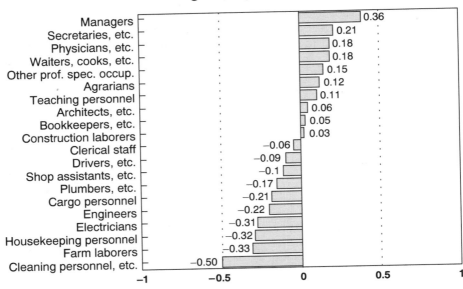

**Occupational Sector
Physical stressors**

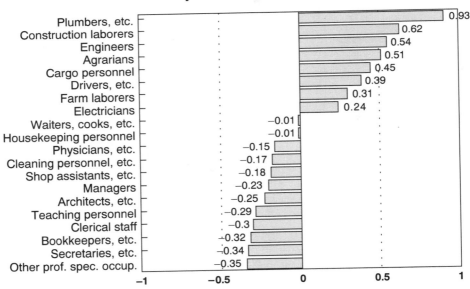

Figure 2. Graphical presentation of the rank order in risk dimensions and health problems for occupational groups. The reference group (the average Dutch employee) constitutes the zero line. Z scores to the right of this zero line indicate that the risk is greater compared with the reference group, whereas Z scores to the left of the zero line

Occupational Sector
Poor intellectual discretion

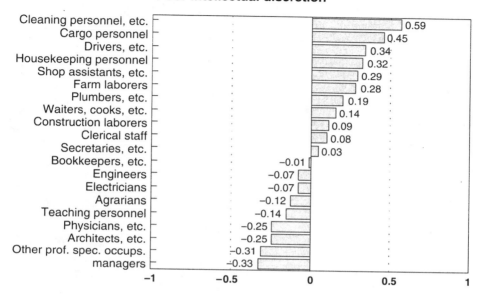

Occupational Sector
Health complaints

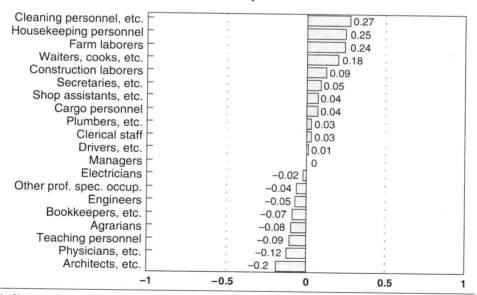

indicate a lower risk compared with the reference group. For high work pace, Z scores $> .18$, $p < .05$; for poor intellectual discretion, Z scores $> .10$, $p < .05$; for physical stressors, Z scores $> .16$, $p < .05$; for health complaints, Z scores $> .10$, $p < .05$.

Table 6. Percentages of Employees Who Work in a High Work Pace; No Proper Fit Between Work, Education, and Experience; and No Proper Promotional Prospects in 1977, 1983, 1986, and 1989 for the Seven Largest Industrial Branches and the Seven Largest Occupational Groups

Branch	1977	1983	1986	1989
	High work pace			
Industrial				
Agriculture and fishing	43	32	42	46
Manufacturing	34	37	41	45
Construction	29	53	46	54
Trade and restaurant–catering services	46	43	52	52
Transport	47	54	44	60
Banking and insurance companies	46	45	53	58
Other services	37	41	48	49
Occupational				
Professional specialty occupations	46	49	53	56
Managers	52	55	77	71
Clerical occupations	43	41	48	55
Commercial occupations	39	43	52	52
Service occupations	33	36	34	42
Agrarians	42	32	42	39
Industrial–transportation occupations	30	40	40	44
	No proper fit between work and education and experience			
Industrial				
Agriculture and fishing	8	27	29	20
Manufacturing	29	36	34	35
Construction	16	34	36	23
Trade and restaurant–catering services	20	43	40	42
Transport	31	44	54	44
Banking and insurance companies	20	34	30	30
Other services	17	27	30	27
Occupational				
Professional specialty occupations	13	16	17	19
Managers	9	18	15	16
Clerical occupations	25	39	42	43
Commercial occupations	19	44	39	37
Service occupations	27	48	45	40
Agrarians	13	27	35	19
Industrial–transportation occupations	26	38	42	36
	No proper promotional prospects			
Industrial				
Agriculture and fishing	54	85	86	84
Manufacturing	60	73	66	69
Construction	52	84	70	68
Trade and restaurant–catering services	59	76	68	75
Transport	58	68	66	80
Banking and insurance companies	41	66	49	59
Other services	49	74	78	80
Occupational				
Professional specialty occupations	43	73	79	76
Managers	43	57	50	63
Clerical occupations	50	70	65	70
Commercial occupations	59	71	64	70
Service occupations	64	77	79	82
Agrarians	60	83	78	83
Industrial–transportation occupations	60	80	75	73

the years. Except for monotonous work, however, one third of the employees report having poor opportunities for personal development and a poor fit between work and education or experience. About two thirds report having poor promotional prospects. The change in poor fit and poor promotional prospects has been an unfavorable one, although both changes appear to be leveling off in recent years.

The changes in physical stressors are also presented in Table 5. The absolute percentages of employees who are confronted with these stressors vary from 7% (dangerous work) to 28% (noise at work), whereas in specific occupations and industrial branches employees are confronted with these risks to a large extent (see Figures 1 and 2). No consistent change in time is shown in these physical risks, except that the percentage of employees that is confronted with dangerous work has declined.

In Table 6 it is shown that the unfavorable developments in work pace, poor promotional prospects, and poor fit appear to be independent of occupation or branch.

Discussion and Conclusions

From the data presented it is clear that an important part of the Dutch working population faces risks for work stress. In 1989 half of the employees worked at a high work pace, almost three quarters had poor possibilities for promotion, and one third had poor possibilities for development and no proper fit between work and education–experience.

Risk groups for a high work pace were found to be employees in the commercial services, health and veterinary services, trade, and road transport and employees in the professions of manager, secretary; physician, nurse, or other health professionals; and caterers. Risk groups for intellectual discretion were found to be employees in road transport (cargo handlers, drivers, etc.), cleaning personnel, and personnel in housekeeping and caring professions. Risk groups for physical stressors are employees in industry, construction, agriculture, and road transport.

Despite what is often stated, blue-collar stressors did not really decrease over time. This is an important notion: It is a popular point of view among human factors and occupational psychologists that, because of automation and computerization, people are living in a mental health era, in which constraints in the work situation are merely of a psychosocial or mental nature. Of course, to some extent this is true. However, large numbers of employees still earn their living under classic blue-collar conditions involving heavy work, noise, and dirty work. Also, static load has become an important health problem in today's offices. Psychologists, with their preoccupation for mental aspects, should bear in mind that, even in industrialized countries, blue-collar stressors are still of particular significance.

Karasek's (1979; Karasek & Theorell, 1990) model predicts the highest stress risk when high demands are combined with low control. Figure 3 plots the 20 professional groups on the two main dimensions from this study: work

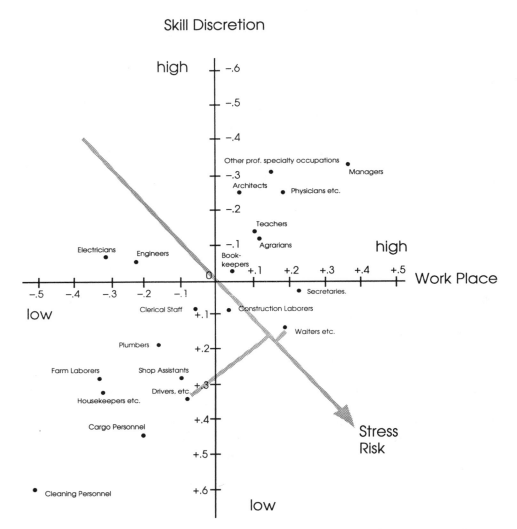

Figure 3. Risk for work stress, as determined by the two risk dimensions work pace and intellectual discretion for the different occupational groups. The scores on the two dimensions are Z-transformed, resulting in 0 for the reference group. The scores of 95% of the Dutch working population are within the range of −1 and +1. The stress risk axis is constructed on the assumption that the stress-related health risk is determined by an equal contribution of work pace and intellectual discretion. The projection on this axis of two occupational groups is indicated.

pace and intellectual discretion. It can be hypothesized that stress-related health risks are best predicted by the combined effect of (high) work pace and (low) discretion. In Figure 3 this combined effect is shown as the projection of the professional groups on the stress-risk axis. This axis is the $x = y$ axis, under the assumption that both axes equally contribute to stress-related health risks.

From this figure it is suggested that the main risk groups for work stress are waiters and cooks, construction laborers, employees in road transport, and secretaries. In this figure managers and physicians are in a less risky situation compared with, for instance, secretaries.

However, at this moment such a conclusion seems at least premature. Although there is a large body of evidence in favor of the demand–control model, it still is unclear to what extent the two risk dimensions interact. In several psychophysiological studies it has been suggested that psychological demands and control are related to different psychological responses (Dienstbier, 1989; Frankenhaeuser, 1983; Obrist et al., 1978). It seems plausible that these pathophysiological mechanisms mediate between risk dimensions for work stress and health problems. Warr (1990) showed that the two risk dimensions are related to different subjective moods: demands being related to tension and control to depressive feelings. When we hypothesize that the different risk dimensions could be associated with (at least partially) different health problems, it is reasonable to identify different risk groups for the different risk dimensions, as is done in this chapter.

Analyses over time show an unfavorable development of some of the stressors, especially high work pace, poor fit between actual work and education or experience and poor promotion prospects. It is tempting to indeed assume unfavorable changes in these risk factors for work stress. However, some alternative explanations should be discussed first. Such an alternative explanation could be found in an increased awareness of psychosocial factors at work or in an increased propensity to complain. Because a universal increase in percentages has not been noted in Table 5, there is not much support for this explanation. There is also no increase in health complaints over time.

It also could be hypothesized that the changes that were reported in this study could be explained by a changed composition of the working population, because of, for instance, an increase in the number of (often part-time) working women.

This hypothesis too seems implausible because the increases in work pace, poor fit, and poor prospects were the same for men and women, for several age groups, and for almost all of the professional groups and branches of industry that were studied (Houtman et al., 1991).

It seems reasonable to conclude that unfavorable changes in the percentages (Table 5) are real and reflect changes in the quality of working life.

There also is circumstantial evidence, especially with regard to high work pace and no proper fit between work and education or experience. In The Netherlands it has been government policy to shorten the average working week by introducing the 36-hour working week. By doing so it was foreseen that more unemployed people would get a job. However, it has become clear that shortening the work week did not lead to an increase of personnel in Dutch companies. In fact, this policy has led to an intensification of work, not only in industrial branches but also in other branches such as health care and transport. In many cases the same (and often a lowered) number of personnel is responsible for a larger output.

It also seems plausible to relate the large number of employees stating a poor fit between actual work and education or experience to, on the one hand, rapid changes in work and work organization (e.g., automation and takeovers) that are in particular a difficulty for older employees and, on the other hand, to the increased levels of training of younger employees who are overtrained for the jobs that are available to them. The average level of education, for both men and women, rose in the 1975 to 1990 period. In 1975 only 25% of men and 28% of the women had a middle or higher level of education. By 1990 these percentages were 69% and 73%, respectively (Bloemhoff & Smulders, 1994).

Because there is a strong adverse trend over time and half of the working population states to work at a high work pace, this factor can be identified as a major stressor for the Dutch working population. This conclusion is supported by a recent survey by the European Foundation (Paoli, 1992), carried out in 12 European countries. In that European study it was concluded that The Netherlands ranks amongst the highest with respect to working at a high work pace.

Despite the increased stress risks, there is no decrease in self-reported health status. It seems plausible that this paradox can be explained by health-based selection processes in the working population (healthy-worker effect). In The Netherlands, by the end of 1990 there were, in a total labor force of around 6.5 million persons, 882,000 people who were declared disabled for work and received disablement benefits (Bloemhoff & Smulders, 1994). This means that 9 out of every 100 people who potentially could work are disabled for work. The main diagnoses in the case of disablement for work are musculoskeletal diseases and mental disorders—psychological dysfunctioning. Both categories make up almost one third of all people who become disabled for work and receive a disablement benefit.

The large number of people disabled for work is partly due to the specific Dutch disability-insurance system enabling industry and the service branch to some extent to discharge those workers who are considered to no longer be fully productive. In fact, the ratio between the number of people working and those people who are disabled for work has become so adverse that there is a major political debate on how the individual and collective costs can be diminished. The Dutch Prime Minister Lubbers announced that he would resign as soon as there were one million disabled workers. When this figure seemed to become a reality, government changed the admission criteria for the insurance system.

Compared with the working population, the health status of these ex-workers is often worse (Bensing, de Bakker, van der Velden, 1991), and it seems likely that those people with major health problems are no longer working, leaving behind a reasonable healthy selection.

References

Bensing, J. M., de Bakker, D. H., & van der Velden, J. (1991). How sick is the WAO? (in Dutch). *Medisch Contact, 37,* 1075–1080.

Bloemhoff, A., & Smulders, P. G. W. (1991). Quality of working life of women and men: Differences and trends 1977–1986 (in Dutch). *Tijdschrift voor Arbeidsvraagstukken, 7,* 4–17.

Bloemhoff, A., & Smulders, P. G. W. (1994). *Work and health: Riskgroups and trends.* Dordrecht, The Netherlands: Kluwer Academic.

Bongers, P. M., de Winter, C. R., Kompier, M. A. J., & Hildebrandt, V. H. (1993). Psychosocial factors of work and musculoskeletal disease: A review of the literature. *Scandinavian Journal of Work Environment and Health, 19,* 297–312.

Cohen, S., Evans, G. W., Krantz, D. S., & Stokols, D. (1980). Physiological, motivational and cognitive effects of aircraft noise in children. *American Psychologist, 35,* 231–243.

Dienstbier, R. A. (1989). Arousal and physiological toughness: Implications for mental and physical health. *Psychological Review, 96,* 84–100.

Frankenhaeuser, M. (1983). The sympathetic-adrenal and pituitary-adrenal response to challenge: Comparison between the sexes. In T. M. Dembroski, T. H. Schmidt, & G. Blümchen (Eds.), *Biobehavioral bases of coronary heart disease* (pp. 91–105). Basel, Switzerland: Karger.

Furda, J., & Meijman, T. F. (1992). Load and threat, control or stress (in Dutch). In J. A. M. Winnubst & M. J. Schrabacq (Eds.), *Handboek arbeid en gezondheidspsychologie* (pp. 127–144). Utrecht, The Netherlands: Lemma.

Gründemann, R. W. M., Nijboer, I. D., & Schellart, A. J. M. (1991). *The work related character of work disablement* (in Dutch). The Hague: Ministerie van SZW, Directoraat Generaal van de Arbeid (S-127).

House, J. S. (1983). *Work stress and social support* (2nd ed.). Reading, MA: Addison-Wesley.

Houtman, I. L. D., Bloemhoff, A., Kompier, M. A. J., & Marcelissen, F. H. G. (1991). *Risk factors for work stress* (in Dutch). The Hague: Ministerie van SZW, Directoraat-Generaal van de Arbeid (S-133).

Joosten, J., & Drop, M. J. (1987). VOEG: Reliability and comparability of three versions (in Dutch). *Gezondheid & Samenleving, 8,* 251–265.

Karasek, R. A. (1979). Job demands, job decision latitude, and mental strain: Implications for job redesign. *Administrative Science Quarterly, 24,* 285–308.

Karasek, R. A., & Theorell, T. (1990). *Healthy work.* New York: Basic Books.

Levi, L. (1983). *Preventing work stress.* Reading, MA: Addison-Wesley.

Obrist, P. A., Gaebelein, C. J., Teller, E. S., Langer, A. W., Grignolo, A., Light, K. C., & McCubbin, J. A. (1978). The relationship among heart rate, carotid dP/dt, and blood pressure in humans as a function of the type of stress. *Psychophysiology, 15,* 102–115.

Paoli, P. (1992). *First European survey on the work environment 1991–1992.* Dublin, Ireland: European Foundation for the Improvement of Living and Working Conditions.

Siegrist, J., Peter, R., Junge, A., Cremer, P., & Seidel, D. (1990). Low status control, high effort at work and ischaemic heart disease: Prospective evidence from blue collar men. *Social Science and Medicine, 31,* 1127–1134.

Van Kamp, I. (1990). *Coping with noise and its health consequences.* Unpublished doctoral dissertation, University of Groningen, Groningen, The Netherlands.

Warr, P. B. (1990). Decision latitude, job demands, and employee well-being. *Work and Stress, 4,* 285–294.

15

Stress-Symptom Factors in Firefighters and Paramedics

Randal Beaton, Shirley Murphy, Kenneth Pike,
and Monica Jarrett

The job-stress "monster in the box" is perhaps no more apparent and menacing than it is for professional firefighters and paramedics. The duties and biodemographics of these closely aligned emergency professionals are continuing to evolve in the 1990s. More women are joining the ranks of firefighting, especially in urban areas, although their numbers are still small (Murphy, Beaton, Cain, & Pike, 1994). Another national trend that has gone largely unnoticed is that professional firefighters respond less often to fire alarms and more frequently to emergency medical calls. In fact, nationwide in 1990, emergency medical calls accounted for nearly 60% of all firefighter alarms (International Association of Firefighters [IAFF], 1992). In Washington State, where our investigation was conducted, all firefighters are certified emergency medical technicians (EMTs) and render emergency medical assistance in response to approximately 80% of their alarms in metropolitan areas. Paramedics in Washington State, with a few exceptions, are also firefighters.

The purposes of this chapter are three-fold. Initially, we summarize the research literature that has previously identified the numerous sources of occupational stress in firefighters and paramedics as well as their adverse health effects. Second, we report on the analyses of survey data from a large sample of firefighters and paramedics that were used to empirically derive statistically distinct stress-symptom factors and to characterize firefighter–paramedic clusters in terms of their stress-symptoms factors. Finally, on the basis of the results of these factor and cluster analyses (and comparisons with a convenience sample of men), we discuss theoretic and practical implications for the design and evaluation of occupational-stress–management interventions for firefighters and paramedics within the context of what is already known about their sources of occupational stress.

Although most available evidence suggests that firefighters and paramedics are at elevated risk to experience a host of stress-related disorders

This research was supported by funds from the University of Washington School of Nursing Biomedical Research Grant, the University of Washington Graduate School Research Grant, and the IAFF Local #106, Bellingham, WA. We also acknowledge the assistance of the Washington State Council of Fire Fighters and the Executive Board of IAFF Local #27, Seattle, WA.

and illnesses related to their exposure to occupational stressors, not all available data are confirmatory. For instance, one study of firefighters, which used the Minnesota Multiphasic Personality Inventory (MMPI), reported that mean firefighter MMPI clinical profiles were within normal limits (Bieliauskas, 1980). This finding contrasted sharply with data collected from urban Canadian firefighters ($N = 636$) with the Brief Symptom Inventory that found statistically significant evaluations on most of the scales of this psychiatric checklist (Corneil, 1993). Our data presented herein suggest that only a fraction of firefighters and paramedics have elevated psychiatric (and other stress-related) complaints. Although epidemiologic data are available that support a relationship between firefighting and the incidence of pulmonary and cardiovascular disease, little is known about the structure of their subjective somatic, behavioral, and cognitive stress symptomatology. This is important to ascertain because it leads to an identification of naturally occurring stress-symptom factors or "stress pathways" in firefighters and paramedics. Then at-risk firefighter–paramedic (FF/PM) subsamples can be identified and categorized on the basis of elevated stress-symptom factor complaints. Identification of these stress factors and at-risk firefighters should help in the construction and targeting of preventive and remedial stress-management programs.

Exposure Risks of Firefighters and Paramedics

Professional firefighting is still one of the most dangerous of all U.S. occupations (IAFF, 1992). Firefighters' 1990 to 1991 rates of injuries and occupational illnesses were the highest of any group of U.S. workers. In terms of lost work hours, U.S. firefighters' on-the-job injury rate was 9.2 times higher than workers in private industry (U.S. Bureau of Labor Statistics, 1990). Line-of-duty deaths are four times greater than in private industry. Although their on-the-job injury rate is the highest of all occupations, it is surprising that the single most prevalent cause of line-of-duty death in firefighters is heart attack and stroke (IAFF, 1992). This statistic is all the more striking when one considers how cardiovascularly fit firefighters must be at the outset of their careers. In 1991, 12.5% of U.S. firefighter mortalities were due to duty-related vehicular accidents (IAFF, 1992; Mitchell & Bray, 1990). Exposure to injured and critically ill people also puts both firefighters and paramedics at risk for airborne and blood-borne infections (e.g., tuberculosis, hepatitis B, and HIV). Although somewhat counter to their macho-hero image, firefighters and paramedics actually expressed considerable apprehension about their own personal safety in a recent anonymous survey (Beaton & Murphy, 1993). Given this partial listing of their dangerous duties and tasks, injuries, and line-of-duty deaths, such fears do not seem unreasonable.

As "crisis workers," firefighters and paramedics are also at risk to experience what Figley (in press) has termed *secondary traumatic stress*. Secondary traumatic stress refers to stress associated with helping or wanting to help a victim of trauma (see Beaton & Murphy, in press). Their exposure to duty-related trauma or "critical incidents" is repetitive and potentially cumulative. Such duty-related critical incidents usually involve overwhelming exposure to injured, multilated, or dead and dying victims (Durham, McCammon, & Allison, 1985; Hartsough & Meyers, 1985; Hytten & Hasle, 1989; McFarlane, 1988a, 1988b, 1988c, 1988d; Mitchell, 1982, 1985). A prospective study of urban firefighters in Canada further suggests that the emotional impact of a series of such critical incidents accumulates across exposures (Corneil, 1992). There is evidence that even "routine" cardiopulmonary resuscitation efforts can result in traumatic symptomatology in emergency workers (Myles, Levine, Ramsden, & Swanson, 1990). Given the intensity, frequency, and ubiquity of occupational stressors for firefighters and paramedics, it is not surprising that research has documented that, as a group, they experience elevated mortality and morbidity. One report in the literature suggests that the average firefighters' life expectancy is foreshortened by nearly a decade compared with community norms (Murdock, 1981). In Washington State, data from the time period from 1950 to 1979 indicate that firefighters experienced greatly elevated proportional mortality rates due to duodenal ulcers (Milham, 1983). In addition, as cited earlier, a sizable fraction of on-the-job fatalities of U.S. firefighters is due to cardiovascular disease (National Fire Protection Agency [NFPA], 1988). Their high levels of stress may also contribute to their high levels of accidental on-the-job injuries (Leiter & Cox, 1992).

Occupational Stressors in Firefighters and Paramedics

Firefighters' and paramedics' elevated risk for myocardial infarctions (MIs) and stroke is likely related to exposure to occupational stressors, such as heavy reliance on team work and low job control. This combination of high demands and low job control supports Karasek and others' classification of firefighters as a high-strain occupation. In their epidemiologic study, high-strain occupations were found to have three to six times' greater prevalence of MIs (Karasek et al., 1988).

Another job-related stressor is the frequent and bothersome sleep disturbance associated with shift work. Most U.S. firefighters and paramedics work 24-hour shifts and are subjected to variable, unpredictable, and unavoidable sleep disruption largely associated with emergency calls and false alarms (Beaton & Murphy, 1993). Firefighters and paramedics may be the only occupations besides military personnel who must respond to a potentially life-threatening emergency from a state of sleep. Some evidence suggests that firefighters experience repetitive adrenaline surges related to their emergency duties. Correspondingly, investigators have reported shift-related increases in 17-ketogenic steroids and adrenaline excretions in both firefighters and paramedics (Dutton, Smolensky, Lorimor, & Leach, 1978; Kalimo, Lehtonen, Daleva, & Kuorinka, 1980).

In stark contrast to critical incidents and more routine emergency calls, firefighters and paramedics must alternatively cope with the boredom and tedium associated with waiting for the next alarm. On any given shift U.S. firefighters spend an average of 22 hours anticipating alarms and only 2 hours at incident sites (Mitchell & Bray, 1990). This time at the station can foment administrative and, to a lesser extent, coworker tensions and conflict. The rigid administrative structures of many fire departments, as well as the necessarily heavy reliance on team work in emergency situations, seems to magnify the toxicity of such organizational conflicts. In fact, of all the job stressors identified in a large-scale anonymous survey of firefighters and paramedics, perceived management—labor conflict was the one that correlated most robustly and consistently with reports of job dissatisfaction and poor work morale (Beaton & Murphy, 1993).

Concerns regarding wages, benefits, and job security are certainly not unique to emergency service workers. From time to time, fire districts face reductions in the force size because of budget cuts. In the wake of affirmative-action programs, another contemporary stressor for public-sector professional firefighters and paramedics has been perceived and actual race and gender-based harassment and even so-called reverse discrimination. Also, partly because of their work schedules and partly because of their incomes, up to 40% of firefighters and paramedics are employed at a second job, generally part-time, and thus are potentially exposed to carryover second-job stress. Another FF/PM stressor is that of conveying news of a tragic death or injury to surviving family and friends. Finally, 80% of firefighters and paramedics are married and have children; thus, they are also prone to experience possible spillover stress from marital and family problems. Although there have been some reports in the literature of even greater job-related stress and strain in paramedics (see Dutton et al., 1978), this was not confirmed in our study of professional firefighters and paramedics in Washington State (Beaton & Murphy, 1993).

Stress Symptoms Associated With Exposure Risks and Occupational Stressors

Besides these resultant mental—physical stress-related diseases and injuries, there are also documented effects of occupational stressors on the mental well-being of firefighters and paramedics. In 1991, approximately 8% of firefighter job disabilities were classified as due to mental stress (IAFF, 1992). The vast majority of firefighters and paramedics experience both acute and chronic secondary trauma symptoms during their careers, including intrusion, avoidance, hypervigilence, disturbed sleep, demoralization, anger, fear or physiological reactivity, marital discord, alcohol abuse, alienation, isolation—withdrawal, delayed loss of confidence, guilt, feelings of insanity—loss of control, and even suicidal thoughts (American Psychiatric Association, 1987; Beaton & Murphy, in press; Dunning & Silva, 1980; Durham et al., 1985; McFarlane, 1988a, 1988b, 1988c, 1988d; Markowitz, Gutterma, Link, & Rivera, 1987; Murphy & Beaton, 1991).

It is unclear exactly how long-term, repetitive exposure to dangerous and even life-threatening situations—coupled with their other occupational stressors—adversely affects the mental and physical health of firefighters and paramedics. However, acute and chronic changes in their neuroendocrine and neurotransmitter systems associated with repeated physiological arousal, frequent circadian disruptions, the potential for constant danger, and associated hypervigilance are undoubtedly contributory. Whatever its etiologic mechanism, we need to know more about the adverse health reactions of firefighters and paramedics if we are to construct and implement appropriate stress-management interventions for these high-strain occupations. The potential costs of not attending to FF/PM stress symptomatology includes their suboptimal task performance and potential compromising of public safety, as well as burnout and foreshortened careers, unnecessary disablement, and elevated morbidity and mortality.

One purpose of this chapter is to empirically identify and delineate the relative frequency–intensity of self-reported somatic, behavioral, and psychological stress-symptom factors in a large sample ($N = 2,042$) of professional FFs/PMs. An assumption made was that the nature and extent of their symptoms of stress reflected their exposure to the numerous and potent occupational stressors identified earlier in this chapter. In conjunction with what is already known about FF/PM job-related stress, these data have theoretic and pragmatic implications for remedial and preventive occupational-stress–management interventions.

Method

Sample and Sampling Procedure

The Symptoms of Stress Inventory was one of several survey measures mailed in late 1989 to more than 4,000 professional FFs/PMs and FFs/EMTs in Washington State. The survey methodology used was a modification of Dillman (1978) and included a follow-up reminder postcard. The Dillman methodology refers to a set of procedures and criteria used to conduct a mail survey. The Dillman mail-survey procedures address item development, sampling, multistage mail-out and follow-up questionnaires, and data collection. Surveys were completed anonymously and mailed back to the investigators. A total of 2,042 surveys were returned for an overall return rate of 51%. Certain data sets for the entire sample and occupational groups were incomplete because of missing entries and statistical-software limitations. The sample, comprising paramedics and firefighters, is described below.

Firefighter–paramedic sample ($N = 1768–1949$). The respondent FF/PM sample comprised 1,730 firefighters (87% of the sample) and 253 paramedics. These FF/PM survey respondents were all professional career firefighters, paramedics, or both. All of the firefighters in this sample were certified EMTs. Nearly all (93%) of the paramedics in this sample were also firefighters. During their past 10 shifts, the paramedic subsample reported that approximately 80% of their on-duty responses were to provide emergency medical services and that about 15% involved fire suppression. The firefighter respondents reportedly provided emergency medical services on nearly 60% of their calls during the past 10 shifts on duty. (In some urban fire districts the percentage of emergency medical service [EMS] calls reported by the firefighters in this survey was in the range of 80% to 90%.) The paramedic subsample was slightly younger (35.6 years old vs. 37.2 years old for firefighters) and had been employed as a firefighter or as a paramedic for fewer years (7.9 years for paramedics vs. 12.3 years for firefighters). Nearly 20% of the firefighter subsample had previously worked as a paramedic for an average of slightly more than a year.

The vast majority of the FF/PM sample was male (97%), White (93%), and married (80%). The average number of years of formal education reported by the FF/PM sample was 2 to 3 years past high school graduation. Approximately 40% of the paramedic subsample and one third of the firefighter subsample reported outside employment (a second job or career) averaging 18 to 25 hours per month. See Beaton and Murphy (1993) for a more detailed description of this respondent sample.

Male comparison sample (*N* = 97). The nonrandom convenience comparison sample was recruited from the Seattle metropolitan area. Participants were asked to compete the Symptoms of Stress (SOS) Inventory anonymously to help student nurses fulfill a course requirement. This nonpatient comparison sample originally comprised 250 women and 97 men. Preliminary testing with the convenience sample, however, uncovered numerous statistically significant gender differences on the dependent variables; therefore, only data collected from the men (*N* = 97) are included in these analyses. The male comparison sample averaged 36.8 years old, were largely from the middle socioeconomic stratum, and were most likely employed as either businessmen or professionals (45.4%) or skilled workers (11.3%). Students made up less than 5% of this male convenience sample.

Symptoms of Stress Inventory

The SOS self-report inventory was used to measure the FF/PM respondents' as well as the male comparison sample's somatic, behavioral, and psychological stress symptomatology (Thompson & Leckie, 1991). FF/PM respondents and the male comparison group participants were asked to rate the frequency with which they may have experienced a particular stress symptom during the past week on a 0- to 4-point scale (0 = *never*, 4 = *frequently*). Scoring of the SOS yields a total score and 10 content-derived scale scores. Prior research studies have shown that the SOS inventory has adequate interim (Cronbach's alpha = .96) and test−retest reliabilities (*r*s for SOS scales ranged from .47 to .86 for a 6-week test−retest interval; Beaton, Burr, Nakagawa, Osborne, & Thompson, 1978; Nakagawa-Kogan & Betrus, 1984). Prior investigations have already documented the SOS's ability to detect the benefits of a stress-management therapy and to differentiate patient and nonpatient samples (Beaton, Egan, Nakagawa-Kogan, & Morrison, 1991; Beaton, Nakagawa-Kogan, Hendershot, & Betrus, 1985). Total SOS scores correlated significantly (*r* = .76) with the Global Symptoms Index of the SCL-90-R in an outpatient sample of clients with stress disorders (Beaton et al., 1978; Derogatis, 1977). The correlation between an appraisal measure of FF/PM job stressors (as measured by a 57-item sources of occupation stress instrument) and the SOS total score was also statistically significant ($r = .60$, $p < .001$) for a sample ($n = 163$) of urban firefighters (Murphy & Beaton, 1991). Thus, in this sample of urban firefighters, a subjective measure of job stressors accounted for approximately 35% of the variance of their reported total SOS scores. The SOS thus appears to have adequate sensitivity and specificity in terms of its capability to measure firefighter and paramedic stress symptomatology. Furthermore, firefighter and paramedic symptoms of stress scores are significantly correlated with their appraised occupational stressors.

Edwards's Social Desirability (SD) Scale

As part of the survey battery, FF/PM respondents were also asked to complete Edwards's SD Scale, a 39-item, true–false measure of the social desirability test-taking bias. Prior research has documented Edwards's SD Scale's essential reliability (Cronbach's alpha = .90) and validity in terms of measuring "conscious/unconscious attempts (of self-report test takers) to give good self-impressions" (Edwards, 1957, 1970). This was important to assess because prior research has shown that such a social desirability test-taking bias can account for up to 50% of the variance of self-report measures of health (Carstensen & Core, 1983).

Results

Similarity of Male and Female and Firefighter and Paramedic Replies

The paramedic subsample's replies on the SOS Inventory did not differ significantly from those of the firefighter respondents (total SOS and all SOS subscale ps were not significant). Therefore, all FF/PM SOS Inventory replies were combined into one FF/PM sample ($N = 1768–1949$ usable replies). (Some FF/PM SOS replies were eliminated from subsequent analyses because of missing data or incomplete data sets.) Female firefighters' SOS data were also included in these analyses because, with only one exception, their mean SOS subscale scores did not differ from those of their male coworkers (Beaton, Murphy, & Pike, 1992).

Edwards's SD Scale Correlates

The social desirability valence of the FF/PM sample's SOS total score was calculated at $r = -.30$ using Edwards's SD Scale. None of the SOS 10 content subscales' SD correlations exceeded $r = -.30$. This meant that the social desirability test-taking bias, as measured by Edwards's SD Scale for the FF/PM sample, accounted for less than 10% of the SOS's total and the subscales' variances.

Table 1. Factor Analysis of Symptoms of Stress for Firefighters–Paramedics
($N = 1,768$)

Scale/item	Factor loading	Scale/item	Factor loading
Apprehension/dread (7 items)		Indigestion/asthma (2 items)	
You get nervous or shaky when approached by a superior	.81	Indigestion	.78
		Increased asthma attacks	.43
Frightening dreams	.76	Percentage of variance explained	1.2
Feeling weak and faint	.76		
Being keyed up and jittery	.73	Pearson correlation coefficient	.11
You become so afraid you can't move	.68		
You are fearful of strangers and/or strange places make you afraid	.66	Gastrointestinal symptoms (6 items)*	
		Nausea	.76
Being uneasy and apprehensive	.64	Constipation	.68
Percentage of variance explained	28.1	Percentage of variance explained	2.4
Cronbach's alpha	.91	Cronbach's alpha	.83
		Generalized anxiety (6 items)*	
Head, neck, and facial tension (8 items)		Worrying about your health	.72
		Stuttering or stammering	.68
Neck tension	.67		
Forehead tension	.64	Percentage of variance explained	2.2
Migraine headaches	.63		
Shoulder tension	.60	Cronbach's alpha	.85
Eye tension	.59		
Jaw tension	.54	Sleeping difficulties (4 items)*	
Blurring of vision	.52	Difficulty in staying asleep	.69
Back tension	.49	Early morning awakening	.64
Percentage of variance explained	4.0	Percentage of variance explained	2.0
Cronbach's alpha	.85	Cronbach's alpha	.80
		Cardiopulmonary (6 items)*	
Anger/"can't think straight" (8 items)		Thumping of your heart	.75
		Rapid or racing heart beats	.71
You become so upset that you hit something	.76	Percentage of variance explained	2.0
Your thinking gets completely mixed up when you have to do things quickly	.73	Cronbach's alpha	.81
Your anger is so great that you want to strike something	.71	Cutaneous/peripheral (5 items)*	
		Sweating excessively even in cold weather	.73
You get directions and orders wrong	.55	Breaking out in cold sweats	.63
You had difficulty in concentrating	.52	Percentage of variance explained	1.9
You become mad or angry easily	.49	Cronbach's alpha	.77

Table 1. (*Continued*)

Scale/item	Factor loading	Scale/item	Factor loading
Anger/"can't think straight" (*continued*)		Agitated depression (5 items)*	
		Pacing	.63
You must do things very slowly to do them without mistakes	.45	Difficulty sitting still	.63
		Percentage of variance explained	1.8
You are unable to keep thoughts from running through your mind	.42	Cronbach's alpha	.82
		Throat and mouth (4 items)*	
Percentage of variance explained	2.9	Hoarseness	.65
Cronbach's alpha	.83	Having to clear your throat often	.64
		Percentage of variance explained	1.7
Headiness (3 items)*			
Sinus headaches	.77	Cronbach's alpha	.76
Spells of severe dizziness	.75		
		Upper respiratory (3 items)*	
Percentage of variance explained	1.7	Colds	.74
Cronbach's alpha	.76	Colds with complications	.74
		Percentage of variance explained	1.6
Intrusive thoughts/no hope (3 items)*		Cronbach's alpha	.70
Frightening thoughts keep coming back	.59		
		Extremity tension (2 times)	
You become suddenly frightened for no good reason	.56	Leg(s) tension	.66
		Hand(s) or arm(s) tension	.57
Percentage of variance explained	1.5	Percentage of variance explained	1.4
Cronbach's alpha	.73	Pearson correlation coefficient	.59
		Hunger (2 items)	
Itchy/rashes (2 items)		Poor appetite	.68
Skin rashes	.83	Increased eating	.62
Severe itching	.79		
		Percentage of variance explained	1.3
Percentage of variance explained	1.4	Pearson correlation coefficient	.74
Pearson correlation coefficient	.59		
		Nervous habits (2 items)	
Exaggerated startle (1 item)		Biting your nails	.66
Sudden noises make you jump or shake	.55	Having to urinate frequently	.47
		Percentage of variance explained	1.2
Percentage of variance explained	1.3	Pearson correlation coefficient	.25

Note. *Only the two highest loading items in the scale are listed. A complete listing of items for all of the symptoms of stress factors is available from the first author.

Table 2. Means, Standard Deviations, and Results of t Testing for Differences Between FF/PM Sample (N = 1903–1918) and Comparison Sample (N = 94–97)

SOS factor scale	FF/PM sample		Comparison male sample			Probability (one-tailed)
	M	SD	M	SD	t value	
Apprehension/dread	9.54	6.05	7.00	4.82	4.99	<.001*
Head, neck, and facial tension	8.71	6.18	7.49	6.11	1.91	.0295
Anger	5.79	4.50	5.25	4.45	1.14	.129
Gastrointestinal symptoms	5.30	4.54	4.13	3.84	2.90	.0025*
General anxiety	4.84	4.28	4.09	3.85	1.88	.031
Sleep difficulties	6.32	4.57	3.81	3.34	5.30	<.001*
Cardiopulmonary	3.68	3.89	3.09	3.33	1.67	.0485
Cutaneous/peripheral	3.73	3.54	3.01	2.95	2.32	.011
Agitated depression	5.26	4.16	4.23	3.53	2.76	.0035
Throat and mouth	3.55	2.91	2.89	2.35	3.08	.0015*
Headiness	0.09	1.70	0.78	1.13	2.51	.0065
Upper respiratory	3.31	2.53	2.86	2.09	2.01	.025
Intrusive thoughts/no hope	1.43	1.89	.97	1.40	3.11	.001*
Extremity tension	1.44	1.77	1.06	1.76	2.05	.0215
Itchy/rashes	0.79	1.48	0.92	1.51	−0.81	.2105
Hunger	2.52	2.21	2.27	1.82	1.29	.099
Exaggerated startle	0.45	0.74	0.38	0.62	1.18	.1205
Nervous habits	1.88	2.23	1.42	1.62	2.02	.004
Indigestion/asthma	0.26	1.48	0.14	0.52	1.78	.0385

Note. FF = firefighter; PM = paramedic; SOS = symptoms of stress.
*Statistically significant with Bonferroni's correction.

Factor Analysis of Symptoms of Stress

A preliminary factor analysis of paramedic responses to all 94 SOS items yielded 20 SOS factors with eigenvalues greater than 1.0. Table 1 shows the results of follow-up principal-components factor analysis with orthogonal rotations generated with only those SOS items from the preliminary factor analysis with factor loadings ≥ .40 (Rummel, 1970). (Also, a few SOS items that did not seem conceptually linked to other factor items were omitted.) This yielded 19 SOS factors with eigenvalues greater than 1; these, together, accounted for 61.8% of the SOS's variance. Table 1 also lists the SOS items for each factor, factor labels (based on each factor's item pool), the variance accounted for by each SOS factor, respective factor item loadings, and each factor's interitem reliability coefficient. The interitem correlations (Cronbach's or Pearson's) varied from .59 to .91 for the SOS factors with only two exceptions. It is important to note that several of the SOS factors that emerged made up only one or two items and cannot be considered scales. They were, however, included in subsequent analyses in this chapter.

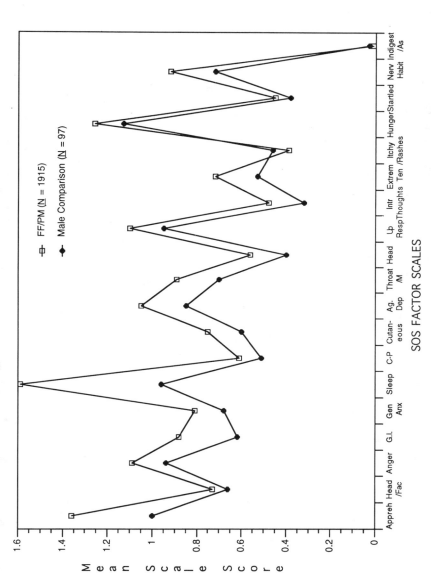

Figure 1. Mean symptoms of stress (SOS) factor scale scores for firefighter/paramedic (FF/PM) sample (N = 1,915) and male comparison group (N = 97). (Mean scale score = total score for scale–number of items in scale.) Appreh = apprehension/dread; Head/Fac = head, neck, and facial tension; Anger = anger/can't think straight; G.I. = gastrointestinal symptoms; Gen Anx = generalized anxiety; Sleep = sleeping difficulties; C-P = cardiopulmonary; Ag. Dep = agitated depression; Throat/M = throat and mouth; Head = headiness; Up Resp = upper respiratory; Intr Thoughts = intrusive thoughts/no hope; Extrem Ten = extremity tension; Startled = exaggerated startle; Nerv Habit = nervous habits; Indigest/As = indigestion/asthma.

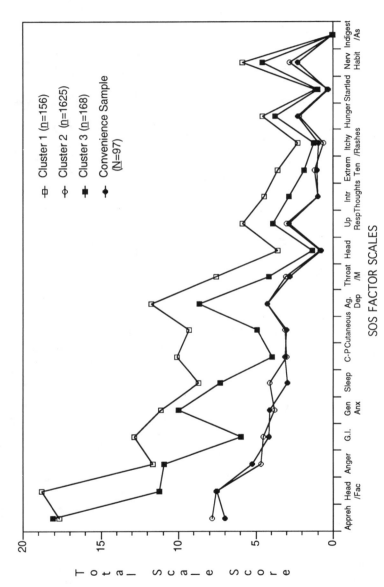

Figure 2. Results of cluster analysis based on firefighter–paramedic symptoms of stress (SOS) factor scale total scores. Data from convenience sample ($N = 97$) are included for comparative purposes. Appreh = apprehension/dread; Head/Fac = head, neck, and facial tension; Anger = anger/can't think straight; G.I. = gastrointestinal symptoms; Gen Anx = generalized anxiety; Sleep = sleeping difficulties; C-P = cardiopulmonary; Ag. Dep = agitated depression; Throat/M = throat and mouth; Head = headiness; Up Resp = upper respiratory; Intr Thoughts = intrusive thoughts/no hope; Extrem Ten = extremity tension; Startled = exaggerated startle; Nerv Habit = nervous habits; Indigest/As = indigestion/asthma.

Differences Between Firefighter–Paramedic and Convenience Sample on SOS Factor Scales

Table 2 shows the SOS factor-scale means, standard deviations, and the results of t testing for differences between the FF/PM and male comparison samples. With Bonferroni's correction, only t values with one-tailed probabilities less than .0026 (.05/19) were considered to be statistically significant (Miller, 1981). Using this conservative Bonferroni correction, a total of five SOS factor scales were significantly elevated in the FF/PM sample. The FF/PM sample scores were significantly higher on the following SOS factor scales: apprehension/dread (Factor 1), gastrointestinal symptoms (Factor 4), sleep difficulties (Factor 6), throat/mouth symptoms (Factor 10), and intrusive thoughts and feelings (Factor 13).

Figure 1 graphically depicts the mean subscale scores (average factor score/number of items) on all of the SOS factor scales for both the FF/PM and male comparison samples. As can be seen graphically, the FF/PM sample scored higher on nearly all (18/19) of these SOS factor scales; this was also significant using a nonparametric sign test, $p < .001$ (Mosteller & Rourke, 1973).

Cluster Analysis

Initially an assumption was made that FF/PM responses to stress could be classified as either somatic, emotionally based, or normal. This assumption, although undoubtedly an oversimplification, was based in part on clinical observations by the first author and reports by Katon, Kleinman, and Rosen (1982) that somatization and somatic complaints were common in firefighters and in distressed patients, respectively. This tripartate assumption was also based on findings of elevated psychiatric complaints in some firefighter populations (Beaton et al., 1992; Corneil, 1993) and reports of psychologic normalcy in other firefighter groups (Bieliauskas, 1980). This led to the generation of a cluster analysis that identified three SOS stress-factor typologies (Norusis, 1988).

Cluster analysis is a statistical procedure that identifies groups or clusters of cases on the basis of their values for a given set of variables. The 19 SOS factor scores were the variables that served as the basis for the cluster analysis. Cluster analysis relies on the concepts of distance and similarity in deciding how cases are alike. Distance measures are small, and similarity measures are large for cases that are similar. The measure of distance used was the squared differences over all of the SOS factor scores. Agglomerative hierarchical clustering, in which clusters are formed by grouping cases into larger and larger clusters until all cases are members of a single cluster, was used to form clusters with the single linkage or nearest neighbor method.

Figure 2 shows the results of this cluster analysis based on SOS factor scores yielding three distinct FF/PM profiles. The SOS raw factor-scale score profile for the male convenience sample is also shown for comparative purposes. This SOS factor-scale cluster analysis identified two FF/PM profile clusters (1 and 3), made up of 8% and 9% of the FF/PM respondent samples, respectively, which were both elevated relative to the vast majority (83%) of FFs/PMs the majority of the male comparison sample. The majority FF/PM profile (Cluster 2) was remarkably similar to that of the male convenience sample in terms of their SOS factor-scale scores.

Discussion and Implications for Treatment

Just as FF/PM job-related stressors are unique, so too is their stress symptomatology. This investigation represents an initial exploratory effort to empirically identify the common stress disorders of professional firefighters and paramedics. Zeller and Carmines (1980) noted that the most difficult decision in factor analysis is to determine the number of factors to include in the analysis. Thus, factor analysis is prone to two types of errors, including too few or too many factors. The former leads to an overly simplistic view of the content domain, whereas the latter results in an overly complicated view of the same content domain. In this investigation, the authors chose to err in the latter direction. As a result, several stress factors potentially unique to FFs/PMs were uncovered. Furthermore, this factor analysis, by categorizing and identifying prevalent somatic, behavioral, and psychological stress symptoms in firefighters and paramedics, may be useful in generating suitable preventive and remedial interventions. FF/PM replies on the SOS inventory yielded a great number (approximately 20) of relatively distinct stress-symptom factors.

Even though these results need to be replicated for other groups of firefighters and paramedics, the large number used in these analyses ($N > 1,700$) suggests that they may be relatively stable and generalizable. SOS Factor 1, consisting of items of subjective apprehension and dread, explained more than a quarter of the SOS's variance and highlighted the centrality of occupational-stress symptomatology for this sample. This SOS factor and a few others (e.g., Factor 13, intrusive thought/no hope) may be related to the inherently dangerous nature of FF/PM work and their repeated exposure to critical incidents. Many of the SOS factors that emerged related to somatic psychophysiologic-stress symptomatology such as gastrointestinal symptoms (Factor 4); head, neck, and facial tension (Factor 2); and cardiopulmonary symptoms (Factor 7). Several of the SOS factors identified in this investigation related to psychologic and behavioral difficulties such as anger (Factor 3), agitated depression (Factor 9), anxiety (Factor 5), and nervous habits (Factor 18).

The FF/PM sample reported a greater number and frequency of symptoms, compared with the convenience sample, on nearly all of stress-factor scales. (It is difficult to determine if and how the white-collar business–professional composition of the male comparison sample may have influenced their symptom reporting.) In any event, on only 5 out of the 19 SOS factor scales were the FF/PM scores significantly higher than the comparison sample's as the result of using a conservative statistical criterion. These elevated SOS factor scales included apprehension/dread (Factor 1), intrusive thoughts and no hope (Factor 13), gastrointestinal symptoms (Scale 4), sleep difficulties (Factor 6), and throat and mouth symptoms (Factor 10). Together, these significantly elevated factor scales suggest that these firefighters and paramedics had an elevated likelihood of problems with symptoms of anxiety, agitation, and irritability. With the exception of their elevated scores on the throat and mouth symptom factor, these elevated stress-symptom factors suggest that FFs/PMs are generally more apprehensive and prone to sleeping difficulties, intrusive thoughts, and anger problems compared with a nonrandom male community sample. Their higher scores on the throat and mouth stress-symptom factor might conceivably be related to their duty-related exposure to smoke at fire-suppression scenes, although they are invariably required to wear respirator gear.

By using cluster analysis on the basis of these stress factors, we anticipated that distinctive, elevated stress profiles would emerge. In fact, two elevated stress-factor cluster groups emerged that differed primary in elevation. Cluster 1, comprising 156 participants, or approximately 8% of the analytic sample, reported higher levels of stress symptomatology on virtually every factor scale relative to Clusters 2 and 3 as well as the convenience sample. Furthermore, Cluster 1 reported a disproportionate number and intensity of somatic stress symptoms including head, neck, and facial tension; gastrointestinal distress; and cardiopulmonary complaints compared with the other FF/PM cluster groups and the convenience sample. Cluster 1 could then be considered the group of FFs/PMs at highest risk. Cluster 3 ($n = 168$) made up approximately 9% of the firefighter sample and showed elevations relative to the comparison sample primarily on psychologic–emotional stress-symptom factors including apprehension/dread, anger, generalized anxiety, and agitated depression. Although Cluster 3 also showed relative elevations on the sleep difficulties and head, neck, and facial tension stress-symptom factors, their primary complaints could be characterized as emotional in nature. Cluster 3 as a group could be considered to be at high risk. In fact, these at-risk FF/PM groups (Clusters 1 and 3), identified by the cluster analysis, represented a substantial *minority* (15% to 20%) of those participating in this survey. Cluster 2, consisting of more than 80% of the firefighter sample ($n = 1,625$), was statistically indistinguishable from the male convenience sample ($N = 97$) in terms of their stress-factor scores. These latter results can be construed to support the conclusion of one investigator that firefighters represent a low-maladjustment population (Bieliauskas, 1980). Although the percentage of at-risk FFs/PMs may be comparable to available community norms, the duties and responsibilities of firefighters and paramedics are by no means normative.

Firefighters and paramedics must cope with an extraordinary number, intensity, and frequency of job stressors identified earlier in this chapter and must render potentially life-saving aid and suppress fires under dangerous and suboptimal conditions. An argument could easily be made that all firefighters and paramedics need a preventive, educational orientation to stress and stress management (Mitchell & Bray, 1990), but at-risk (or those in the high-stress–symptom clusters) firefighters and paramedics may need more intensive and extensive interventions. In the first instance, these high-risk FFs/PMs need to be identified, perhaps through screening, without possibility of penalty or stigmatization. Second, remedial interventions need to be tailored and offered to these firefighter and paramedic groups.

The development of appropriate interventions for at-risk FFs/PMs requires a determination of what they are at risk for. The highest risk cluster group (1) in this investigation reports more somatic and mental health symptoms. The high-risk cluster (3) seems to be primarily plagued by just only emotional difficulties. Both of these at-risk clusters (1 and 3) could benefit from a broadly based psychoeducational intervention, perhaps provided through a group format, focusing on identified sources and symptoms of their stress. Ideally, such a program would intervene at both the organizational and the individual levels and would include work redesign and coping-skills training. Relevant treatment modules might include relaxation training to counter their reported stress symptoms of apprehension and dread and generalized anxiety; principles of cardiovascular health to stem their incidence of cardiovascular morbidity and mortality; and conflict-resolution training to teach firefighters and supervisors the skills needed to mediate their inevitable interpersonal conflicts.

Prior reports have shown that firefighters' conflicts with their administrative supervisors were strongly associated with firefighter job dissatisfaction and low worker morale (Beaton & Murphy, 1993). Organizational leadership training emphasizing more humane and egalitarian management styles might be one cost-effective way to reduce the stress level of an entire fire department. The highest risk group (Cluster 1) might also need and benefit from one-to-one biofeedback training and stress-reduction techniques for their identified psychophysiological stress disorders (e.g., their muscle tension and gastrointestinal complaints; Mason, 1985). Sleep hygiene information—including education about circadian regulation, the effects of shift work, bedtime rituals and routines, and the influence of drugs on sleep—should also be provided to all firefighters and paramedics because sleep disturbance is one of their preeminent job-stress complaints (Beaton & Murphy, 1993).

Summary and Conclusions

The results of this factor analysis suggest that FF/PM stress syndromes are empirically numerous and diverse. These results suggest that, in addition to stress symptoms relatable to critical incidents, firefighters and paramedics report many other distinct somatic, emotional, and behavioral stress pathways. Most of the prevailing models of job stress are not too helpful in predicting which stress symptoms are most likely to emerge in at-risk occupational groups. These FF/PM data certainly seem congruent with the model developed by Karasek and others that categorizes firefighting as a high-strain occupation (Karasek & Theorell, 1990; Karasek et al., 1988). They are also consistent with the systems model of occupational stress developed by Hurrell and others at the National Institute for Safety and Health (Hurrell, 1987).

A comprehensive approach to stress management in firefighters and paramedics must necessarily be more broadly based than critical-incident stress debriefings. Moreover, the results of this investigation suggest that perhaps only 15% to 20% of firefighters and paramedics are at risk and in need of intensive stress-management treatment. Perhaps by studying the mediating variables that seem to be protective for the majority of firefighters and paramedics, we can better develop preventive programs for all FFs/PMs and remedial programs for the at-risk groups. How do some firefighters and paramedics, for instance, cope with frequent challenges and occasional outright violations of their cognitive "assumptions" of safety and predictability? (see Janoff-Bulman, 1992). Individual personality, cognitive appraisal, social support, and organizational variables have already been implicated as potential mediating factors for firefighters and other rescue workers (Beaton & Murphy, 1991; Hartsough & Myers, 1985; McCammon, Durham, Allison, & Williamson, 1988; McFarlane, 1988a, 1988b, 1988c, 1988d; Murphy & Beaton, 1991; Raphael, 1986).

It should be noted that this investigation was exploratory and preliminary. The SOS factors derived here need to be further developed and tested. Nearly one half of the professional FFs/PMs in Washington State did not participate in this survey, and we do not know how their participation and inclusion might have influenced these results. Finally, the replies of firefighters and paramedics from Washington State may not be representative of those obtained from FFs/PMs working in other regions of the United States or in other countries.

References

American Psychiatric Association. (1987). *Diagnostic and statistical manual of mental disorders* (3rd ed. rev.). Washington, DC: Author.

Beaton, R., Burr, R., Nakagawa, H., Osborne, O., & Thompson, E. (1978). Empirical inconsistencies of stress response indices: Some preliminary findings. *Communicating Nursing Research, 11,* 73–74.

Beaton, R., Egan, K., Nakagawa-Kogan, H., & Morrison, K. (1991). Self-reported symptoms of stress with temporomandibular disorders: Comparisons to healthy men and women. *Journal of Prosthetic Dentistry, 65,* 289–293.

Beaton, R., & Murphy, S. (1991, July). *Social support and relationship conflict in fire fighters.* Paper presented at the third biannual Psychosocial Nursing Conference, University of Washington, Seattle, WA.

Beaton, R., & Murphy, S. (1993). Sources of occupational stress among firefighter/EMTs and firefighter/paramedics and correlations with job-related outcomes. *Prehospital and Disaster Medicine, 8,* 140–150.

Beaton, R., & Murphy, S. (in press). Research implications of working with people in crisis. In C. Figley (Ed.), *Compassion fatigue: Coping with secondary traumatic stress disorder in those who treat the traumatized.* New York: Brunner/Mazel.

Beaton, R., Murphy, S., & Pike, K. (1992, November). *Symptoms of stress in male and female firefighters/paramedics.* Poster presentation at the second American Psychological Association/National Institute for Occupational Safety and Health Conference on Occupational Stress, Washington, DC.

Beaton, R., Nakagawa-Kogan, H., Hendershot, S., & Betrus, P. (1985). Psychological benefits of multimodal EMG biofeedback therapy for patients with musculoskeletal pain. *Proceedings of the 16th Annual Meeting of the Biofeedback Society of America* (pp. 14–17). New Orleans, LA.

Bieliauskas, L. (1980). Life events, 17-OHCS measures & psychological defensiveness in relation to aid-seeking. *Journal of Human Stress, 6,* 28–36.

Carstensen, L., & Core, J. (1983). Social desirability and the measurement of psychologic well-being in elderly persons. *Journal of Gerontology, 38*, 713–715.

Corneil, W. (1992, June). *Prevalence and etiology of post-traumatic stress disorders in firefighters.* Symposium on Public Safety Personnel. First World Conference on Trauma and Tragedy, The Netherlands.

Corneil, W. (1993). *Prevalence of post traumatic stress disorders in a metropolitan fire department.* Unpublished doctoral dissertation, Johns Hopkins University, Baltimore, MD.

Derogatis, L. (1977). *SCL-90 administration, scoring and procedures manual I-for the revised version and other instruments of the psychophysiology rating scale series.* Baltimore, MD: Johns Hopkins University Press.

Dillman, C. (1978). *Mail and telephone surveys: The total design method.* New York: Wiley.

Dunning, C., & Silva, M. (1980). Disaster-induced trauma in rescue workers. *Victimology: An International Journal, 5*, 287–297.

Durham, T., McCammon, S., & Allison, E. (1985). The psychological impact of disaster on rescue personnel. *Annals of Emergency Medicine, 14*, 664–668.

Dutton, L., Smolensky, M., Lorimor, R., & Leach, C. (1978). Stress levels of ambulance paramedics and firefighters. *Journal of Occupational Medicine, 20*, 111–115.

Edwards, A. (1957). *The social desirability variable in personality assessment and research.* New York: Dryden.

Edwards, A. (1970). *The measurement of personality traits by scales and inventories.* New York: Holt, Rinehart & Winston.

Figley, C. (in press). *Compassion fatigue: Coping with secondary traumatic stress disorder in those who treat the traumatized.* New York: Brunner/Mazel.

Hartsough, D., & Myers, D. (1985). *Disaster work and mental health: Prevention and control of stress among workers.* Washington, DC: National Institute of Mental Health, Center for Mental Health Studies of Emergencies.

Hurrell, J. (1987). An overview of organizational stress and health. In L. Murphy & P. Schoenborn (Eds.), *Stress management in work settings* (pp. 31–45; DHHS [NIOSH] Publication No. 87-111). Washington, DC: Department of Health and Human Services.

Hytten, K., & Hasle, A. (1989). Firefighters: A study of stress and coping. *Acta Psychiatry–Scandanavia Supplement, 355*, 50–55.

International Association of Firefighters. (1992). 1991 death and injury survey. *International Firefighter, 74*, 13–15.

Janoff-Bulman, R. (1992). *Shattered assumptions.* New York: Free Press.

Kalimo, R., Lehtonen, A., Daleva, M., & Kuorinka, I. (1980). Psychological and biochemical strain in fireman's work. *Scandinavian Journal of Work and Environmental Health, 6*, 179–187.

Karasek, R., & Theorell, T. (1990). *Healthy work stress, productivity and the reconstruction of working life.* New York: Basic Books.

Karasek, R., Theorell, T., Schwartz, J., Schnall, P., Pieper, C., & Michaela, J. (1988). Job characteristics in relation to the nonrelevance of myocardial infarction in the U.S. Health Examination Survey (HES) and the Health and Nutrition Examination Survey (HANES). *American Journal of Public Health, 78*, 910–918.

Katon, W., Kleinman, A., & Rosen, G. (1982). Depression and somatization: A review, Part 1. *American Journal of Medicine, 72*, 127–135.

Leiter, M., & Cox. (1992, November). *Prevention of stress-related accidents in health care workers.* Paper presented at the second American Psychological Association/National Institute for Safety and Health Conference, Washington, DC.

Markowitz, J., Gutterman, E., Link, B., & Rivera, M. (1987). Psychological response of firefighters to a chemical fire. *Journal of Human Stress, 13*, 84–93.

Mason, L. (1985). *A guide to stress reduction.* Berkeley, CA: Celestial Arts.

McCammon, S., Durham, T., Allison, E., & Williamson, J. (1988). Emergency workers' cognitive appraisal and coping with traumatic events. *Journal of Traumatic Stress, 1*, 353–372.

McFarlane, A. (1988a). The aetiology of post-traumatic stress disorders following a natural disaster. *British Journal of Psychiatry, 152*, 116–121.

McFarlane, A. (1988b). Relationship between psychiatric impairment and a natural disaster: The role of distress. *Psychological Medicine, 18*, 129–139.

McFarlane, A. (1988c). The phenomenology of post-traumatic stress disorders following a natural disaster. *Journal of Nervous and Mental Disease, 176,* 22–29.

McFarlane, A. (1988d). The longitudinal course of post-traumatic morbidity: The range of outcomes and their predictors. *Journal of Nervous and Mental Disease, 176,* 30–39.

Milham, S. (1983). *Occupational mortality in Washington State, 1950–1979* (DHHS Publication No. 83-116). Washington, DC: U.S. Department of Health and Human Services.

Miller, R. (1981). *Simultaneous statistical inference.* New York: Springer-Verlag.

Mitchell, J. (1982). The psychological impact of the Air Florida 90 disaster on fire-rescue, para-medic, and police officer personnel. In *Mass casualties: Lessons learned—Approach, accidents, civil disorder, natural disasters, terrorism* (DOT Pub. No. HS806302). Washington, DC: Department of Transportation.

Mitchell, J. (1985). Helping the helper. *Proceedings from a workshop: Role stressors and supports for emergency workers* (pp. 105–118). Rockville, MD: National Institute of Mental Health.

Mitchell, J., & Bray, G. (1990). *Emergency service stress.* Englewood Cliffs, NJ: Prentice Hall.

Mosteller, F., & Rourke, R. (1973). *Study statistics, nonparametrics and order statistics.* Reading, MA: Addison-Wesley.

Murdock, J. (1981, September). What a chief can do. *Fire Chief Magazine,* pp. 43–48.

Murphy, S., Beaton, R., Cain, K., & Pike, K. (1994). Gender differences in firefighter job stress and symptoms of stress. *Women & Health, 22,* 55–69.

Murphy, S. A., & Beaton, R. (1991). *Counteracting effects of trauma in everyday life: Leisure patterns among firefighters.* Paper presented at the seventh annual meeting of the Society for Traumatic Stress Studies, Washington, DC.

Myles, G., Levine, J., Ramsden, V., & Swanson. (1990). The impact of providing help: Emergency workers and cardiopulmonary resuscitation attempts. *Journal of Traumatic Stress, 3,* 305–313.

Nakagawa-Kogan, H., & Betrus, P. (1984). Self-management: A nursing mode of therapeutic influence. *Advance Nursing Science, 6,* 55–73.

National Fire Protection Agency. (1988). *Annual report of firefighters deaths and injuries.* Quincy, MA: Author.

Norusis, M. (1988). *Quick cluster procedure: SPSS/PC+ advanced statistics V2.0.* Chicago: SPSS.

Raphael, B. (1986). *When disaster strikes.* New York: Basic Books.

Rummel, R. (1970). *Applied factor analysis.* Evanston, IL: Northwestern University Press.

Thompson, E., & Leckie, M. (1991). *Therapeutic manual for stress response management.* Unpublished manuscript, University of Washington, Seattle.

U.S. Bureau of Labor Statistics. (1990). *Occupational injuries and illnesses in the United States by industry* (Bulletin 2399). Washington, DC: Author.

Zeller, R., & Carmines, G. (1980). *Measurement in the social sciences.* Cambridge, England: Cambridge University Press.

16

Work-Related Stress and Depression in Emergency Medicine Residents

Dennis A. Revicki and Theodore W. Whitley

Physicians are at increased risk for work-related stress and the various psychological and physical effects of working in stressful situations. Early research on job demand and health outcomes demonstrated that physicians report the highest workloads, greatest responsibility for other people, and highest levels of job complexity compared with other professions (Caplan, Cobb, French, Van Harrison, & Pinneau, 1975). There is considerable evidence that psychological distress is an occupational hazard for physicians (Cartwright, 1979; Gallery, Whitley, Klonis, Anzinger, & Revicki, 1992; Krakowski, 1982; May & Revicki, 1985; McCue, 1982; Revicki & May, 1985). Physicians in training and those practicing in the community have rates of suicide, substance abuse, and psychological disorders that exceed rates in the general population. Although not seriously impaired, many physicians are still troubled and dissatisfied with their work (Mawardi, 1979).

Physicians frequently encounter stresses that represent an intrinsic part of medical practice (McCue, 1982). Working with intensely emotional aspects of medical care, such as suffering, fear, and death and handling difficult patients, contributes to uncertainty within medical practices (Revicki & May, 1985). Medical residents, during their training, may be vulnerable to stress because of new responsibilities for patient care, uncertainty about the best course of action, inexperience, and confusion about their roles in the health care setting. Butterfield (1988) and others (Asch & Parker, 1988; Levin, 1988; McCue, 1985; Reuben, 1985; Whitley et al., 1991) have documented the stressors associated with residency training. The transition from medical student to practicing physician is also inherently stressful (Koran & Litt, 1988). Previous studies have also found that first-year residents (Keller & Koenig, 1989; McCue, 1985), female residents (Janus, Janus, Price, & Adler, 1983; Whitley, Gallery, Allison, & Revicki, 1989), and unmarried residents (Adler, Werner, & Korsch, 1980; Kelner & Rosenthal, 1986; Whitley et al., 1989, 1991) report greater work-related stress.

Emergency physicians, because of the unpredictable nature of their work and practice environment, may experience a greater number of potentially stressful situations compared with primary-care physicians. Gallery et al. (1992), in a survey of 750 emergency medicine physicians, found that the stress of working in the emergency department was associated with plans to leave the profession. Previous research has demonstrated that increased perceptions of work-related stress are associated with increases in depression and psychological distress in primary-care physicians (May & Revicki, 1985; Revicki & May, 1985) and emergency physicians (Gallery et al., 1992; Revicki, Whitley, Gallery, & Allison, 1993).

Problems with work-related stress are exacerbated in the emergency department where unexpected and often serious medical conditions, severe trauma, and life and death situations are commonplace. Residents frequently perceive emergency medicine rotations as stressful (Schwartz, Black, Goldstein, Jozefowicz, & Emmings, 1987). Several studies demonstrate a relationship between work-related stress and depression and morbidity in emergency medicine residents (Revicki et al., 1993; Whitley et al., 1989, 1991; Zun, Kobernick, & Howes, 1988).

Despite evidence that rotations in emergency departments are highly stressful (Levin, 1988; Schwartz et al., 1987; Zun et al., 1988) and that residents have been depressed following rotations in emergency departments (Reuben, 1985), there is little research on the work-related stress experienced by emergency medicine residents. This small number of studies is surprising in light of predictions that physical and emotional distress would lead to attrition from the specialty (Anwar, 1983; Whitley et al., 1991; Zun et al., 1988). Several recommendations have been made to reduce stressors in emergency medicine training, including 12-hour shifts for residents working in emergency departments and the staffing of emergency departments by physicians who have completed 3 years of postgraduate training and are trained to evaluate and care for emergency patients (Asch & Parker, 1988).

Revicki et al. (1993) completed a cross-sectional study of 484 emergency medicine residents who were members of the Emergency Medicine Residents Association. Using structural equation modeling, the findings suggest that there is a direct relationship between measures of occupational stress and symptoms of depression. Support from other residents and the cohesiveness of the work group decreased levels of perceived stress. Role ambiguity is an important predictor of work-related stress among emergency medicine residents. The cohesiveness of the work group, level of role clarity in the hospital environment, and amount of occupational stress are all associated with job satisfaction.

Most of the research on physician occupational stress and psychological distress is based on cross-sectional designs. The existing longitudinal studies are based on small samples from restricted settings or geographic areas. Clearly, longitudinal studies with psychometrically sound measures of important variables are needed to more fully understand the association between work-related stress and depression. Our study examined the relationship between task and role ambiguity, work-group support, work-related stress, and depression by using a longitudinal sample of emergency medicine residents.

The theoretical model underlying this investigation is based on previous research on work-related stress by Revicki and his colleagues (Revicki & May, 1985, 1989; Revicki, Whitley, Landis, & Allison, 1988; Revicki et al., 1993).

It was hypothesized that residents experiencing task and role ambiguity and little support from other emergency department physicians and staff were more likely to report work-related stress. Research based in hospitals and other complex organizations confirm that role ambiguity and conflict result in increased occupational stress and decreased performance (Cartwright, 1979; Gray-Toft & Anderson, 1985; House & Rizzo, 1972; Kahn, Wolfe, Quinn, Snoek, & Rosenthal, 1964; Revicki & May, 1989; Revicki et al., 1988). Occupational stress was associated with increased symptoms of depression. Strong and cohesive work groups decrease work-related stress and moderate the stress—psychological distress relationship. For example, social support from other physicians and coworkers was a significant intervening variable in the relationship between work-related stress and depression in family physicians (Revicki & May, 1985). This model of organizational characteristics (e.g., task and role conflict or ambiguity and work-group function), work-related stress, and psychological distress has been applied in cross-sectional studies of hospital nurses (Gray-Toft & Anderson, 1985; Revicki & May, 1989), emergency medical technicians (Revicki et al., 1988), and emergency medicine residents (Revicki et al., 1993). We examined these relationships with longitudinal data on emergency medicine residents over three waves of postgraduate medical training.

Method

Sample

Three cohorts of emergency medicine residents were recruited for this study. In 1989, 1990, and 1991, all emergency medicine residents who were beginning their first year of postgraduate medical training were surveyed. Mailing lists provided by the American College of Emergency Physicians were used each year to identify and contact the approximately 500 residents beginning training (cf. Gallery & Allison, 1990). The survey was mailed to all residents at the same time each year. The final sample had 556 first-year residents, 369 second-year residents, and 192 third-year residents (cohorts 1989 and 1990 only). The longitudinal study sample consists of 20% to 37% of all emergency medicine residents in the United States, and previous analysis suggests that the sample is representative of this group of residents (Gallery et al., 1992).

Measures

A mail survey was constructed to gather data on demographic characteristics; work-group function; and support, task and role clarity, work-related stress, and depression. Age was measured in years. Gender was coded as a 1 for men and a 0 for women. Marital status was dichotomized as a 1 for those married and as a 0 for not married.

Measures of work-group support and task and role clarity were based on instruments developed by Gray-Toft and Anderson (1985). The work-group support scale measures perceptions about the cohesiveness and support among residents and other health professionals in an occupational setting. Role and task ambiguity, or conflict, occurs when an individual is unclear about job expectations or responsibilities and position in the work group and is uncertain of the response to her or his behavior during work. High scores on this scale represent task and role clarity. Modifications were made in the content of some of the items to make them more applicable for residents in the emergency department setting. These modified scales have shown good reliability and validity in previous studies of emergency medicine residents (Revicki, May, & Whitley, 1991; Revicki et al., 1993; Whitley et al., 1989). Internal-consistency reliability for work-group function and task and role clarity scales were .84 and .78, respectively.

The Work-Related Strain Inventory (WRSI; Revicki et al., 1991) was used to measure occupational stress. The WRSI is an 18-question, Likert scale that requests the respondent to indicate the extent to which a statement applies to her or his work situation. The total scale score is a global assessment of perceived work-related stress symptoms. Internal-consistency reliability coefficients range from .85 to .91 for a number of different health professional samples (Revicki et al., 1991). Internal-consistency reliability for this group of emergency medicine residents was .84. The WRSI has good construct, discriminant, and convergent validity (Gallery et al., 1992; May & Revicki, 1985; Revicki & May, 1985, 1989; Revicki et al., 1989, 1991).

The Center for Epidemiologic Studies-Depression (CESD) Scale (Radloff, 1977) was used to measure symptoms of depression. The CESD is a brief self-report scale designed to measure common symptoms of depression in general populations. There is extensive evidence supporting the validity of the CESD for a number of psychiatric and general-population groups (Radloff, 1977). The internal consistency reliability for the CESD in this sample was .91.

Statistical Analysis

An analysis of covariance (ANCOVA) was used to evaluate whether there were any statistically significant differences in task-role clarity, work-group support, WRSI, and CESD scores between the three cohorts (1989, 1990, and 1991) by residency year (1, 2, and 3) to determine whether the groups could be collapsed. Adjustments were made for gender, age, and marital status. Bonferroni corrections were made for multiple comparisons; therefore, a probability value of .004 (i.e., .05/14) was used for all statistical tests.

Ordinary least squares regression analysis was used to evaluate the impact of the demographic variables, task and role clarity, work-group support, and work-related stress on depression symptoms. At baseline, age, gender, marital status, task and role clarity, and work-group support were regressed on WRSI scores, and the demographic variables, task and role clarity, work–group support, and WRSI scores were regressed on CESD scores. Identical cross-sectional regression analyses were performed for data collected at Residency Years 2 and 3.

For Residency Years 2 and 3, the regression models used CESD scores as the dependent variables, and independent variables included the demographic variables; baseline CESD; and task and role clarity, work-group support, and WRSI scores from the previous measurement occasion. Interaction terms were constructed between the task and role clarity, work-group support, and work-related stress and were included in the regression models. Interaction terms were constructed with deviation scores as specified by Finney and colleagues (Finney, Mitchell, Cronkite, & Moos, 1984).

Results

At the time these analyses were conducted, there were complete data on 556 first-year residents, 369 second-year residents, and 192 third-year residents. The reason for the smaller number of third-year residents was that data for the 1991 cohort's third year of residency were not available at the time of analysis. Average age of the residents at the start of the study was 30 years ($SD = 3.6$) and ranged from 24 to 44 years. Seventy-four percent were men, and the majority were White (92%). Fifty-six percent were married when they began their residency program. The percentage of married residents increased to 63% by Year 2 and to 61% by Year 3. The sample is comparable to the universe of all emergency medicine residents (Gallery et al., 1992).

Table 1 summarizes the means and standard deviations for the main study variables for each residency year. The means for WRSI and CESD are comparable for each residency year. Using the criterion of a CESD score greater than 16 as indicative of significant depression (Boyd, Weissman, Thompson, & Myers, 1982; Radloff, 1977; Roberts & Vernon, 1983), we found that 27% of first-year, 23% of second-year, and 22% of third-year residents were depressed.

Cohort Comparisons

Cohort differences on WRSI, CESD, task and role clarity, and work-group support scores were evaluated with an ANCOVA, after controlling for age, gender, and marital status. Only 3 of the 12 ANCOVAs reached statistical

Table 1. Descriptive Statistics for Task-Role Clarity, Work-Group Support, WRSI, and CESD Scores by Residency Years

	Residency Year					
	1		2		3	
Variable	M	SD	M	SD	M	SD
N	556		369		192	
Task-role clarity	40.2	3.6	41.9	3.5	42.9	3.6
Work-group support	35.1	6.4	34.4	6.3	34.7	6.5
WRSI	31.8	7.9	32.1	8.4	31.4	8.7
CESD	11.9	9.3	10.8	8.7	10.3	8.5

Note. WRSI = Work-Related Strain Inventory; CESD = Center for Epidemiologic Studies-Depression Scale.

significance, CESD in Year 1 ($p < .035$), WRSI in Year 2 ($p < .0035$), and CESD in Year 2 ($p < .005$). However, after correction for multiple comparisons, only Residency Year 2 WRSI scores demonstrated statistically significant differences between cohorts. The differences between the means were very small, 0.34 points between the 1989 and 1990 cohorts, 0.40 points between the 1989 and 1991 cohorts, and 0.74 points between the 1990 and 1991 cohorts. Given the relatively few statistically significant differences between the cohorts by residency year and the small magnitude of mean differences where there was statistical significance, we decided to combine cohorts to maximize sample size for the regression analyses.

Cross-Sectional Regression Analyses

Table 2 summarizes the regression analyses for WRSI scores for each year. Task and role clarity and work-group support were the only statistically significant predictors of WRSI at Year 1. Increased task and role clarity and greater support from others in the emergency department resulted in lower work-related stress scores. The interaction term for work-group support and task and role clarity was also significant ($p < .05$). Emergency medicine residents with low work-group support and low task-role clarity had the highest WRSI scores ($M = 38.7, SD = 7.8$), whereas those with supportive work groups and high task-role clarity had the lowest WRSI scores ($M = 29.3, SD = 6.9$). Residents with high work-group support and low task-role clarity had WRSI scores similar to those with low work-group support and high task-role clarity ($M = 32.2, SD = 8.3$ vs. $M = 33.3, SD = 7.0$).

The results of the regression analyses for WRSI in Years 2 and 3 were similar to Year 1 (see Table 2). Task-role clarity and work-group support were the only consistent predictors of WRSI. No significant Task-Role Clarity ×

Table 2. Cross-Sectional Regression Analyses of WRSI and CESD Scores

	Residency year					
	1		2		3	
Variable	WRSI b^a	CESD b^a	WRSI b^a	CESD b^a	WRSI b^a	CESD b^a
Age (years)	0.13	−0.05	0.23*	0.01	0.01	0.11
Gender (man = 1)	−0.33	−0.31	−0.28	−0.98	−0.01	−1.63
Marital status (married = 1)	−0.49	−1.82**	−0.21	−1.48*	−1.04	−2.48*
Task-role clarity	−0.52***	−0.08	−0.43***	−0.16	−0.75***	−0.54***
Work-group support	−0.42***	−0.13*	−0.51***	−0.07	−0.59***	−0.02
WRSI	—	0.71***	—	0.62***	—	0.49***
R^2	0.22	0.44	0.22	0.42	0.36	0.47

Note. WRSI = Work-Related Strain Inventory; CESD = Center for Epidemiologic Studies-Depression Scale.
[a] Unstandardized regression coefficients.
*$p < .05$. **$p < .01$. ***$p < .001$.

Work-Group Support interaction was found for Year 2, but there was a statistically significant interaction in Year 3 ($p < .02$). As in Year 1, residents with low work-group support and low task-role clarity had the highest WRSI scores ($M = 40.4$, $SD = 8.6$), whereas those with supportive work groups and high task-role clarity had the lowest WRSI scores ($M = 27.8$, $SD = 6.8$). Residents with high work-group support and low task-role clarity had WRSI scores similar to those with low work-group support and high task-role clarity ($M = 32.1$, $SD = 7.6$ vs. $M = 34.0$, $SD = 9.1$). The regression models (Table 2) explained 22% to 36% of the variance in WRSI scores.

The regression analyses for depression scores are reported in Table 2. The regression analyses suggest that not being married and having increased work-related stress results in more symptoms of depression. Between 42% and 47% of the variance in CESD scores was explained by the model. There was no evidence of a work-group support–task and role clarity interaction for any year. Cross-sectional regression analyses for the Year 2 and Year 3 data had comparable findings. The only exception was that task–role clarity was significantly associated with CESD scores in Year 3. Greater task and role clarity results in lower depression scores.

Endpoint Regression Analyses

Regression analysis was used to examine the impact of work-related stress on depression symptoms, after adjusting for task and role clarity and work-group support and baseline depression (see Table 3). During the second residency year, baseline CESD was the only statistically significant predictor ($p < .0001$), although WRSI nearly reached statistical significance ($p = .054$). Thirty-two percent of the variance in Year 2 CESD scores was explained by the regression model. No evidence of statistically significant interactions were found.

For the third year of residency, depression scores were also affected by gender ($p < .02$) and measures of work-related stress ($p < .0001$; Table 3, Model 3). Women in emergency medicine training programs and residents experiencing high levels of occupational stress reported more depression symptoms. About 38% of the variance in Year 2 CESD scores was accounted for by the regression model.

The only statistically significant interaction was for task-role clarity and work-group support ($p < .05$); gender, previous year CESD scores, and WRSI scores were also significant contributors in the model (Table 3, Model 4). Residents with supportive work groups and a greater sense of task–role clarity were less likely to be depressed ($M = 7.4$, $SD = 6.6$). Those residents with low support and low task and role clarity had more symptoms of depression ($M = 13.9$, $SD = 12.4$). Regardless of level of work-group support, residents with low task–role clarity reported more depression symptoms (CESD score of 13.9 vs. 13.5). Even in situations in which there was little work-group support, high task and role clarity resulted in lower CESD scores ($M = 11.5$, $SD = 7.3$).

Table 3. Endpoint Regression Analysis for CESD Scores at Residency Year 2 ($n = 369$) and Year 3 ($n = 192$)

Variable	CESD Year 2		CESD Year 3	
	Model 1 b^a	Model 2 b^a	Model 1 b^a	Model 2 b^a
Age (years)	0.19	0.18	0.03	0.03
Gender (man = 1)	-1.16	-1.17	-2.59^*	-2.25^*
Marital status (married = 1)	-1.16	-1.06	-1.77	-1.97
CESD (Year 1)	0.43^{***}	0.43^{***}	—	—
CESD (Year 2)	—	—	0.22^{**}	0.23^{**}
Task-role clarity (Year 1)	-0.03	-0.02	—	—
Task-role clarity (Year 2)	—	—	-0.14	-0.18
Work-group support (Year 1)	-0.11	-0.11	—	—
Work-group support (Year 2)	—	—	-0.02	-0.01
WRSI (Year 1)	0.13	0.14^*	—	—
WRSI (Year 2)	—	—	0.37^{***}	0.33^{***}
Task-Role Clarity × Work-Group Support (Year 1)	—	-0.32	—	—
Task-Role Clarity × Work-Group Support (Year 2)	—	—	—	-1.23^*
Work-Group Support × WRSI (Year 1)	—	-0.49	—	—
Work-Group Support × WRSI (Year 2)	—	—	—	-0.47
Task-Role Clarity × WRSI (Year 1)	—	0.18	—	—
Task-Role Clarity × WRSI (Year 2)	—	—	—	-0.96
R^2	0.32	0.32	0.38	0.40

Note. WRSI = Work-Related Strain Inventory; CESD = Center for Epidemiologic Studies-Depression Scale.
[a] Unstandardized regression coefficients.
$^*p < .05.$ $^{**}p < .01.$ $^{***}p < .001.$

Discussion

The results of this longitudinal study of emergency medicine residents support the relationship between work-group support and task–role clarity and work-related stress and the relationship between work-related stress and increased symptoms of depression. This study confirms previous research on primary-care physicians (May & Revicki, 1985; Revicki & May, 1985), emergency physicians (Gallery et al., 1992), emergency medicine residents (Revicki et al., 1993; Whitley et al., 1989, 1991), nurses (Gray-Toft & Anderson, 1985; Revicki & May, 1989), and emergency medicine technicians (Revicki et al., 1988). This study extends previous analyses of cross-sectional data and provides further insight into the relationship between work-related stress and psychological distress in physicians in training.

Residents who report task and role clarity in their positions and who have supportive peers and cohesive work groups are less likely to also report high levels of work-related stress. A structural equation model analysis by Revicki et al. (1993), based on cross-sectional data on a different group of emergency medicine residents, found that work-group support directly affects task and role clarity and that both variables directly affect perceptions of work-related stress. Research in hospital and other complex organizations have also found a link between role conflict and ambiguity and increased work-related stress, increased psychological distress, and reduced job performance (Cartwright, 1979; Gray-Toft & Anderson, 1985; House & Rizzo, 1972; Kahn et al., 1964; Revicki & May, 1989; Revicki et al., 1988, 1993).

High levels of work-related stress and task–role ambiguity result in psychological distress. Previous studies by Revicki and his colleagues have also found evidence for the strong relationship between occupational stress and mental health outcomes (Gallery et al., 1992; May & Revicki, 1985; Revicki & May, 1985, 1989; Revicki et al., 1988, 1993; Whitley et al., 1989, 1991). For example, Revicki et al. (1993) found that work-related stress was a significant direct contributor to a measure of depression in a sample of 484 emergency medicine residents. In this study, WRSI scores were the strongest predictors of depression.

A potential alternative explanation for the strong association between WRSI scores and depression is that there may be some content overlap between the two measures. Revicki et al. (1991), however, showed that the correlation between WRSI scores and measures of work-group support, role ambiguity, and job satisfaction were only slightly reduced after adjusting for depression symptoms. Clearly, this suggests that the WRSI is tapping a different construct distinct from depression.

There was a significant interaction between task–role clarity and work-group support in the regression models for depression. Emergency medicine residents who perceived both greater peer support and cohesion and high clarity regarding their role in the emergency department also reported lower levels of depression. Residents experiencing significant role and task ambiguity, in the presence of low support, reported more symptoms of depression. These findings are supported by previous research in the health professions (Cartwright, 1979; Gray-Toft & Anderson, 1985; Revicki & May, 1985, 1989; Revicki et al., 1988, 1993). In addition, social support resources modify the effect of stress on mental health and exert a direct, positive effect on psychological well-being (Aneshensel & Stone, 1982; Broadhead et al., 1983; Cohen & Wills, 1985; Kessler & McLeod, 1985; Revicki & May, 1985).

More interesting is the finding that task and role clarity, regardless of level of social support in the emergency department, appear to have an impact on depression. Emergency medicine residents in situations with much ambiguity regarding their roles and responsibilities and little task clarity, even in situations with high work-group support, reported more depression compared with residents with high task–role clarity. The lowest levels of depression were reported for those residents with high social support and high task–role clarity. In work settings with considerable role ambiguity, residents report higher levels of depression than in environments with task and role clarity. Strong work-group cohesion in these work environments cannot entirely eliminate the negative effects of role ambiguity on psychological distress. This is not surprising given the previous research on role ambiguity and conflict in complex work environments (Cartwright, 1979; Gray-Toft & Anderson, 1985;

House & Rizzo, 1972; Kahn et al., 1964; Revicki & May, 1989; Revicki et al., 1993).

Clear perceptions of roles and responsibilities may be more critical in practice environments where physicians work fairly independently. May and Revicki (1985) found that family physicians working in the community were more likely to report higher work-related stress compared with family medicine residents and faculty physicians. Task–role clarity makes a larger difference when there is little work-group cohesion and support. The most psychologically distressing situations are those in which physicians work alone, without a lot of contact or support from other health care providers and with no clear indication about their responsibilities within the organization.

These results also have further implications for postgraduate training of emergency medicine physicians. Recognition of the unique stressors connected with residency training and work in emergency departments have resulted in the creation of programs to assist residents in coping with the training setting. These programs encourage the provision of clear expectations about roles and responsibilities in the emergency department. The Resident Services Committee (1988) recommended the development of orientation programs to clearly specify the goals and responsibilities of residency training and formal meetings between residents and training-program directors to evaluate resident performance and to address problems early. Residency training programs need to describe residency training as a job and need to have realistic job descriptions to reduce unrealistic expectations. Program directors need to monitor resident progress and be alert to symptoms of psychological distress. Interventions and activities designed to improve support among residents, attending physicians, and other health care providers working in the emergency department can help decrease the incidence of depression among residents.

To summarize, on the basis of longitudinal data from emergency medicine residents, we found that work-related stress was strongly related to the development of depression symptoms. Task and role clarity was an important factor in reducing psychological distress. It is clear that individuals working in inherently stressful occupational settings, such as emergency departments, are more likely to be at risk for adverse mental health outcomes. However, psychological distress resulting from occupational stress is less likely to be a problem in settings where there is clear understanding of and expectations about roles and responsibilities.

References

Adler, R., Werner, E. R., & Korsch, B. (1980). Systematic study of four years of internship. *Pediatrics, 66*, 1000–1008.

Aneshensel, C. S., & Stone, J. D. (1982). Stress and depression: A test of the buffering model of social support. *Archives of General Psychiatry, 39*, 1392–1396.

Anwar, R. A. H. (1983). A longitudinal study of residency-trained emergency physicians. *Annals of Emergency Medicine, 12*, 20–24.

Asch, D. A., & Parker, R. M. (1988). The Libby Zion case: One step forward or two steps backward. *New England Journal of Medicine, 318*, 771–775.

Boyd, J. H., Weissman, M. M., Thompson, D., & Myers, J. K. (1982). Screening for depression in a community sample: Understanding the discrepancies between depression symptom and diagnostic scales. *Archives of General Psychiatry, 39*, 1195–1200.

Broadhead, W., Kaplan, B., James, S., Wagner, E., Scheonbach, V., Grimson, R., Heyden, S., Tibblin, G., & Gelbach, S. (1983). The epidemiologic evidence for a relationship between social support and health. *American Journal of Epidemiology, 117*, 521–537.

Butterfield, P. S. (1988). The stress of residency: A review of the literature. *Archives of Internal Medicine, 148*, 1428–1435.

Caplan, R. D., Cobb, S., French, J. R. P., Van Harrison, R., & Pinneau, S. R. (1975). *Job demands and worker health* (Department of Health, Education and Welfare [NIOSH] Publication No. 75-160). Washington, DC: U.S. Government Printing Office.

Cartwright, L. K. (1979). Sources and effects of stress in health careers. In G. C. Stone, F. Cohen, & N. E. Adler (Eds.), *Health psychology* (pp. 419–446). San Francisco: Jossey-Bass.

Cohen, S., & Wills, T. A. (1985). Stress, social support, and the buffering hypothesis. *Psychological Bulletin, 98*, 310–357.

Finney, J. W., Mitchell, R. E., Cronkite, R. C., & Moos, R. H. (1984). Methodological issues in estimating main and interactive effects: Examples from coping/social support and stress field. *Journal of Health and Social Behavior, 25*, 85–98.

Gallery, M. E., & Allison, E. J. (1990). Manpower needs in academic emergency medicine. *Annals of Emergency Medicine, 18*, 1157–1161.

Gallery, M. E., Whitley, T. W., Klonis, L. K., Anzinger, R. K., & Revicki, D. A. (1992). A study of occupational stress and depression among emergency medicine physicians. *Annals of Emergency Medicine, 21*, 58–64.

Gray-Toft, P. A., & Anderson, J. G. (1985). Organizational stress in the hospital: Development of a model for diagnosis and prediction. *Health Services Research, 19*, 753–774.

House, R. J., & Rizzo, J. R. (1972). Role conflict and ambiguity as critical variables in a model of organizational behavior. *Organizational Behavior and Human Performance, 7*, 467–505.

Janus, C. L., Janus, S. S., Price, S., & Adler, D. (1983). Residents: The pressure's on the women. *Journal of the American Medical Womens Association, 38*, 18–21.

Kahn, R. L., Wolfe, E. M., Quinn, R. P., Snoek, L., & Rosenthal, R. (1964). *Organizational stress: Studies in role conflict and ambiguity*. New York: Wiley.

Keller, K. L., & Koenig, W. J. (1989). Management of stress and prevention of burnout in emergency physicians. *Annals of Emergency Medicine, 18*, 42–47.

Kelner, M., & Rosenthal, C. (1986). Postgraduate medical training, stress, and marriage. *Canadian Journal of Psychiatry, 31*, 22–24.

Kessler, R. C., & McLeod, J. D. (1985). Social support and mental health in community samples. In S. Cohen & S. L. Syme (Eds.), *Social support and health* (pp. 219–240). San Diego, CA: Academic Press.

Koran, L. K., & Litt, L. F. (1988). House staff well-being. *Western Journal of Medicine, 148*, 97–101.

Krakowski, A. J. (1982). Stress and the practice of medicine. *Journal of Psychosomatic Research, 26*, 92–98.

Levin, R. (1988). Beyond "The Men of Steel": The origins and significance of house staff training stress. *General Hospital Psychiatry, 10*, 114–121.

Mawardi, B. H. (1979). Satisfactions, dissatisfactions, and causes of stress in medical practice. *Journal of the American Medical Association, 241*, 1483–1486.

May, H. J., & Revicki, D. A. (1985). Professional stress among family physicians. *Journal of Family Practice, 20*, 165–171.

McCue, J. D. (1982). The effects of stress on physicians and their medical practice. *New England Journal of Medicine, 306*, 458–463.

McCue, J. D. (1985). The distress of internship: Causes and prevention. *New England Journal of Medicine, 312*, 449–452.

Radloff, L. S. (1977). The CES-D Scale: A self-report depression scale for research in the general population. *Applied Psychological Measurement, 1*, 385–401.

Residents Services Committee, Association of Program Directors in Internal Medicine. (1988). Stress and impairment during residency training: Strategies for reduction, identification, and management. *Annals of Internal Medicine, 109*, 154–161.

Reuben, D. B. (1985). Depression symptoms in medical house officers: Effects of level of training and work rotation. *Annals of Internal Medicine, 145,* 286–288.

Revicki, D. A., & May, H. J. (1985). Occupational stress, social support, and depression. *Health Psychology, 4,* 61–77.

Revicki, D. A., & May, H. J. (1989). Organizational characteristics, occupational stress, and mental health in nurses. *Behavioral Medicine, 15,* 30–36.

Revicki, D. A., May, H. J., & Whitley, T. W. (1991). Reliability and validity of the Work-Related Strain Inventory among health professionals. *Behavioral Medicine, 17,* 111–120.

Revicki, D. A., Whitley, T. W., Gallery, M. E., & Allison, A. J. (1993). Organizational characteristics, perceived work stress, and depression in emergency medicine residents. *Behavioral Medicine, 19,* 74–81.

Revicki, D. A., Whitley, T. W., Landis, S. S., & Allison, A. J. (1988). Organizational characteristics, occupational stress, and depression in rural emergency medicine technicians. *Journal of Rural Health, 4,* 73–83.

Roberts, R. E., & Vernon, S. W. (1983). The Center for Epidemiologic Studies Depression Scale: Its use in a community sample. *American Journal of Psychiatry, 140,* 41–46.

Schwartz, A. J., Black, E. R., Goldstein, M. G., Jozefowicz, R. F., & Emmings, F. G. (1987). Levels and causes of stress among residents. *Journal of Medical Education, 62,* 744–753.

Whitley, T. W., Allison, A. J., Gallery, M. E., Heyworth, J., Cockington, R. A., Gaudry, P., & Revicki, D. A. (1991). Work-related stress and depression among physicians pursuing postgraduate training in emergency medicine: An international study. *Annals of Emergency Medicine, 20,* 992–996.

Whitley, T. W., Gallery, M. E., Allison, A. J., & Revicki, D. A. (1989). Factors associated with stress among emergency medicine residents. *Annals of Emergency Medicine, 18,* 1157–1161.

Zun, L., Kobernick, M., & Howes, D. S. (1988). Emergency physician stress and morbidity. *American Journal of Emergency Medicine, 6,* 370–374.

17

Burnout, Technology Use, and ICU Performance

Wilmar B. Schaufeli, Ger J. Keijsers, and Dinis Reis Miranda

> A stranger on entering an ICU is at once bombarded with a massive array of sensory stimuli, some emotionally neutral but many highly charged. Initially the greatest impact comes from the intricate machinery with its flashing lights, buzzing and beeping monitors, gurgling suction pumps and whooshing respirators. Simultaneously one sees many people rushing around busily performing life saving tasks. The atmosphere is not unlike that of a tension charged strategic war bunker. One becomes aware of desperately ill, sick and injured human beings and they are hooked up to the machinery. And in addition to the mechanical stimuli one can discern moaning, crying, screaming and the last gasps of life. Sights of blood, vomitus, excreta, exposed genitals, mutilated and wasted bodies, and unconscious and helpless people assault the sensibilities. Many are neither alive nor dead. Most have tubes in every orifice. Their sounds and action or inaction are almost inhuman. (Hay & Oken, 1972, p. 112)

This vivid, impressionistic observation suggests that working in an intensive care unit (ICU) is stressful. ICU staff are confronted with human suffering, grief, and death and are exposed to distasteful, degrading, and sometimes even disgusting sights. What is perhaps even more characteristic for ICUs, however, is the surreal environment that is dominated by sophisticated equipment. More than other hospital wards, ICUs have developed into high-tech environments that require complex cognitive skills such as monitoring the equipment and responding to alarms, in addition to traditional nursing (Fitter, 1987).

Aside from emotional demands and the use of advanced technology, various stressors have been identified in ICUs, such as conflicting communications with physicians, administrators, and other nurses; heavy workload; inadequate knowledge and skill; ethical problems; and responsibility for life and death decisions (for a review, see Caldwell & Weiner, 1981). Viewed from this perspective, it is not surprising that, one decade ago, burnout was listed among the top research priorities for ICUs (Lewandowski & Kositsky, 1983).

Burnout is considered to be a long-term stress reaction (Maslach & Schau-

---

This study was supported by Grant TA 87-34 from the Dutch Ministry of Health and by the Foundation for Research on Intensive Care in Europe (FRICE).

feli, 1993). Although different definitions of burnout exist, it is most commonly described as

> a psychological syndrome of emotional exhaustion, depersonalization, and reduced personal accomplishment that can occur among individuals who work with other people in some capacity. Emotional exhaustion refers to feelings of being emotionally overextended and depleted of one's emotional resources. Depersonalization refers to a negative, callous, or excessively detached response to other people, who are usually the recipients of one's services or care. Reduced personal accomplishment refers to a decline in one's feelings of competence and successful achievement in one's work. (Maslach, 1993, pp. 20–21)

Despite the claims that nursing in ICUs is particularly stressful, and thus causes burnout, comparisons with other hospital wards are inconclusive. Harris (1989) reviewed 23 studies that compared ICUs and non-ICUs on several stress-related outcomes (e.g., job dissatisfaction, burnout, turnover, alienation, and diminished organizational commitment) that were measured by self-reports. Fifteen studies found no differences between ICUs and non-ICUs, 3 studies reported fewer stress reactions in ICUs, and only 5 studies indicated higher stress-related outcomes in ICUs. Nevertheless, Harris (1989) observed some interesting patterns across all units:

> Nurses who are burned out have less hardiness; have higher stress, anxiety, and turnover; are younger, less experienced, more hassled, less educated, less involved with working conditions, and less able to anticipate problems at work; and have feelings of alienation, powerlessness, and lack of control, as well as somatic complaints. (pp. 24–25)

In summary, the evidence that levels of experienced stress, including burnout, are higher among ICU nurses than among non-ICU nurses is inconclusive. However, consistent relationships have been reported between burnout and other variables in ICUs and non-ICUs. Accordingly, it appears that burnout is a general problem in nursing, rather than a specific problem in ICUs.

Unlike other (e.g., clerical and blue-collar) jobs, the impact of technology on stress has barely been studied in ICUs (for a review, see Kumashiro, Kamada, & Miyake, 1989). This is all the more surprising because the use of medical technology is considered to be one of the most typical stressors in ICUs (Huckaby & Jagla, 1979). In their review of the literature, Karasek and Theorell (1990) concluded that the introduction of new technologies has led to increased stress because of "deskilling" and reduction of decision latitude, particularly in lower status administrative, technical, and manufacturing jobs. The report of the European Foundation for the Improvement of Living and Working Conditions (1988), concerned with the impact of new technology on workers in health care, concluded that nurses are increasingly dependent on the technology. According to the report, this deskilling has "particularly stressful consequences in the event of machine unreliability or breakdown, when a nurse might have difficulty switching from a passive role to active responsibility for patients" (European Foundation for the Improvement of Living and Working Conditions, 1988, p. 54).

More specifically, Fitter (1987) reviewed six case studies about the impact of technology use in ICUs that were performed in several European countries (Denmark, Ireland, Italy, the United Kingdom, The Netherlands, and Germany). He identified four common stress factors that are directly related to the use of new technology: enhanced cognitive demands (e.g., constant vigilance), poor design and equipment failures (e.g., false alarms), lack of adequate training, and ethical dilemmas (e.g., euthanasia). Accordingly, intensive use of technology can be considered a specific indicator of qualitative workload. Following this line of reasoning, it can be hypothesized that burnout is positively associated with the use of technology in ICUs.

It is expected that depersonalization occurs in ICUs where much sophisticated equipment is used. Depersonalization is considered to be a way of coping with emotional exhaustion through mental distancing (Maslach, 1993). Following this line of reasoning, it is likely that the use of advanced equipment fosters a detached and impersonal attitude toward patients.

Burnout and Job Performance

As Maslach and Schaufeli (1993) pointed out in their recent review of the historical and conceptual development of burnout, from the onset, it was postulated that workers who feel burned out are not able to perform on an adequate level. Some authors have even considered poor performance to be an aspect of burnout, rather than its consequence (e.g., Pearlman & Hartman, 1978). At any rate, the relevance of burnout for organizations is largely determined by the crucial assumption that it impairs job performance. However, empirical tests of this assumption are generally lacking. To date, the burnout–performance relationship is still a blind spot, which is illustrated by Kahill (1988), who concluded in her review of empirical burnout research, "The impact of burnout on job performance . . . is the area with perhaps the greatest practical and ethical implications, and has been addressed frequently in the anecdotal literature, yet has been largely neglected by researchers" (p. 295).

As far as human services are concerned, only three studies on burnout included job performance. Lazaro, Shinn, and Robinson (1985) studied 82 childcare workers from several agencies and found that burnout was more strongly (negatively) associated with self-rated performance than with supervisor-rated performance. Unfortunately, they used an unusual composite burnout score that included scales for job alienation, job satisfaction, psychological symptoms, and somatic symptoms. A more appropriate operationalization of burnout was used by Randall and Scott (1988), who used the well-known Maslach Burnout Inventory (MBI; Maslach & Jackson, 1986). In their study of 248 nurses at a general hospital, they found that burnout was related to poor self-rated performance, whereas its relationship with supervisor-rated performance was nearly absent. Finally, and most interestingly, Roelens (1983) investigated 261 ICU and non-ICU nurses. As predicted, burnout—as measured with the MBI— was negatively related to the nurses' own ratings of their performance. Quite remarkably, performance ratings by the head nurse agreed with this pattern in non-ICU settings, but in ICUs supervisor ratings were positively related to burnout. So, the better the nurses performed according to the assessment of their superior, the higher their burnout scores. Roelens speculated that in dehumanizing settings of the ICU, depersonalization may be an effective coping strategy, allowing nurses to focus on the technical aspects of their jobs. In other words, dehumanizing patients—a crucial aspect of burnout—is necessary for ICU nurses to survive psychologically.

Unfortunately, these three studies used subjective assessments of job performance that are plagued by many shortcomings. As far as we know, only one study used objective criteria of performance in relation to burnout. Golembiewski and Munzenrider (1988) studied the productivity of 48 work units of a U.S. federal service agency. In addition to individual performance ratings, assessments of qualitative and quantitative performances of work units were included. Qualitative performance was measured by headquarters ratings and by clients assessments of the quality of the services provided by the unit. Quantitative performance was calculated by multiplying all activities of the unit's members by their corresponding standard times (e.g., answering an incoming phone call was assigned a standard time of 4 min). Next, these multiplicands were added and divided by the total time resources that were allocated to that unit. Accordingly, an objective measure of unit effectiveness was constructed. Golembiewski and Munzenrider found mixed results regarding productivity when comparing units where more than 50% of the employees were in advanced stages of burnout with more healthy units. Work units with many burned-out employees were assessed significantly less productive by the headquarters and by the employees themselves. Besides, the qualitative performance (i.e., unit effectiveness) of these units was slightly, but nonsignificantly, poorer than that of the units with less burned-out workers. No differences were found in clients' assessments of the quality of the services provided. Interestingly, the employee's subjective performance rating was unrelated to the other more objective performance measures, except the clients' ratings ($r = .20$).

In summary, burnout is consistently associated with poor self-rated performance, whereas its relationship to performance appraisals of others (i.e., supervisors, clients, and headquarters) is much weaker or inconsistent. Furthermore, some very limited indications were found that burnout is associated with poor objective performance.

The General Research Model

To date, burnout is predominantly studied in relation to other self-reported variables (cf. Maslach & Schaufeli, 1993). Because similar subjective methods are used to measure the antecedents, symptoms, and consequences of burnout, common method variance that inflates relationships cannot be ruled out. Only objective measures avoid what has been called "the triviality trap." Therefore, in our study, the focus was on objective measures of work demands and performance that were assessed independently from the participant. A general model was explored that assumes that the nurses' level of burnout plays an intermediate role between particular job demands (e.g., the intensive use of technology) and ICU performance. It is expected that the higher the demands (e.g., the more intensively sophisticated the technology), the higher the level of burnout and the lower the unit's performance. In addition to the indirect relationship to burnout, the model assumes that high job demands may have a direct negative effect on unit performance. In our model, excessive use of technology is considered to be an indicator of qualitative work overload that impairs work performance. Several reasons have been suggested for the negative relationship between stress and performance (Cohen, Evans, Stokolos, & Krantz, 1986). For instance, overload causes a narrowing of attention that can result in poor judgment, a high propensity to commit errors, and an inability to distinguish the trivial from the important. This view is compatible with Jamal (1984), who suggested that coping with stress drains nurses' energy that is needed for maximum performance on the job. Although our research model suggests causal relationships, the current study can offer only cross-sectional evidence.

Method

Participants

The data used in our study are part of a larger investigation that was conducted among 39 Dutch ICUs that contain 21% of all 317 ICU beds in the country (Reis Miranda & Spangenberg, 1992). Because 200 or more admissions per ICU are needed as an adequate sample size for calculating the objective performance criteria (Zimmerman, 1989), 19 ICUs had to be excluded because of a failure to meet minimum patient admissions. Accordingly, 20 ICUs with 210 beds remained, covering 14% of the national ICU capacity. In the 7 months of data collection from February to August 1990, 7,126 patients were admitted to these ICUs.

Moreover, self-report data are available from 508 ICU nurses (43% men, 57% women) who voluntarily completed a questionnaire (response rate: 75%). To investigate the representativeness of the present subsample, the nurses who were included in our study ($N = 508$) were compared with the nurses ($N = 262$) from the 19 ICUs that were not included in the study. No significant differences were found for age, $t(768) = 0.02$ (ns), sex, $\chi^2(1) = .04$ (ns), proportion of part-time employed nurses, $\chi^2(1) = 0.61$ (ns), proportion of registered nurses, $\chi^2(1) = 1.48$ (ns), emotional exhaustion, $t(768) = 1.42$ (ns), depersonalization, $t(768) = 0.21$ (ns), and personal accomplishment, $t(768) = -0.36$ (ns). Only one significant difference between the two subsamples was observed: Nurses included in the present study perceived their units to be more effective than their colleagues who were not included in the study, $t(768) = -2.68$, $p < .01$. The present sample consisted of 43% male and 57% female nurses, of whom about 60% worked full time. The mean age of the sample was 33.4 years ($SD = 5.5$). About 90% were registered as an ICU nurse.

Measures

The use of technology in an ICU is reflected by the percentage of patients who were given mechanic ventilation during the period of investigation. The nursing of these patients is particularly demanding because their respiration is executed by sophisticated equipment. In intensive care medicine, this measure is generally considered to be an objective indicator of the technological demands ICU nurses are facing (Spangenberg, Van der Poel & Gaetano, 1990).

Burnout was assessed with the MBI (Maslach & Jackson, 1986), which consists of three subscales: Emotional Exhaustion (9 items; Cronbach's α = .84), Depersonalization (5 items; α = .65), and Reduced Personal Accomplishment (8 items; α = .75). Scores range from *never* (0) to *every day* (6). Recently, Schaufeli and Van Dierendonck (1993) demonstrated that the reliability and construct validity of the Dutch version is comparable to the original American version. The MBI was completed by each nurse individually, but the three burnout scores were aggregated on unit level by computing means per ICU.

ICU performance was measured both objectively and subjectively. Two objective indicators of performance were calculated: effectiveness and efficiency. *Effectiveness* refers the degree to which goals and objectives are successfully met. This is assessed by the standard mortality ratio (SMR), which is the ratio of observed versus predicted death rates (Zimmerman, 1989). The predicted mortality is based on a comparison with a U.S. reference group that includes more than 17,000 ICU patients. SMR explicitly controls for a number of medical, physiological, and biographical characteristics. Hence, SMR is an indicator of clinical effectiveness that is adjusted for several patient characteristics such as the severity of the illness, age, chronic health status, and medical diagnosis.[1] For the purpose of this study, SMR scores have been reversed, so that scores greater than 1.0 indicate good performance; the observed death rate of the ICU is smaller than the predicted death rate.

Efficiency refers to the degree to which goals and objectives are met at low costs (Scott & Shortell, 1988). This is estimated by the patient's length of stay. The shorter patients stay at an ICU, the more efficient the ICU is operating. Like mortality, length of stay has to be standardized for illness-related patient characteristics because, for instance, more severely ill patients are likely to stay longer than less severely ill patients. Accordingly, a standardized length-of-stay ratio (SLR) was computed similar to the SMR. SLR is the ratio of observed versus predicted length of stay. Again, the predicted length of stay is based on the American reference group and controls for several patient

---

[1]More particularly, the predicted death rate is derived from the Acute Physiology and Chronic Health Evaluation, Version 3 (APACHE III) predictive equations (Zimmerman, 1989). APACHE III is designed to provide accurate relative risk stratification for acutely ill hospitalized adults with medical and surgical diagnoses. The APACHE III score consists of a cardinal index risk number varying from 0 to 299 points. Points are tabulated from weights assigned to acute physiologic derangements (0 to 252 points), significant comorbidities influencing a patient's immunologic status (0 to 23 points), and the patient's chronological age (0 to 24 points).

The statistical evaluation of the patient data and the calculation of the mortality and length of stay ratios have been conducted by APACHE Medical Systems, Inc. (Reis Miranda & Spangenberg, 1992).

characteristics such as the severity of the illness, age, chronic health status, and medical diagnosis. An SLR greater than 1 indicates good ICU efficiency; patients stay a shorter time than was predicted.

Perceived unit effectiveness (PUE) is measured by asking the nurses to what extent they believe their unit is successful in achieving several goals (e.g., "Our unit is capable of reaching its goals in relation with patient care"; Shortell, Rousseau, Gillies, Devers, & Simons, 1991). For psychometric reasons, three original items had to be deleted. The remaining five items—scored on a 5-point rating scale ranging from *completely agree* (1) to *completely disagree* (5)—constitute an internally consistent scale ($\alpha = .70$). Similar to burnout, the nurses' perceived effectiveness scores were aggregated on unit level.

Results

Table 1 shows the levels of burnout among ICU nurses in comparison to a sample of non-ICU nurses from several health care settings ($N = 667$): general hospitals (15%), mental hospitals (25%), hospices (17%), community nursing (31%), institutions for people with mental retardation (9%), and other health care institutions (2%). Although this composite sample is not likely to represent all types of other nursing, it is homogeneous as far as levels of burnout are concerned. Only one significant difference was observed between the subsamples: Psychiatric nurses report stronger feelings of diminished accomplishment than do community nurses (Schaufeli & Peeters, 1990). Compared with nurses from other fields, the ICU nurses in the present study reported significantly more feelings of depersonalization and lower levels of personal accomplishment. Accordingly, they exhibited more burnout symptoms on two of the three dimensions.

Table 2 shows the means, standard deviations, and correlations between the aggregated variables at unit level. The pattern of correlations displayed in Table 2 is investigated with the LISREL VII computer program. A so-called linear structural model is tested that is based on our general research model. In this model, burnout is considered to be a latent variable or hypothetical construct that is measured by three manifest variables (i.e., emotional exhaustion, depersonalization, and reduced personal accomplishment). Moreover, ICU performance is assessed by three different kinds of indicators that are

Table 1. Burnout Among ICU Nurses ($N = 508$) and Non-ICU Nurses ($N = 667$)

Variable	ICU nurses		Non-ICU nurses		
	M	*SD*	*M*	*SD*	*t*
EEX	16.3	6.9	16.7	8.5	−0.86
DEP	7.2	3.7	5.9	3.9	5.8*
PAC	30.4	3.6	32.4	4.9	−7.8*

Note. ICU = intensive-care unit; EEX = emotional exhaustion; DEP = depersonalization; PAC = personal accomplishment.
*$p < .001$.

Table 2. Means, Standard Deviations and Correlations Between Variables in the Model ($N = 19$)

Variable	M	SD	MVT	EEX	DEP	PACr	SUE	SMR
					Product−moment correlations			
MVT	23.0	21.9	1.00					
EEX	14.9	2.9	.30	—				
DEP	7.0	1.0	.48	.57	—			
PACr	30.5	1.8	.40	.65	.75	—		
PUE	3.8	0.2	−.50	−.44	−.36	−.41	—	
SMR	1.3	0.5	−.13	.26	.12	−.01	−.31	—
SLR	1.0	0.2	−.30	.49	.17	.18	.01	.48

Note. MVT = mechanical ventilation (%); EEX = emotional exhaustion; DEP = depersonalization; PACr = personal accomplishment (reduced); PUE = perceived unit effectiveness; SMR = standardized mortality ratio; SLR = standardized length of stay ratio; for $r > .45$, $p < .05$; for $r > .57$, $p < .01$; for $r > .66$, $p < .001$.

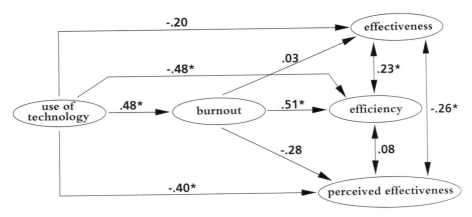

Figure 1. Use of technology, burnout, and intensive-care unit−performance (standardized LISREL solution).

supposed to be weakly positively related: effectiveness (SMR), efficiency (SLR), and a subjective indicator (PUE). Although the model is tested on only 19 cases, the aggregated data come from samples that include more than 500 nurses and more than 7,000 patients. Consequently, the aggregated variables in the model can be considered reliable estimates.

According to the chi-square goodness-of-fit statistic, the postulated model fits well to the empirical data, $\chi^2(11) = 16.60$, $p = .177$. Low values of chi-squares that produce high probability values are indicative of a good fitting model. It should be noted, however, that the chi-square index of fit depends on the sample size. The smaller the sample, the less powerful the statistic. Nevertheless, the model explains substantial percentages of variance in performance measures: effectiveness (31%), efficiency (43%), and perceived effectiveness (46%). Figure 1 shows the path coefficients (standardized regression coefficients β) that result from the LISREL analysis. For reasons of economy, only latent variables are displayed. However, the three manifest burnout dimensions are closely related to the underlying construct as is shown by their significant standardized regression coefficients: emotional exhaustion (β = .75), depersonalization (β = .88), and reduced personal accomplishment (β = .89).

The path coefficients between the latent variables show that, as expected, the use of technology is positively related to the nurses' level of burnout. However, contrary to expectations, the path coefficients in Figure 1 show that technology use is negatively related to two of the three performance indicators (i.e., efficiency and perceived effectiveness). Accordingly, the higher the technological demands, (a) the higher the mean level of nurse burnout, which is particularly because of depersonalization (see Table 2); (b) the less efficient the ICU operates (the longer the patients stay); and (c) the poorer the effectiveness of the ICU is evaluated by the nurses. Unfortunately, the negative relationship with the objectively assessed effectiveness criterion (SMR) does not reach significance. It should be noted that the objective performance criteria are adjusted for several patient characteristics such as severity of illness and medical diagnosis. Accordingly, the finding that the length of stay is longer in ICUs where a high proportion of patients are mechanically ventilated cannot be explained by the fact that more seriously ill patients are treated in these units.

Burnout relates differently to each of the three performance indicators. As expected, burnout is related negatively to subjective performance. Unfortunately, the path coefficient just failed to reach significance. Nurse burnout is unrelated to effectiveness; in ICUs where nurses are more burned out about as many patients die (according to the SMR) than in ICUs where nurses are less burned out. Quite surprising, and somewhat counterintuitive, burnout is positively related to the units' efficiency; in ICUs where nurses report higher levels of burnout, patients stay for a shorter period.

Instead of being weakly positively related, the relationships among the three performance indicators are more complex. This is caused by the nurses' perceived unit effectiveness; both objective measures (i.e., SMR and SLR) are, as expected, weakly but significantly positively related. Thus, in ICUs where fewer patients die than is expected on statistical grounds, patients stay for shorter periods. Again, it should be noted that both performance measures are standardized for patient characteristics. Somewhat surprising, the nurses' perceived unit effectiveness is unrelated to ICU efficiency and negatively related to objectively assessed ICU effectiveness.

In summary, burnout plays a mediating role in the job demands–performance relationship, but only as far as efficiency is concerned. However, this role is unexpected because nurse burnout that results from qualitative workload seems to have a positive rather than a negative impact on ICU efficiency.

Discussion

In this final section, five main conclusions are discussed that can be drawn from the current study on burnout, use of technology, and ICU performance.

First, the use of technology—an objective measure of qualitative workload—is positively related to burnout. In ICUs where technology is more intensively used, nurses are more likely to experience burnout symptoms. As expected, this is particularly true for depersonalization (see Table 2). In units where many patients are mechanically ventilated, nurses tend to view their patients as impersonal objects. In contrast to Roelens (1983), we do not believe that nurses use depersonalization as an effective coping strategy to deal with the emotional demands of their jobs. Rather, we consider depersonalization as an obvious response to the highly technological environment where patients, particularly when they are mechanically ventilated, are easily regarded as merely extensions of the medical equipment. The major reason behind this interpretation is the fact that ICU nurses do not experience higher levels of emotional exhaustion than non-ICU nurses, although their depersonalization scores are significantly higher (see Table 1). However, some caution has to be taken because the composite sample of non-ICU nurses is not representative for other types of nursing.

Second, as expected, the use of technology has a direct negative impact on subjective and objective performance and most notably on perceived unit effectiveness and on efficiency (i.e., the patient's length of stay). Obviously, a high qualitative workload (i.e., an intensive use of sophisticated technology) puts high pressure on the nurse, so that as a result not only the perceived effectiveness but also the units' objectively assessed efficiency declines (i.e., the patient's length of stay increases). Following Cohen et al. (1986), it can be speculated that nurses under pressure make more mistakes and their communication and coordination with other team members is impaired, which might result in less efficient unit performance. Indeed, unfamiliarity with sophisticated equipment, lack of adequate training in handling advanced technology, and interpersonal difficulties among ICU team members are among the major stressors that have been identified by ICU nurses (Caldwell & Weiner, 1981).

Third, the nurses' level of burnout is not significantly related to the unit's objectively measured effectiveness. In fact, this result agrees with Golembiewski and Munzenrider (1988), who conducted the only other study in which an objective performance criterion (i.e., unit effectiveness) was used in relation to burnout. Although the authors claimed throughout their book that burnout affects productivity, close inspection reveals that differences in performances between units with many and those with few burned-out employees are nonsignificant, with one exception: the headquarters' rating of the unit (Golembiewski & Munzenrider). It is unlikely that the nonsignificant relationship between burnout and effectiveness is due to measurement problems because the validity of the Dutch version of the MBI (Schaufeli & Van Dierendonck, 1993) and the SMR (Keijsers et al., 1994) has been convincingly demonstrated.

Fourth, contrary to expectations, burnout is positively related to ICU efficiency; the higher the burnout levels, the more efficient the ICU operates. A tentative explanation is that nurses in the more efficient ICUs are in the process of burning out because of the high qualitative job demands they are facing. It is likely that social affiliation and comparison processes foster the development of burnout symptoms in ICUs. Recently, Buunk and Schaufeli (1993) found that nurses under stress who perceive symptoms of burnout among their colleagues take on these symptoms, reasoning that these symptoms are apparently normal given their stressful job situation. This process of symptom contagion might explain the virulent nature of burnout that has also been observed in work units of a U.S. federal service agency (Golembiewski & Munzenrider, 1988). According to Golembiewski and Munzenrider, the burnout process usually starts when feelings of depersonalization develop. Beyond some undefinable point, depersonalization undercuts personal accomplishment and eventually leads to growing emotional exhaustion. This interpretation is supported by the finding that the ICU nurses who are included in the present study show significantly more feelings of depersonalization and reduced personal accomplishment compared to nurses from other fields, whereas no differences in emotional exhaustion were observed (see Table 1). However, despite the fact that ICU nurses might have entered an early phase of burnout, their negative mental state does not impede the medical performance of the ICU. Although their levels of burnout lead the nurses to evaluate the effectiveness of their units negatively (albeit not significantly), their objective performance in terms of effectiveness and efficiency is not impaired. Quite to the contrary, they perform well, particularly in term of efficiency. One can speculate that the units' performance improves as a result of the same process of social affiliation that is responsible for the spreading of burnout symptoms. It is plausible that social affiliation facilitates coordination and communication between ICU staff, hence improving the units' performance. For instance, Knaus, Draper, Wagner, and Zimmerman (1986) found that objectively assessed ICU performance was positively related to the interaction and coordination between nurses and physicians. Accordingly, the unexpected finding that burnout is positively related to ICU efficiency might be explained by referring to social affiliation processes within ICUs that simultaneously produce higher burnout levels and higher efficiency rates.

Fifth, subjective and objective measures of performance seem to tap different aspects of reality. Both objective performance measures (i.e., effectiveness and efficiency) share a relatively small but significant percentage of their variances (23%). This is likely to be caused by a third variable. For instance, it could be speculated that a favorable organizational climate, including adequate nurse–physician coordination, fosters the unit's effectiveness as well as its efficiency. The unexpected negative relationship between objective and subjective effectiveness might look somewhat puzzling at first glance. In units that are less effective according to our objective criterion (SMR), nurses believe that their unit is more effective, and vice versa. However, keep in mind that the objective performance criterion is unobservable by the nurses by its very nature. Instead of a distal and calculated SMR, nurses observe actual mortality. It is remarkable that the unstandardized morality rate (i.e., the number of patients who have actually died) is significantly and positively correlated with the nurses' perceived unit effectiveness ($r = .47$, $p < .05$). Thus, the more patients who actually die in an ICU, the less effective this unit is evaluated by the nurses. This clearly makes sense from a psychological point of view.

Obviously, by standardizing actual mortality rates and transforming them into an abstract output ratio, the measure is disposed of its psychological quality.

So, taken together, a high qualitative workload has a direct negative effect on ICU efficiency as well as an indirect positive effect. However, this positive effect has its price—nurse burnout. This conclusion is tentatively supported by the observation that the total costs that are spent per ICU bed are positively correlated with objective ICU performance (SMR: $r = .78$; SLR: $r = .38$) and with burnout $(.46 < r < .62)$.[2] Accordingly, allocating more financial resources to ICUs might increase medical performance as well as burnout.

Although our study is unique by including standardized objective performance indicators, it also has two weak points. First, only a limited number of ICUs are included, so the power of the statistical tests is weak. Second, the present study is cross sectional, so that no causal relationships between the variables can be studied. For instance, an alternative explanation can be given for the unexpected positive relationship between burnout and efficiency by reversing the causal order. It can be speculated that in the presence of a challenge, ICU nurses rise to the occasion and work more efficiently, but in the process of doing so they are likely to experience burnout.

Nevertheless, our study has demonstrated the fruitfulness of including simultaneously objective indicators of job demands and organizational performance and subjective experiences (i.e., burnout). In doing so, we hope that this investigation has contributed to the illumination of a blind spot in burnout research.

References

Buunk, A. P., & Schaufeli, W. B. (1993). Burnout: A perspective from social comparison theory. In W. B. Schaufeli, C. Maslach, & T. Marek (Eds.), *Professional burnout: Recent developments in theory and research* (pp. 53–69). New York: Taylor & Francis.

Caldwell, T., & Weiner, M. F. (1981). Stresses and coping in ICU nursing: A review. *General Hospital Psychiatry, 3,* 119–127.

Cohen, S., Evans, G. W., Stokolos, D., & Krantz, D. (1986). *Behavior, health, and environmental stress.* New York: Plenum.

European Foundation for the Improvement of Living and Working Conditions. (1988). *The impact of new technology of workers and patients in the health services.* Dublin, Ireland: Shankill.

Fitter, M. (1987). The impact of new technology on nurses and patients. In R. Payne & J. Firth-Cozens (Eds.), *Stress in health professionals* (pp. 211–229). New York: Wiley.

Golembiewski, R. T., & Munzenrider, R. F. (1988). *Phases of burnout: Developments in concepts and applications.* New York: Praeger.

Harris, R. B. (1989). Reviewing nursing stress according to a proposed coping-adaptation framework. *Advances in Nursing Science, 11,* 12–28.

Hay, D., & Oken, D. (1972). The psychological stress of intensive care nursing. *Psychosomatic Research, 34,* 109–118.

Huckaby, L. M. D., & Jagla, B. (1979). Nurse's stress factors in intensive care unit. *Journal of Nursing Administration, 9,* 21–32.

---

[2]Unfortunately, the financial data of the ICUs are incomplete. Therefore, the correlations are based on only nine units.

Jamal, M. (1984). Job stresses and job performance controversy: An empirical assessment. *Organizational Behavior and Human Performance, 33*, 1–21.

Kahill, S. (1988). Symptoms of professional burnout: A review of the empirical evidence. *Canadian Psychology, 29*, 284–297.

Karasek, R., & Theorell, T. (1990). *Healthy work: Stress, productivity, and the reconstruction of working life.* New York: Basic Books.

Keijsers, G. J., Schaufeli, W. B., Reis Miranda, D., Spangenberg, J. F. A., Devers, K. J., Gillies, R. R., & Shortell, S. M. (1994). *Psychological climate in intensive care units: The relationship of staff interaction with objective performance.* Manuscript submitted for publication.

Knaus, W. A., Draper, E. A., Wagner, D. P., & Zimmerman, J. E. (1986). An evaluation of outcome from intensive care in major medical centers. *Annals of Internal Medicine, 104*, 410–418.

Kumashiro, M., Kamada, R., & Miyake, S. (1989). Mental stress with new technology at the workplace. In M. J. Smith & G. Salvendy (Eds.), *Work with computers: Organizational, management, stress and health aspects* (pp. 270–277). Amsterdam: Elsevier.

Lazaro, C., Shinn, M., & Robinson, P. E. (1985). Burnout, job performance, and job withdrawal behaviors. *Journal of Health and Human Resources Administration, 7*, 213–234.

Lewandowski, L. A., & Kositsky, A. M. (1983). Research priorities for critical care nursing: A study by the American Association of Critical-Care Nurses. *Heart & Lung, 12*, 35–44.

Maslach, C. (1993). Burnout: A multidimensional perspective. In W. B. Schaufeli, C. Maslach, & T. Marek (Eds.), *Professional burnout: Recent developments in theory and research* (pp. 19–32). New York: Taylor & Francis.

Maslach, C., & Jackson, S. E. (1986). *MBI: Maslach Burnout Inventory; manual research edition* (2nd ed.). Palo Alto, CA: Consulting Psychologists Press.

Maslach, C., & Schaufeli, W. B. (1993). Historical and conceptual development of burnout. In W. B. Schaufeli, C. Maslach, & T. Marek (Eds.), *Professional burnout: Recent developments in theory and research* (pp. 1–16). New York: Taylor & Francis.

Pearlman, B., & Hartman, A. E. (1978). Burnout: Summary and future research. *Human Relations, 35*, 283–305.

Randall, M., & Scott, W. A. (1988). Burnout, job satisfaction, and job performance. *Australian Psychologist, 23*, 335–347.

Reis Miranda, D., & Spangenberg, J. F. A. (1992). *Kwaliteit, doelmatigheid en organisatie van intensive care units in Nederland* [Quality, efficiency and organization of intensive care units in The Netherlands]. Groningen, The Netherlands: Foundation for Research on Intensive Care in Europe.

Roelens, A. (1983). Job stress and burnout among staff nurses in acute care hospitals (Doctoral dissertation, New York University, 1983). *Dissertation Abstracts International, 44*, 4578.

Schaufeli, W. B., & Peeters, M. C. W. (1990, September). *The measurement of burnout.* Paper presented at the European Network of Organizational Psychologists conference on occupational burnout, Krakow, Poland.

Schaufeli, W. B., & Van Dierendonck, D. (1993). The construct validity of two burnout measures. *Journal of Organizational Behavior, 14*, 631–647.

Scott, W. R., & Shortell, S. M. (1988). Organizational performance: managing for efficiency and effectiveness. In S. M. Shortell & A. D. Lauzny (Eds.), *Health care management: A text in organizational theory and behavior* (2nd ed., pp. 418–457). New York: Wiley.

Shortell, S. M., Rousseau, D. M., Gillies, R. R., Devers, K. J., & Simons, T. L. (1991). Organizational assessment in intensive care units (ICUs): Construct development, reliability and validity of the ICU nurse-physician questionnaire. *Medical Care, 29*, 709–727.

Spangenberg, J. F. A., Van der Poel, J. H. R., & Gaetano, J. (1990). Management and control in the ICU. In D. Reis Miranda, A. Williams, & P. Loirat (Eds.), *Management of intensive care: Guidelines for better use of resources* (pp. 103–123). Dordrecht, The Netherlands: Kluwer Academic.

Zimmerman, J. E. (1989). APACHE III study design: Analytic plan for evaluation of severity and outcome in intensive care unit patients. *Critical Care Medicine, 17*(Suppl. 2), 169–221.

18 ⸻

Patient Assaults on Psychologists: An Unrecognized Occupational Hazard

Jane Y. Fong

Occupational stress is a rapidly growing concern in professional psychology. Many psychologists conduct stress research in numerous occupational settings, identify stress factors, and create programs for helping millions of workers cope with stress. However, psychologists tend to minimize or deny major stresses in their own professional lives. One serious and neglected occupational hazard that has received minimal professional attention is the occurrence of patient or client assaults on mental health workers, including psychologists.

Many reasons may explain the dearth of reports on patient assaults in the professional literature: lack of reporting mechanisms, personal feelings of embarrassment, shame or guilt, countertransference, clinician denial of his or her vulnerability or status as a victim of aggression by a patient, lack of ability or lack of interest to understand the dynamics or meanings of patient assaults. Or, as explained by a respondent in this present study, an assaultive experience "goes with the territory." A review of the professional literature that follows clearly demonstrates that safety issues have not received adequate attention.

In 1985, two psychiatrists in Oregon were killed by patients in the normal course of their professional duties. One was attacked by a psychotic inpatient shortly after the psychiatrist evaluated him. The other was shot in his private outpatient office by a former patient with a history of violence. Violent deaths of mental health professionals are not reported in professional journals; rather, they are typically reported in the popular press (Bloom, 1989).

Prior to 1970 few articles on assaults by patients appeared in professional and scientific journals. In a comprehensive review article, Rosenbaum (1991) surveyed the literature by culling through five standard psychiatry texts and performing computer searches of MEDLINE reference databases. He found no references to patient violence and assaults until 1966. He wrote, "until the 1960's violent incidents may not have been frequent enough or serious enough,

This research was conducted while the author was in private clinical practice in the Washington, DC, metropolitan area. Dr. Fong relocated to Atascadero, California, in June 1993.

The author gratefully acknowledges the invaluable assistance of Ms. Susan Phillips of Fairfax, VA, in the data collection.

or considered important enough to become subjects for clinical investigation" (Rosenbaum, 1991, p. 117).

During the past 20 years, reports of serious assaults on mental health workers have been published with great regularity. A majority of articles in this time period describe patient violence against psychiatrists, psychiatric nurses, psychiatric technicians, or other line staff working in inpatient psychiatric wards (see Carmel & Hunter, 1991; Lion & Reid, 1983; Davis, 1991; Rosenbaum, 1991).

The literature contains few research reports on patient assaults on professionals in outpatient settings. In an exhaustive review of the literature, Bloom (1989) estimated rates ranging between 14% and 48% of mental health professionals reporting experiences of assaults by patients. Dubin, Wilson, and Mercer (1988) surveyed psychiatrists and reported a range between 20% and 74% (with a mean of 42%) of those reporting at least one assault experience in their careers.

Both the Bloom (1989) and Dubin et al. (1988) studies suggest that the actual incidence of assaults is underreported. The lack of reporting, or low reporting, is clearly portrayed in the survey research conducted by Dubin and his colleagues: Out of 3,800 questionnaires sent to psychiatrists in Pennsylvania, New Jersey, and Delaware, only 91 questionnaires were returned. This low response rate (2%) was further compromised by respondents' vague answers, items left blank on the questionnaires, or other forms of poor reporting. Dubin et al. speculated on the possibility of discomfort psychiatrists have about aggressive acts from patients and about reporting violent incidents.

Patient Assaults on Psychologists: An Exploratory Survey

In response to the lack of literature on patient assaults on psychologists, I conducted an exploratory survey with psychologists regarding experiences that they may have had with client assaults.

Psychologists work in many professional settings: psychiatric inpatient wards, medical rehabilitation facilities, residential treatment centers, university counseling centers, and community mental health centers. Additionally, many clinical psychologists are engaged in privately owned outpatient clinical practices.

Psychologists, like other mental health professionals, encounter hostile transference reactions from patients during the course of their careers and are also likely to experience verbal assaults, threats, or aggressive actions from their patients. As stated earlier, the lion's share of pertinent articles in the professional literature reports research studies, surveys, or theoretical papers generated from assault incidents observed in institutional settings. To date, the literature shows no comprehensive survey or empirically valid and reliable research that has been conducted on incidents of patient assaults on psychologists (or on mental health professionals) in general. The work reported here is an exploratory survey to assess occurrences of assaultive incidents that psychologists experience, regardless of work setting.

Method

A brief survey instrument was developed to interview psychologists who attended the annual American Psychological Association convention in Washington, DC, in August 1992.

An assistant researcher[1] sought out psychologists in various locations of the convention (i.e., in hotel lobbies or lounges, outside conference rooms, on the streets, or areas near exhibits). To minimize any interference with the psychologists' schedules, she attempted to interview psychologists who were between conference activities. The researcher approached psychologists in a causal, yet professional, manner, introduced herself as a research assistant working on an issue relevant to psychologists' occupations, and asked for a few moments of their time.

All psychologists who consented to the interview were asked demographic information: age, marital status, state of residence, and primary occupational setting. They were asked whether they had experienced one or more of the following assault incidents by patients or clients: received phone calls that threatened bodily harm; been threatened with bodily harm in person; been physically attacked; or had personal or business property attacked, destroyed, or otherwise defiled.

If participants stated they had experienced any of these incidents, the researcher interviewed them further about the incidents. She probed and discussed these events gently. Time allotted for interviews varied, depending on how little or how much information participants were willing to discuss. Respondents were also asked about medical or psychological consequences they suffered, coping strategies used following the incidents, and their thoughts on how to prevent patient assaults.

Results

A total of 108 respondents were interviewed over a 2-day period. Of these, 18 (17%) reported one or more of the four categories of assault defined above. Demographic data are exhibited in Table 1. The *yes* respondents were psychologists who reported having had one or more assaultive experiences; *no* respondents were psychologists who reported no assaultive experience. Percentages are rounded off to the next whole number.

The two groups had similar characteristics in age range and primary work setting. In the *yes* group, there was a clustering of psychologists engaged in solo or group practice, and 78% were psychologists in outpatient clinical settings.

Table 1 also illustrates differences in marital status between the two groups: The *yes* group contained more than twice the number of single than married people; the *no* group contained equal numbers of single and unmarried people. This brings up the question of why single, unmarried people may demonstrate vulnerability different from married people. Alternatively, sin-

[1]Susan Phillips of Fairfax, VA, provided invaluable assistance in this study.

Table 1. Demographic Data

Demographic characteristic	Yes respondents (n = 18)	No respondents (n = 90)
Age		
20–30 yrs	1 (6%)	11 (12%)
31–40 yrs	7 (39%)	43 (48%)
41–50 yrs	8 (44%)	24 (27%)
51–60 yrs	1 (6%)	9 (10%)
61 + yrs	1 (6%)	3 (3%)
Gender		
Male	9 (50%)	44 (48%)
Female	9 (50%)	46 (51%)
Marital status		
Single	12 (67%)	42 (47%)
Married	6 (33%)	46 (51%)
Widowed	0	2 (2%)
Primary work setting		
Academic–teaching	1 (6%)	14 (16%)
Academic–research	1 (6%)	7 (8%)
Academic counseling center	1 (6%)	14 (16%)
School psychologist	0	4 (4%)
Solo practice	9 (50%)	22 (24%)
Group practice	5 (28%)	28 (31%)
Residential treatment center	1 (6%)	0
Hospital	0	1 (1%)

gle people may feel more vulnerable to hostile actions from others, or patients with a history of aggression may act out their impulses more often toward single people who may show signs of personal vulnerability. The trend found in this survey deserves further research. Note that the male:female ratio in both *yes* and *no* groups were nearly equivalent, about half male and half female. In view of the random method of selecting respondents to interview, this male:female balance may reflect only the gender ratio of conference attendees. Special attention to female clinicians' unique vulnerability to assault experiences is discussed by Binder (1991).

Table 2 exhibits data on the number of assault types reported by the 18 respondents. The tabulations are based on the yes–no responses for each, or for combinations, of the four assault types surveyed.

Table 2. Summary of Single and Multiple Assault Types Reported by 18 Psychologists

Received phone calls that threatened bodily harm	6 (22%)
Threatened with bodily harm in person	10 (37%)
Been physically attacked	5 (19%)
Had personal/business property attacked, destroyed, or defiled	6 (22%)
Total assault types reported	27

The data are impressive considering the size of the sample. The largest reported assault type (Type B, threatened with bodily harm in person), appears nearly twice the size (37%) of the other three types reported (compared with 19% for Type C, being physically attacked, and 22% for Type A, received phone calls that threatened bodily harm, and Type D, had personal/business property attacked, destroyed, or defiled). The number of physical attacks on the psychologist's body added to the number of attacks on property made up 41% of assault-incident types surveyed.

Multiple assaults were reported by 5 respondents: Two had experienced all four types; 2 experienced threats of bodily harm on one occasion and were physically attacked on another occasion; and 1 psychologist reported receiving phone calls that threatened bodily harm and was threatened with harm in person.

Occupational stress is apparent: The victimized respondents reported psychological, emotional, and medical consequences of their experiences. They reported statements such as the incident "made me feel tense and vulnerable," "I still feel anxious 2 years later," or "I was afraid to walk home from work for a long time." Only 2 of the 18 respondents reported that they "felt safe" at the time of their incidents.

The respondents were asked, "What have you done to deal with these concerns or feelings?," "What did you do to cope more effectively?," and "What did you do to cope with the assault?" Some of their responses came from a checklist on the survey instrument; many responses were from verbal statements or descriptions the respondents made during interviews.

Most of the respondents reported increased use of defensive and preventive measures: "I am much more self-protective and cautious. . . . When the assailant got out of jail, I took a week off to be sure he would not return." Another respondent reported, "I changed work hours." A third reported, "I upgraded security measures at the office and at home." Three participants did not give responses to these questions.

Table 3 exhibits the variety of coping strategies 15 psychologists used after assaultive events.

Table 3. Coping Strategies Used by 15 Psychologist–Victims After Assaultive Incidents

Became more cautious, more self-protective (e.g., established firm rules and limits on patient behavior, changed work hours, upgraded security)	8[a]
Reacted with denial, indifference, overcompensation "not surprised," "no time to handle it," "goes with territory," "he's a patient"	6
Got support from peers, supervisors, others	6
Involved authorities (police, lawyers)	5
Took time to analyze nature of work	3
Reinforced plan to change work or job	3
Discussed incident with patient	2
Took time off from work	2
Created a support group or network	2

[a]Number of psychologists who used each coping method.

Discussion

This exploratory survey clearly demonstrates that assaults by patients exist in the lives of psychologists. Although the sample number of respondents interviewed was small ($N = 108$), the findings are noteworthy: Despite the random sampling procedure, the fact that 17% (18 psychologists) of those surveyed reported they had experienced assaultive incidents suggests that these experiences are not random and do not occur merely by chance. Assaults by patients raise questions of serious occupational risk or hazard in the mental health workplace. Who or what groups bear major responsibility for assuring safety in psychologists' work settings?

Organizational and Legal Efforts to Assure Safety

Some of the onus belongs to governmental and legal authorities, who can further investigate the extent to which patient assaults on mental health workers constitute an occupational-safety issue. Safety definitions as set forth by the Occupational Safety and Health Administration (OSHA) in its creation in 1970 may no longer be relevant to the workplaces of the 1990s.

Federal OSHA regulations, for example, encourage employers in industry and business to submit reports on personal injuries. These reports include rates of lost work days, medical treatment, loss of consciousness, restriction of work or motion, termination of employment, or transfer to another job.

The same incident reports are required from mental health treatment institutions and facilities (Hanson & Balk, 1992). To what extent worker injuries are associated with patient assaults on mental health professionals may or may not be clearly indicated on report forms. Or, individuals who complete incident report forms do not consistently note that patients' actions were responsible for worker injuries. Serious reviews of these forms and new reporting procedures are necessary to redefine safety. For clinicians in outpatient practice, however, no current avenues exist for reporting assaultive events to the federal government. And even if assaultive incidents are reported, there are no methods of redress or compensation for victims' suffering.

Legal aspects also play an important role in psychologists' occupational stress: A "Patient's Bill of Rights," as espoused by the Joint Commission on the Accreditation of Hospital Organizations, advocates for patients in institutions and organized community mental health centers. With recourse to this bill, especially when it is reinforced by patient-advocate representatives, patients frequently take the position that their diagnosis of mental illness protects them from the consequences of their behavior, including violent actions. Although the bill is useful for the protection of patients, it can also limit a professional's ability to protect himself or herself for fear of future reprisal by a litigious patient or the possibility of offending the patient advocate.

Some professionals advocate holding assaultive patients responsible for their behaviors. This position carries its own complex dilemmas and problems (K. L. Applebaum & P. S. Applebaum, 1991; P. S. Applebaum, 1983). Nevertheless, it is important for mental health workers to have some sense of personal control in their situations, especially in instances in which the assailant did not appear to be psychotic or did not have a diagnosis of psychosis or schizophrenia at the time of the incident. To date, no mental health worker's (psychologist's) Bill of Rights exists. Sadly, organizational and legal efforts for safety reform in the mental health field, including any serious proposal and enactment of a professional bill of rights, do not appear to be forthcoming in the near future. Until government, institutions, and laws genuinely advocate for the safety of all mental health workers, safety guidelines must come from other sources. The most effective and reliable measures of personal safety must first come from individual practitioners.

Personal Efforts to Assure Safety

Mental health professionals in general, or psychologists in particular, can take responsible actions to prevent risks and use effective coping strategies.

Recognize one's own vulnerability to stress, regardless of age, sex, training, or work environment. Far too often the psychologist's defensive structure includes denial, projection, rationalization, or other styles of minimizing stress associated with his or her work and with assaultive incidents. One respondent in my survey, for example, responded to his incident with "It goes with the territory." Another stated, "I was pissed off at him." A third responded, "I was not surprised."

Be alert to patient transference and therapist countertransference dynamics. It is important that the clinician fully examine and understand his or her perceptions, attitudes, feelings and management of his or her own hostile–aggressive impulses and how these may have an impact on work with clients (Binder, 1991; Conn & Lion, 1983; Davis, 1991; Dubin, 1989; Felthous, 1984). Familiarity with one's own dynamics regarding aggression and hostility enables a clearer understanding and treatment of patients' aggressive impulses.

Binder (1991) suggested that female clinicians may have special risks. Women who had past experiences of sexual or physical assaults are likely to be more sensitive to violence, female clinicians may be the objects in male patients' rape fantasies, and pregnant female clinicians are likely to stir up complex maternal transference material. Binder cautioned women to be especially alert to gender characteristics that suggest unique risks to their safety.

Practice effective methods of patient management. This method can begin even before the first appointment. The wise clinician obtains information on the patient's treatment background (if any) as completely as possible and as quickly as possible. Safety may be compromised if the psychologist does not have adequate background information from previous therapists or from referral sources.

One psychologist in the sample reported that he was treating a "severe borderline" man who revealed at 3 months into treatment that he had threatened to kill his former therapist. The referral source apparently did not share this vital piece of information with the psychologist, who had been a victim of physical assault 2 years earlier. The psychologist did not seek out sufficient detail about the patient's prior treatment. The anxiety generated by the patient reactivated the psychologist's earlier trauma. If the psychologist had obtained relevant information on his new patient, he would have approached treatment differently or referred the patient elsewhere.

At onset of treatment, comprehensive structured clinical interviews with new patients should be conducted to obtain thorough past and present histories. Interviews with the patients' significant others, who can verify or nullify information patients themselves offer, should be conducted. The use of collaborative histories enables the clinician to arrive at useful, and often times more accurate, diagnostic formulations during early stages of treatment.

Thorough admissions background information should include past history of aggressive acting out or violence, substance abuse, some forms of psychosis or schizophrenic disturbance, severe personality disorders, legal involvement, organic brain dysfunction, acute stress or trauma, and psychiatric syndromes secondary to major medical conditions.

If the professional chooses to work with patients who have histories suggestive of aggressive or violent behavior, measures can be taken to minimize occupational risk to the clinician and also enhance therapeutic benefits for these patients: referral for medications to manage impulse or psychotic disorders, if appropriate; use of structured versus psychodynamic treatment techniques; use of group versus individual treatment; and the setting of appointments during daylight hours or between other patient appointments.

If the therapist is not fully experienced in working with an individual presenting a particular diagnostic syndrome, he or she would benefit from consultation and supervision with more experienced professionals or may choose to refer the patient to another specialist.

To address physical and environmental safety, psychologists can implement practical strategies: Establish or improve physical security measures in one's place of work and around one's home; learn and use physical-contact self-defense skills; set firm limits and mutual agreements with patients on appropriate behavior in the clinical setting; arrange appointments on days when several other patients are seen; be directly connected to crisis centers, inpatient facilities, or residential treatment facilities; be familiar with county civil mental commitment procedures; and have a support network or responsive peer group.

These methods are useful to all clinicians in all types of settings. When clinicians take direct responsibility to ensure their own safety, aggressive acting out from patients is minimized or eliminated in daily professional practice.

References

Applebaum, K. L., & Applebaum, P. S. (1991). A model hospital policy on prosecuting patients for presumptively criminal acts. *Hospital and Community Psychiatry, 42*, 1233–1237.

Applebaum, P. S. (1983). Legal considerations in the prevention and treatment of assault. In J. R. Lion & W. H. Reid (Eds.), *Assaults within psychiatric facilities* (pp. 173–190). New York: Grune & Stratton.

Binder, R. L. (1991). Women clinicians and patient assaults. *Bulletin of the American Academy of Psychiatry and the Law, 19,* 291–296.

Bloom, J. D. (1989). The character of danger in psychiatric practice: Are the mentally ill dangerous? *Bulletin of the American Academy of Psychiatry and the Law, 17,* 241–255.

Carmel, H., & Hunter, M. (1991). Psychiatrists injured by patient attack. *Bulletin of the American Academy of Psychiatry and the Law, 19,* 309–316.

Conn, L. M., & Lion, J. R. (1983). Assaults in a university hospital. In J. R. Lion & W. H. Reid (Eds.), *Assaults within psychiatric facilities* (pp. 61–70). New York: Grune & Stratton.

Davis, S. (1991). Violence by psychiatric inpatients: A review. *Hospital and Community Psychiatry, 42,* 585–590.

Dubin, W. R. (1989). The role of fantasies, countertransference, and psychological defenses in patient violence. *Hospital and Community Psychiatry, 40,* 1280–1283.

Dubin, W. R., Wilson, S. J., & Mercer, C. (1988). Assaults against psychiatrists in outpatient settings. *Journal of Clinical Psychiatry, 49,* 338–345.

Felthous, A. R. (1984). Preventing assaults on a psychiatric inpatient ward. *Hospital and Community Psychiatry, 35,* 1223–1226.

Hanson, R. H., & Balk, J. A. (1992). A replication study of staff injuries in a state hospital. *Hospital and Community Psychiatry, 43,* 836–837.

Lion, J. R., & Reid, W. H. (1983). *Assaults within psychiatric facilities.* New York: Grune & Stratton.

Rosenbaum, M. (1991). Violence in psychiatric wards: The role of the lax milieu. *General Hospital Psychiatry, 13*(2), 115–121.

19

Musicians: A Neglected Working Population in Crisis

David J. Sternbach

By any measure, stress and stress-related illnesses and injuries are pandemic among professional musicians today, and the problems of musicians and other performers have, until recently, gone virtually unnoticed and untreated. This chapter presents an overview of the primary work-related stressors in the lives of performing musicians—primarily, but not exclusively, symphony and opera orchestra players—and discusses prospects for addressing these concerns.

In 1971, Tucker, Faulkner, and Horvath reported that "the average age of musicians at death was 54 compared to the normal life expectancy of 69 years," in a study contrasting those populations (covering the years 1959 to 1967), with coronary heart disease accounting for almost 3% more deaths among the musicians (pp. 321–322). No more recent data concerning this alarming statistic of nearly 22% earlier mortality among musicians have been examined to see whether this disparity remains as wide or whether it has changed for the better or the worse in the ensuing 28 years. A survey (Fishbein, Middlestadt, Ottati, Straus, & Ellis, 1985) of health problems among classical musicians that polled 4,025 members of 48 orchestras garnered a 55% response rate (2,212 of 4,025), 82% of whom reported experiencing at least one medical problem. A remarkable 76% reported levels of pain sufficient to affect their performance. Nearly 30% of those responding acknowledged using beta-blockers in performance to control stage fright, although this medication was originally developed to control high blood pressure. "In the vast majority of cases," musicians are using this medication without medical supervision (Fishbein et al., 1985).

This sampling did not address those who left the profession with physical or psychological problems that made continued participation in a major orchestra impossible, and it does not include a substantially larger number whose overuse injuries or audition anxiety kept them from competing successfully for orchestra positions. From the mid-1980s on there have been many articles and studies that report the high incidence and severity of injuries, illness, and psychological problems that musicians are subject to (Calderon et al., 1986; Charness, Parry, Markison, Rosegay, & Barbaro, 1985; Harman, 1982, 1987, 1988; Salmon, Schrodt, & Wright, 1989).

Anyone, from the entry-level young professional to the seasoned performer is affected by performance anxiety. Singer Barbra Streisand returned to the stage after a 20-year struggle with stage fright, and cellist Pablo Casals suffered from stage fright during his entire career (Seligman, Namuth, & Miller, 1994). How many working people are involved? There are over 150,000 members of the American Federation of Musicians in the United States and Canada alone. Union officials estimate that the actual figures for working musicians is far higher, probably 10 times this number when those not affiliated with the union are counted. These musicians are drawn mostly from ranks in the entertainment fields, including dance-band, rock-and-roll, and some recording-studio musicians (A. Pollard & L. Waldeck, personal communication, June 10, 1993; W. Moriarty, personal communication, March 17, 1994).[1] The musicians in these populations are those who have the least adequate health coverage and are the least well informed about, and have the lowest rates of access to, appropriate music medicine resources or, for that matter, health programs in general. Finally, musicians in the popular music fields are those about whose health habits researchers know the least.

There is another large population affected by similar workplace concerns: music teachers in elementary and secondary schools, colleges and conservatories, and large numbers of private studio teachers. This is a substantial population of working people whose private vocation is teaching music but who are also active performers. These teachers comprise a large population who perform part time but are also subject to stress and stage fright that is often more severe because of the infrequency of performance opportunities.

Something in the musicians' work environment is causing too many injuries, and something is killing them too soon. Although substantial research is required to discover the critical factors in musicians' worklife that may be responsible, many believe that stress plays a major role in musicians' health problems. Stress is regarded as playing a contributory role in all the major causes of death in the United States. Studies on stress and occupational health present convincing evidence of the relationship between a variety of workplace stressors and the costs to working people in terms of heightened stress and stress-related illnesses (Goldberger & Breznitz, 1982; Keita & Sauter, 1992; Quick, Murphy, & Hurrell, 1992). Among the general population, "more than two thirds of doctors' visits are for stress-related symptoms. Many of the most frequently prescribed medications, among them Prozac, Tagamet, and Valium, are designed to relieve depression or ease anxiety" (Nucho, 1988, p. 5).

In the music profession, as in business and industry, stress-related health problems translate into lost work hours, accidents, disability, and ever-higher health insurance costs. One out of every five Fortune 500 companies has stress-management programs, and most now have employee assistance programs (EAPs). However, there are few such corresponding services for musicians. There are a handful of EAPs for musicians in the United States, serving a modest number of symphony orchestras. Aside from the New York musicians' union, however, which has an on-site counseling and referral service, the absence of such programs in other cities leaves the population of freelance

---

[1]Pollard, Musicians' Union official, Local 161-710, DC; Waldeck, head, American Federation of Musicians, Symphonic Services Division; and Moriarty, Musicians' Union, Local 802, NY.

musicians; club-date players; and jazz, rock, and recording artists without access to any kind of assessment and referral services designed specifically for them.

It may come as a surprise to associate musicians with the term *occupational stress*. Musicians are generally regarded as possessing a high degree of work satisfaction. Strongly inner-directed, working in careers that are self-selected, and enjoying what many audiences romanticize as a glamorous life with opportunities for self-expression and self-actualization, musicians should theoretically display low levels of occupational stress.

There are certainly many musicians to whom these terms apply, who manage to find ways to adapt to the stressors involved in this career. But there are many who are less stress resistant and whose lives reveal a far different picture. What this survey of musicians' workplace issues is intended to demonstrate is that there are a great number of elements that contribute to high stress levels in this population.

Three in particular stand out, which in combination are sufficient to create a high-stress work environment unique to this group.

First, musicians perform before the public and must deal, usually throughout their careers, with all of the anxieties associated with stage fright.

Second, they work under the constant scrutiny of conductors and band leaders, in rehearsals as well as in concert. Their work is exposed to supervisory review and criticism from moment to moment by conductors, many of whose own perfectionist agendas result in micromanagement.

Finally, musicians are expected to produce virtually note-perfect performances. Recordings have long since become a standard against which live performances are measured, which creates an atmosphere of unrealistic audience expectancies and intense performance pressures for musicians, particularly classical performers.

Musicians in other fields experience similar pressures and, additionally, have their own unique stressors to deal with. Jazz musicians are expected to stand up on a stage and be endlessly creative, four to six hours at a time, night after night. Freelance and club-date musicians live a precarious economic existence that demands great flexibility. Routinely hired for single engagements, they will go to a job, often not knowing in advance the other musicians with whom they will be working. If they cannot blend in with the band or otherwise satisfy the expectations of the hiring agent or conductor, they are unlikely to be called back again. Recording-studio time is expensive, and recordings are usually made under tight deadlines. Studio musicians are expected to get their parts right, on the first take. Retakes to achieve cosmetic perfection are a luxury reserved for the star soloists alone. In the popular and entertainment fields, musical styles and public tastes change constantly, leaving older players less familiar and increasingly less comfortable with these styles. Musicians in all fields devote substantial unpaid practice hours of each work week to maintain their playing skills and to keep up with the demands of new repertoire.

Taken together, these stressors along with many others, in particular in the classical music field, create a unique, highly stressful working environment. Professional athletes, by contrast, perform before the public but work with broader tolerances for error. A major league baseball player with a .300 batting average is a star, but no orchestra or audience would tolerate a musician who missed 7 out of every 10 notes.

Diamond cutters work under close and even more unforgiving tolerances but can do their work quietly, away from the public gaze. They can take their breaks as they need them. This is not the case, however, for a player of a solo part in a symphony that requires unremitting concentration for about 35 to 110 minutes. Playing in Mozart's *Marriage of Figaro* demands split-second timing by all players that must be sustained for nearly 4 hours.

Performing in public is risky business; no matter how well one rehearses, something can always go wrong. When one performs in an ensemble of 90 musicians, many things can go wrong. Mental fatigue becomes a cumulative stress issue when a performer has been taking risks in public, year after year. Sustained levels of high stress over long periods of time can set the stage for any number of degenerative conditions.

There are a number of other workplace factors that contribute to stress, among them irregular work schedules, shifting work locations, constantly rotating conductors with different demands, vulnerability to physical injury and disablement, and the perennial financial insecurity of the arts.

Holt (1982) documented nearly 60 types of occupational stressors, assembled from a bibliography of nearly 200 studies of stress in the workplace. Aspects of musicians' work life are reflected in virtually every one of these items to varying degrees.

Holt grouped occupational stressors into categories of objective and subjective types of stressors. For the purposes of this chapter, musicians' occupational stress is classified into three categories: environmental hazards, intrapersonal and interpersonal factors, and stress factors unique and intrinsic to the lives of performing artists.

Environmental Hazards

Musicians' workplace stress factors include "the physical properties of the working environment, including physical hazards, chronic dangers, pollution and less immediate dangers, extremes of heat, cold, humidity, pressure, noise, bad machine-man design" (Holt, 1982, p. 422). The notion of physical hazards associated with performing music may appear an odd one. Hazardous working conditions are more generally associated with meatpackers, lumberjacks, or other working populations in manifestly dangerous occupations.

Musicians are like professional athletes; they use their bodies in the performance of their jobs. They, like athletes, need physical strength, flexibility, and endurance and are vulnerable to injury. Athletes talk about "the moment," referring to the accident or injury that may sideline them for a game, a week or two, a season, or for life (Freeman, 1991). Musicians experience many sorts of injuries, brought on by overuse (Fry, 1986), parasthesias (Schwartz & Hodson, 1980), various neuropathies (Charness et al., 1985), muscular strains, carpal tunnel syndrome, focal dystonia, and "fiddler's neck," as well as the more common garden varieties of stress-related disorders including ulcers, high blood pressure, skin rashes, headache and muscle spasms, and anxiety disorders (Fishbein et al., 1985).

Very little is required to disable musicians. With a sore lip, a bruised finger, or a sore throat, most people can get through the work day and regard such injuries as trivial, but not a trumpet player, a violinist, or a singer. In addition, as a specialized worker, there is nothing else that an injured musician can do at work.

Injuries that affect players even temporarily carry psychological freight. A musician's identity is closely tied to his or her art. Aside from immediate issues of loss of income and concern for the future, a measure of depression and anxiety is frequently encountered in such patients, a consequence of their loss of access to their primary emotional and expressive medium. Traditionally, medical treatment has underestimated and often left unaddressed the psychological aspects of injury, disability, and recovery.

Playing a musical instrument is hard work and can impose significant stress on the physiology. Davis (1975), telemetering electrocardiograms of musicians in performance, has documented arrhythmias and tachycardias in brass players, with valsalva-like responses.

Hearing loss and tinnitus affect many musicians (Santucci, 1990; Westmore & Eversden, 1981), and these hazards are not confined to rock musicians. Symphony, opera, and pit-orchestra musicians seated near the brass or percussion sections are at high risk; for instance, in response to petitions from the musicians, the Chicago Symphony Orchestra management now provides custom-designed acoustic ear plugs to any players requesting them. It is common knowledge among musicians that Pete Townsend of the rock group The Who has for years been obliged to limit performing on stage for more than ten minutes at a time, his hearing having been permanently damaged by exposure to high volumes of sound. Many rock musicians feel caught up in a collision between the tastes of the public and their concern for their own auditory risks.

Tours, a way of life for most performers, expose them not only to the usual inconveniences but also to risks associated with travel. The musical world has lost some of its greatest artists in travel accidents, including Billie Holiday, the young jazz musician Bill Chase and members of his band, the famous French horn soloist Dennis Brain, and the young conductor Guido Cantelli.

Backstage areas, especially in older concert halls and theaters, are often found to be contaminated with asbestos. Halls may have inadequate ventilation, and most seating is poorly designed for performance tasks, significantly aggravating postural problems. Onstage, TV lights may produce glare directly in the faces of players, whereas cramped and uncomfortably crowded seating in theater pits and poor music-stand lighting leads to eye strain and often neck strain as players lean forward in their efforts to see.

Even modest temperature changes affect the tuning of string and wind instruments, and halls too hot or too cold affect players' ability to perform. Most instruments are poorly designed from an ergonomic standpoint and contribute to muscle strain. Many figurations for piano require sustained ulnar deviation; a sustained posture involving significant hip rotation is required for playing harp and French horn. Most instruments place unequal demands on right- and left-sided muscle systems, and instruments have become heavier over the years as they have evolved to meet the increasing demands of composers and the player's need to project in larger halls. Heavier instruments place more static load on the player. The valveless horn of the 18th century weighed under two pounds; the modern double horn weighs over six. As orchestras and musical scores have become larger and more complex, the physical effort required for sound production has become more demanding, placing more strain on the entire physiology. The piano Chopin played required less than one third the finger effort to depress a key compared with the force required on the modern concert grand piano.

There is overload. Many 20th-century works make physical demands that push players beyond reasonable limits; this, in combination with the increasing length of the symphony orchestras' performing seasons, has made musicians more susceptible to overuse and repetitive motion injuries. Research findings by Wilson (1988, 1989) have demonstrated that focal dystonia can be triggered by musicians attempting to learn new musical works whose technical requirements go so far beyond what was previously required they place abnormal strain on the physiology. Careers have been ended with the onset of this syndrome.

Stress Associated With Time Pressures

Musicians are routinely subject to the effects of "time variables, change in time zone or length of workday, nonstandard working hours or shift work, deadlines, and time pressures" (Holt, 1982, p. 422), effects that not only have a direct impact on workers' health but also indirectly affect them through emotional wear and tear.

Musicians may travel eight hours, cross three time zones, and perform the same evening. Freelance musicians may on any given day rehearse in the morning, record in the afternoon, and play a concert that evening, and their schedules change from one day to the next. Recording sessions may find players working against time pressures in a studio 24 hours or longer until the final takes are finished. Musical theater runs provide one day off in a work week of eight performances, two days of which have back-to-back afternoon matinees and evening shows.

Time pressures are implicit in the very nature of live performances scheduled for given times. Most concert halls book several programs a day, often years in advance. Concerts cannot be delayed a few hours, a half day, or two days, and if canceled, they are not easily rescheduled. The old adage "the show must go on" refers not only to dedication to audiences, but also to the pressures of the business side of the entertainment field. Finally, in terms of time pressure, live performance before the public means no second chances.

Add to these factors other workplace stressors—among them irregular work schedules, shifting work locations, and one particularly challenging stressor, constantly rotating conductors. Few working people in business offices or industrial settings would find it congenial to have to adapt to constantly changing supervisors, but musicians, from one week to the next in symphony orchestras, nightly in opera houses, and often two or three times in a single day, must work with and have the flexibility to adapt to many different conductors, all with different technical styles, artistic demands, and distinctly unique personalities.

Intrapersonal and Interpersonal Factors

Often referred to as subjectively defined occupational stressors, this category takes in those aspects that may not be immediately threatening to the performer's physical health but that contribute to emotional wear and tear. Stress of this kind can be interpersonal or transactional.

A certain amount of temperament among those involved in the arts is not necessarily a negative trait, and the personality collisions among creative individuals may be an indispensable ingredient of the creative process. However, such clashes can also be wearing, as well as productive, to great artistic achievements. Under the pressures of preparing and presenting artistic productions under time pressure, differences will arise. They arise between strong egos, over artistic differences almost as deeply held as religious convictions, and these can produce dramatic levels of friction and conflict. In the Renaissance in Italy, men fought duels over differing theories of instrument tuning.

Today, there are other differences that arouse strong passions: those between orchestra players and conductors. There are conductors whose styles with the orchestras that they direct are models of respect and collegial courtesy (e.g., Andre Previn, Kurt Sanderling, Erich Leinsdorf, and many others). But there are also those whose difficult temperaments, poor communication skills, and often abusive personal styles are notorious stressors that musicians consistently list as their primary work stressor.

Anxiety exacerbated in this respect is not confined to performance before the public. Every note musicians play in rehearsals is scrutinized by conductors and subject to criticism, and studies of telephone workers demonstrate "increased stress levels in workers subject to overmanagement" (Smith & Carayon, 1990, p. 12). Orchestra and opera conductors and band leaders who abuse their positions of authority create highly charged, anxiety-ridden rehearsal and performance conditions for their players. One musician, a solo player in major orchestras for 30 years, once said that for him, concerts were actually less stressful than rehearsals under the autocratic style of his orchestra's director: "It came as a relief to play the concert. At least then he couldn't stop you and criticize you, in front of the entire orchestra. And he never criticized people in a kindly way" (Farkas, personal communication, April 1963).

Until relatively recently, symphony conductors had sole authority to hire and fire and could dismiss players or singers on the spot if so inclined. The worst abuses have been alleviated in recent years as a result of the efforts by organized labor representing musicians in contract negotiations, but emotional abuse is more difficult to negotiate away. Referring to the history of conductor–orchestra relations, Andre Previn said, "American unions have protected musicians here from very violent things that have been done to them in the past" (Epstein, 1987, p. 42). One can infer, from this careful choice of words, the number of crushed egos, ruined careers, and resentments in the community of orchestral musicians. The situation nearly everywhere in the entertainment field is less enlightened; there, the individual band leader still reigns supreme, hiring and firing at will.

Musicians in orchestras are given little opportunity for input into artistic decisions and interpretation, a domain reserved by conductors for themselves: "You don't initiate anything in an orchestra. That's the conductor's job," said one seasoned violinist in the Boston Symphony. "You're very much imprisoned" (Epstein, 1987, p. 216).

As managements strive to increase earnings, traditional orchestra programs give way to more with popular appeal. They bring in large audiences but represent a significant compromise in aesthetic values for the musicians, prompting one humorous soul to label orchestra playing "a life of sin" (Epstein, 1987, p. 219).

Negotiating and resolving artistic or personality conflicts with conductors and colleagues can be frustrating and distracting when they involve the musician in business affairs that take them outside their area of expertise and training. Music schools offer few courses that teach young students how to negotiate contracts, deal with publicity agents, work through interpersonal conflicts effectively, or manage finances and career-development strategies as self-employed workers.

Employee abuses by management continue to occur, even among the top symphony orchestra organizations. One major ensemble returned home from a three-week tour of the Far East, arriving around midnight on a flight from Tokyo, with a 9:00 a.m. rehearsal scheduled for the following morning. Organizational decisions of this kind exacerbate relationships between management and orchestra personnel.

Labor–management issues compound musicians' problems in other ways. Every year, an average of 37 work weeks are lost in U.S. orchestras because of strikes and lock-outs (L. Waldeck, personal communication, Sept. 14, 1991). Most American ensembles are underfunded, and in budget crises managements frequently turn to the most obvious target for deficit reduction—musicians' salaries.

Issues Around Employment Insecurity and Compensation

Aging principal players face the prospect of forced demotion with loss of direct and associated earnings and loss of status; there are many conductors who openly express prejudices against older musicians in general. The specter of unemployment is literally a day-to-day issue for the self-employed musician. Even those with steady positions under contract and protected by tenure and appeal systems are aware that their playing must be maintained at the highest levels, continuously throughout their careers. Even when musicians are performing well, economic uncertainties affect employment, just as shop workers in factories may be laid off—not through any failures on their parts, but because of larger economic forces operating in the marketplace.

Musicians work as hard off the work site as on. Job compensation does not cover the hours of practice at home, study of scores, repair and maintenance of instruments, reed making, travel and expenses connected with master classes, and training that musicians consider essential to sustain their technical skills, advance their artistic abilities, and renew inspiration.

In this respect, compensation ranges from excellent to poor, especially after factoring in the time expended to maintain playing skills. The best-paid orchestra musicians in the top orchestras can earn $65,000 to $75,000 a year or more. Players in low-budget regional orchestras or per-service ensembles may earn no more than $5000 a year from their music and must regularly support themselves with other employment.

Stress Associated With Workload

Machine pacing, a notorious stressor in industry, has its analog in musicians' lives. Live performances are compared critically with note-perfect recordings, which can benefit from as many retakes and judicious splicings as needed to achieve perfection. Musicians now also find themselves competing with synthesizers, a computer-generated music product, whereas dance and club-date musicians' work is steadily being displaced by disc jockeys.

The workload for musicians is highly demanding. Music making is hard physical and mental work. Few people outside the profession can fully appreciate how difficult it is to maintain performance standards at the levels of excellence now routinely expected by the public. Players of solo parts in any ensemble have total job responsibility; if they miss the entrance cue, that moment is gone. There can also be monotony even when performing difficult works. Pit musicians in long-running musicals might play the same challenging show material several thousand times. Opera musicians may play *La Bohème* 20 times a season, for 25 or 30 years.

Stress Associated With Changes in Work

Musicians are as vulnerable as any group of working people to the threat of change or loss of job, demotion, qualitative changes in job, or overpromotion, which may propel a player from a minor ensemble into a position with a top orchestra. In such a job transfer, a player faces new pressures that may include recordings, more demanding conductors, a higher level of playing to conform to, live radio and TV broadcasts, and more demanding audiences. Careers have been destroyed by sudden leaps upward in employment, pushing players beyond their zone of psychological comfort.

Transfer of work to a new city brings all the concomitant stressors associated with any relocation, generally without the relocation support that large companies can provide. Lack of control over their work schedules creates substantial stress for self-employed freelance musicians, especially those attempting to raise families.

Labor–Management Conflicts

Low wages, poor or nonexistent benefits, discrimination in hiring, and arbitrary management policies were all typical of the American symphony orchestra scene well into the 1970s. In all these areas, the United States lagged behind most other Western industrialized countries, information I brought to musicians' attention in articles contrasting European and American symphony and opera house employment conditions (Sternbach, 1975a, 1975b). Although working conditions for many symphony and opera orchestras have improved, these gains have been threatened in recent years as orchestras have incurred greater deficits in overall economic atmosphere of increasing scarcity of funding for the arts. Many professional musicians have never enjoyed the protection of secure contracts.

Stress Associated With Self-Criticism

Musicians constantly evaluate their own performance. One trumpeter said, "If I haven't practiced for a day, I know it. Two days, and my colleagues notice. Three days, and everybody knows it." Musicians monitoring themselves continually, with persistent self-observation untempered by tolerance for imperfection, can exact a cruel price. It may result in an obsessive, life-long dissatisfaction with one's own products, robbing the performer of any joy in playing and shattering self-confidence. A crisis of confidence may befall any working person, but the consequences for a public performer are disastrous. Loss of self-confidence leaves a musician vulnerable to attacks of stage fright that can literally be crippling.

Performance Anxiety

In surveys asking Americans their 10 worst fears, respondents place public speaking at the top of the list (Wallace, Walleschinsky, & Wallace, 1977). But anxieties associated with speaking in public, where one can stumble over a word, stop, make a correction and continue do not compare with the pressure experienced by musicians when a false note once played cannot be taken back and corrected without disrupting a performance.

Musicians live with stage fright, a kind of semiphobic condition that manifests itself in three different but clearly associated categories. There is anticipatory anxiety that involves concern over future performances, then the actual experience of stage fright in performance itself, and finally, postperformance anxieties. All are potentially devastating, each in different ways, and most musicians suffer from all three.

Steven Hough, a concert pianist, observed,

> First, there are the nerves, or the nervousness, one feels before a performance which dissipate when the concert begins. Then there is the confidence which suddenly fails the artist when he or she walks out on stage. Or the failure can come in the middle of the performance whether through tiredness or distraction when the performer begins to question the value of tonight's playing and wonders why things aren't going well. The mind and the nerves can play various tricks on anyone. I know; at different times I've been the victim of all of them. (March 1988, p. 137)

The degree to which performing anxiety affects people can vary enormously from one individual to another and in any one person throughout their career. In its milder forms stage fright can elicit a degree of excitation that can enhance a performance, transforming it from the merely competent into something unforgettable.

At the other extreme, a performer may experience a full-blown anxiety attack. Behavioral, physiological, and psychological manifestations can include tremors producing a shaking and uncontrollable bow, palpitations and loss of wind support that can ruin the efforts of a wind player, numbness in the fingers causing inaccurate passage work, memory blanks, accelerated heart rates or tachycardias, dizziness, transient limb paralysis, black-outs, and even cardiac arrest in the most extreme cases. All this can be accompanied by racing thoughts, memory loss, inability to keep place rhythmically, and a pervasive sense of disaster.

Janina Fialkowska, a pianist, related her feelings experienced during a concert appearance while listening to a long orchestral introduction: "I felt as though a black sheet had fallen over my head. I just didn't know how to start it, and I didn't seem to know where I was or what I was doing there. The thought came that I should run off the stage immediately" (March 4, 1988, p. 66).

Anticipatory, or preperformance, anxiety can affect musicians just moments before walking on stage or hours, days, even weeks or months before a critical performance. Thought processes before a concert or audition may include calamitizing and catastrophising, fantasies of failure or blunders onstage that are visualized destroying not only the performance but also one's career. The Russian virtuoso Emil Gilels said, "I have always been nervous before concerts, and I continue to this day to be so. I've never found a cure for it. But I find that by being reflective and meditative about it all, I can do it" (March 1988, p. 123).

There is always, it would seem, something with which a performer can be dissatisfied, regardless of how well a concert may appear to have gone to others. The third aspect of performance anxiety arises after the concert, with remorse over real or imagined errors.

"I'm never satisfied with a concert" said Dusset, a concert artist, echoing a sentiment many musicians share (March 1988, p. 196). Mental review of a concert or audition can range from a relatively detached and objective assessment of one's strong and weak points with strategies for future improvement to wholesale self-condemnation. The brief periods of time provided in auditions and solo competitions appear to aggravate this tendency. A candidate for a university teaching position may, following a selection process after submission of credentials and references, be invited to a campus for a full day of meetings with department heads, other faculty, and deans, and be offered seminar or teaching assignment, and have ample time to overcome initial anxieties.

By comparison, musicians prepare for years to audition for positions in orchestras or participate in competitions, which can be an entry to a concert career. Over years, they invest untold hours of energy and dedication, and expend considerable funds to train themselves for an audition that may last 5 to 15 minutes. In this regard, they face the same competitive pressures as Olympic athletes, whose performance tensions are far more evident to the general public.

> The concert artist Murray Perahia spoke for many soloists when he said, My initial reaction, once I got there (to the site of a competition), was to get sick. I don't really hate competitions, at least not as much as some of my colleagues do, but I certainly would not have entered one on my own. It's just that I do not find them a pleasant activity. Yet I know that competitions, or at least a certain number of them, are necessary to help artists get playing engagements. (March 1988, p. 215)

Many famous names in music are on record concerning their opinions of the entire competitive process. "Competitions are for horses, not for artists," said Bela Bartok. "The effect of inexplicable failures, with their attendant damage to the young performer's morale, more than outweighs the success of the few," revealed Joseph Szigeti. "I suffer agony to see young artists go through the humiliation of a competition . . . the joy of those who succeed is spoiled by the sorrow of those who have been hurt . . . it cannot be useful to discourage a hundred merely to encourage one," said Gregor Piatagorsky. And Glenn Gould admitted, "auditions inflict 'spiritual lobotomy.'" (all in Horowitz, 1990, p. 16).

Musicians may enter many auditions. The failed applicants, with little or no evaluative feedback, are left to guess at how the selection process was made. One psychiatrist who has worked extensively with musicians reported that symptoms of musicians who fail critical auditions in many regards

> resemble those of individuals who have been exposed to hostage situations, assault, muggings, even rape. They feel victimized by chance and experience loss of sense of self, loss of control, anguish, flashbacks, and frequently overwhelming feelings of helplessness, conditions resembling posttraumatic stress disorder. (J. Buffington, personal communication, May 1987)

These reactions are exacerbated by the sudden-death conditions of orchestra auditions or competitions in which one may be dismissed during the process at any time. Managements of orchestras openly stipulate this as a condition of the audition.

Significant numbers of young musicians, burned out by the experience of orchestral auditions or competitions, desert the profession every year.

Even after winning a position in an orchestra, a musician's worries are far from over. Besides the strain of working under constant supervision in rehearsals, musicians are acutely conscious of the role that critics can play with negative reviews of their work. Careers can be destroyed with a single review.

One consequence of micromanagement, which is responsible for serious rifts between many conductors and orchestras, should be noted in this context. Office and line workers in industry understandably react with resentment to negative supervisory styles. However, for musicians, the problem of poor management style takes on an added dimension. Performers open themselves up to others to achieve rapport, to explore at a deep level the emotional content of a piece, and to reach an audience emotionally. At such moments, a musician with lowered psychological boundaries is vulnerable. Ill-timed criticism and the abusive styles of some conductors are particularly destructive. Constant exposure to this kind of insensitivity has in great measure been responsible for the troubled relationships between many conductors and orchestras.

How Musicians Deal With Pain and Injuries

Musicians have tended historically to disguise injuries, illness, and stage fright. They will play hurt, play through their pain or their panic, and do so for years because the alternative might be temporary or permanent unemployment. Given the lack of job security for many musicians in an overcrowded and fiercely competitive field, few feel comfortable in speaking openly about their physical or psychological problems.

This secretiveness has the unfortunate effect of also operating to keep many performers from obtaining appropriate medical and psychological help. This is changing as musicians become better acquainted with information about their problems reported at music medicine conferences and in articles in musicians' publications. But many still consult with physicians or therapists in an atmosphere of secrecy, justifying this by their concern for the potential damage to their marketability with concert managers. There have been dramatic successes for many such patients, but confidentiality is reserved by artists who feel there is more to lose than to be gained in any public revelation. Although their positions are understandable, their silence inhibits other injured and anxious musicians, especially younger ones, from seeking treatment under the mistaken notion that no one else in their profession would ever need such help, and certainly not the top performers.

It is also an unfortunate fact that inadequate awareness of the dangers of performing while ill or injured may lead a busy musician to procrastinate in seeking out appropriate treatment. "Such delays often lead to medical complications which involve more treatment procedures and reduce prospects for a full and speedy recovery" (Rozmaryn, 1995, p. 6). Such delays have, on a number of occasions, contributed to the premature end to the careers of many musicians. Finally, an important factor that keeps many artists from seeking out health care is financial. Health benefits have been slow in coming to musicians, and for that matter, to the general public in the United States, as opposed to a long tradition of such protections afforded citizens in most European countries.

Stressors Intrinsic to a Performer's Life

I now turn to stressors that, although not strictly workplace hazards, are inseparable aspects that accompany the choice of a life as a performing artist. Career decisions that have such a profound effect on one's entire life, if made solely on a rational basis, would be weighed in terms of benefits and costs, an evaluative process for which few budding young performers are equipped to make from a perspective that only many years of experience can provide. Rather, Freud (1910/1961) proposed that important life decisions are made from deep within the unconscious, only partially subject to mediation by the conscious mind. Early in life, the decision to perform appears to be made for them, almost as if the art selects them, rather than the other way around.

It is only later, already deeply committed to this career choice, that most discover and begin dealing with the inevitable frustrations that accompany any career choice. Many learn to deal in mature ways with such issues, but some never do, instead developing maladaptive strategies in response to the inevitable and many frustrations of a career as a performing artist. It is these individuals who are at high risk for emotional illness and substance abuse problems.

"Playing the French horn is like driving a fast car on an oily road" (B. Tuckwell, personal communication, December 1976). Every instrument has its limitations. Musicians are, in a sense, married to their instruments and must learn not only how to cultivate the finest expressive qualities from them but also to come to terms with and tolerate the limitations imposed by them. Some, even famous artists, never come to terms with their ambivalence. One famous artist told of having sustained an injury to his left hand by a falling rock and thinking, just as it happened, "Thank God, I'll never have to play the cello again." He then remarked that "dedication to one's art does involve a sort of enslavement, and then too, of course, I have always felt such dreadful anxiety before performances" (Casals, 1970, p. 105).

The High Price of the Pursuit of Excellence

Living with perfectionist ideals and imperfect execution is the lot of the artist. Although striving to bring into reality one's most highly developed artistic ideals is life enhancing and brings a richness and depth to life that is the special gift of creativity, it also demands a certain stability to tolerate this frustration and continue to pursue ever higher goals throughout one's creative life.

Many artists accommodate these tensions, and the best of them continuously push their own limits, but not without stress. The predicament of the performing artist is well expressed in *Babette's Feast*, "It is terrible," writes the opera singer, "for an artist to be encouraged to do, to be applauded for doing, his second best. Through all the world there goes one long cry from the heart of artist; give me leave to do my utmost" (Dinesen, 1985, p. 68).

The violinist Fritz Kreisler said that in his youth he had a certain ideal of violin playing, but once he had achieved this in his 20s, the ideal was replaced by another, more complex notion of playing. Once he felt that he had accomplished this level of performance, he discovered that yet another, higher level of playing seemed possible. And so it went throughout his life. In his 70s, he said, he had gotten quite close to his ideal, closer than ever before, but it still lay beyond him (Lochner, 1950).

Two Life Cycles in the Lives of Musicians

Musicians deal with two developmental processes. Meeting the stepped-developmental challenges Erikson (1980) referred to as *the life cycle*, musicians also find themselves dealing with the unfolding of their art, which has a developmental life of its own. This is of a different nature than absorption in one's career, which can occur in many other kinds of work. The unique, driving talent present in any prodigy impels young musicians into an involvement with something quite apart from their personal life or career and economic concerns. The young artist's ego needs collide with the imperatives of a talent that can consume one's life. One singer referred to her voice as "a monster" (C. Williams, personal communication, December 1966).

The risk that one's talent will take precedence over one's character is not simply material for drama and literature; such conflicts are commonplace for performing artists throughout their lives. Young musicians practice alone when they would prefer to be socializing with their peers. Young musicians may have to refrain from certain activities, fearing injuries that could abruptly terminate a budding career. Life can pass performers by while they follow the direction that their talent takes them.

Age takes its toll on the athleticism of performers, while their artistic capacities deepen. Placido Domingo said, "with years, you lose some things; flexibility, stamina." The American baritone Sherill Milnes commented, "while some purely physical prowess diminishes, we find ourselves able to say more with a text. We've lived, learned, had tragedy in our lives. . . . [But] I don't have the stamina I had. I cannot sing as well as often as I used to" (both in Tommasini, 1994, p. H31).

The psychological task of reconciliation to the gulf between one's capacities and one's artistic vision adds a poignant dimension to the Eriksonian life stage of reconciliation to aging.

Aside from the tensions of balancing two developmental cycles throughout one's life, there is the issue of loneliness. Musicians devote many hours in isolation to perfecting their skills in youth, to the maintenance of those skills throughout their careers, to studying scores and to mastering a new repertoire. Loneliness is a condition of the performer's work life and may lead to a sense of alienation without access to a rich network of friendships and connection to community.

Prospects for Treatment and Remediation

There are several areas that appear to be appropriate directions for development. Sauter, Murphy, and Hurrell (1992), in reviewing the need for more emphasis on prevention of work-related stress disorders, suggested strategies that include training, education, and the development of training and educational materials; dissemination of information; and mobilization and coordination of relevant organizations. These policies apply equally to the population of musicians and other performers.

The past decade has seen established a new area of medical specialization, music medicine, in response to the growing recognition of musicians' physical problems. There now exist music medicine clinics in major cities in the United States and in Canada, specialists treating musicians' overuse and repetitive motion problems, journals addressing health issues of performers, conferences and newsletters, and a growing bibliography of articles on this subject. Many explore stress issues in the lives of musicians as well, but as yet there is no separate discipline that directly targets musicians' mental health issues in its own right.

The Development of Training and Educational Materials

There already exist a broad range of treatment modalities for the kinds of psychological problems performers present. There is a need for training programs to acquaint mental health professionals with short-term approaches that can help musicians and other performers reduce their stress levels, modulate their stage fright to controllable levels and, in the long term, develop more stress-resistant lifestyles.

Researchers now know that most performance anxiety can be successfully treated without medication. Some treatment modalities successful in helping performers deal with stage fright include systematic desensitization (Wolfe, 1989); response stopping, cue-controlled relaxation response, and deep-muscle–relaxation techniques (Benson, 1975); stress reduction and cognitive restructuring (Steptoe & Fidler, 1987); education about the nature of stress (Desberg & March, 1988); focusing techniques; and, above all, training in imagery rehearsal enhanced by light trance states.

Programs in stress management would help musicians become more flexible and stress resistant. Counseling can help to change distorted belief systems, reduce perfectionistic and obsessive styles, and moderate an excessive need for approval and acceptance by others that drives many performers. Cognitive–behavioral therapies provide skills in developing coping statements and reframing.

Mobilization and Coordination of Relevant Organizations

Because musicians are exposed to significant numbers of occupational stressors, it would seem to be an appropriate investment on the part of public health agencies to reevaluate more closely the workplace settings of performers and propose further remedies through employer education or through regulatory processes. Because early intervention practices are known to be efficient in terms of both early recovery and lower treatment costs, the eventual provision of EAP resources to all performers would be a good objective. Such programs would be available to musicians not only in their home cities, but on tours as well.

This is essential because travel is a fact of life for most musicians. Potential disruption from medical or psychological problems is of more serious consequence on tours than at home, where substitute players are known and are potentially available. An alliance between public health agencies, existing music medicine organizations, the national musicians' union, and the various players' organizations would greatly expedite the successful achievement of these objectives.

Education and Dissemination of Information

Education of this population to an awareness of the risks that they face associated with workplace stress are needed. Over the past 15 years, the reduction of heart disease and extension of life expectancy in the United States offers clear evidence of the role that public-health education can play in helping citizens develop healthier lifestyles. When educated to recognize how their physical and emotional health affects their creativity and productivity as artists, musicians are likely to prove themselves highly motivated to change lifestyle habits.

In the treatment of musicians at music medicine centers, there is a clear role in the intake and assessment process for injured performers for a thorough psychosocial assessment by a mental health professional; those findings should be routinely integrated into the workup and treatment design.

Health professionals treating the medical problems of musicians should be encouraged to be stronger advocates for stress-management skills. Appropriate referrals should be made routinely to mental health professionals trained in techniques designed to help performers to control stage fright and develop more stress-resistant styles, providing them with the potential for careers and personal lives that are healthier, longer, and more productive.

In addition to establishing better treatment programs, another target is the education of young musicians. This agenda has the potential for yielding significant improvements in the mental health of musicians in the years to come. Educational institutions now training musicians should be encouraged to establish courses in stress management and in the skills that can help regulate performance anxiety.

Ample opportunity exists for basic research into the lifestyles of musicians, not only to establish the most significant workplace stress factors that place working musicians at high risk for physical and emotional problems. Research will be equally productive that targets those traits in the lifestyles of the highly stress-resistant musicians that help them maintain their immunity to the negative effects of excess stress in this challenging and difficult profession. These aims would benefit from a coordinated approach, if an integrated remedial effort is to be mounted successfully.

Broader Implications for the General Public

Information about this population has other applications; there are shifts in the nature of work in the general American population. More and more it seems, working people in business and industry are beginning to resemble freelance musicians, facing the same kinds of generic stressors that have long existed in the lives of musicians. These include economic uncertainty, the erosion of job security, and increasing workplace injuries from overuse and repetitive motion syndromes. Workers in the home are experiencing higher stress brought on by isolation, and the pressure to overproduce—long a feature in the American workplace—seems to be increasing. What is learned about musicians can potentially be of benefit to the larger working population.

The young men and women who set out to build careers as performing musicians enter this career hoping and expecting to live rich and fulfilling creative lives. It comes as a shock to them to eventually realize that the achievement of their career and artistic goals may be at the cost of their physical and emotional health. Sadly, this appears to be the case for growing numbers of performers. The price that many musicians now pay for living a creative life is too high. We can help substantially to reduce the health costs in injuries, disability, and stress to those who bring so much beauty and enjoyment into all our lives.

References

Benson, H. (1975). *The relaxation response.* New York: Murrow.

Calderon, P., Calabrese, L., Clough, J., Lederman, R., Williams, G., & Leatherman, J. (1986). A survey of musculoskeletal problems encountered in high-level musicians. *Medical Problems of Performing Musicians, 1*, 136–139.

Casals, P. (1970). *Joys and sorrows.* New York: Simon & Schuster.

Charness, P., Parry, G., Markison, R., Rosegay, H., & Barbaro, N. (1985). Entrapment neuropathies in musicians [abstract]. *Neurology, 35*(suppl. 1), 74.

Davis, S. (1975). Stressed musicians. *Senza Sordino, 13*(6), 2.

Desberg, P., & March, G. (1988). *Controlling stage fright.* Oakland, CA: New Harbinger.

Dinesen, I. (1985). Babette's feast. In *Anecdotes of destiny.* New York: Vintage.

Epstein, H. (1987). *Music talks: Conversations with musicians*. New York: McGraw-Hill.

Erikson, E. (1980). *Identity and the life cycle*. New York: Morton.

Fishbein, M., Middlestadt, S., Ottati, V., Straus, S., & Ellis, A. (1985). Medical problems among ICSOM musicians: Overview of a national survey. *Senza Sordino, 25*(26), 1–8.

Freeman, M. (June, 1991). Ultimate fear: "The moment." *Washington Post*, pp. D1, D6.

Freud, S. (1961). *Five lectures on psychoanalysis, Leonardo and other works*. London: Hogarth Press. (Original work published 1910)

Fry, H. (1986). Incidence of overuse syndrome in the symphony orchestra. *Medical Problems of Performing Artists, 3*, 1–8.

Goldberger, L., & Breznitz, S. (Eds.). (1982). *The handbook of stress*. New York: Free Press.

Goode, D., & Knight, S. (1991). Identification, retrieval, and analysis of arts medicine literature. *Medical Problems of Performing Artists, 6*, 3–7.

Harman, S. (1982). Occupational diseases of instrumental musicians. *Maryland Medical Journal, 39*, 42–47.

Harman, S. (1987). Bibliography of occupational disorders in instrumental musicians. *Medical Problems of Performing Artists, 2*, 155–162.

Harman, S. (1988). Bibliography for occupational diseases of instrumental musicians: Update. *Medical Problems of Performing Artists, 3*, 163–165.

Holt, R. (1982). Occupational stress. In L. Goldberger & S. Breznitz (Eds.), *The handbook of stress* (pp. 419–444). New York: Free Press.

Horowitz, J. (1990). *The ivory trade*. New York: Summit Books.

Keita, G., & Sauter, S. (Eds). (1992). *Work and well-being: An agenda for the 1990s*. Washington, DC: American Psychological Association.

Lochner, L. (1950). *Fritz Kreisler*. New York: Knopf.

Nucho, A. (1988). *Stress management*. Springfield, IL: Charles C Thomas.

Quick, J., Murphy, L., & Hurrell, J. (Eds.). (1992). *Stress and well-being at work*. Washington, DC: American Psychological Association.

Rozmaryn, L. D. (1995, March 31). Hand surgery outcome in musicians [Abstract]. In S. Harmon (Ed.), *Proceedings of the 3rd Conference on Performing Arts Medicine* (p. 6). Baltimore, MD: Maryland Medical Society.

Salmon, P., Schrodt, G. R., & Wright, J. (1989). A temporal gradient of anxiety in a distressful performance context. *Medical Problems of Performing Artists, 4*, 77–80.

Santucci, M. (1990). Musicians can protect their hearing. *Medical Problems of Performing Artists, 5*, 136–138.

Sauter, S., Murphy, L., & Hurrell, J. (1992). Prevention of work-related psychological disorders. In G. Keita & S. Sauter (Eds.), *Work and well-being: An agenda for the 1990s* (pp. 31–33). Washington, DC: American Psychological Association.

Schwartz, E., & Hodson, A. (1980). A viola paresthesia. *Lancet, 2*, 156–158.

Seligman, J., Namuth, T., & Miller, M. (1994, May 23). Drowning on dry land. *Newsweek*, pp. 64–66.

Smith, M., & Carayon, J. (1990). *Electronic monitoring of worker performance: A review of the potential effects on job design and stress*. Madison: University of Wisconsin.

Steptoe, A., & Fidler, H. (1987). Stage fright in orchestral musicians: A study of cognitive and behavioral strategies in performance anxiety. *British Journal of Psychology, 78*, 241–249.

Sternbach, D. (1975a). The American and European orchestra: A comparative study, Part 1. *Senza Sordino 13*(5), 1–2.

Sternbach, D. (1975b). The American and European orchestra: A comparative study, Part 2. *Senza Sordino 13*(6), 1–2.

Tommasini, A. (1994, Oct. 9). As the limelight fades, a star lowers his sights. *The New York Times*, pp. H31, H38.

Tucker, A., Faulkner, M. E., & Horvath, S. (1971). Electrocardiography and lung function in brass instrument players. *Archives of Environmental Health, 23*, 327–334.

Wallace, A., Walleschinsky, D., & Wallace, I. (1977). *The book of lists*. New York: Morrow.

Westmore, G. A., & Eversden, I. D. (1981). Noise-induced hearing loss and orchestral musicians. *Archives of Otolaryngology, 107*, 761–764.

Wilson, F. (1988). Teaching hands, treating hands. *Piano Quarterly*, *141*, 34–41.
Wilson, F. (1989). Acquisition and loss of skilled movement in musicians. *Seminars in Neurology*, *9*, 146–151.
Wolfe, M. (1989). Coping with musical performance anxiety: Problem-focused and emotional-focused strategies. *Medical Problems of Performing Artists*, *5*, 33–36.

20

Exhilarating Work: An Antidote for Dangerous Work?

Nancy J. McIntosh

Substantial research indicates a relationship between the nature of work and experiences of strain in the workplace (see, e.g., House, Wells, Landerman, McMichael, & Kaplan, 1979; Karasek, 1979). Earlier studies (Farid & Lirtzman, 1991; Jermier, Gaines, & McIntosh, 1989; McIntosh & Atkins, 1991; McIntosh, Gaines, & Jermier, 1989) have demonstrated that workers' perceptions of the characteristics of their jobs are related to the amount of work-related stress that they report. An anomalous finding in this research is that physically dangerous work has both a negative (direct) relationship and a positive (indirect) relationship to strain. A suggested explanation of the unexpected positive impact of dangerous work is that it is somehow exhilarating and exciting as well as threatening.

In the research cited above, Jermier et al. (1989) concluded that for police danger was a characteristic of work distinct from other work dimensions, workers' perceptions of danger were related to the objective danger present, and those perceptions were related to higher incidence of emotional exhaustion. However, although the indirect effect of objectively dangerous work, mediated by perceived physical danger, was increased emotional exhaustion, the direct effect of objectively measured danger was lower levels of emotional exhaustion. In addition, objective danger was related to the motivating potential of the task (Hackman & Oldham, 1975, 1976).

In a subsequent study of workers from multiple occupations and organizations (McIntosh et al., 1989) objectively measured danger again was significantly related to perceived danger, which in turn was related to increased emotional exhaustion and report of physical symptoms. However, objectively measured danger was directly related to decreased reported physical symptoms. These findings were replicated in a study of nurses (McIntosh & Atkins, 1991). These results, along with evidence from other studies, particularly of policing (e.g., Reiss, 1971; VanManaan, 1974), suggests that workers identify a positive as well as a negative component of the danger in their jobs. It was

Lou Ann Atkins contributed significantly to an earlier version of this chapter. Earlier theoretical and empirical work on physical danger in collaboration with Jeannie Gaines and John Jermier of the University of South Florida was the springboard for this inquiry.

A complete factor analysis table, which was edited to conserve space, may be requested from the author.

hypothesized that the positive component is an exhilarating, exciting dimension of work perceived by workers as a task characteristic distinct from both danger and task-motivating potential. This study investigated the concept of exhilarating work and its relationship to other aspects of work and responses to work.

Dangerous Work

Dangerous work, whether physical or emotional, is characterized by a probability that a worker will suffer harm from exposure to a hazardous agent or activity (McIntosh et al., 1989). Physical danger is defined as "exposure to agents that can cause bodily pain, injury, illness and/or death." Emotional danger is defined as "exposure to human tragedy, pain, misery and suffering" (Jermier et al., 1989, p. 16).

Dangerous work has both objective and subjective components. Objective danger exists in the environment (e.g., toxic chemicals, machinery, and noise) independent of whether it is perceived and is a significant predictor of the variance in workers' perceptions of danger in their work (Brody, 1988; Farid & Lirtzman, 1991; Jermier et al., 1989; McIntosh & Atkins, 1991; McIntosh et al., 1989). However, the full impact of objectively measured danger is not reflected in measures of perceived danger. Objective danger is also related to positive worker affect and reduced strain. This component may represent a social and symbolic construction of the work designed to increase perceptions of autonomy and prestige or status (see Jermier et al., 1989, p. 17). This study attempted to capture in its measure of exhilarating, exciting work the component of objective danger that is associated with lower levels of strain.

Nursing as Dangerous Work

Physical hazards for nurses include exposure to body fluids, ionizing radiation, X-rays, lasers, noise, electricity, infectious diseases, and chemical hazards. Nurses are also subject to injury from lifting, from handling equipment, and from disruption in circadian rhythm and are exposed to situations that make their work emotionally dangerous, regularly encountering pain, suffering, and tragedy.

Although danger reflects realities of the nature of the work, the amount of work is also related to strain for nurses. For example, McIntosh (1984) reported that workload and exposure to dying patients are separate stressors for nurses. Because workload is a consistently reported stressor for nurses, its effect relative to that of task characteristics was explored.

The Current Study

Interpretations of previous studies of physical danger suggest that exhilarating work is a discreet task characteristic, distinguishable from enriched work and emotional and physical danger. The purpose of this study was to determine whether nurses identify exhilarating work as a discreet task characteristic and to explore its impact on strain. It was anticipated that exhilarating work would have a direct effect on workers' experiences of strain and that the effect would be in addition to that of other task characteristics and other previously identified workplace stressors. The excitement generated by the work will influence workers to feel more positive about the work. When work is exhilarating, it may also reduce or neutralize the impact of more negatively assessed properties of work. For example, when the worker finds an element of excitement in doing the work, heavy workload and dangerous work will not seem as onerous.

In addition, exhilarating work may moderate the relationship between known stressors and strain either by buffering the impact or by serving as a coping mechsnism. Buffering (House, 1981) occurs when the relationship between a stressor and a strain is not significant in the presence of the buffering dimension but is significant in the absence of the buffering dimension. That is, workload may not be related to burnout when the work is exhilarating but will be related to burnout when the job offers little excitement. Lazarus and Folkman (1984), in their model of coping, suggest that individuals cognitively appraise situations to determine whether they represent threat or challenge. The exhilarating work concept may reflect a cognitive appraisal of work as challenge rather than threat and, therefore, facilitate coping with the situation. A coping effect of exhilarating work will be reflected in a stronger relationship between exhilarating work and strains when workload is heavy and danger is high than in the case of lower workload and less danger.

Two affective responses to work generally thought to capture important components of the worker's experience are job satisfaction and burnout. Job satisfaction refers to the affective response to the overall assessment of the job. Exhilarating work, because it is a positively valued characteristic of the task, was expected to be associated with increased satisfaction and to buffer the impact of more negative dimensions of work on strain. That is, if the job is described as exhilarating, the impact of workload and danger on satisfaction will not be as great as when work is not exciting.

Burnout, a strain often experienced by helping professionals, reflects an emotional and psychological state characterized by emotional exhaustion (feelings of being used up), reduced sense of personal accomplishment, and depersonalization of patients. The stimulation of exciting work was expected to result in lower levels of burnout and to provide a way of coping with heavy workload and dangerous work. That is, the role of exhilarating work will be more pronounced when the workload is high and the work is dangerous. At those points, nurses will appraise their situation and decide that even though the work is stressful it is exciting and that makes coping with the stressors possible.

Method

Participants

Respondents were 200 nurses employed at a regional veterans' medical center in the Southeastern United States. Thirty-four of the respondents were licensed practical nurses (LPNs), and 166 were registered nurses (RNs). Seventy-five percent of the respondents were between 36 and 55 years of age, with a median nursing tenure of 18 years. A subgroup of this sample (100 nurses) was derived from those who provided information about the specific unit on which they work. Twenty units of the 23 in the hospital were represented in the reduced sample, with nine as the high number for one unit and one as the minimum for each unit. This group did not differ significantly from the total group on any of the study variables, except that they were slightly older than the total sample.

Procedure

The 300 nurses who received survey packets containing a 37-page question-naire, a letter, and instructions from the researchers represented a randomly selected stratified sample of the 600 nurses employed by the hospital. The nurses knew that a study had been approved by the Institutional Review Board and were encouraged by their supervisors to participate. The 200 completed surveys, representing a 67% response rate, were returned to a central location. There was no way to identify respondents. Because of missing data on some variables, some analyses were based on 180 responses. Respondents used self-selected codes for identification and were promised feedback on their own scores on selected variables, along with comparative data from other samples.

Measures

Stressors. Stressors included exhilarating work, perceived physical danger, emotional danger, enriched work, workload, and objectively measured physical danger. Reliabilities reported, except where noted, were calculated using Cronbach's alpha.

Exhilarating work was assessed using a 7-item scale (see Table 1 for items) developed for this study to ascertain to what extent there were exciting, exhilarating, status-enhancing qualities in the job itself. Cronbach's alpha for the exhilarating work scale was .83. Perceived physical danger was measured using a 6-item scale developed by Jermier et al. (1989). The items refer to the amount of danger in the job itself. Reliability of the scale in this sample was .75. The 16-item emotional-danger scale (Jermier, McIntosh, & Gaines, unpublished) was specifically designed to inquire about exposure to pain, suffering, and tragedy in the job itself. Cronbach's alpha for the scale was .90. All of these scales were written with the intent that the job and not the response to it would be the referent for description. Enriched work was measured using

Table 1. Varimax-Rotated Factor Loadings for Representative-Task Characteristics

	Factor			
Item	I EMD	II EXJ	III PPD	IV TMP
My work involves dealing with tragedy.	.7728			
On my job, I observe suffering or pain.	.6926			
My work gives me a sense of anticipation		.7952		
My work provides a sense of excitement.		.7510		
My work can be exhilarating.		.7375		
My work gives me energy.		.7140		
My work helps keep me going psychologically.		.6703		
My work has a certain amount of glamour in the eyes of others.		.5787		
My job is risky, but that's part of why it's important.		.4430	.4433	
My job is physically dangerous.			.7926	
I am *directly* exposed to physical harm in carrying out my job.			.7805	
How much *autonomy* is there in your job?				.5261
In general, how significant or important is your job?				.5234

Note. EMD = emotion danger; EXJ = exhilarating job; PPD = perceived physical danger; TMP = task-motivating potential.

Hackman and Oldham's (1976) 15-item task-motivating potential scale score, which examines the extent to which the job has task identity, significance, autonomy, variety, and provides feedback. Reliability of the scale was .73. Workload, the amount and difficulty of tasks, and the availability of resources for doing them was measured using four items developed by Quinn and Shepard (1974). Cronbach's alpha for the scale in this sample was .80.

Objective physical danger, used in the reduced-sample analyses only, was measured with ratings assigned independently by five nurses familiar with all units but not assigned to a specific unit of the hospital. A 5-point scale, ranging from *almost no danger* to *a great deal of danger*, was used to rate each unit. Interrater reliability, evaluated using the Kendall coefficient of concordance, was significant ($p < .00$).

Strains. Job satisfaction, an indicator of general affective response to a job, was measured with the 20-item short form of the Minnesota Satisfaction Questionnaire (Weiss, Dawis, England, & Lofquist, 1966). Burnout was measured with the 22-item Maslach Burnout Inventory (Maslach & Jackson, 1981). Reliabilities were .89 for satisfaction and .81 for burnout.

Analyses

Means, standard deviations, reliabilities, and intercorrelations were calculated for all study variables, followed by analyses to explore whether exhilarating work is a discreet task characteristic that mediates the relationship between objectively measured danger and strain, has a main effect on strain in addition

to the impact of previously identified stressors, buffers the relationship between stressors and strain, and is used as a coping mechanism. In all regression
analyses, organizational tenure was held constant, and pairwise deletion of
missing data was specified.

Exhilarating work as a task characteristic. To determine whether exhilarating work is a distinct characteristic of the task, items from the exhilarating-work, enriched-work, physical-danger, and emotional-danger scales were
subjected to principal-components analysis with varimax rotation and four
factors specified.

Exhilarating work as a mediator. Hierarchical regression analyses were
used to determine whether the pattern of both a direct and an indirect effect
of objectively measured work found in earlier studies (Jermier et al., 1989;
McIntosh & Atkins, 1991) was replicated in this study and whether exhilarating work as well as perceived danger mediates the relationship of objective
danger to strain.

In separate equations (Figure 1), perceived physical danger and exhilarating work were regressed on objective physical danger. Then, to assess direct
and indirect effects of objective danger, the strains were regressed on objective
danger and perceived physical danger. Finally, to determine whether exhilarating work accounted for a significant portion of the strain-reducing effect
of objective physical danger, burnout and job satisfaction were regressed on
exhilarating work, controlling for objective danger and perceived physical danger. A mediating effect of exhilarating work would be indicated by a positive
relationship in the first model between objective danger and exhilarating work
and a reduced impact of objective danger when exhilarating work was added as
a predictor with objective danger and perceived danger statistically controlled.

Direct effect of exhilarating work. A hierarchical regression procedure was
used to determine whether exhilarating work has a direct effect on strain in
addition to the effect of previously known stressors. Holding tenure constant,
physical danger, emotional danger, and enriched work were entered as the
first block of predictors, workload as the second, and exhilarating work as the
third. A significant relationship between exhilarating work and strain, with
the other predictors statistically controlled, indicates a direct effect of exhilarating work.

Buffering effect of exhilarating work. Subgroup analysis was used to test
for buffering effects of exhilarating work. The sample was divided into subgroups on the basis of high and low scores on workload, emotional danger, and
perceived danger. Job satisfaction and burnout were regressed on exhilarating
work in each subgroup. A significant relationship between exhilarating work
and strain in the low-stressor subgroup is indicative of a buffering effect.

Coping effects of exhilarating work. To test for coping effects of exhilarating
work, the sample was divided into subgroups on the basis of high and low

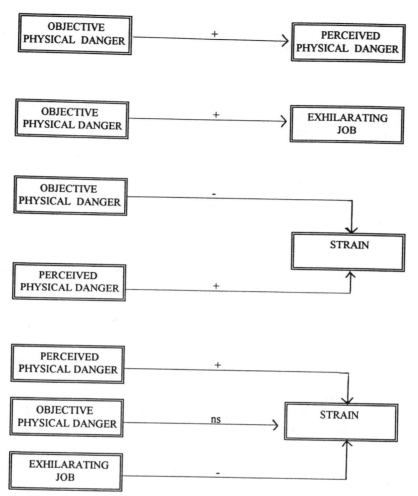

Figure 1. Expected relationships if both perceived danger and exhilarating job mediate the relationship of objective danger to strain.

scores on exhilarating work. In each subgroup, job satisfaction and emotional
exhaustion were regressed on emotional danger, physical danger, and workload. A significant relationship between stressor and strain in the low, but not
the high, exhilarating-work subgroup indicates the use of exhilarating work
as a coping mechanism.

Results

Descriptive statistics, including means, standard deviations, actual and possible scale ranges, and reliabilities, are reported in Table 2. Neither the low
scores on job satisfaction nor the very high scores on the burnout scale appeared
in this sample, which indicates moderately restricted range for these strains.

Table 2. Means, Standard Deviations, Possible and Actual Ranges, and Sample Size

Variable	M	SD	Possible range	Actual range	n
1. Perceived physical danger (PPD) (6 items)	16.79	4.59	6–30	7–29	198
2. Emotional danger (EMD)	43.92	10.74	16–80	24–79	191
3. Exhilarating job (EXJ) (7 items)	23.89	5.05	7–35	7–35	195
4. Task-motivating potential (TMP) (15 items)	172.47	64.35	1–343	23–343	193
5. Workload (WKLOAD) (4 items)	14.43	2.84	4–20	6–2	195
6. Job satisfaction (JOBSAT) (20 items)	75.99	9.18	20–100	43–98	197
7. Burnout (MBI) (22 items)	30.65	16.45	0–132	5–7	193

Correlations (Table 3) do not suggest excessive multicollinearity among predictor variables.

Exhilarating work as a task characteristic. Factor analysis (see Table 1 for representative items) revealed, as expected, that exhilarating work is a task characteristic that is statistically and conceptually distinct from physical danger and emotional danger and from enriched work. Emotional-danger items made up the first factor, explaining 7.7% of the common variance. Exhilarating job items loaded as a second factor, explaining 12.2% of common variance. Task-variety items loaded on the exhilarating-work factor, suggesting that variety contributes to the excitement of work.

Exhilarating work as a mediator. Objectively measured danger explained 5% of variance in perceived physical danger, $F(2, 90) = 6.85, p < .01$, and 6% of the variance in exhilarating job, $F(2, 90) = 6.08, p < .05$. As in earlier studies, perceived physical danger was negatively related to job satisfaction, $F(3, 89) = 5.26, p < .05$, and objective physical danger was positively related

Table 3. Bivariate Correlations of All Variables

Scale	1	2	3	4	5	6	7
1. PPD	—						
2. EMD	.322	—					
3. EXJ	−.092	−.013	—				
4. TMP	−.297	−.039	.338	—			
5. WKLOAD	−.025	.201	.034	.064	—		
6. JOBSAT	−.181	−.047	.453	.566	.091	—	
7. MBI	.153	.301	−.357	−.341	.256	−.454	—

Note. PPD = perceived physical danger; EMD = emotional danger; EXJ = exhilarating job; TMP = task-motivating potential; WKLOAD = workload; JOBSAT = job satisfaction; MBI = burnout.
$p \le .01$, if $r \ge .25$. $p \le .05$, if $r \ge .20$.

Table 4. Regression of Burnout and Job Satisfaction on Task Characteristics, Workload, and Exhilarating Job

	Strain			
	Burnout		Job satisfaction	
Stressor	β	F	β	F
Tenure	−.07	1.31	−.01	0.02
PPD	−.03	0.17	−.00	0.00
EMD	.25	13.79***	−.04	0.32
TMP	−.26	13.91***	.46	49.41***
WKLOAD	.23	13.34***	.06	0.92
EXJ	−.29	18.09***	.30	22.09***
	$R^2 = .30$***		$R^2 = .38$***	

Note. N = 180; PPD = perceived physical danger; EMD = emotional danger; TMP = task-motivating potential; WKLOAD = workload; EXJ = exhilarating job.
*$p \le .05$. **$p \le .01$. ***$p \le .001$.

to job satisfaction, $F(3, 89) = 4.47$, $p < .05$. Perceived physical danger was positively related to burnout, $F(3, 89) = 4.10$, $p < .05$, and objective danger was negatively related to burnout, $F(3, 89) = 4.84$, $p < .05$. Perceived and objective danger explained 4% of variance in both job satisfaction and burnout.

When exhilarating job was added to the models, objective danger was not significantly related to job satisfaction, perceived physical danger remained a significant predictor of reduced job satisfaction, $F(4, 88) = 17.58$, and exhilarating job was a significant predictor of increased satisfaction, $F(4, 88) = 17.58$, $p < .001$. Neither objective nor perceived danger continued to be significantly related to burnout when exhilarating job, $F(4, 88) = 9.10$, $p < .01$, was added to the model. The full model explained an additional 8% of variance in burnout and 10% of variance in satisfaction beyond that explained by perceived and objective danger alone. The results demonstrate that exhilarating work does mediate the relationship between objective physical danger and strain.

Direct effects of exhilarating work. The regression of job satisfaction and burnout (Table 4) on emotional danger, perceived physical danger, task-motivating potential, workload, and exhilarating job revealed that exhilarating work does explain variance in strains beyond that explained by previously identified stressors. The three task characteristics and workload, which were forced to enter the regression model before exhilarating work, explained 23% of the variance in burnout. Task-motivating potential was related to reduced burnout, $F(6, 173) = 13.91$, $p < .001$. Emotional danger, $F(6, 173) = 13.79$, $p < .001$, and workload, $F(6, 173) = 13.34$, $p < .001$, were positively related to burnout. With the other stressors held constant, exhilarating work was related to reduced burnout, $F(1, 178) = 13.74$, $p < .000$, explaining an additional 7% of variance in burnout.

Perceived physical danger, emotional danger, task-motivating potential, and workload explained 31% of the variance in job satisfaction. Task-moti-

Table 5. Buffering Analysis: Relationship of Stressors to Strain in High and Low Exhilarating-Job Subgroups

	Burnout							
	High exhilarating job				Low exhilarating job			
Subgroups Predictor	β	F	R^2	n	β	F	R^2	n
PPD	.14	1.33	.01	67	.13	1.49	.00	91
EMD	.23	3.38	.02	67	.37	13.73***	.12***	89
WKLOAD	.28	5.48*	.05	67	.20	3.68*	.02	91

	Job satisfaction							
	High exhilarating job				Low exhilarating job			
Subgroups Predictor	β	F	R^2	n	β	F	R^2	n
PPD	$-.39$	12.07***	.14**	69	$-.01$	-0.01	.01	93
EMD	$-.04$	0.12	.02	68	$-.02$	0.01	.02	89
WKLOAD	.10	0.69	.01	68	.12	1.29	.00	91

Note. Twelve regression equations were specified. *n*s within subgroups differ because of missing data. *n* totals less than sample because median scores were not included in either subgroup. PPD = perceived physical danger; EMD = emotional danger; WKLOAD = workload.
$*p \leq .05.$ $**p \leq .01.$ $***p \leq .001.$

vating potential was positively related to job satisfaction, $F(6, 173) = 49.41$, $p < .001$. With other task characteristics and workload held constant, exhilarating work was significantly and positively related to job satisfaction, $F(1, 178) = 19.34$, $p < .000$, and explained an additional 7% of variance.

Interaction of exhilarating work with stressors. Subgroup analysis (Table 5) of effects of exhilarating work revealed only one buffering relationship: Emotional danger was significantly related to burnout when the job was not exhilarating, $F(2, 86) = 13.73$, $p < .001$, but unrelated when the job was exhilarating. In addition, perceived physical danger was related to satisfaction when the job was exhilarating, $F(2, 90) = 12.97$, $p < .001$, but not in the absence of exhilarating work. Subgroup analyses for coping (Table 6) revealed that exhilarating work aided in coping with the impact of heavy workload on burnout and job satisfaction.

Summary of results. Analyses revealed that in this sample exhilarating work is a task characteristic that is distinct from enriched work, physical danger, and emotional danger and is a mediator variable through which objectively measured physical danger is related to reduced burnout and increased job satisfaction. In addition to its mediating effect, exhilarating work contributes to reduced burnout and increased satisfaction beyond the effects of other known stressors. Exhilarating work buffers the relationship between emotional danger and burnout and assists in coping with workload.

Table 6. Coping Analysis: Relationship of Exhilarating Job to Strain in High and Low Stressor Subgroups

| | Burnout | | | | | | | |
| | High stressors | | | | Low stressors | | | |
Stressor	β	F	R^2	n	β	F	R^2	n
PPD	−.35	12.31***	.10**	94	−.38	12.94***	.13**	74
EMD	−.32	8.51**	.09*	76	−.46	21.84**	.20**	89
WKLOAD	−.30	5.47*	.07*	59	−.35	8.27**	.12**	64

| | Job satisfaction | | | | | | | |
| | High stressors | | | | Low stressors | | | |
Stressor	β	F	R^2	n	β	F	R^2	n
PPD	.40	17.44***	.14***	96	.53	28.26***	.27***	74
EMD	.43	17.02***	.16***	80	.52	29.02***	.24***	89
WKLOAD	.35	7.80**	.10*	59	.49	18.49***	.21***	65

Note. Twelve regressions were specified. *n*s within subgroups differ because of missing data. *n* totals less than sample size because median scores were not included in either subgroup. PPD = perceived physical danger; EMD = emotional danger; WKLOAD = workload.
*$p \leq .05$. **$p \leq .01$. ***$p \leq .001$.

Discussion

Understanding dangerous work has become increasingly important to organizational researchers as the implications of modern technologies and exposure to emotionally threatening work situations are being recognized. Exhilarating work has been suggested as an important and previously unmeasured characteristic of work useful for understanding and predicting the impact of danger as well as other stressors at work.

Certainly, care needs to be taken to avoid overinterpreting these results because all data except the objective-danger measure were provided by respondents on a single instrument, providing potential for common-method variance, and the cross-sectional nature of the data mandates caution in inferring cause–effect relationships. However, the relatively modest correlations between variables that are somewhat similar seem to suggest a minimum of common-method variance, and earlier longitudinal studies have suggested that there is a causal relationship between the more frequently investigated stressors and strains included in the study. Even with some caution in interpretation, the data provide some interesting insights.

Having work that is exciting provides some anticipation, energy, and exhilaration and is perceived by others to have some glamour has a variety of positive implications for the worker. First, exhilarating work is experienced as conceptually and empirically distinct from other perceived work dimensions, including emotional and physical danger and the motivating potential of the job. Second, the impact of exhilarating work is robust: As one of many dimensions in the complex of task characteristics, it has a direct and positive effect on affective responses to work regardless of other facets of the work. Third, exhilarating work has a moderating effect, buffering the relationship between emotional danger and burnout and serving as a coping mechanism when nurses are faced with heavy workload. Finally, although exhilarating work moderates the impact of dangerous work on experiences of burnout, high levels of danger and high levels of excitement in work interacted in this sample to produce lower levels of satisfaction.

The study results represent another piece in the puzzle of understanding the dynamic that previous empirical and ethnographic research has suggested: Work that is dangerous is perceived to have both a negative and a positive component. Perceived physical danger reflects the negative interpretation of dangerous work, and exhilarating work captures the positive aspects of objectively dangerous work, as demonstrated by the fact that the relationship of objective danger to burnout was reduced to nonsignificance when exhilarating job was also included in the regression model.

Several theoretical perspectives may help explain the fact that dangerous work is fear-inducing and threatening to workers and, at the same time, a source of exhilaration, excitement, glamour, and prestige. A number of researchers (e.g., Farid & Lirtzman, 1991; Viscusi, 1979) have suggested that the negative impact of dangerous work is offset by the fact that the market reflects the extent of danger to the worker in the economic-compensation scale. Perhaps the increased reward adds glamour to the job in the eye of the worker who perceives that this is also true as others view the work. However, this perspective alone cannot account for the fact that dangerous work has a mixed impact on worker affect because many kinds of work that are objectively very dangerous (e.g., commercial fishing and construction) provide primarily low-paying jobs.

Another perspective on dangerous work suggests that certain personality types may enjoy dangerous work, thus serving as moderators of the dangerous job–affective response relationship. Farley (1986) suggested that in addition to Type A and Type B personalities, there is a Type T (thrill-seeking) personality. He posited that personality exists on a continuum from those who actively seek thrills to those who avoid risk and stimulation. He further asserted that the thrill-seeking personality may seek either mental or physical stimulation, both of which may contribute to either creative or destructive behavior to society, depending on the type of stimulation sought. Although previous studies examining other (primarily demographic) individual-differences factors have not been particularly useful (Farid & Lirtzman, 1991), exploration of the Type T personality concept merits exploration.

Another perspective is the concept of "edgework" discussed by Lyng (1990) as a means of understanding voluntary risk taking. Lyng suggested that edgework—carried out on the border between order and chaos and reflecting both psychological and contextual factors—provides workers in dangerous occupations a sensation of being in control and permits demonstrating important survival skills. This mechanism seems similar to descriptions given by critical-care nurses of their feelings about their work in times of emergency. Recognizing the importance of both individual sensations and feelings and the political economic factors involved in the dynamic of dangerous working situations reflects the complexity of the experience and should be investigated further.

It is suggested that future research on the mixed impact of dangerous work concentrate on exploration of theoretical perspectives that illuminate the meaning of dangerous work to those who engage in it. Among questions to be answered are whether it is perceived by the worker to be voluntary risk taking, whether the exhilaration is directly associated with the doing of the work or is mediated by economic or other factors, and whether the interpretation of dangerous work is contingent on individual differences. Inquiry into response to dangerous work in occupations that have not been "professionalized" and may not have developed a romanticized social construction of danger, as has apparently occurred in policing and nursing, should provide further enlightenment about the mechanisms by which dangerous work is or is not considered exciting.

In addition, the concept of exhilarating work itself merits further exploration. For example, one effect of the renewed emphasis on productivity, which by definition requires more work of fewer people, has been an increase in stress-related illness and behavior. If, as jobs are redesigned, they are made more exciting without concurrently increasing perceptions of danger, some of these symptoms may be avoided. This requires further examination of factors that make work exhilarating.

References

Brody, J. (1988). Responses to collective risk: Appraisal and coping among workers exposed to occupational health hazards. *American Journal of Community Psychology, 16*, 645–663.

Farid, M., & Lirtzman, S. (1991). Effects of hazard warning on workers' attitudes and risk-taking behavior. *Psychological Reports, 68*, 659–673.

Farley, F. (1986, May). The big T in personality. *Psychology Today*, pp. 44–52.

Hackman, J., & Oldham, G. (1975). Development of the Job Diagnostic Survey. *Journal of Applied Psychology, 60*, 159–170.

Hackman, J., & Oldham, G. (1976). Motivation through the design of work: Test of a theory. *Journal of Applied Psychology, 55*, 259–286.

House, J. (1981). *Work stress and social support.* Reading, MA: Addison-Wesley.

House, J., Wells, J., Landerman, L., McMichael, A. & Kaplan, B. (1979). Occupational stress and health among factory workers. *Journal of Health and Social Behavior, 20*, 139–160.

Jermier, J., Gaines, J., & McIntosh, N. (1989). Reactions to physically dangerous work: A conceptual and empirical analysis. *Journal of Organizational Behavior, 10*, 15–33.

Karasek, R. (1979). Job demand, job decision latitude, and mental strain: Implications for job redesign. *Administrative Science Quarterly, 24*, 285–307.

Lazarus, R., & Folkman, S. (1984). *Stress, appraisal and coping.* New York: Springer.

Lyng, S. (1990). Edgework: A social psychological analysis of voluntary risk taking. *American Journal of Sociology, 95*, 851–886.

Maslach, C., & Jackson, S. (1981). The measurement of experienced burnout. *Journal of Occupational Behavior, 2*, 99–113.

McIntosh, N. (1984). *The relationship of client characteristics to burnout among helping professionals.* Unpublished doctoral dissertation, University of Florida, Tallahassee.

McIntosh, N., & Atkins, L. (1991, August). *The relationship of danger at work to affective responses of nurses.* Paper presented at the Academy of Management National Meeting, Miami.

McIntosh, N., Gaines, J., & Jermier, J. (1989, August). *Organizational determinants of dangerous work: An emerging social issue*. Paper presented at the Academy of Management National Meeting, Washington, DC.

Quinn, R., & Shepard, L. (1974). *The 1972–1973 Quality of Employment Survey*. Ann Arbor: Survey Research Center Institute for Social Research, University of Michigan.

Reiss, A., Jr. (1971). *The police and the public*. New Haven, CT: Yale University Press.

VanManaan, J. (1974). Working the street: A developmental view of police behavior. In H. Jacobs (Ed.), *Annual review of criminal justice: The potential for reform* (Vol 3, pp. 83–130). Newbury Park, CA: Sage.

Viscusi, W. (1979). Job hazards and worker quit rates: An analysis of worker adaptive behavior. *Industrial Labor Relations Review, 20*, 29–58.

Weiss, D., Dawis, R., England, G., & Lofquist, L. (1966). *Manual for the Minnesota Satisfaction Questionnaire* (Minnesota Studies in Vocational Rehabilitation: 23). Minneapolis: University of Minnesota, Industrial Relations Center.

IDENTIFYING RISK FACTORS FOR JOB STRESS

Part V

Methodological Developments

Introduction

Perhaps one of the most visible—if not most important—methodological concerns in the study of job stress today is the suitability of methods for assessing workers' exposures to suspected risk factors in the workplace. The most common technique is to seek worker self-reports of working conditions with a questionnaire survey. This part's first two chapters, by Schonfeld, Rhee, and Xia and by Chen, Spector, and Jex, recount and demonstrate the hazards of this approach, showing how such reports are subject to contamination by dispositional factors such as negative affectivity and by emotional response to the job itself, including degree of job satisfaction. The result increased the opportunity for confounding or inflation of presumed cause–effect relationships in stress research. This problem can be exacerbated by common method variance in cross-sectional study designs that use self-report measures of health outcomes or by conceptual–semantic overlap between independent and dependent measures. For these reasons, Chen and colleagues express considerable reservation about the use of individual-level perceptions of working conditions in job-stress research, asserting that such information tells more about the worker than the job and calling for increased use of multimethod and longitudinal study designs to overcome these problems. The Schonfeld et al. chapter expresses similar concerns and provides specific suggestions for minimizing these problems but notes that even longitudinal study designs may not fully prevent contamination of job ratings by dispositional factors. These suggestions are timely and important, recognizing that questionnaire methodologies are unlikely to be abandoned given their expediency in public health research (not to mention problems associated with more "objective" assessments of working conditions, which are beyond the scope of the current discussion).

The chapter by Carayon extends the discussion of exposure assessment to an important subject that has received insufficient attention in job-stress research. Specifically, Carayon notes that metrics for most rating scales of job attributes do not enable an assessment of chronicity or accumulated exposure. Carayon presents data showing that for some job characteristics, such as controllability, chronic exposures are considerably more important than acute or episodic exposures in determining risks for negative health outcomes. Although this effect seems to be intuitive and implicit in stress research, Carayon's analyses suggest that for some factors such as work pressure, acute exposure is as salient as chronic exposure in eliciting adverse mood effects.

The concluding chapter by Adelmann contributes to the present discussion by providing a psychometric method for assessing emotional labor (need to actively manage one's emotions), a construct that is capturing increasing attention as a risk factor for job stress. Adelmann operationalizes emotional labor in a manner applicable to most forms of human-service work and explores its relationship with a variety of other job characteristics and with job satisfaction.

21

Methodological Issues in Occupational-Stress Research: Research in One Occupational Group and Wider Applications

Irvin S. Schonfeld, Jaesoon Rhee, and Fang Xia

The purpose of this chapter is to address a number of important methodologic issues that are relevant to occupational-stress researchers. The issues addressed have arisen in the context of an ongoing research program involving cross-sectional and longitudinal studies of stress in teachers; the issues, however, apply to occupational research in general. The first issue involves measurement strategies required in operationalizing the stress process. The focal concern of this section of the chapter is the reduction of confounding in measures of the work environment. The second issue encompasses the question of whether to sample new or veteran workers. In some circumstances there are advantages to research designs in which new workers are sampled. The third issue applies to types of job stressors. The discussion of the three issues coalesce in a section describing a study of confounding in measures of various occupational stressors encountered by new teachers. Finally, some of the wider implications of reducing confounding are discussed.

A supplementary issue bearing on a great deal of the occupational-stress literature, including the literature on teachers, has been the largely cross-sectional nature of study designs. From the standpoint of developing causal models of the effects of working conditions, cross-sectional designs are very weak. The chapter speaks to the necessity of longitudinal designs in occupational-stress research.

Operationalizing the Stress Process

A problem in much of the literature on teachers has been the absence of a satisfactory conceptualization of the stress process. Many investigators have

Preparation of this chapter was supported by NIOSH/CDC grants 1 01 OH02571 and PSC-CUNY Award Program grants 6-67401, 6-68419, 669416, and 661251. We thank Mark Davies, Edwin Farrell, and Pearl Knopf for their comments on an earlier version of this chapter.

conceptualized stress as an overly inclusive construct embracing both the working conditions that are suspected of provoking psychological distress and the distress those conditions are thought to provoke (DeFrank & Stroup, 1989; Dunham, 1984; Farber, 1984; Fimian & Santoro, 1983; Galloway, Panckhurst, Boswell, Boswell, & Green, 1984; Gold, 1985; Kyriacou & Sutcliffe, 1978, 1979; Maslach & Jackson, 1981; Needle, Griffen, & Svendsen, 1981; Seiler & Pearson, 1984). A commonly used stress questionnaire having an item structure that reflects this blurring of independent and dependent variables comes from Kyriacou and Sutcliffe (1978, 1979): "As a teacher, how great a source of stress are these factors? Inadequate disciplinary policy of school; Pupils' poor attitudes to work" (pp. 159–160). Another problem with the items is that they provide no information on the extent or duration of the exposures.

In a different sense burnout scales (Fimian, 1983; Gold, 1984, 1985; Iwanicki & Schwab, 1981; Johnson, Gold, & Knepper, 1984; Malanowski & Wood, 1984; Maslach & Jackson, 1981, 1984; Meier, 1984; Zabel & Zabel, 1982) also confound presumed cause and effect (see Schonfeld, 1990a, 1992a, 1992b, in press). Burnout scales are typically used with helping professionals. Burnout involves the attribution to one's job of a syndrome centered on feelings of psychological exhaustion, a poor sense of personal accomplishment, and the depersonalizing of the individuals whom the professional is supposed to serve. Schonfeld (in press) adduced evidence from the published literature to indicate that burnout lacks construct validity. He showed that burnout measures cover much the same ground as well-validated depressive symptom scales and that there is evidence to suggest that depression and burnout are operationally redundant.

A related problem is that cross-sectional correlations of (a) stress scales with measures of distress and (b) burnout scales with measures of job conditions are likely to be overestimates because stress and burnout measures— albeit to different degrees—include items that refer to both difficulties at work and the distress engendered by those difficulties (a problem relating to lagged correlations is discussed later). Teacher-stress measures (e.g., Fimian & Santoro, 1983), vulnerable to similar overestimation errors, ask respondents to indicate how bothered or annoyed they are by various school and classroom conditions.

Stressor-Rating Scales

Some measures of occupational (and nonoccupational) stress in other samples of working people require respondents to indicate if a condition occurred and to rate its impact, positively or negatively, on a Likert-type scale (e.g., Bhagat, McQuaid, Lindholm, & Segovis, 1985; Brief, Burke, George, Robinson, & Webster, 1988). Occupational-stress scales are created by summing the negative ratings on various work-related conditions. These scales, however, are open to confounding with preexisting distress. Respondents are also vulnerable to attribution errors (Cohen, Karmarck, & Mermelstein, 1983). Procedures that have respondents identify conditions by their stressful consequences are better suited for pilot or exploratory research than for research on the etiologic significance of stress (Schonfeld, 1992a).

Negative Affectivity

The problem of confounding is also underlined in the personality literature. Watson and Clark (1984) adduced evidence for the view that negative affectivity (NA) is a major dimension of personality. NA is a stable disposition toward a dysphoric mood that permeates much of the individual's attitudes and behavior. Long-term psychological distress may be reasonably characterized as NA. For example, NA is highly related to measures of depressive symptoms (e.g., Brief et al., 1988). NA is likely to color an individual's evaluation of perceived stress (Watson & Pennebaker, 1989). Brief et al. (1988) found that NA is confounded with typical measures of work and nonwork stress and distorts the zero-order relation between stress and distress. Work-environment scales comprising "How stressed are you?" types of items or summated stressor-rating scales such as the ones described above (e.g., Bhagat et al., 1985; Brief et al., 1988) tap NA and thus are likely to overestimate cross-sectional correlations with measures of current distress.

Reducing Confounding

Kasl (1978, 1987) suggested that one way to minimize circularity in measuring occupational stress is to banish the stress concept. In place of measuring occupational stress, an investigator would do better to obtain independently measures of the hypothesized adverse environmental exposures (i.e., the stressors) and current psychological distress (e.g., depressive symptoms). The advantage of this conceptualization of the stress process is that the independent and dependent variables are kept distinct. From a public-health standpoint, it is important to be able to alter identifiable exposures that may affect the well-being of workers (Kasl, 1987). When stress measures become too subjective or if the independent and dependent variables are blurred, the targets of remedial actions become less identifiable.

An independent measure of psychological distress. In two studies, one of veteran teachers (Schonfeld, 1990a, 1990b) and the other of newly appointed teachers (Schonfeld 1992a, 1992b), stressors and outcomes were measured independently. Psychological morbidity, an important outcome variable, was measured with the Center for Epidemiologic Studies-Depression Scale (CES-D; Radloff, 1977; Weissman, Sholomskas, Pottenger, Prusoff, & Locke, 1977), a depressive symptom scale that makes no reference to working conditions. The CES-D has two other advantages. First, normative landmark scores are well-known from general-population surveys (Schonfeld, 1990b). Second, it can be used for the purpose of psychiatric case finding (see Schonfeld, 1992a).

Neutral self-reports. Adverse working conditions, the stressors, were measured with neutrally worded self-report items. Consistent with Kasl's (1983) critique of existing self-report stress instruments, a strategy was employed in which the items used to assess school-related conditions were worded with a minimum of reference to the distress they have been hypothesized to cause (e.g., "You encountered students involved in a fight ... not at all, once per month, once per week, 2–4 times per week, daily"). In addition, items were written to minimize the amount of inference making required by the teacher incumbents (e.g., "You were assaulted by a student or an intruder? No, Yes"). Later in this chapter, we evaluate the potential for confounding with preexisting psychological distress, the neutrally worded self-reports on school conditions that newly appointed teachers encounter.

Objective data. One source of objective, external measures of working conditions is the *Dictionary of Occupational Titles* (*DOT*; U.S. Department of Labor, 1965). The *DOT* provides average values on work characteristics across job titles. Measures such as the *DOT*, however, are better suited for between- than for within-occupations research. Other types of objective measures may be sought for within-occupations designs. In one of the within-teachers studies, data obtained from the reports of teachers who work in New York City public schools will eventually be linked to officially collected records of assaults, larcenies, and sex offenses against teachers. One of us reported elsewhere (Schonfeld, 1992b), however, that such so-called objective measures have deficiencies including lack of candor on the part of administrators reporting on violence against teachers (also see Dillon, 1994).

Partitioning the sample. A complementary strategy that can reduce confounding between measures of stress and distress, in longitudinal research, is to limit samples to individuals who, initially, are relatively undistressed. Depue and Monroe (1986) advanced the view that individuals who are high and low in psychological symptoms represent different populations and should therefore be examined separately in research linking risk factors to later distress. In an investigation of social support in women making the transition from college to work, Schonfeld (1991) limited a number of his longitudinal analyses to women whose symptom scores at the beginning of the study suggested that they were initially free of high levels of distress. He found that social companionship was more strongly (and inversely) related to later symptoms when women who initially were highly symptomatic were excluded from the sample than when no exclusionary criteria were imposed. This finding was not merely an artifact of reduced variance in the covariate owing to the exclusionary criteria. Three other social support measures—tangible, appraisal, and self-esteem support scales—were unrelated to future symptoms whether highly symptomatic women were excluded from the analyses.

By also examining subsamples of individuals who, initially, are relatively more highly distressed, two other important research questions can be addressed. First, investigators can study the extent to which later job conditions aggravate or reduce preexisting distress. Of particular interest is the issue of identifying work environments that lead to a diminution of initial distress. Schonfeld (1992b) advanced the view that work environments that offer teachers a sense of control as well as physical safety will result in new lower levels of distress compared with preemployment baseline levels. More research on this issue, however, needs to be conducted.

Second, investigators, using longitudinal designs, can more generally study the relation of high levels of psychological distress or NA to health-related sequelae (cf. Vassend, 1989) and other outcomes. Research on NA has largely been cross sectional. Longitudinal designs could be used to examine the effects of preexisting psychological distress, either directly or in interaction with adverse job conditions, on later physical and mental health. Other outcomes worthy of study include the propensity to encounter, or overreport, adversity at the workplace.

Psychological distress should be treated as a variable to be studied in its own right, rather than as a mere nuisance variable that needs to be controlled before other, more interesting questions can be examined. What we do not want to lose sight of is the issue of how working conditions are related to temporal changes in psychological distress and a host of other aspects of health.

Studies of New and Veteran Workers

The general occupational-stress literature has relied heavily on veteran-worker samples. Longitudinal research on veteran workers is especially important when the effects of job conditions on incumbents are insidious and apparent only after many years of exposure. Selection into occupational categories is not likely to be a problem. In the context of slow, long-term effects of exposures and in the absence of self-selection by subclinical disease and other risk factors, longitudinal research on veteran-worker samples is particularly suited to the field of chronic-disease epidemiology.

Studies of veteran workers can be problematic when findings are susceptible to selection-based explanations. Compared with research on physical health, selection is a relatively more important problem in research linking working conditions to mental health because preemployment records of conditions such as depressive symptoms are less available than medical records with, say, preemployment blood pressures. Investigators often have little or no knowledge of the functioning of veteran workers before they obtained their jobs, making it difficult to determine if mental health problems in particular occupational groups resulted from exposures to adverse working conditions or if less healthy individuals selected themselves into occupational roles with ostensibly the most adverse exposures. Research with newly employed workers allows for a test of the selection hypothesis.

A related advantage of following new workers is the opportunity afforded for controlling confounding in measures of the work environment and psychological distress, provided new workers are evaluated before they assume their jobs and several times after. In his research on newly appointed teachers, Schonfeld (1992a, 1992b) used preemployment measures of depressive symptoms as a baseline against which to measure change in functioning. One component of the preemployment depressive symptoms measure is likely to be trait depression or NA (Watson & Clark, 1984), depending on the perspective (psychosocial epidemiologic or personality) of the investigator.

Importance of Preemployment Baseline Data

Longitudinal studies of new workers may be problematic without preemployment baseline measures. If, among new workers, the effects of the work-related exposures on distress occur relatively immediately after entry into the work role (an immediate-exposure effects model), longitudinal designs that begin after workers assume their new work roles are incapable of disentangling relations among work-environment factors and distress (this notion is also discussed below in the context of causal modeling). In an immediate-exposure effects model, a Time 1 correlation between the measures of the work environment and psychological distress may truly reflect a causal pathway from environment to distress; however, without preemployment baseline distress data, the Time 1 relation cannot be deciphered satisfactorily.

Moreover, within the framework of such a model, a partial regression coefficient assessing the relation of the Time 1 work environment to Time 2 psychological morbidity may underestimate the corrosive effects of poor working conditions when Time 1 symptoms are controlled. In the regression equation, controlling for Time 1 symptoms amounts to controlling for the unfolding causal process. In this model, elevations in Time 2 symptoms are the result of a process that developed at Time 1. For individuals who remain stably employed but encounter poor working conditions as soon as they commence work, Time 2 symptoms are high because (a) the symptom elevations originate at Time 1 with the relatively immediate impact of adverse features of the work environment, and (b) the bad environment is unremitting, maintaining the symptoms over time. Making sense of the process occurring at Time 1 is critical.

An example of an occupational group in which immediate work-environment effects are evident is teachers. Using preemployment symptom data, Schonfeld (1992b) adduced evidence that among new teachers the effects of adverse job conditions occur relatively soon after the teacher assumes her new work role. New female teachers who obtained jobs in the "best" and "worst" schools did not differ in preemployment depressive symptoms but did differ markedly in symptoms during the first months on the job. If much of the action of the work environment on distress occurs at Time 1 and endures through the worker's tenure on the job, without preemployment baseline data it may be difficult to discern effects even with two or more waves of data collection through the duration of employment. Teachers in well- and poorly run schools may differ from one another at Time 1 and Time 2; however, without the leverage afforded by Time 0 preemployment morbidity data, there will be little opportunity to rule out selection-based explanations of the differences in symptoms (through either self-selection or selection by administrative gatekeepers). More important, in the absence of Time 0 group differences in morbidity, large

Time 1 morbidity differences are more plausibly linked to Time 1 differences in working conditions.

Nursing (Parkes, 1982), social work (Satyamurti, 1981), and corrections (Cullen, Link, Wolfe, & Frank, 1985) are examples of other fields in which within-occupation stress research has been conducted. They are also apt contexts in which to conduct prospective research on new entrants into those fields. Prospective research would be aided by the inclusion of a preemployment data collection period if there is reason to suspect that working conditions exert immediate effects on incumbents. Parkes's (1982) work on nurses is exemplary because she (a) examined the same student nurses rotating through both medical and surgical units and (b) obtained prerotation baseline measures of psychological symptoms in addition to measures obtained during each of the two rotations. She found that work in medical wards was linked to marked increases in depressive symptoms and job dissatisfaction.

A disadvantage of the first author's (Schonfeld, 1990a, 1990b) study of veteran New York City teachers is that the sample was likely to overrepresent individuals who made successful adaptations to their jobs, despite the teachers' relatively high levels of depressive symptoms. The average experience of these teachers was 13 years. The teachers necessarily excluded from the sample because of attrition in the school system were likely to be the major casualties of job stress (cf. Kasl, 1983). These are the teachers who left the profession before the investigator recruited his sample. Thus, the study probably underestimated teacher distress. In response to the problems inherent in research with veteran workers, a later study (Schonfeld, 1991, 1992a, 1992b) followed newly appointed teachers and obtained key preemployment symptom data as well as data on expected job satisfaction.

Episodic and Ongoing Stressors

Some general life-stress investigators (e.g., Brown & Harris, 1978; Pearlin, Lieberman, Menaghan, & Mullan, 1981) underline the distinction between episodic and ongoing stressors; that distinction, however, is often absent in the occupational-stress literature. Stressful events are unscheduled, episodic, and undesirable (Dohrenwend, Krasnoff, Askenasy, & Dohrenwend, 1982; Pearlin et al., 1981). In Pearlin's terminology (Pearlin et al., 1981; Pearlin & Schooler, 1978), strains refer to enduring, threat-arousing problems (also see Brown & Harris, 1978).

To fully sample the array of stressful conditions teachers encounter, Schonfeld (1992a, 1992b) measured both events and strains, including a range of areas that are more or less problematic for teachers. For example, a fight erupting between students or an insult from a colleague would constitute a stressful event. An ongoing threat of involuntary transfer or excessive noise in the ambient environment would constitute a strain. In view of the above discussion of confounding in stress scales, we present findings bearing on the relation of work-related event and strain items to preemployment psychological symptoms and morale.

A Study of Confounding

As part of an ongoing longitudinal study of stress in newly appointed teachers, subject recruitment was conducted at several colleges with a history of staffing local school districts. Recruitment took place during the late winter and the spring in upper-level, senior-year education classes (1987 to 1990) that were identified by faculty and administrative informants as likely to include graduating seniors who would go on to obtain teaching jobs in the September following their graduation. The September following June and August graduations is ordinarily the month during which new teachers begin work. The college classes in which recruitment took place were classes students typically attend en route to obtaining teacher certification.

The teachers came from largely middle-class homes (average social class of origin as measured on the Hollingshead, 1974, scale was 2.7), 30% were married, and 77% were White. The mean age of the teachers was 27 years, which is consistent with national and local trends regarding the aging of the undergraduate population (Schonfeld & Ruan, 1991). To maximize stable differences in exposures to a variety of working conditions, the sample was limited to 198 women who were full-time teachers in the fall, remained full-time teachers in the same schools in the spring, and contributed the preemployment data described below. Past reports on this data set (Schonfeld, 1992a, 1992b) were limited to cohorts graduating before 1990 and to combined samples of full-time and part-time female teachers, including those who changed schools.

Participants completed questionnaires in the summer (preemployment period or Time 0), fall (Time 1), and spring (Time 2). At Times 0, 1, and 2 depressive symptoms (alpha $\geq$ .91 Time 0 to Time 2) were measured with the 20-item CES-D (Radloff, 1977; Weissman et al., 1977). At Time 0 expected job satisfaction was assessed with one Likert-type item ("Overall, how satisfied do you expect to be in the job you are about to get?") specially modified from the Quality of Employment Surveys (QES; Quinn & Staines, 1979). By contrast, at Times 1 and 2 a job-satisfaction scale was constructed from three Likert-type QES items (alphas = .78 and .74 at Time 1 and Time 2, respectively).

Three measures of teachers' working conditions consisted of neutrally worded self-report items administered at Time 1. The Teacher Event Inventory assessed the extent to which teachers encountered episodically occurring stressors (Schonfeld, 1990a, 1990b, 1992a, in press; Schonfeld & Ruan, 1991). The response alternatives for the event items were (0) *not at all*, (1) *once per month*, (2) *once per week*, (3) *2–4 times per week*, and (4) *daily*. The Teacher Strain Inventory assessed the extent to which teachers encountered ongoing difficulties (Schonfeld, 1990a, 1990b, 1992a, in press; Schonfeld & Ruan, 1991). The response alternatives for the strain items were (0) *not at all*, (1) *to a minimal extent*, (2) *to a small extent*, (3) *to a moderate extent*, and (4) *to a great extent*. To reduce the likelihood of response set, the event and strain items included positive conditions. The alpha coefficients for the event and strain scales created from these items were both .80. The Crime Inventory consisted of a series of yes–no items that assess whether teachers have been the victim of an assault or robbery in or near their school (Schonfeld, 1990a). In addition, assaults against teacher colleagues were also ascertained. A crime scale was created by counting the number of different types of crimes of which the respondent (or, in the case of one item, a colleague) was a victim.

Confounding in the Items

Among the full-time female teachers, we examined the relation of the Time 1 event, crime, and strain items to the preemployment (Time 0) CES-D. Three of the 22 event items attained conventional levels of significance (see Table 1 for a sample of the items). One of the eight crime items (excluding one item with no variance) was significantly related to prior depressive symptoms. Seven of the 32 strain items were significantly related to prior symptoms. Although the significant strain-related correlations tended to be small, averaging .17 (corrected for the direction of the coefficient), these tallies indicate that it was more difficult to develop unconfounded strain items than items that assess the occurrence of events and crimes.

The relation of the Time 1 event, crime, and strain items to the Time 0 expected job satisfaction measure was also examined. Two of the 22 event items were significantly related to Time 0 expected satisfaction. In contrast to the relations between the strain items and the Time-0 CES-D, 3 of the 32 strain items were related to Time 0 expected satisfaction. No crime item was related to expected satisfaction.

The findings show that it is practically impossible to obtain self-report measures of the work environment that are perfectly uncorrelated with prior depressive symptoms or prior expectations about work. The findings, however, indicate that work-environment measures that tap discrete events such as episodes of vandalism and the occurrence of crimes are somewhat less likely to be correlated with preemployment depressive symptoms than are measures of ongoing working conditions (strains).

Reprise of the Problem of Confounding

An explanation of the relation of the work-environment items to prior distress calls for a closer look at the event and strain items. The response alternatives for the strain items were *not at all, to a small extent, to a minimal extent, to a moderate extent,* and *to a great extent.* The response alternatives for the event items were *not at all, once per month, once per week, 2–4 times per week,* and *daily.* Compared with the strain items, the event items were more closely anchored to estimable frequencies. Although prior mental state could have colored the respondents' estimates of event frequencies, the strain items, with their more subjective extent alternatives, were more affected.

One would expect the response to the crime items to be the least confounded with prior depressive symptoms because self-knowledge of one's status as a crime victim is relatively unambiguous. It is of note that one of the crime items (property damage) was weakly, but significantly, related to prior depressive symptoms. Although it is possible that individuals who experienced

Table 1. The Item-Level Relation Between School Environment Measures and Preexisting Depressive Symptoms: Systematic Sample of Half the Items

Items	Correlation with preemployment depressive symptoms
Event items	
A student threatened you with personal injury	−.11
You were confronted by an insolent student	−.05
Materials or books you selected were disapproved by a supervisor	−.03
An episode of vandalism occurred in your class	.05
Several students failed to complete their classwork	.06
A student expressed appreciation for your teaching	.08
Several students failed to complete their homework	.02
A student used vulgar language in class	.07
A fellow teacher insulted you	.17*
You broke up a fight	−.16*
Crime items	
Were you assaulted by a student or an intruder?	−.07
Was anything of yours stolen in school?	−.11
Were you harassed on your way to or going from school?	.07
Were you assaulted in the neighborhood of your school?	.03
Your class activities must be planned on an individual basis	.01
Your class activities are closely controlled by supervisors	−.15*
You are safe to walk alone in the neighborhood surrounding your school	−.05
You are in jeopardy of being *involuntarily* transferred to another school or building	.20**
The noise level in the school is excessive	−.03
Underprepared students attend your class(es)	.03
Your fellow teachers are friendly	−.08
It is unsafe to be alone in the school building	.08
In general, school personnel enforce sanctions against rule breakers	−.14*
Administrators routinely give teachers too much information	.09
Your paperwork is excessive	−.03
Administrators give you information discourteously	.19**
Several fellow teachers tend to be lazy	.11
You teach low ability students	−.01
Administrators criticize you unfairly	−.05

Note. The response alternatives for the event items were $0 = not\ at\ all$; $1 = once\ per\ month$; $2 = once\ per\ week$; $3 = 2-4\ times\ per\ week$; $5 = daily$. The response alternatives for the crime items were $0 = no$ and $1 = yes$. The response alternatives for the strain items were $0 = not\ at\ all$; $1 = to\ a\ minimal\ extent$; $2 = to\ a\ small\ extent$; $3 = to\ a\ moderate\ extent$; $4 = to\ a\ great\ extent$.
*$p < .05$. **$p < .01$.

property damage were somehow more likely to have been singled out for victimization because of their mental state, this hypothesis is unlikely in view of the absence of significant correlations between the Time 0 CES-D and other crime items. It is implausible that prior mental state plays a role in making teachers vulnerable to one type of crime but not to others. The relation of the property-damage item to prior symptoms probably reflected a Type I error.

Another Self-Report Measure

Although it is not the purpose of this chapter to review all types of self-report instruments that have been designed to assess working conditions, it is important, within the context of a discussion of confounding, to mention one of the more prominent instruments, Hackman and Oldham's (1975) Job Diagnostic Survey (JDS). Levin and Stokes (1989) found that "NA was significantly and inversely correlated with six of the seven [dimensions of] job characteristics" that were obtained from the JDS (p. 756). Levin and Stokes (1989) suggested that, compared with individuals lower in NA, high-NA individuals cognize their work environments differently. The authors speculated that high-NA workers more often selectively attend to negative aspects of their jobs, distort in negative ways their perceptions of their jobs, and store in memory negative aspects of their jobs.

Other findings are consistent with those of Levin and Stokes (1989). Brousseau (1978) found that temporal change in a personality dimension labeled *freedom from depression* was more closely related to JDS scales than were other personality dimensions. Schnake and Dumler (1985), in a factor analytic study, found JDS scales to be subtly biased by affective state.

To attempt to reduce confounding with affective state, stress researchers may consider administering to workers neutrally worded self-report items, although such a strategy may be more amenable to within- than between-occupations designs. In view of the notion that a depressed affective state can bias cognitions negatively, the self-report items should be developed to minimize the amount of inference making required of incumbents who are asked to characterize their work environments. Slightly more inference making is required of JDS items because the JDS was designed to assess relatively broad dimensions of the work environment across a wide variety of occupations (Hackman & Oldham, 1975). Because of the teacher study's within-occupation design, neutrally worded items could be tailored specifically to assess working conditions teachers encounter. An approach we recommend is that focused (e.g., Teacher Event Inventory and a comparable social worker inventory) and broad-band scales (e.g., the JDS) be used within the same study to investigate the effects of within-occupation stressors and to allow comparisons across occupations (e.g., teachers vs. social workers).

Data Analytic Considerations

It might be argued that the problem of constructing highly distinct measures of the work environment and distress should not be a high priority. After all, the beauty of regression procedures is that they can estimate the impact of one risk factor on psychological morbidity outcomes, controlling for the influence of other risk factors. Consider, however, the situation in which two risk factors (e.g., initial adverse job conditions and preemployment depressive symptoms) influence a later morbidity outcome (e.g., Time 2 depressive symptoms), and the two risk factors are themselves positively correlated. Because each predictor variable carries information about the outcome that is also carried by the other predictor variable, Cohen and Cohen (1983) described this condition as "partial redundancy" and noted that it constituted "by far the most common pattern of relationship in nonexperimental research in the behavioral sciences" (p. 94).

The standardized regression coefficient for X_1 in a two-predictor regression equation is as follows:

$$\beta_1 = [r_{yx_1} - r_{yx_2}r_{x_1x_2}]/[1 - r_{x_1x_2}^2].$$

If each of the bivariate correlations involving X_1, X_2, and Y is positive (as is likely with multiple risk factors), the size of the zero-order relation between X_1 and X_2 will affect the partial regression coefficient representing the influence of X_1 on Y.[1] For example, if $r_{yx_1} = .4$, $r_{yx_2} = .4$, and $r_{x_1x_2} = .1$, then β_1 = .36. By contrast, if $r_{x_1x_2} = .4$, with the other two bivariate correlations held constant, then β_1 would be reduced to .29. Similar results can be shown with the unstandardized regression coefficients.

Often enough, redundancy among predictor variables is difficult to avoid. The view advanced here is that, when possible, redundancy in the predictors should be minimized. We should refrain from using items that ask "How stressed are you by student fighting?" Similarly, we should refrain from using summated stressor scales that depend on participants' ratings of stressor negativity (e.g., Bhagat et al., 1985; Brief et al., 1988). When we covary for prior psychological distress, the stress scale will lose power to predict future psychological distress. The penalty for avoidable redundancy will typically be reduced effect sizes and, concomitantly, lower power. The aim in constructing work-environment measures that were based on neutral self-reports (in contrast to the more traditional "How stressed are you?" measures) was to reduce redundancy in the work-environment and preemployment distress scales.

It is worth reiterating here that redundancy has an opposite effect in the case of cross-sectional correlations between "How stressed are you?" measures of the work environment and summated stressor-rating scales, on one hand, and psychological distress, on the other. As mentioned earlier, cross-sectional correlations (or lagged correlations without a distress covariate) are likely to be overestimates because of the content overlap in the measures. The correlation coefficient is inflated because both predictor and predicted variables reflect psychological distress.

---

[1] The focal concern of this discussion is how commonly found redundancy can weaken effect sizes. Other less common conditions can arise such as one in which r_{yx_1}, and $r_{x_1x_2}$ are positive; however, the product of r_{yx_2} and $r_{x_1x_2}$ is large enough to make the numerator $[r_{yx_1} - r_{yx_2}r_{x_1x_2}]$ negative, forcing β_1 to be negative, the sign opposite the sign of the zero-order relation (r_{yx_1}). See Cohen and Cohen (1983) for a discussion of various patterns of association in the regression context.

Another advantage of developing measures that reduce redundancy is that such measures enable investigators to test models of reciprocal causation. Two-stage least squares (Kenny, 1979) and reciprocal LISREL (Jöreskog & Sörbom, 1989) models require instrumental variables. Instrumental variables are factors that explain one causal variable but are relatively independent of another causal variable of interest (Kenny, 1979). For example, in an earlier study (see Figure 1) Time 0 (preemployment) depressive symptoms were significantly related to Time 1 (fall) depressive symptoms but were uncorrelated with the Time 1 school environment measures (Schonfeld & Ruan, 1991). Thus, the Time 0 symptoms measure was used as an instrumental variable in a causal

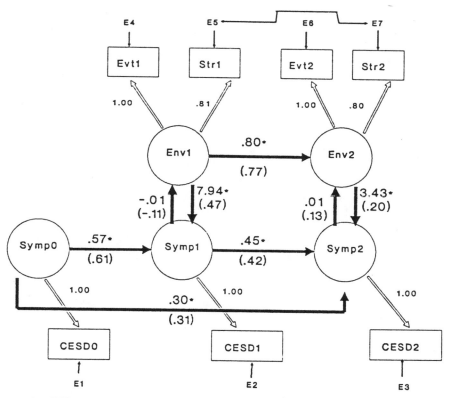

Figure 1. LISREL-generated path diagram depicting reciprocal relations between depressive symptoms and school work environments. Symp0, Symp1, and Symp2 represent depressive symptoms in the summer, fall, and spring, respectively, adjusted for measurement error; CESD0, CESD1, and CESD2 represent raw scores on the Center for Epidemiologic Studies-Depression Scale. Env1 and Env2 represent adversity in the school environment in the fall and spring. Evt1 and Evt2 represent fall and spring scores on the Event Inventory, a measure of episodically occurring job stressors; Str1 and Str2 represent fall and spring scores on the Strain Inventory, a measure of ongoing job stressors. Unstandardized coefficients are presented above each path, and standardized coefficients are presented below each path in parentheses. Asterisks indicate a significant causal path ($p < .001$). From Schonfeld and Ruan, 1991. Reprinted with permission.

model of reciprocal effects between Time 1 symptoms and the Time 1 school environment. The Time 1 path from symptoms to the school-environment variable can be construed as a halo effect representing response distortion associated with the reporting on school conditions by symptomatic teachers. Note the effect size associated with the halo was small and nonsignificant. The effect size for the Time 1 path from the school environment to symptoms was large and significant. Similar findings were obtained for the Time 2 (spring) school-environment and symptoms measures. Although the model depicted in the figure fit the data satisfactorily, an alternative model in which the two paths representing the symptoms-to-environment halos were deleted fit somewhat better. The model that included the halo effects is shown here to demonstrate the potency of environment-to-symptoms effects even when the potential for response distortion is controlled.

The model depicted in the figure fit the data better than a lagged model (not shown) that incorporated an effect, such as the one described earlier, from the Time 1 school environment to Time 2 depressive symptoms. In other words, the most apt model depicted a process in which the effects of working conditions on teachers occur relatively soon after entry into the work role. A causal process in which adverse school conditions engender depressive symptoms relatively soon after the individual's entry into the work role is highly plausible. Qualitative research conducted by Blase (1986) suggests that many veteran teachers' work environments can be characterized by an absence of control that leads to great disappointment. The problems in many urban schools are not isolated to certain parts of the building or limited to the least experienced teachers. The problems in these schools are pervasive.

Quantitative research (Schonfeld, 1990a) also underlines the dangers and lack of control faced by many veteran teachers. When the characteristics of the work environment sharply contradict the expectations beginning workers bring to their jobs, one would expect elevated risk for depression (cf. Brown & Harris, 1989). By the same reasoning, it is expected that working conditions in which individuals are free of danger and allowed to exercise control will promote high morale.

Summary

We outline a number of methodologic strategies with which investigators can more clearly operationalize the stress process. The development of independent measures of stressors and distress is important. When self-report instruments are used, neutrally worded items (Kasl, 1978, 1987) that assess work-environment exposures are less likely to be confounded with preemployment distress. By contrast, traditional "How stressed are you?" measures and summated rating scales of stressor impact are more confounded with psychological distress or negative affectivity. A complementary approach to reducing confounding in stressor and distress measures involves following longitudinally samples that have been limited to workers who, initially, are relatively free of distress (cf. Depue & Monroe, 1986).

Research with newly employed female teachers illustrates the difficulty in developing unconfounded self-report measures of work-environment exposures. Neutrally worded self-report measures, however, can be constructed to be reasonably unconfounded with preemployment distress. Reduced confounding in stressor scales and distress covariates pays off in increased statistical power to detect stressor-related changes in later distress. In addition, longitudinal research with new workers on whom preemployment baseline morbidity data are collected is especially important in detecting workplace effects that develop relatively soon after the individual's entry into the work role. Another advantage of combining baseline morbidity data with an independent assessment of working conditions is the opportunity this research design affords for testing causal models of reciprocal effects.

References

Bhagat, R. S., McQuaid, S. J., Lindholm, H., & Segovis, J. (1985). Total life stress: A multimethod validation of the construct and its effect on organizationally valued outcomes and withdrawal behaviors. *Journal of Applied Psychology, 70,* 202–214.

Blase, J. J. (1986). A qualitative analysis of sources of teacher stress: Consequences for performance. *American Educational Research Journal, 23,* 13–40.

Brief, A. P., Burke, M. J., George, J. M., Robinson, B. S., & Webster, J. (1988). Should negative affectivity remain an unmeasured variable in the study of job stress? *Journal of Applied Psychology, 73,* 193–198.

Brousseau, K. R. (1978). Personality and job experience. *Organizational Behavior and Human Performance, 22,* 235–252.

Brown, G. W., & Harris, T. (1978). *The social origins of depression.* New York: Free Press.

Cohen, J., & Cohen, P. (1983). *Applied multiple regression/correlation analysis for the behavioral sciences.* Hillsdale, NJ: Erlbaum.

Cohen, S., Kamarck, T., & Mermelstein, R. (1983). A global measure of perceived stress. *Journal of Health and Social Behavior, 24,* 385–396.

Cullen, F. T., Link, B. G., Wolfe, N. T., & Frank, J. (1985). The social dimensions of correctional officer stress. *Justice Quarterly, 2,* 505–533.

DeFrank, R. S., & Stroup, C. A. (1989). Teacher stress and health: Examination of a model. *Journal of Psychosomatic Research, 33,* 99–109.

Depue, R. A., & Monroe, S. M. (1986). Conceptualization and measurement of human disorder in life stress research: The problem of chronic disturbance. *Psychological Bulletin, 99,* 36–51.

Dillon, S. (1994, July 7). Report finds more violence in the schools: Board says principals covered up incidents. *New York Times,* pp. B1, B7.

Dohrenwend, B. S., Krasnoff, L., Askenasy, A. R., & Dohrenwend, B. P. (1982). The Psychiatric Epidemiology Research Interview Life Events Scale. In L. Goldberger & S. Breznitz (Eds.), *Handbook of stress: Theoretical and clinical aspects* (pp. 332–363). New York: Free Press.

Dunham, J. (1984). *Stress in teaching.* Beckenham, England: Croom Helm.

Farber, B. (1984). Stress and burnout in suburban teachers. *Journal of Educational Resarch, 77,* 325–331.

Fimian, M. J. (1983). A comparison of occupational stress correlates as reported by teachers of mentally retarded and non-mentally retarded handicapped children. *Education and Training of the Mentally Retarded, 18,* 62–68.

Fimian, M. J., & Santoro, T. M. (1983). Sources and manifestations of occupational stress as reported by full-time special education teachers. *Exceptional Children, 49,* 540–543.

Galloway, D., Panckhurst, F., Boswell, K., Boswell, C., & Green, K. (1984). Mental health, absences from work, stress, and satisfaction in a sample of New Zealand primary school teachers. *Australian and New Zealand Journal of Psychiatry, 18,* 359–363.

Gold, Y. (1984). The factorial validity of the Maslach Burnout Inventory in a sample of California elementary and junior high school classroom teachers. *Educational and Psychological Measurement, 44*, 1009–1016.

Gold, Y. (1985). The relationship of six personal and life history variables to standing on three dimensions of the Maslach Burnout Inventory in a sample of elementary and junior high school teachers. *Educational and Psychological Measurement, 45*, 377–387.

Hackman, J. R., & Oldham, G. R. (1975). Development of the Job Diagnostic Survey. *Journal of Applied Psychology, 60*, 159–170.

Hollingshead, A. B. (1974). *Four-factor index of social status.* New Haven, CT: Yale University Press.

Iwanicki, E. F., & Schwab, R. L. (1981). A cross validation study of the Maslach Burnout Inventory. *Educational and Psychological Measurement, 41*, 1167–1174.

Johnson, A. B., Gold, V., & Knepper, D. (1984). Frequency and intensity of professional burnout among teachers of the mildly handicapped. *College Student Journal, 18*, 261–266.

Jöreskog, K. G., & Sörbom, D. (1989). *LISREL 7: Users reference guide.* Mooresville, IN: Scientific Software.

Kasl, S. V. (1978). Epidemiological contributions to the study of work stress. In C. L. Cooper & R. Payne (Eds.), *Stress at work* (pp. 3–48). New York: Wiley.

Kasl, S. V. (1983). Pursuing the link between stress life experiences and disease: A time for reappraisal. In C. L. Cooper (Ed.), *Stress research* (pp. 79–102). New York: Wiley.

Kasl, S. V. (1987). Methodologies in stress and health: Past difficulties, present dilemmas, future directions. In S. V. Kasl & C. L. Cooper (Eds.), *Stress and health: Issues in research methodology* (pp. 307–318). New York: Wiley.

Kenny, D. A (1979). *Correlation and causation.* New York: Wiley.

Kyriacou, C., & Sutcliffe, J. (1978). Teacher stress: Prevalence, sources, and symptoms. *British Journal of Educational Psychology, 48*, 159–167.

Kyriacou, C., & Sutcliffe, J. (1979). Teacher stress and satisfaction. *Educational Research, 21*, 89–96.

Levin, I., & Stokes, J. P. (1989). Dispositional approach to job satisfaction: Role of negative affectivity. *Journal of Applied Psychology, 74*, 752–758.

Malanowski, J. R., & Wood, P. H. (1984). Burnout and self-actualization in public school teachers. *Journal of Psychology, 117*, 23–26.

Maslach, C., & Jackson, S. (1981). *Maslach Burnout Inventory.* Palo Alto, CA: Consulting Psychologists Press.

Maslach, C., & Jackson, S. (1984). Burnout in organizational settings. *Applied Social Psychology Annual, 5*, 133–153.

Meier, S. T. (1984). The construct validity of burnout. *Journal of Occupational Psychology, 53*, 211–219.

Needle, R. H., Griffen, T., & Svendsen, R. (1981). Occupational stress: Coping and health problems of teachers. *Journal of School Health, 51*, 175–181.

Parkes, K. R. (1982). Occupational stress among student nurses: A natural experiment. *Journal of Applied Psychology, 67*, 784–796.

Pearlin, L. I., Lieberman, M. A., Menaghan, E. G., & Mullan, J. T. (1981). The stress process. *Journal of Health and Social Behavior, 22*, 337–356.

Pearlin, L. I., & Schooler, C. (1978). The structure of coping. *Journal of Health and Social Behavior, 19*, 2–21.

Quinn, R. P., & Staines, G. L. (1979). *The 1977 Quality of Employment Survey: Descriptive statistics with comparison data from the 1960-70 and the 1972-73 surveys.* Ann Arbor: Survey Research Center, Institute for Social Research, University of Michigan.

Radloff, L. S. (1977). The CES-D Scale: A self-report depression scale for research in the general population. *Applied Psychological Measurement, 1*, 385–401.

Satyamurti, C. (1981). *Occupational survival.* Oxford, England: Basil Blackwell.

Schnake, M. E., & Dumler, M. P. (1985). Affective response bias in the measurement of perceived task characteristics. *Journal of Occupational Psychology, 58*, 159–166.

Schonfeld, I. S. (1990a). Coping with job-related stress: The case of teachers. *Journal of Occupational Psychology, 63*, 141–149.

Schonfeld, I. S. (1990b). Distress in a sample of teachers. *Journal of Psychology, 123*, 321–338.

Schonfeld, I. S. (1991). Dimensions of functional social support and psychological symptoms. *Psychological Medicine, 21,* 1051–1060.

Schonfeld, I. S. (1992a). Assessing stress in teachers: Depressive symptoms scales and neutral self-reports on the work environment. In J. Quick, L. Murphy, & J. Hurrell, Jr. (Eds.), *Work and well-being: Assessments and instruments for occupational mental health.* Washington, DC: American Psychological Association.

Schonfeld, I. S. (1992b). A longitudinal study of occupational stressors and depressive symptoms in first-year teachers. *Teaching and Teacher Education, 8,* 151–158.

Schonfeld, I. S. (in press). Burnout in teachers: Is it burnout or is it depression? *Human Stress: Current and Selected Research, 5.*

Schonfeld, I. S., & Ruan, D. (1991). Occupational stress and preemployment measures: The case of teachers. *Journal of Social Behavior and Personality, 6,* 95–114.

Seiler, R. E., & Pearson, D. A. (1984). Stress among accounting educators in the United States. *Research in Higher Education, 21,* 301–316.

U.S. Department of Labor. (1965). *Dictionary of occupational titles* (3rd ed.). Washington, DC: U.S. Government Printing Office.

Vassend, O. (1989). Dimensions of negative affectivity, self-reported somatic symptoms, and health-related behaviors. *Social Science and Medicine, 28,* 29–36.

Watson, D., & Clark, L. A. (1984). Negative affectivity: The disposition to experience aversive emotional states. *Psychological Bulletin, 96,* 465–490.

Watson, D., & Pennebaker, J. W. (1989). Health complaints, stress, and distress: Exploring the central role of negative affectivity. *Psychological Review, 96,* 234–254.

Weissman, M., Sholomskas, M., Pottenger, M., Prusoff, B., & Locke, B. (1977). Assessing depressive symptoms in five psychiatric populations: A validation study. *American Journal of Epidemiology, 106,* 203–214.

Zabel, R. H., & Zabel, M. K. (1982). Factors in burnout among teachers of exceptional children. *Exceptional Children, 49,* 261–263.

22

Effects of Manipulated Job Stressors and Job Attitude on Perceived Job Conditions: A Simulation

Peter Y. Chen, Paul E. Spector, and Steve M. Jex

Over the past few decades, there has been increasing interest in stress across many areas including the job domain (e.g., Cooper & Marshall, 1978; Lazarus, 1966). Most job-stress studies assume that work environments cause employee strains, which result in health symptoms and disease (Cox, 1978). This proposition has been described clearly by several job-stress models such as Beehr and Newman (1978) and Ivancevich and Matteson (1980).

Because of the constraints on manipulating job stressors in organizational settings and the difficulties of measuring objective stressors in job contexts (e.g., autonomy), researchers and practitioners often measure perceived job stressors with the hope that such measures reflect objective job stressors. After perceived job stressors and outcomes are measured, the relationships between them are used to infer the impact of objective job stressors on strain outcomes.

Question of Causality From Objective Job Stressors

Many laboratory studies and field experiments have shown that objective job stressors induce perceived job stressors and various outcomes (e.g., Anderson, 1976). However, several researchers have either explicitly or implicitly addressed the question of whether perceived job conditions (e.g., perceptions of either job stressors or job characteristics) or outcomes (e.g., job satisfaction) were caused solely by actual work environments (Adler, Skov, & Salvemini, 1985; Caldwell & O'Reilly, 1982; Hall & Spector, 1991; O'Reilly, Parlette, & Bloom, 1980; Spector, 1992; Spector, Dwyer, & Jex, 1988; Spector & Jex, 1991; Taber & Taylor, 1989). For example, Spector reported a meta-analysis of convergent validities of job conditions (e.g., autonomy and role ambiguity) derived from alternative sources. His data suggested that, at the individual level, about 80% to 90% of the variance could not be attributed to objective job conditions. Taber and Taylor also found that the majority of variance in Job Diagnostic Survey (JDS; Hackman & Oldham, 1975) scores were unexplainable by objective tasks.

Caldwell and O'Reilly (1982) and O'Reilly et al. (1980) deliberately controlled the variation of job characteristics by selecting respondents who held the same job. They found that perceived job characteristics and job scope varied as a function of job attitudes (e.g., overall job satisfaction). As pointed out by Spector (1992), job dimension–job satisfaction correlations in O'Reilly and associates' samples, which were highly homogeneous, do not differ from those found in two meta-analysis studies (Fried & Ferris, 1987; Loher, Noe, Moeller, & Fitzgerald, 1985) or those with heterogeneous job samples (e.g., Spector & Jex, 1991). Similar to Caldwell and O'Reilly's methodology, Hall and Spector (1991) found that stressor–strain relations between their homogeneous employees and heterogeneous respondents in other studies were similar in magnitude. Theoretically, the magnitude of correlations in Hall and Spector and O'Reilly and associates' studies should have been attenuated because of the restricted range in objective job characteristics. Their findings suggest that objective job environments might not have much impact on observed stressor–strain relations.

If objective job stressors are not the only important determinant of observed stressor–strain relations, what other factors may contribute to the covariation between perceived job stressors and strains? Although research has not focused on this question in the job-stress literature, there are other possible variables proposed in other research domains. These include response consistency, priming, and social information cues (Salancik & Pfeffer, 1977), dispositions (e.g., negative affectivity; Watson, Pennebaker, & Folger, 1987), transient moods (e.g., Kraiger, Billings, & Isen, 1989), and job attitudes (Staw, 1975).

Among these variables, job attitudes such as job satisfaction have an important implication for job-stress researchers because job attitudes are often studied as the outcomes of job stressors in the job-stress literature (e.g., Caplan, Cobb, French, Harrison, & Pinneau, 1975). In addition, attitudinal variables, especially job satisfaction, have been studied in the laboratory as the potential cause of perceptions and ratings in job characteristics and performance-appraisal studies (e.g., Adler et al., 1985; Caldwell & O'Reilly, 1982; Smither, Collins, & Buda, 1989).

Experimental (Adler et al., 1985; Caldwell & O'Reilly, 1982) and correlational (James & Jones, 1980; James & Tetrick, 1986; Kohn & Schooler, 1982) evidence has suggested that perceived job conditions (mainly perceived job characteristics) might vary as a function of job satisfaction. For example, Adler et al. manipulated job satisfaction by randomly providing engineering students with incorrect information about job-satisfaction norms. Participants who believed their satisfaction scores were higher than the norms reported significantly higher task satisfaction, more skill variety, task identity, and autonomy after performing a simulated job than did those who believed that their satisfaction scores were lower than the norms. Likewise, Caldwell and O'Reilly randomly assigned part-time master's of business administration students to two groups: satisfied and dissatisfied. All participants were instructed to imagine that they were either satisfied or dissatisfied with their job. Participants then reviewed the same job description of a retail-store manager and rated the job on four job dimensions (autonomy, identity, variety, and feedback). Satisfied participants perceived significantly more task identity, skill variety, task feedback and autonomy than dissatisfied participants. Neither of these studies, however, manipulated actual job dimensions in either the simulated job or the job description.

Kohn and Schooler (1982) investigated reciprocal effects of working conditions and individual outcomes in a 10-year longitudinal study. They argued that working conditions such as one's position in the hierarchy or cleanliness of the workplace led to distress. Distress feelings then led to "actual or perceived" (p. 1282) job conditions such as time pressure. A similar notion has also been investigated by James and Jones (1980) and James and Tetrick (1986). James and Jones found evidence that job satisfaction was both the cause and the effect of job perceptions. Furthermore, James and Tetrick compared three different models posing the potential causal relations among job conditions, job perceptions, and job satisfaction. They concluded that job environments determine individuals' initial job perceptions. Job perceptions then influence job satisfaction, and finally job satisfaction reciprocally affects their perceptions.

The findings from the above studies indicate that job attitudes such as job satisfaction may be one possible cause of perceived job conditions. If it is a viable proposition, the covariance between job attitudes and perceived job conditions cannot be solely attributed to objective job conditions. Because this phenomenon has been observed in job characteristics studies (e.g., Adler et al., 1985; Caldwell & O'Reilly, 1982), it would be reasonable to expect similar findings in the job-stress domain.

The Current Study

Our study attempted to examine the roles of job attitude (operationalized by job satisfaction) and stressful job conditions on individuals' affective reactions (feelings of stress, frustration, and job satisfaction), perception of job stressors (role ambiguity, role conflict, work load, and autonomy), and task perceptions (skill variety, feedback, task identity, and task significance). A simulated laboratory design was used. Participants were asked to review one of nine job descriptions that varied across levels of job stressors and job attitude of the incumbent. Their affective reactions, perceived job stressors, and task perceptions were assessed at the end of the session. In one sense, it is a replication of Caldwell and O'Reilly's (1982) study because participants were asked to imagine they were working on a simulated job, and their task perceptions were evaluated. The imagination method was derived from role-playing techniques that have been applied in different areas such as attitude and habit change (e.g., Culbertson, 1957). The implicit assumption of this approach is that participants can vicariously experience and empathize with the situation of others. Such a line of reasoning is strongly supported by social learning theory and the research of Bandura (1965).

The current study also expands on Adler et al.'s (1985) and Caldwell and O'Reilly's (1982) studies in four ways. First, three levels of stressful job conditions were manipulated. Second, interactions of manipulated job stressors and job attitude were explored. Third, richer and more detailed scenarios were embedded in the job description. It minimized the superficiality, to some extent, compared with Caldwell and O'Reilly's study. Fourth, the potential impact of manipulated job stressors on task perceptions were explored, whereas none of the four job dimensions (skill variety, feedback, task identity, and task significance) were varied.

The advantage of the laboratory strategy used here was to control extraneous and irrelevant variables so that results would indicate possible directions of causality. It should also be noted that our research was designed to test a "can it happen?" hypothesis (Ilgen, 1986). In other words, we wanted to examine whether simulated job stressors and job attitude would have an effect on reports of job affect and perceived job conditions. The ultimate goal is to use current results to evaluate the conventional job-stress model applied in organizational research and practice. In addition, the empirical data are used to supplement the findings from correlational studies (James & Tetrick, 1986; Spector et al., 1988).

We proposed three hypotheses: (a) There would be significant effects of simulated job stressors on affective reactions and perceived job conditions. Participants who read the job description embedded with a high level of job stressors would report more negative affect, more perceived job stressors, and lower levels of task characteristics than those who read the job description with a low level of job stressors; (b) job attitude (operationalized by job satisfaction) would have an effect on affective reactions and perceived job conditions. Participants reading a job description embedded with a positive job attitude would report more positive affect, lower levels of perceived job stressors, and higher levels of task characteristics than those with a job description indicating a negative job attitude; and (c) simulated job stressors and job attitude would have an interactive effect on affective reactions and perceived job conditions. It would be reasonable to expect a consensus among participants about the job condition if the condition was highly stressful. Therefore, participants were anticipated to report the observed conditions regardless of the job-attitude condition. However, participants might interpret same job conditions differently if the conditions were less stressful. For example, people with negative affect tend to focus on negative aspects of the world and make negative evaluation (Watson et al., 1987). As a result, under less stressful conditions, participants in the negative attitude condition are expected to report more negative experiences than those in the positive attitude condition.

Method

Participants

Three hundred twenty-three college students participated in the study in exchange for course credits. Ages ranged from 18 to 54 years, with a median age of 21 years. There were 25.9% male participants, and 83.3% were advanced undergraduate and graduate students (44% junior, 38.7% senior, and 0.6% graduate). With regard to ethnicity, 84% were White, 5% were African American, 7% were Hispanic, and 4% were Asian.

Study Design

The study used a 3 × 3 experimental design. Three levels of job stressors and three levels of job attitude were manipulated. The manipulated job-stressor conditions were high stressful, medium, and low stressful. The job-attitude conditions were satisfied, neutral, and dissatisfied.

Development of Stimulus Materials

Participants were given a detailed job description for the job of social work supervisor. Embedded in the description were the combinations of one of three job-stressor profiles and one of three job-satisfaction profiles.

Job-satisfaction profiles. Satisfied and dissatisfied job profiles were written on the basis of statements from Spector's (1985) job-satisfaction scale. One item each was randomly chosen from six facets (i.e., pay, promotion, benefits, contingent rewards, coworkers, and nature of work) of the scale. For example, "you think that your efforts are rewarded the way they should be" was one of the statements used in the satisfied job profile. There was no profile presented in the neutral job-satisfaction condition.

Job-stressor profiles. Three versions of job-stressor profiles (i.e., low stressful, medium, and high stressful) were constructed. First, five workload items, six role conflict items, and three autonomy items and three role ambiguity items, which were able to distinguish perceived high and low stressor groups in Jex's (1988) data, were extracted from a workload scale (Spector et al., 1988), a role ambiguity and conflict scale (Rizzo, House, & Lirtzman, 1970), and an autonomy scale (JDS; Hackman & Oldham, 1975). These variables have been studied in the job-stress literature (e.g., Ivancevich & Matteson, 1980) and were viewed as job stressors in our study.

All items were rewritten to be as objective and behaviorally oriented as possible. These statements were then mixed randomly and presented to seven advanced graduate students in industrial–organizational psychology. According to the retranslation procedure (Smith & Kendall, 1963), each student was asked to sort these statements back into four carefully defined categories, namely, role conflict, role ambiguity, workload, and autonomy. Additionally, each student evaluated the extent to which each statement could be verified through direct observation from working environments. Two items within the final sorted categories were chosen on the basis of three criteria: agreement among judges in correct categories, a high mean, and a low standard deviation in the rating.

After that, high stressful and low stressful profiles were written according to a job description (which was developed from a job analysis and used as the medium stressful profile) of a social work supervisor in a community mental health center. The previously selected statements were embedded in the job description with appropriate scenarios. Twenty-seven advanced graduate students in psychology randomly received either high stressful or low stressful profiles and evaluated the degree of role ambiguity, role conflict, workload, and autonomy the job had. A series of analyses of variance indicated that the high stressful profile possessed significantly more job stressors than the low stressful profile.

Dependent Measures

There were 11 dependent variables collected at the end of the experiment, which included scales to measure affective reactions (i.e., job satisfaction, feelings of stress, and feelings of frustration), perceived job stressors (i.e., work load, role ambiguity, role conflict, and autonomy), and perceived job characteristics (i.e., skill variety, task significance, task identity, and feedback). All measures were slightly modified so that they could fit into the current context. It should be noted that the items used as dependent variables were different from the ones used in developing stimulus materials.

Affective outcomes. All affective scales had six response choices ranging from *strongly disagree* to *strongly agree*. The job-satisfaction measure (Cammann, Fichman, Jenkins, & Klesh, 1979) was a 3-item scale. A high score reflected high satisfaction with the job in general. Feelings of frustration were measured by Peters and O'Connor's (1980) 3-item scale. Feelings of stress were measured by Chen and Spector's (1991) 3-item scale. High scores indicated high frustration and stress.

Perceived job stressors. A 3-item workload and a 4-item role-ambiguity scale were used (Beehr, Walsh, & Taber, 1976). Role conflict was measured by Quinn and Shepard's (1974) 3-item scale. Autonomy was measured by Dossett and Lee's (1989) 6-item autonomy scale (3-item work-method autonomy and 3-item work-scheduling autonomy subscales). All scales, except for the role-conflict scale, had the same response categories as the job-satisfaction scale. The role conflict scale had six response choices ranging from *never* to *extremely often*. High scores reflected that respondents perceived high workload, role ambiguity and conflict, and autonomy in the job.

Perceived job characteristics. Four job characteristics were measured by Idaszak and Drasgow's (1987) revised Job Diagnostic Survey. Each subscale contained three items with the same response categories as the job-satisfaction scale. High scores implied that respondents perceived high task identity, skill variety, task significance, and feedback in the job.

Procedure

Participants were randomly assigned to one of nine conditions. At the beginning of the experiment, all participants read one of three randomly assigned job-attitude profiles. According to the assigned profiles, they were instructed to imagine that they had worked in a social work supervisor position for 1 year. Following that, they continued reading one of three randomly assigned job-stressors profiles, which was embedded in the social work supervisor job description obtained from a job analysis. Finally, they filled out a questionnaire containing the measures described in the Measures section.

Results

Among studied variables, most coefficient alphas were reasonably high (8 out of 11 were over .80). The lowest was .69 for skill variety. In addition, the observed ranges for all variables covered almost the entire possible ranges. Thus, the problem of restriction of range was minimized. On the basis of pooled within-group correlations (which control for group differences) described in Table 1, it was found that job satisfaction was negatively related to feelings of frustration and stress. Most of the correlations between job satisfaction and perceived job stressors and characteristics were statistically significant but quite small. Feelings of frustration and stress were modestly related to perceived job stressors and characteristics. With the exception of skill variety and task significance, perceived job stressors and job characteristics were significantly correlated with one another.

Table 1. Pooled Within-Group Correlations Among Study Variables

Variables	1	2	3	4	5	6	7	8	9	10	11
1. RA	—										
2. RC	24	—									
3. WL	38	25	—								
4. AU	−25	−16	−23	—							
5. TI	−26	−16	−21	32	—						
6. FB	−42	−16	−23	35	61	—					
7. TS	−06	03	−06	12	19	35	—				
8. SV	−01	05	04	18	17	26	59	—			
9. JS	−15	−07	−25	12	13	21	12	16	—		
10. ST	15	24	46	−16	−11	−04	10	16	28	—	
11. FR	17	27	37	−16	−10	−12	07	08	−23	68	—

Note. $n = 314$. Correlations equal or greater than .11 are significant at the .05 level, two tailed. The decimal points have been removed from the correlations. RA = role ambiguity; RC = role conflict; WL = workload; AU = autonomy; TI = task identity; FB = feedback; TS = task significance; SV = skill variety; JS = job satisfaction; ST = feelings of stress; FR = feelings of frustration.

Hypothesis Tests

Three 3×3 between-subjects multivariate analyses of variance (MANOVAs) were performed on three groups of dependent variables to ensure sufficient power. These groups were conceptually different in the study. The first group included job satisfaction, feelings of stress, and frustration; the second was workload, role ambiguity, role conflict, and autonomy; and the third was skill variety, task identity, task significance, and feedback. A total of 321 participants were retained in the MANOVA after deleting cases with missing data. The numbers of participants in each cell ranged from 34 to 37. With the use of unweighted means approach and Wilks's criterion, significant main effects ($p < .05$) on the prior three groups of dependent variables were all found, with $F(6, 620) = 26.0$, $F(8, 616) = 46.2$, and $F(8, 612) = 16.6$ in the stressor manipulation, and with $F(6, 620) = 13.0$, $F(8, 616) = 5.2$, $F(8, 612) = 3.0$ in the job-attitude manipulation. A significant interactive effect on the second group of dependent variables was also found with $F(16, 942) = 2.3$.

Main effects of manipulated job stressors. It was found that each univariate F test reached significance except for skill variety. Cell means for each significant variable, compared using least significant difference (LSD) tests, are reported in Table 2. Specifically, the high stressful condition led respondents to report more dissatisfaction, stress, and frustration than the medium or low stressful conditions. In addition, respondents perceived more workload, role ambiguity, role conflict, and less autonomy in the high stressful condition than in the other conditions. These data also suggested the manipulation of job-

Table 2. Mean Comparisons on Dependent Variables Across Three Levels of Job Stressors

Dependent variables	Stressful conditions		
	Low	Medium	High
Job satisfaction	12.4[ac]	11.0[b]	7.8
Stress	10.7[ac]	13.1[b]	14.9
Frustration	11.2[ac]	13.3[b]	14.8
Workload	8.4[ac]	10.6[b]	12.5
Role ambiguity	12.3[c]	12.3[b]	17.3
Role conflict	7.1[ac]	9.4[b]	11.0
Autonomy	28.2[ac]	24.1[b]	17.3
Task identity	12.2[ac]	9.8[b]	7.8
Task significance	15.6[c]	15.5[b]	14.4
Feedback	12.1[c]	11.7[b]	8.9

Note. The p level was less than .05 for all significant comparisons. The skill-variety variable was excluded because of the nonsignificant omnibus F test.
[a]There are significant mean differences between the low stressful condition and the medium condition.
[b]There are significant mean differences between the medium condition and the high stressful condition.
[c]There are significant mean differences between the low stressful condition and the high stressful condition.

stressors profiles succeeded. Furthermore, the high stressful condition led respondents to report less feedback, task identity, and task significance compared with the medium and low stressful job conditions. In summary, the hypotheses about the main effects of job stressors on the affective outcomes, perceived job characteristics, and perceived job stressors were supported.

Main effects of job attitude. All but skill variety were significantly affected by job-attitude profiles based on univariate analyses. Cell means for each significant variable compared by LSD tests are reported in Table 3. Specifically, dissatisfied respondents reported less job satisfaction and more feelings of stress and frustration than the neutral or satisfied respondents. These data further implied that the manipulation of job attitude was successful. Additionally, dissatisfied respondents perceived more workload, role ambiguity, and role conflict and less autonomy, task identity, task significance, and feedback than other respondents. In summary, the hypotheses of the impact of job attitude on affective reports, perceived job stressors, and job characteristics were supported.

Interaction of job stressors and job attitude. As reported, only an omnibus interaction effect on the second group of variables was significant. By means of a series of univariate F tests, all interactions were significant at $p < .05$, with $F(4, 311) = 2.7$, $MS_E = 12.6$ for role ambiguity; $F(4, 311) = 5.1$, $MS_E = 4.7$ for role conflict; $F(4, 311) = 2.7$, $MS_E = 9.0$ for work load; and $F(4, 311) = 4.1$, $MS_E = 28.9$ for autonomy. Cell means for these variables across job stressors and job attitude are reported in Table 4. It was further shown through LSD tests that there were no mean differences between satisfied and dissatisfied people under high stressful conditions. However, in the medium stressful condition, satisfied respondents reported significantly lower levels of job stressors

Table 3. Mean Comparisons on Dependent Variables Across Three Levels of Job Attitude

Dependent variables	Satisfied	Neutral	Dissatisfied
Job satisfaction	12.1[ac]	10.8[b]	8.3
Stress	11.6[ac]	13.1[b]	14.0
Frustration	12.2[ac]	13.2[b]	14.0
Workload	9.4[ac]	10.5[b]	11.6
Role ambiguity	13.6[c]	13.5[b]	14.9
Role conflict	8.6[c]	9.0[b]	10.0
Autonomy	24.0[c]	23.5	22.0
Task identity	10.7[c]	9.8	9.3
Task significance	15.3[c]	15.5[b]	14.7
Feedback	11.3[c]	11.2[b]	10.2

Note. The p level was less than .05 for all significant comparisons. The skill-variety variable was excluded because of the nonsignificant omnibus F test.

[a]There are significant mean differences between the satisfied condition and the neutral condition.

[b]There are significant mean differences between the neutral condition and the dissatisfied condition.

[c]There are significant mean differences between the satisfied condition and the dissatisfied condition.

Table 4. Means on Role Ambiguity, Role Conflict, Workload, and Autonomy Across Three Levels of Job Stressors and Job Attitude

Variable	Low stressors			Medium stressors			High stressors		
	H	N	L	H	N	L	H	N	L
		Attitude			Attitude			Attitude	
Role ambiguity									
M	12.0	11.6	13.3	11.1	11.5	14.3	17.6	17.3	17.1
n	36	34	34	36	36	36	36	35	37
Role conflict									
M	6.3	7.3	7.5	8.3	8.9	11.1	11.3	10.7	11.2
n	36	34	34	36	36	36	36	35	37
Workload									
M	7.4	8.7	9.2	8.9	10.3	12.6	12.1	12.6	12.8
n	36	34	34	36	36	36	36	35	37
Autonomy									
M	28.9	27.9	27.6	25.8	25.8	20.8	17.3	16.6	18.1
n	36	34	34	36	36	36	36	35	37

Note. H = high; N = neutral; L = low.

than the dissatisfied group. Furthermore, there were significant mean differences, with the exception of role ambiguity and autonomy, between satisfied and dissatisfied respondents under low stressful condition. As predicted, the satisfied people reported observing less job stressors than the dissatisfied people. For ease of interpretation, Figure 1 depicts the interactions of job stressors and job attitude on role ambiguity (figures of the interactive effects on role conflict and work load were not presented because of their similarity) and autonomy. In summary, results in the interaction partially supported the hypothesis.

Discussion

The results of this study generally supported the hypotheses that manipulated job attitude and job stressors would affect reports of job affect and job conditions. Consistent with prior job-characteristics studies (Adler et al., 1985; Caldwell & O'Reilly, 1982), task perceptions were affected by manipulated job satisfaction. Manipulated job attitude also influenced the way respondents perceived the stressors embedded in the job profiles. These findings demonstrate the generalizability of job-attitude effects, at least in laboratory designs, from job-characteristics to job-stress domains. The results also supported prior correlational studies that proposed that perceived job conditions might be the cause, as well as the effect, of job attitudes (James & Jones, 1980; James & Tetrick, 1986; Kohn & Schooler, 1982; Spector et al., 1988). These data further imply that the relationships between perceived job stressors and outcomes (e.g., feelings of stress and frustration or job satisfaction) may be attributed not only to work environments but also to individuals' attitudes (e.g., job satisfaction in this case) about their jobs. Most important, the findings indicate that the

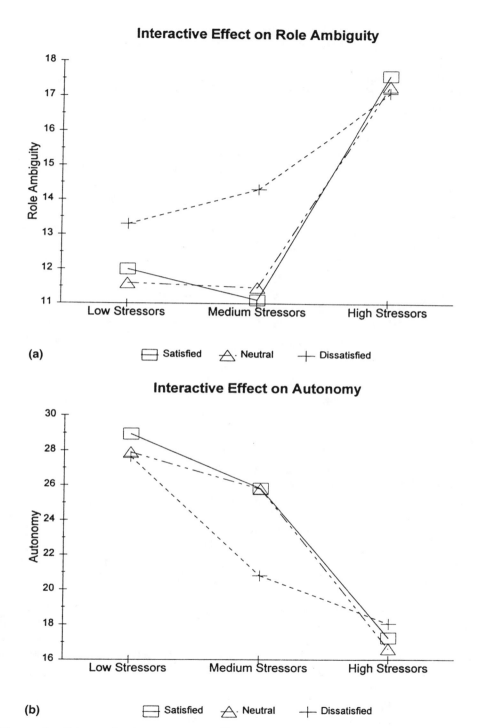

Figure 1. Perceived role ambiguity and autonomy vary as a function of job stressor and job attitude.

conventional job-stress models (e.g., Cox, 1978; French & Kahn, 1962) might be misspecified. Furthermore, the exploration of interaction effects was also partially supported. The results suggest that under highly stressful conditions, people tend to evaluate some job conditions negatively, regardless of their job attitude. However, under medium or low stressful conditions, people with different attitudes may evaluate the conditions differently.

How did job attitude (i.e., manipulated job satisfaction) influence respondents' perceptions of stressors? Four possible reasons were presented. First, similar to other self-reports, job-stressor scales often require employees to go well beyond objective job stressors and to engage in a process that includes recall, weighting, inference, prediction, interpretation, and evaluation (Podsakoff & Organ, 1986). This process has been shown to be influenced by internal affective experiences (Zajonc, 1984). Zajonc contended that cognition and affective states might influence each other. The affective component (Organ & Near, 1985; Watson et al., 1987) of job satisfaction hence would very likely affect respondents' perceptions of job stressors in the current study. James and Jones (1980) further proposed that job satisfaction may function as a major cognitive filter that would guide the recall of situational events when employees are requested to describe their work environment.

The second possible reason is the general good-mood effect proposed by Adler et al. (1985). The good-mood effect hypothesizes that satisfied employees may have a positive frame of reference in their minds and that they tend to evaluate everything positively. Kraiger et al. (1989) found that the manipulation of positive affect had an impact on individuals' task perception ratings. Positive-affect respondents rated simulated jobs better than neutral-affect ones.

The third possible reason is that job-satisfaction conditions provide individuals information with which they may redefine the relevant job conditions of the simulated job. For example, satisfied employees caused by either dispositional factors (e.g., Watson et al., 1987), mood (e.g., Kraiger et al., 1989), genetic factors (e.g., Arvey, Bouchard, Segal, & Abraham, 1989), or satisfaction levels of other employees (Salancik & Pfeffer, 1977) may redefine, reconstruct, or infer the relevant job contexts. This proposition is extended from the logic of Salancik and Pfeffer's social information-processing theory and Landy's (1989) cognitive-attribution hypothesis derived from Schachter and Singer's (1962) theory of emotions. The final possible reason is simply demand characteristics (Orne, 1969). Respondents might have guessed what we wanted them to say.

The manipulated profiles contain four job stressors. Conditions related to task identity, task significance, skill variety, and feedback were kept constant in the profiles, but significant effects of job stressors on most of these task perceptions were found. Why did manipulated job stressors influence task perceptions? There are at least three possible explanations.

First, the significant effect on task perceptions may have resulted from subjects' conceptual similarities between job-stressors and job-characteristics categories. For example, participants might believe role-ambiguity items should negatively covary with feedback items. This speculation is expanded from the systematic distortion hypothesis (Shweder & D'Andrade, 1980). This hypothesis proposes that individuals' recall processes are systematically distorted by the illusory covariance among rated categories (Cooper, 1981). Hence, the belief of covariations may explain why some perceived job stressors were correlated with some task perceptions, even though job characteristics were not varied in the profiles.

Another possible factor may be attributed to problems of scale contamination. As described previously, job stressors embedded in the profiles were modified from job-stressor scales (e.g., role ambiguity and conflict scales). It is possible that those scales measured something else (e.g., feedback or task identity), as well as role ambiguity and conflict. As a result, the correlations between perceived job stressors and task perceptions appeared because of poor discriminant validities.

The third possible reason may be the spillover effects of manipulated job stressors. The high stressful condition might make people redefine, believe, or experience the simulated job as less attractive than the medium or low stressful conditions. O'Reilly et al. (1980) observed that individuals' frame of reference (e.g., perceived stressors in the current case) may result in different perceptions and definition of the same job. Griffin (1983) also pointed out that individual responses are often based on a gestalt impression of the job rather than one well-defined category.

The significant findings of this study must be interpreted carefully in light of methodological constraints. The potential biases resulting from artificial contexts, demand characteristics, and a student population may impede the generalizability of these results. However, our data can supplement the increasing evidence that people's reports of job conditions may reflect attitudes as well as the environment (James & Jones, 1980; James & Tetrick, 1986; Spector, 1992; Spector et al., 1988). In addition, the data suggest that employees' perceptions of job stressors may, in part, be a joint function of attitudes and environments.

The major implication of this study is that researchers and practitioners should be cautious in using correlations between perceived job stressors and strains to infer the impact of objective job conditions. Our results suggest that correlational findings should be applied cautiously when used for purposes such as job design or stress management. These findings also highlight the necessity of reevaluating the objectives of stress-management programs at the needs-assessment stage. For instance, given moderately stressful or low stressful conditions, programs such as stress management or job design may offer limited help reducing strain outcomes (e.g., anxiety) or changing perception of job stressors if they were influenced by job attitude. Instead, attitude change should provide employees and employers with more benefit.

More longitudinal or multimethod research is needed to clearly specify the job-stress process. Unfortunately, a growing body of research (e.g., Gupta & Beehr, 1982; McGrath, 1982; Podsakoff & Organ, 1986) has cast doubt about the construct validity of incumbents' reports as indicators of objective features of jobs. In light of this research, we conclude that measures of individual perceptions provide much more information about the person rather than the content of the work he or she is performing. If the work is our interest, reports solely from employees at an individual level are probably not sufficient. Other information about job conditions from job analysis, supervisors, or other employees should be used to supplement individual self-reports. However, because people do act largely on the basis of their perceptions, self-reported job stressors are still very important.

References

Adler, S., Skov, R. B., & Salvemini, N. J. (1985). Job characteristics and job satisfaction when cause becomes consequence. *Organizational Behavior and Human Performance, 35*, 266–278.

Anderson, C. R. (1976). Coping behaviors as intervening mechanisms in the inverted-U stress-performance relationship. *Journal of Applied Psychology, 61*, 30–34.

Arvey, R. D., Bouchard, T. J., Segal, N. L., & Abraham, L. M. (1989). Job satisfaction: Environmental and genetic components. *Journal of Applied Psychology, 74*, 187–192.

Bandura, A. (1965). Vicarious processes: A case of no-trial learning. In L. Berkowitz (Ed.), *Advances in experimental social psychology* (Vol. 2). San Diego, CA: Academic Press.

Beehr, T. A., & Newman, J. E. (1978). Job stress, employee health, and organizational effectiveness: A facet analysis, model, and literature review. *Personnel Psychology, 31*, 665–699.

Beehr, T. A., Walsh, J. T., & Taber, T. D. (1976). Relationship of stress to individually and organizationally valued states: Higher order needs as a moderator. *Journal of Applied Psychology, 61*, 41–47.

Caldwell, D. F., & O'Reilly, C. A., III (1982). Task perceptions and job satisfaction: A question of causality. *Journal of Applied Psychology, 67*, 361–369.

Cammann, C., Fichman, M., Jenkins, D., & Klesh, J. (1979). *The Michigan Organizational Assessment Questionnaire.* Unpublished manuscript, University of Michigan, Ann Arbor.

Caplan, R. D., Cobb, S., French, J. R. P., Jr., Harrison, R. V., & Pinneau, S. R., Jr. (1975). *Job demands and worker health: Main effects and occupational differences.* Washington, DC: U.S. Government Printing Office.

Chen, P. Y., & Spector, P. E. (1991). Negative affectivity as the underlying cause of correlations between stressors and strains. *Journal of Applied Psychology, 76*, 398–407.

Cooper, C. L., & Marshall, J. (1978). Sources of managerial and white collar stress. In C. L. Cooper & R. Payne (Eds.), *Stress at work* (pp. 81–105). New York: Wiley.

Cooper, W. H. (1981). Ubiquitous halo. *Psychological Bulletin, 90*, 218–244.

Cox, T. (1978). *Stress.* Baltimore: University Park Press.

Culbertson, F. M. (1957). Modification of an emotionally held attitude through role playing. *Journal of Abnormal and Social Psychology, 54*, 230–233.

Dossett, D. L., & Lee, J. (1989, April). *Cross-cultural validation of work autonomy scales.* Paper presented at the Fourth Annual Conference of the Society for Industrial and Organizational Psychology, Boston.

French, J. R. P., & Kahn, R. L. (1962). A programmatic approach to studying the industrial environment and mental health. *Journal of Social Issues, 18*, 1–47.

Fried, Y., & Ferris, G. R. (1987). The validity of the job characteristics model: A review and meta-analysis. *Personnel Psychology, 40*, 287–322.

Griffin, R. W. (1983). Objective and social sources of information in task redesign: A field experiment. *Administrative Science Quarterly, 28*, 184–200.

Gupta, N., & Beehr, T. A. (1982). A test of the correspondence between self-reports and alternative data sources about work organizations. *Journal of Vocational Behavior, 20*, 1–13.

Hackman, J. R., & Oldham, G. R. (1975). Development of the Job Diagnostic Survey. *Journal of Applied Psychology, 60*, 159–170.

Hall, J. K., & Spector, P. E. (1991). Relationships of work stress measures for employees with the same job. *Work & Stress, 5*, 29–35.

Idaszak, J. R., & Drasgow, F. (1987). A revision of the job diagnostic survey: Elimination of a measurement artifact. *Journal of Applied Psychology, 72*, 69–74.

Ilgen, D. R. (1986). Laboratory research: A question of when, not if. In E. A. Locke (Ed.), *Generalizing from laboratory to field settings* (pp. 257–267). Lexington, MA: Lexington Books.

Ivancevich, J. M., & Matteson, M. T. (1980). *Stress and work: A managerial perspective.* Glenview, IL: Scott, Foresman.

James, L. R. & Jones, A. P. (1980). Perceived job characteristics and job satisfaction: An examination of reciprocal causation. *Personnel Psychology, 33,* 97–135.

James, L. R., & Tetrick, L. E. (1986). Confirmatory analytic tests of three causal models relating job perception to job satisfaction. *Journal of Applied Psychology, 71,* 77–82.

Jex, S. M. (1988). *The relationship between exercise and employee reactions to work stressors: A test of two competing models.* Unpublished doctoral dissertation, University of South Florida, Tampa, FL.

Kohn, M. L., & Schooler, C. (1982). Job conditions and personality: A longitudinal assessment of their reciprocal effects. *American Journal of Sociology, 87,* 1257–1286.

Kraiger, K., Billings, R. S., & Isen, A. M. (1989). The influence of positive affective states on task perceptions and satisfaction. *Organizational Behavior and Human Decision Processes, 44,* 12–25.

Landy, F. J. (1989). *Psychology of work behavior* (4th ed.). Pacific Grove, CA: Brooks/Cole.

Lazarus, R. S. (1966). *Psychological stress and the coping process.* New York: McGraw-Hill.

Loher, B. T., Noe, R. A., Moeller, N. L., & Fitzgerald, M. P. (1985). A meta-analysis of the relation of job characteristics to job satisfaction. *Journal of Applied Psychology, 70,* 280–289.

McGrath, J. E. (1982). Methodological problems in research on stress. In H. W. Krohne & L. Laux (Eds.), *Achievement, stress, and anxiety* (pp. 19–48). New York: Hemisphere.

O'Reilly, C. A., Parlette, C. N., & Bloom, J. R. (1980). Perceptual measures of task characteristics: The biasing effect of differing frames of reference and job attitudes. *Academy of Management Journal, 23,* 118–131.

Organ, D. W., & Near, J. P. (1985). Cognition vs affect in measures of job satisfaction. *International Journal of Psychology, 20,* 241–253.

Orne, M. T. (1969). Demand characteristics and the concept of quasi-controls. In R. Rosenthal & R. L. Rosnow (Eds.), *Artifact in behavioral research* (pp. 143–179). San Diego, CA: Academic Press.

Peters, L. H., & O'Connor, E. J. (1980). Situational constraints and work outcomes: The influences of a frequently overlooked construct. *Academy of Management Review, 5,* 391–397.

Podsakoff, P. M., & Organ, D. W. (1986). Self-reports in organizational research: Problems and prospects. *Journal of Management, 12,* 531–544.

Quinn, R. P., & Shepard, L. J. (1974). *The 1972–73 quality of employment survey: Descriptive statistics with comparison data from the 1969–70 survey of working conditions.* Ann Arbor, MI: Survey Research Center.

Rizzo, J. R., House, R. J., & Lirtzman, S. I. (1970). Role conflict and ambiguity in complex organizations. *Administrative Science Quarterly, 15,* 150–163.

Salancik, G. R., & Pfeffer, J. (1977). An examination of need-satisfaction models of job attitudes. *Administrative Science Quarterly, 22,* 427–456.

Schachter, S., & Singer, J. E. (1962). Cognitive, social, and physiological determinants of emotional state. *Psychological Review, 69,* 379–399.

Shweder, R. A., & D'Andrade, R. G. (1980). The systematic distortion hypothesis. In R. A. Shweder & D. W. Fiske (Eds.), *New directions for methodology of behavioral science: Fallible judgment in behavioral research* (pp. 37–58). San Francisco: Jossey-Bass.

Smith, P. C., & Kendall, L. M. (1963). Retranslation of expectations: An approach to the construction of unambiguous anchors for rating scales. *Journal of Applied Psychology, 47,* 149–155.

Smither, J. W., Collins, H., & Buda, R. (1989). When ratee satisfaction influences performance evaluations: A case of illusory correlation. *Journal of Applied Psychology, 74,* 599–605.

Spector, P. E. (1985). Measurement of human service staff satisfaction: Development of the Job Satisfaction Survey. *American Journal of Community Psychology, 13,* 693–713.

Spector, P. E. (1992). A consideration of the validity and meaning of self-report measures of objective job characteristics. In C. L. Cooper & I. T. Robertson (Eds.), *International review of industrial and organizational psychology.* New York: Wiley.

Spector, P. E., Dwyer, D. J., & Jex, S. E. (1988). Relation of job stressors to affective, health, and performance outcomes: A comparison of multiple data sources. *Journal of Applied Psychology, 73,* 11–19.

Spector, P. E., & Jex, S. M. (1991). Relations of job characteristics from multiple data sources with employee affect, absence, turnover intentions and health. *Journal of Applied Psychology*, *76*, 46–53.

Staw, B. M. (1975). Attribution of the "causes" of performance: A general alternative interpretation of cross-sectional research on organization. *Organizational Behavior and Human Performance*, *13*, 414–432.

Taber, T. D., & Taylor, E. (1989, April). *Psychometric properties of the job diagnostic survey*. Paper presented at the Fourth Annual Conference of the Society for Industrial and Organizational Psychology, Boston.

Watson, D., Pennebaker, J. W., & Folger, R. (1987). Beyond negative affectivity: Measuring stress and satisfaction in the work place. In J. M. Ivancevich & D. C. Ganster (Eds.), *Job stress: From theory to suggestion* (pp. 141–157). New York: Haworth Press.

Zajonc, R. B. (1984). On the primacy of affect. *American Psychologist*, *35*, 151–175.

23

Chronic Effect of Job Control, Supervisor Social Support, and Work Pressure on Office Worker Stress

Pascale Carayon

The stress literature differentiates between acute and chronic stressors or between episodic and chronic stressful events (Bailey & Bhagat, 1987). *Acute stressors* are events that are temporary or transitory in nature but may have a major emotional effect. The literature on life events is concerned with these acute stressors, such as death of a spouse or divorce, that can affect well-being and health (Friedman, Rosenman, & Carroll, 1958; Holmes & Rahe, 1967). In the work-stress literature, one can find many studies of acute stressors, such as job loss (Cobb & Kasl, 1977), computer shutdown and breakdown (Caplan & Jones, 1975; Eden, 1990), computer breakdown (Johansson & Aronsson, 1984), and technological change (Amick & Celentano, 1991). Some of these studies show that acute stressors are often accompanied by chronic stressors, such as increased workload (Amick & Celentano, 1991) and uncertainty regarding one's future (Cobb & Kasl, 1977). Some authors have argued that more attention should be paid to chronic stressors that employees have to face day after day (Bailey & Bhagat, 1987; Lazarus & Cohen, 1977).

Many theories of work stress implicitly assume that job stressors are chronic stressors. The role theory (Kahn, Wolfe, Quinn, Snoek, & Rosenthal, 1964) and the person–environment fit theory (Caplan, Cobb, French, Harrison, & Pinneau, 1975; Harrison, 1978) emphasize that permanent or long exposure to stressors (e.g., role ambiguity, role conflict, workload, and lack of participation) may lead to psychological, physiological, and behavioral strain that may produce mental and physical illness. The job–strain model (Karasek, 1979) states that a combination of high workload and low control puts the individual at higher risk for stress and illness. The stressful effect is likely to be due to the chronic or lasting exposure of the individual to the combination of high workload and low control. The concept of daily hassles proposed by Lazarus and his colleagues provides an interesting framework for understanding the effect of chronic job stressors on worker stress (Lazarus & Cohen, 1977; Monat & Lazarus, 1977).

Lazarus and his colleagues have developed a theory of stress based on the idea that minor stressors experienced day after day are likely to affect health (Kanner, Coyne, Schaefer, & Lazarus, 1981; Lazarus & Cohen, 1977; Monat

& Lazarus, 1977). They called such minor stressors *daily hassles*, defined as "the irritating, frustrating, distressing demands that to some degree characterize everyday transactions with the environment" (Kanner et al., 1981, p. 3). Studies have shown that daily hassles are more powerful predictors of negative affect (Kanner et al., 1981), self-reported mental health (Kanner et al., 1981), and self-reported health (DeLongis, Coyne, Dakof, Folkman, & Lazarus, 1982) than life events. In this study, I was interested in daily hassles in the work context.

Chronic job stressors can be conceptualized as daily hassles at work. If the individual is exposed to a job stressor for a short period of time, then the stressor may not cause stress. However, when the individual is exposed to the chronic stressor constantly, day after day, he or she might experience stress. It may take some time for the stressors to cause stress, but the effects of chronic job stressors are likely to be long lasting. The stress effect can be conceptualized as the cumulative effect of chronic stressors. Certain stress effects are more likely to result from such a cumulative process. For instance, physical and mental disorders, such as hypertension and depression, take some time to develop, whereas other stress reactions, such as adverse mood states and increased heart rate, are more immediate. However, the cumulative effect of these more immediate stress effects may lead to long-term stress outcomes.

When studying chronic stressors, it is important to examine the temporal dimension of chronic stressors, that is, to determine the level of exposure of the worker to the stressor. Most studies of work stress examine the intensity or strength of stressors: Stressors of higher intensity or strength are hypothesized to cause higher stress than low-intensity stressors. For instance, studies have shown that high workload and work pressure and low job control and social support are related to high levels of stress (Johnson, 1989; Karasek, 1979). However, very few studies have examined the effect of the duration of exposure to stressors—that is, the length of time that the individual is exposed to the stressor—in addition to the strength of the stressor (Heaney, Israel, & House, 1994; House, Strecher, Metzner, & Robbins, 1986; Johnson, Hall, Stewart, Fredlund, & Theorell, 1991).

Mortality rates as of 1978 and 1979 were computed for a subsample of the Tecumseh Community Health Study that was interviewed first in 1967–1969 and again in 1970 (House et al., 1986). The 1967 to 1969 interview included a measure of job tension. The 1970 interview included a measure of job pressure that was moderately correlated with the 1967 to 1969 measure of job tension ($r = .45$). Both measures were trichotomized, and their joint relationship with mortality was examined. Individuals who experienced persistently elevated job tension–pressure levels at both points in time had a mortality rate of 8.7% versus 2.9% for all other men (i.e., those with persistently low or very labile levels of job tension or pressure). Similar analyses for measures of job satisfaction revealed no significant effects on mortality. This study showed that people with persistently high job stressors have a higher mortality rate than people with persistently low job stressors or labile job stressors.

In a longitudinal study of 207 automobile workers, Heaney et al. (1994) studied the impact of chronic job insecurity on job satisfaction and health. Questionnaire data were collected at two points in time separated by about one year. The immediate, lagged, and chronic effects of job insecurity were examined in relation to the measures of job satisfaction and health at Time 2. The immediate effect was defined as the measure of job insecurity at Time 2, whereas the measure of job insecurity at Time 1 defined the lagged effect. A dichotomous measure of chronic job insecurity was built using the measures of job insecurity at Times 1 and 2. Individuals with chronic job insecurity were defined as those with high job insecurity at both Times 1 and 2. Regression analyses showed that Time 2 job insecurity was related to decreased job satisfaction, but not with increased physical symptoms. On the other hand, chronic job insecurity was related to both decreased job satisfaction and increased physical symptoms. This study demonstrated that job insecurity can become a stressor as the time of exposure increases; in other words, job insecurity can be a chronic stressor.

Johnson and his colleagues have examined the exposure to low control over the life course on cardiovascular disease (Johnson et al., 1991; Johnson & Stewart, 1993). They developed a methodology to measure work organization exposure over the life course based on cross-sectional data (Johnson & Stewart, 1993). Respondents were asked to recall their past work experiences and the duration of time each job was held. On the basis of this information and on data from the 1977 and 1979 Swedish Survey of Living Conditions, individuals could be categorized in four quartiles: high control, medium high control, medium low control, and low control. Individuals in the high control category held jobs with high control for a long time, whereas individuals in the low control category had jobs with low control during their entire work history. The medium-high control and medium-low control categories included individuals with varying levels of control. Johnson et al. (1991) showed that individuals in the low control category had higher probability of dying of cardiovascular disease than individuals in the high control category.

Longitudinal research designs are powerful designs to examine the temporal dimensions of work stressors, stress, and the relationship between stressors and stress. If data are collected on work stressors and stress several times on the same group of people (longitudinal panel design), the following time issues can be studied: (a) comparison of instantaneous, lagged, and chronic effects of stressors on stress; (b) the relationship between change in stressors and change in stress; (c) the stability of the relationship between stressors and stress; (d) causal analysis; and (e) the effect of change on stressors and stress.

As stated earlier, longitudinal design has been used for studying chronic stressors among blue-collar workers in a single manufacturing facility (Heaney et al., 1994) and among a sample of workers in different jobs (House et al., 1982). In this chapter, I present data regarding the relationship between chronic stressors and stress among office workers. Along with my colleagues (Carayon, 1992; Carayon, Yang, & Lim, in press), I have reported results of a study that examined the stability of the relationship between stressors and stress. Marcelissen, Winnubst, Buunk, and Wolff (1988) used a longitudinal design with three data collection points to examine the causality of the relationships among social support and physiological strain (high blood pressure, high cholesterol, and being overweight), psychological stress, and health complaints.

They used LISREL to assess the nature of the causal relationships between social support and stressors (e.g., role conflict) or stress. There was not much evidence for the causal effect of social support on stressors and stress. Actually, stress had a causal effect on coworker social support. This study showed the important role that longitudinal research designs can play in improving the understanding of the causal relationship between stressors and stress. Another powerful application of longitudinal research design is the study of changes, such as technological change (Lindström, 1993). In this study, I used a longitudinal research design to compare the instantaneous and chronic effects of job stressors on worker stress.

Specifically, I examined the chronic-stress effects of lack of job control and lack of social support from supervisor and work pressure. Many studies have shown the stress effects of lack of job control (Karasek, 1979, 1990; Carayon-Sainfort, 1991), lack of social support (House, Cynthia, & Helen, 1982; Johnson, 1989; LaRocco, Tetrick, & Meder, 1989), and work pressure (Karasek, 1979; Margolis, Kroes, & Quinn, 1974). Studies of office workers have also demonstrated the importance of these three job stressors (Piotrkowski, Cohen, & Coray, 1992; Sauter, Gottlieb, Rohrer, & Dodson, 1983; Smith, Carayon, Sanders, Lim, & LeGrande, 1992; Smith, Cohen, & Stammerjohn, 1981).

It can be hypothesized that workers who are exposed to high levels of chronic stressors for a long time are more likely to experience stress than workers who are not exposed to such high levels of the stressors or who are exposed to the stressors for a shorter period of time. To examine both exposure duration and strength, it is necessary to have data on past experiences (Johnson & Stewart, 1993) or longitudinal data (Heaney et al., 1994; House et al., 1986). This chapter examines longitudinal data from an ongoing office-automation study to examine the combined effect of exposure duration and strength of stressors on stress reactions of office workers (Carayon et al., in press). Figure 1 shows the relationship between strength and duration of exposure and their effects on stress reactions. It was expected that individuals with consistently high levels of stressor during the study period (individuals in Group 5) would report higher levels of stress than individuals with consistently low levels of stressor during the study period (individuals in Group 1), individuals with consistently medium levels of stressor (individuals in Group 3), or individuals with varying levels of stressor (individuals in Groups 2 and 4).

Method

Sample

A group of office workers from a public-service organization participated in a 3-year longitudinal study of office automation (Carayon et al., in press). Data were collected at three points in time, separated by about 1.5 years. The response rate was 85% at Time 1 ($n = 177$), 73% at Time 2 ($n = 151$), and 71% at Time 3 ($n = 148$). Seventy-six people participated in all three rounds of data collection. This subset was used to examine the duration and strength

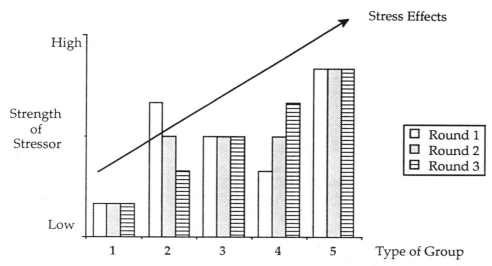

Figure 1. Hypothesized effect of strength and duration of exposure of stressor on stress. 1 = group with low levels of stressor at all three rounds; 2 = group of individuals with high stressor at Round 1, medium stressor at Round 2, and low stressor at Round 3; 3 = group of individuals with medium levels of stressor at all three rounds; 4 = group of individuals with low stressor at Round 1, medium stressor at Round 2, and high stressor at Round 3; 5 = group of individuals with high levels of stressor at all three rounds.

hypotheses. To determine if there were unique demographic characteristics of this sample, it was compared with data from employees who participated in only one or two rounds of the study. There was a lower proportion of part-time employees in the group of people who participated in the subset than in the whole sample. Participants in the three rounds had longer tenure with their employer, more experience in their position, and less years of education than the comparison sample. There were no specific aspects of the subset demographics that were so unique as to influence the study results regarding stress responses.

The demographic data for the subset were for the first round of data collection. The average age was 38.2 years (SD = 9.3 years). Seventy-two percent of the participants were women. All study participants were White. About half of them were married (51%). The majority had permanent (96%) and full-time (93%) jobs. The employees had an average tenure with the company of 10.5 years (SD = 6.0 years) and an average experience with current position of 6.3 years (SD = 5.5 years). The average number of years of school was 7.9 (SD = 1.3 years). Study participants performed a range of office tasks and included clerical workers (e.g., data-entry operator and secretary), professionals (e.g., programmer and engineer), and managers.

Measures

Measures of job stressors and worker-stress reactions were obtained through a questionnaire that included questions used in previous studies (Caplan et al.,

1975; Carayon, 1994; Sainfort, 1990; Smith et al., 1981). The measure of job control was the sum of five items (Carayon, 1994; Sainfort, 1990). The Cronbach alpha scores for job control for the three rounds were .70 (Round 1), .63 (Round 2), and .71 (Round 3). The measure of supervisor social support was the sum of four items (Caplan et al., 1975; Carayon, 1994; Sainfort, 1990). Cronbach alpha scores for supervisor social support for the three rounds were .85, .89, and .89, respectively. The measure of work pressure was the sum of six items (Carayon, 1994; Sainfort, 1990). The Cronbach alpha scores for work pressure for the three rounds were .82, .78, and .72, respectively.

The measures of worker-stress reactions included four measures derived from a factor analysis of the National Institute for Safety and Health (NIOSH) health checklist (Sainfort & Carayon, 1994; Smith et al., 1981): musculo-skeletal discomfort (15 items), respiratory problems (6 items), anxiety (7 items), and distress (4 items). The measures were obtained by computing the sum of the items divided by the number of items. The Cronbach alpha scores for the three rounds were .91, .90, and .91, respectively, for musculoskeletal discomfort; .70, .81, and .77, respectively, for respiratory problems; .84, .84, and .79, respectively, for anxiety; and .57, .73, and .54, respectively, for distress. Questions on the NIOSH health checklist ask respondents to report the frequency of various symptoms experienced "within the past year." Given the time frame of the question, one can assume that these measures are capturing the long-term stress reactions. Therefore, they are adequate measures to examine the chronic effect of job stressors on worker stress. As a contrasting measure of short-term stress, we used the Daily Life Stress Scale of Reeder, Schrama, and Dirker (1973). The Cronbach alpha scores for the measure of daily life stress were .85 for Round 1, .88 for Round 2, and .84 for Round 3.

Procedures

One public-service organization agreed to participate in a longitudinal study of office automation. The target population of the study was all office workers excluding the top management level. The list of names of potential participants was provided by the organization, and participation in the study was voluntary. All employees were asked to participate in the study by filling out a questionnaire. The response rates for the three rounds were 85%, 73%, and 71%, respectively. Most of the questionnaires were handed out and collected in person by a researcher. Other data collection methods included having a company contact person distribute and collect the questionnaires or leaving the questionnaire in the person's mailbox and having the person send it back to the researcher by mail. Employees were given time on the job to fill out the questionnaire.

Analyses

I computed a measure of chronic stressors by taking the sum of the measures of stressors at the three rounds. This measure was a cumulative score of the strength and duration of exposure of the stressors. Individuals with high scores on this measure were exposed to strong stressors during the entire study period. Individuals with low scores on this measure were exposed to low stressors during the entire study period. Individuals with medium scores were exposed either to medium stressors during the study period or to varying levels of stressors during the study period.

The correlations between worker-stress reactions and the chronic measure of stressors were computed. In addition, the correlations for just the last round of measurement (Time 3) were computed. To ensure that the effect of the chronic measure of stressors on worker-stress reactions was not due to the instantaneous effect of the Time 3 measure, I computed partial correlations between worker stress and the chronic measure of stressors, partialing out the effect of the Time 3 measure. I then performed regression analyses of the five measures of worker stress with the Time 3 measure and the chronic measure as independent variables. These regression analyses were meant to examine the concomitant effect of the instantaneous stressors (Time 3 measure) and the chronic stressors (chronic measure). Finally, the chronic measure was split into three levels of strength and duration: high, medium, and low. Individuals with high scores were exposed to high stressors during the entire study period, whereas the individuals with low scores were exposed to low stressors during the entire study period. The individuals with medium scores were exposed either to varying levels of stressors (e.g., high at Time 1 and then low at Times 2 and 3) or to medium stressors during the entire study period. Analyses of variance (ANOVAs) were performed to compare the three groups on the five measures of worker stress. I expected the individuals in the chronically high-stressor category to report high stress.

Results

Correlation Analyses

Pearson correlations were computed between the measures of stressors and the five measures of worker stress for each of the three rounds (see Table 1). A correlational analysis was also conducted to compare the relationship between the measure of stressors at Time 3, the chronic measures of stressors, and the measures of worker stress. The correlation analysis showed that low job control at Time 3 was correlated with three of the five measures of worker stress: musculoskeletal discomfort ($r = -.36$, $p < .01$), respiratory problems ($r = -.28$, $p < .05$), and distress ($r = -.32$, $p < .01$). Individuals with low job control reported high levels of musculoskeletal discomfort, respiratory prob-

Table 1. Results of Pearson Correlation Analyses Between Stressors and Worker Stress for Each of Three Rounds

Variable	MUSCUL	RESP	ANX	DIST	DSTRESS
Round 1					
Job control	−.28*	−.16	−.30**	−.26*	−.28*
Supervisor social support	−.18	−.21	−.21	−.14	−.37***
Work pressure	.06	−.12	.21	−.06	.32***
Round 2					
Job control	−.34**	−.24**	−.13	−.05	−.22
Supervisor social support	−.41***	−.24*	−.15	−.09	−.30*
Work pressure	.10	−.07	.01	.06	.26*
Round 3					
Job control	−.36**	−.28*	−.22	−.14	−.37***
Supervisor social support	−.15	.02	−.08	−.13	−.44***
Work pressure	.04	−.01	.11	.15	.49***

Note. MUSCUL = musculoskeletal discomfort; RESP = respiratory problems; ANX = anxiety; DIST = distress; DSTRESS = daily life stress.
*$p < .05$.   **$p < .01$.   ***$p < .001$.

lems, and distress. The chronic measure of job control was correlated with three measures of worker stress: musculoskeletal discomfort ($r = -.36$, $p < .01$), anxiety ($r = -.35$, $p < .01$), and distress ($r = -.37$, $p < .01$). Individuals exposed to low job control for a long period of time reported high stress, such as musculoskeletal discomfort, anxiety, and distress. When the effect of job control at Time 3 was partialed out, these chronic correlations dropped to −.17 (*ns*) for musculoskeletal discomfort, −.29 ($p < .05$) for anxiety, and −.21 ($p < .10$) for distress.

With regard to supervisor social support, the Time 3 measure was correlated with only one of the five measures of worker stress: daily life stress ($r = -.44$, $p < .001$). Individuals with low support from their supervisors reported higher daily life stress than individuals with high supervisor support. The chronic measure of supervisor social support was correlated with four measures of worker stress: musculoskeletal discomfort ($r = -.28$, $p < .05$), anxiety ($r = -.26$, $p < .05$), distress ($r = -.26$, $p < .01$), and daily life stress ($r = -.47$, $p < .001$). Individuals who had little support from their supervisors for a long period of time reported higher musculoskeletal discomfort, anxiety, distress, and daily life stress than individuals with high supervisor support during the entire study period. The partial correlations between worker stress and the chronic measure of supervisor social support given the Time 3 measure of social support yielded significant correlations for the following measures of worker stress: musculoskeletal discomfort ($r = -.21$, $p < .10$), anxiety ($r = -.24$, $p < .05$), distress ($r = -.25$, $p < .05$), and daily life stress ($r = -.28$, $p < .05$).

The correlation analyses of work pressure showed that the Time 3 measure and the chronic measure of work pressure were correlated with the measure of daily life stress ($r = .49$, $p < .001$, and $r = .30$, $p < .01$). Individuals with high work pressure reported high daily life stress. When the Time 3 measure was partialed out, the correlation between the chronic measure of work pressure and daily life stress dropped to .03 (*ns*).

Regression Analyses

The results of the regression analyses are shown in Table 2. For each of the five measures of worker stress, a separate regression analysis was conducted for the three stressors. The independent variables were the Time 3 measure of the stressor and the chronic measure of the stressor. The Time 3 measure of job control was a statistically significant predictor of respiratory problems, whereas the measure of chronic job control was a predictor of anxiety. The measure of chronic supervisor social support was a significant predictor of three measures of worker stress: anxiety, distress, and daily life stress. The Time 3 measure of work pressure was a significant predictor of daily life stress.

Effect of Chronic Stressors on Worker Stress

As indicated before, the measure of chronic stressors was split in three levels: high, medium, and low. Comparisons between these three groups on the five measures of worker stress were conducted. The results of this analysis are in Table 3. The first part of Table 3 shows the comparison between groups who were exposed to different levels of job control for different periods of time. In this table, the high group is the group with high job control during the entire study period. The low group includes individuals with low job control during the entire study period. The medium group includes individuals with medium or varying levels of job control. The means of the three groups were compared using ANOVA and Scheffé tests. Results show that individuals exposed to

Table 2. Results of Regression Analyses

Independent variable	MUSCUL	RESP	ANX	DIST	DSTRESS
Job control					
Time 3	−.16	−.38*	.12	−.09	−.08
Chronic	−.24	.12	−.44*	−.30	−.09
Adjusted R^2	12%**	6%*	10%*	11%**	0%
Supervisor social support					
Time 3	−.01	.19	.12	.08	−.22
Chronic	−.27	−.25	−.33*	−.33*	−.33*
Adjusted R^2	5%	1%	5%	5%	23%***
Work pressure					
Time 3	.08	.13	.03	.24	.49**
Chronic	.04	−.20	.12	−.10	−.04
Adjusted R^2	0%	0%	0%	1%	19%***

Note. The entries in the table are the beta coefficients of the regression analyses. MUSCUL = musculoskeletal discomfort; RESP = respiratory problems; ANX = anxiety; DIST = distress; DSTRESS = daily life stress.
*$p < .05$. **$p < .01$. ***$p < .001$.

Table 3. Chronic Effect of Job Control, Supervisor Social Support, and Work
Pressure on Worker Stress

	Level of Chronic Stressor			Results of F and
Stress variable	High	Medium	Low	Scheffé tests
		Job control		
n	16	39	21	
MUSCUL	21.4	21.4	27.3	**, low > high, medium
RESP	9.2	8.1	9.6	ns
ANX	11.6	10.5	13.1	**, low > high, medium
DIST	4.8	4.6	5.6	**, low > high, medium
DSTRESS	2.0	2.0	2.3	ns
		Supervisor social support		
n	32	34	10	
MUSCUL	21.4	23.4	26.8	.10
RESP	8.6	8.6	9.7	ns
ANX	10.6	12.0	12.3	.07
DIST	4.5	5.1	5.4	*, low, medium > high
DSTRESS	1.8	2.2	2.4	***, low, medium > high
		Work pressure		
n	13	42	21	
MUSCUL	24.6	23.0	21.8	ns
RESP	8.5	8.5	9.5	ns
ANX	11.8	11.6	11.0	ns
DIST	5.0	4.9	4.9	ns
DSTRESS	2.4	2.0	1.9	*, high > low

Note. The entries in the table are the means of worker stress for each of the three groups (high,
    medium, and low). MUSCUL = musculoskeletal discomfort; RESP = respiratory problems;
    ANX = anxiety; DIST = distress; DSTRESS = daily life stress; ns = not significant.
*$p < .05$. **$p < .01$. ***$p < .001$.

low job control during the entire study period reported higher musculoskeletal
discomfort, more anxiety, and more distress than the rest of the participants.
    The second part of Table 3 displays the comparison between groups who
were exposed to different levels of supervisor social support for different periods
of time. In this table, the high group is the group with high social support
during the entire study period. The low group includes individuals with low
social support during the entire study period. The medium group includes
individuals with medium or varying levels of social support. Individuals with
high supervisory social support during the entire study period reported lower
distress and daily life stress than the rest of the sample.
    The third part of Table 3 shows the comparison between groups who were
exposed to different levels of work pressure for different periods of time. In
this table, the high group is the group with high work pressure during the
entire study period. The low group includes individuals with low work pressure
during the entire study period. The medium group includes individuals with
medium or varying levels of work pressure. The three groups were significantly

different on only one of the five measures of worker stress. Workers with chronically high work pressure reported higher daily life stress than workers with low work pressure during the entire study period.

Discussion

My results show that lack of job control and lack of social support from supervisors may act as chronic job stressors. The chronic measure of job control was correlated with three of the five measures of worker stress, and two of these three correlations were still statistically significant after the effect of the Time 3 measure of job control was partialed out. The comparison between the high, medium, and low groups showed that individuals with low job control during the entire study period had higher levels of stress (three of the five measures of stress) than the rest of the sample. With regard to social support, although the Time 3 measure of social support was correlated with only one measure of worker stress, the chronic measure of social support was correlated with four measures of worker stress. Individuals with high social support during the entire study period reported lower levels of stress (two of the five measures) than the rest of the sample. However, the chronic measure of work pressure was not related to the measures of worker stress. It seems that work pressure has an instantaneous effect on stress and that this instantaneous effect affects only short-term stress (i.e., daily life stress).

Although lack of job control and lack of social support appeared to be chronic job stressors, their chronic effect on worker stress seems to be different. With regard to job control, the highest levels of stress were related to lack of job control over the entire study period. Individuals with either high or varying levels of job control had similar levels of stress (see Table 3). The effect of social support is the opposite. Individuals with the highest levels of stress reported either low social support during the study period or medium-to-varying levels of social support. The lowest levels of stress were reported for individuals with high social support from their supervisor during the entire study period (see Table 3). Being exposed to conditions of low job control over and over may lead to increased stress, whereas receiving low or medium support from a supervisor either for a long period of time or intermittently may lead to increased stress. Lack of job control seems to lead to stress if one is exposed to this stressor for a long period of time. Supervisor social support is a positive factor that, if sustained over time, can protect the individual from high stress. In Lazarus's (Lazarus & Cohen, 1977) terminology, lack of job control may be considered a daily hassle, whereas supervisory social support may be a daily uplift.

This study has shown the importance of considering not only the strength of stressors but also the duration of exposure to stressors. The Time 3 measure of supervisor social support was correlated with only one of the five measures of worker stress, whereas the chronic measure of social support was correlated with four measures of stress. If one considers only the instantaneous effect of supervisor support, one would erroneously conclude that supervisor social support does not affect worker stress. Supervisor support seems to affect stress mainly as a chronic stressor. This result indicates that findings from cross-sectional studies of worker stress may not be valid if one considers only the strength of the stressors. Thus, researchers need to develop and test theories of work stress that differentiate between the strength and duration of exposure of stressor.

This study examined only three chronic stressors: lack of job control, lack of social support from supervisor, and work pressure. Other studies of chronic stressors have examined only one stressor at a time. Johnson et al. (1991) examined the effect of chronic lack of control among Swedish workers, whereas Heaney et al. (1994) studied chronic job insecurity among automobile workers and House et al. (1986) examined the chronic effect of job tension–pressure on mortality rate in a subsample of the Tecumseh Community Health Study. According to the theory of daily hassles put forth by Lazarus and colleagues (Lazarus & Cohen, 1977), the number of daily hassles experienced is an important determinant of one's well-being and physical health: The more daily hassles one experiences, the lower one's psychological well-being (Kanner et al., 1981) and the more physical symptoms one reports (DeLongis et al., 1982). Therefore, workers who are exposed to many chronic job stressors are more likely to experience stress. A cross-sectional study by Carayon (1994) showed that some jobs have more stressors than others and that these jobs are associated with high levels of stress. Therefore, to further understand the effect of chronic job stressors or daily hassles at work, researchers have to examine the range of job stressors that the individual experiences and the interactions between these job stressors.

The model of the work system proposed by Smith and Carayon-Sainfort (1989) provides a good framework for conceptualizing the variety of stressors to which an individual can be exposed. The work system is conceptualized as a system with five elements: task, organizational factors, technology, physical and social environment, and the individual. The task, organizational factors, technology, and environment have negative aspects that can create a stress load on the individual. The greater the load, the more substantial the stress reactions will be. The accumulation of negative aspects (e.g., lack of control and poor environment), if not compensated by positive aspects (e.g., resources and support), can lead to stress reactions and diseases with chronic exposure. This model provides a holistic framework for studying job stressors that encompasses many of the stressors of previous stress models (e.g., Caplan et al., 1975; Karasek, 1979) as well as ergonomic factors, aspects of the physical environment, and technology characteristics.

This study has some weaknesses that limit the generalizability of the results. The sample size of 76 individuals was relatively small. Longitudinal studies are open to such a problem because of attrition. Also, data were collected from office workers in only one organization; therefore, results may not be generalizable to other organizations or to other jobs. This study demonstrated the importance of having a longitudinal design that allows researchers to examine the strength and duration of exposure of job stressors on worker stress. Further research is needed to replicate the findings of this study.

References

Amick, B. C., III, & Celentano, D. D. (1991). Structural determinants of the psychosocial work environment: Introducing technology in the work stress framework. *Ergonomics, 34*, 625–646.

Bailey, J. M., & Bhagat, R. S. (1987). Meaning and measurement of stressors in the work environment: An evaluation. In S. V. Kasl & C. L. Cooper (Eds.), *Stress and health: Issues in research methodology* (pp. 207–229). New York: Wiley.

Caplan, R. D., Cobb, S., French, J. R. P., Harrison, R. V., & Pinneau, S. R. (1975). *Job demands and worker health*. Washington, DC: U.S. Government Printing Office.

Caplan, R. D., & Jones, K. W. (1975). Effects of work load, role ambiguity, and Type A personality on anxiety, depression, and heart rate. *Journal of Applied Psychology, 60*, 713–719.

Carayon, P. (1992). A longitudinal study of job design and worker strain: Preliminary results. In J. C. Quick, L. R. Murphy, & J. J. Hurrell, Jr. (Eds.), *Stress and well-being at work: Assessments and interventions for occupational mental health* (pp. 19–32). Washington, DC: American Psychological Association.

Carayon, P. (1994). Stressful jobs and non-stressful jobs: A cluster analysis of office jobs. *Ergonomics, 37*, 311–323.

Carayon, P., Yang, C. L., & Lim, S.-Y. (in press). Examining the relationship between job design and worker strain over time in a sample of office workers. *Ergonomics*.

Carayon-Sainfort, P. (1991). Stress, job control and other job elements: A study of office workers. *International Journal of Industrial Ergonomics, 7*, 11–23.

Cobb, S., & Kasl, S. V. (1977). *Termination: The consequences of job loss*. Washington, DC: U.S. Government Printing Office.

DeLongis, A., Coyne, J. C., Dakof, G., Folkman, S., & Lazarus, R. S. (1982). Relationship of daily hassles, uplifts, and major life events to health status. *Health Psychology, 1*, 119–136.

Eden, D. (1990). Acute and chronic job stress, strain, and vacation relief. *Organizational Behavior and Human Decision Processes, 45*, 175–193.

Friedman, M., Rosenman, R. H., & Carroll, V. (1958). Changes in the serum cholesterol and blood clotting time in men subjected to cyclic variation of occupational stress. *Circulation, 17*, 852–861.

Harrison, R. V. (1978). Person–environment fit and job stress. In C. L. Cooper & R. Payne (Eds.), *Stress at work* (pp. 175–205). New York: Wiley.

Heaney, C. A., Israel, B. A., & House, J. S. (1994). Chronic job insecurity among automobile workers: Effects on job satisfaction and health. *Social Science Medicine, 38*, 1431–1437.

Holmes, T. H., & Rahe, R. H. (1967). Social Readjustment Rating Scale. *Journal of Psychosomatic Research, 11*, 213–218.

House, J. S., Cynthia, A. R., & Helen, L. M. (1982). The association of social relationships and activities with mortality: Prospective evidence from the Tecumseh Community Health Study. *American Journal of Epidemiology, 116*, 123–140.

House, J. S., Strecher, V., Metzner, H. L., & Robbins, C. A. (1986). Occupational stress and health among men and women in the Tecumseh Community Health Study. *Journal of Health and Social Behavior, 27*, 62–77.

Johansson, G., & Aronsson, G. (1984). Stress reactions in computerized administrative work. *Journal of Occupational Behaviour, 5*, 159–181.

Johnson, J. V. (1989). Control, collectivity and the psychosocial environment. In S. L. Sauter, J. J. Hurrell, Jr., & C. L. Cooper (Eds.), *Job control and worker health* (pp. 55–74). New York: Wiley.

Johnson, J. V., Hall, E. M., Stewart, W., Fredlund, P., & Theorell, T. (1991). Combined exposure to adverse work organization factors and cardiovascular disease: Towards a life-course perspective. In L. Factor (Eds.), *Proceedings of the 4th International Conference on the Combined Effects of Environmental Factors* (pp. 117–122).

Johnson, J. V., & Stewart, W. F. (1993). Measuring work organization exposure over the life course with a job exposure matrix. *Scandinavian Journal of Work, Environment and Health, 19*, 21–28.

Kahn, R. L., Wolfe, D. M., Quinn, R. P., Snoek, J. D., & Rosenthal, R. A. (1964). *Organizational stress: Studies in role conflict and role ambiguity*. New York: Wiley.

Kanner, A. D., Coyne, J. C., Schaefer, C., & Lazarus, R. S. (1981). Comparison of two modes of stress measurement: Daily hassles and uplifts versus major life events. *Journal of Behavioral Medicine, 4*, 1–39.

Karasek, R. (1979). Job demands, job decision latitude, and mental strain: Implications for job redesign. *Administrative Science Quarterly, 24*, 285–307.

Karasek, R. (1990). Lower health risk with increased job control among white-collar workers. *Journal of Organizational Behavior, 11*, 171–185.

LaRocco, J. M., Tetrick, L. E., & Meder, D. (1989). Differences in perceptions of work environment conditions, job attitudes, and health beliefs among military physicians, dentists, and nurses. *Military Psychology, 1*, 135–151.

Lazarus, R. S., & Cohen, J. B. (1977). Environmental stress. In I. Altman & J. F. Wohlwill (Eds.), *Human behavior and the environment: Current theory and research* (pp. 89–127). New York: Spectrum.

Lindström, K. (1993). Well-being and job demands after data system changes with work reorganization in the service sector. In H. Luczak, A. Cakir, & G. Cakir (Eds.), *Work with display units 92* (pp. 454–458). Amsterdam: Elsevier Science.

Marcelissen, F. H. G., Winnubst, J. A. M., Buunk, B., & de Wolff, C. J. (1988). Social support and occupational stress: A causal analysis. *Social Science in Medicine, 26*, 365–373.

Margolis, B., Kroes, W. M., & Quinn, R. (1974). Job stress: An unlisted occupational hazard. *Journal of Occupational Medicine, 16*, 654–661.

Monat, A., & Lazarus, R. S. (1977). *Stress and coping: An anthology.* New York: Columbia University Press.

Piotrkowski, C. S., Cohen, B. G. F., & Coray, K. E. (1992). Working conditions and well-being among women office workers. *International Journal of Human–Computer Interaction, 4*, 263–282.

Reeder, L. G., Schrama, P. G., & Dirker, J. M. (1973). Stress and cardiovascular health: An international cooperative study. *Social Science Medicine, 7*, 753–784.

Sainfort, F., & Carayon, P. (1994). Self-assessment of VDT operator health: Validity analysis of the NIOSH health checklist. *International Journal of Human–Computer Interaction, 6*, 235–252.

Sauter, S. L., Gottlieb, M. S., Rohrer, K. M., & Dodson, V. N. (1983). *The wellbeing of video display terminal users.* Madison: Department of Preventive Medicine, University of Wisconsin.

Smith, M. J., and Carayon-Sainfort, P. (1989). A balance theory of job design for stress reduction. *International Journal of Industrial Ergonomics, 4*, 67–79.

Smith, M. J., Cohen, B. G. F., & Stammerjohn, L. W. (1981). An investigation of health complaints and job stress in video display operations. *Human Factors, 23*, 387–400.

Smith, M. J., Carayon, P., Sanders, K. J., Lim, S. Y., & LeGrande, D. (1992). Employee stress and health complaints in jobs with and without electronic performance monitoring. *Applied Ergonomics, 1*, 17–28.

24

Emotional Labor as a Potential Source of Job Stress

Pamela K. Adelmann

It has been estimated that at least one third of American workers engage in *emotional labor* that is required by their jobs (Hochschild, 1983). That is, they are paid not only for the physical and mental labor they perform at work but also for the emotion they display, and often must feel.

Emotional labor has been defined as paid labor requiring "the management of feeling to create a publicly observable facial and bodily display" (Hochschild, 1983, p. 7). A limited amount of research has been undertaken to examine the nature of emotional labor in selected occupations, the organizational transmission of emotional labor norms, and the organizational consequences of emotional labor, but the effects on individuals of performing emotional labor largely have been overlooked.

The focus of this chapter is whether emotional labor is a potential source of employee job stress. I developed a measure of emotional labor in a sample of workers employed in an occupation requiring a high degree of emotional labor and explored how the type and amount of emotional labor are related to employee job reactions.

Work, Emotion, and Employee Well-Being

Little evidence exists on the consequences of emotional experience on the job for workers. Occupations as diverse as police officer (Arther & Caputo, 1959), physician (M. Bell, 1984), and bill collector (Hochschild, 1983) require some degree of emotional labor. In service jobs, the most rapidly expanding segment of the labor force (D. Bell, 1973; Riddle, 1986; Shelp, 1981), emotional labor has become such a normative part of job performance that it is an established focus in many job-training programs (Albrecht, 1988; Czepiel, Solomon, & Surprenant, 1985; Riddle, 1986).

Some evidence suggests that emotional aspects of the job may play an important part in job stress. Repetti and Crosby (1984) found that positive and negative emotions at work were correlated with employee depression, whereas Spector, Dwyer, and Jex (1988) found that anxiety and frustration at work were linked with lower job satisfaction and performance, more health symptoms, and higher intent to quit the job. George (1989) found that mood at work is related to absence. Others (Payne, Jabri, & Pearson, 1988) have proposed that affect at work should be considered in studies of job characteristics and job stress.

In the studies cited above, affective experience at work may have arisen from any number of sources, including relations with boss and coworkers, physical conditions, and other job characteristics. Few studies have focused specifically on the nature or consequences of emotional labor—expression and feelings that are required as part of the job.

Most of the existing research on emotional labor is concerned with its organizational aspects. Smith and Kleinman (1989), for example, described how medical students learn the unspoken rules and means for managing emotions in their contacts with the human body. Descriptive accounts of emotional labor also have been published about police detectives (Stenross & Kleinman, 1989), waiters (Mars & Nicod, 1984), and bill collectors (Sutton, 1991). Sutton and Rafaeli (1988) examined organizational sales in relation to emotional labor by convenience-store clerks, and Rafaeli (1989) analyzed the nature of emotional labor by store clerks as a function of customer, clerk, and workplace attributes.

The consequences of emotional labor for employees have been investigated less thoroughly. Hochschild (1983), who coined the term *emotional labor*, reported in qualitative research among flight attendants and bill collectors that emotional labor was linked to such problems as substance abuse, headaches, absenteeism, and sexual dysfunction, which clearly suggests that emotional labor may be a major source of job stress. More recently, Richman (1988) reported psychological distress among beginning female medical students whose norms for emotional expressivity deviated from the medical school norms.

To date, however, the relation between emotional labor performed as part of the job and employee job reactions has not been fully investigated. The research described in this chapter explores these issues in a sample of table servers. Below, two theoretical perspectives bearing on the association between emotional labor and employee well-being are described.

Theoretical Perspectives on Emotional Labor and Job Stress

That emotional labor may have consequences for employee well-being was proposed by Hochschild (1983) in her book *The Managed Heart*. In it, she defined *emotional labor* as "the management of feeling to create a publicly observable facial and bodily display; emotional labor is sold for a wage and therefore has *exchange value*" (p. 7). It involves contact with the public, it requires the worker to produce an emotional state in another person, and it allows the employer or work situation to exercise control over the emotional activities of the employee.

Hochschild (1983) explained that often what must be displayed and what is really felt in such occupations are at odds; persistent dissonance produces alienation from one's own emotions. She argued that this alienation led to the array of psychological and interpersonal problems revealed in her samples. Although Hochschild's argument is compelling and her data richly textured, both would be strengthened by supporting quantitative data on emotional labor with established measures of job-related well-being.

A separate body of theory and research suggests that it may not be emotional labor itself but the type of emotional expression required that is important to well-being. William James (1884/1922) contended that in emotion, "the bodily changes follow directly the perception of the exciting fact, and that our feeling of the same changes as they occur is the emotion" (p. 13). Modern emotion theorists have developed from this notion the facial-feedback hypothesis, which proposes that facial expression alters or initiates subjective feeling through a physiological feedback mechanism (Gellhorn, 1964; Izard, 1971; Tomkins, 1962). In a review of the research on facial feedback, Adelmann and Zajonc (1989) concluded that "intensification of a congruent facial pattern enhances subjective experience, while an inhibited congruent pose or the pose of an incongruent emotion reduces subjective experience" (p. 269).

The facial-feedback hypothesis suggests that the effect of emotional expression required by the job should be an emotional experience that is consistent with the expression. In other words, as Rafaeli and Sutton (1987) noted, "employees who are expected to smile may benefit from feelings of elation and exuberance" (p. 32). Only those who must display negative affect as part of the job, such as funeral directors and bill collectors, should experience distress as a consequence of the emotional labor they perform.

Although the two camps differ in the overall association that would be expected between emotional labor and occupational well-being, they are in some agreement that the effects of emotional labor may depend on consonance between expression and feeling. Ekman and Friesen (1982), in the facial-feedback domain, argued that voluntary or posed emotional expressions are qualitatively different from spontaneous or "felt" facial expressions. They are innervated through different physiological pathways (Miehlke, 1973) and differ in timing, laterality, and intensity (Ekman & Friesen, 1982). A "felt" smile (in which the person actually experiences a positive emotion) differs in all these regards, as well as in its muscular pattern, from a "phony" smile (in which nothing is felt), and from a "masking" smile (in which negative emotion is concealed; Ekman & Friesen, 1982). The implication for emotional labor is that only when a required smile closely approximates a spontaneous expression may facial feedback of a positive emotion take place; under other conditions, positive emotional labor should not have particularly positive consequences for employees. In addition, although Hochschild (1983) suggested that any emotional labor has potentially damaging consequences for employees, she specified that distress is primarily due to dissonance between expression and feeling.

Goals of the Study

The overall goal of this study was to explore emotional labor as a potential source of job stress. My specific aims were to develop a measure of emotional labor, to examine employee perceptions of emotional labor, and to test the association between emotional labor and job-related well-being.

Table servers were selected for this study for three reasons. First, the display of positive affect is required of more workers than is negative affect, and as the service economy continues to grow this will be true of more and more workers. Second, the work that table servers perform is similar to that performed by Hochschild's (1983) sample of flight attendants and, therefore, offers the opportunity to closely replicate her findings. Finally, occupations requiring emotional labor involving positive affect allow the two hypotheses to be contrasted. The *alienation hypothesis* proposes that any emotional labor is detrimental to well-being; the *facial-feedback hypothesis* suggests that displaying positive affect should have positive outcomes for workers.

Method

Sample

Data were gathered from responses to a questionnaire mailed to a sample of table servers working in Washtenaw County, Michigan. The sample was obtained from the Michigan Restaurant Association membership list. One fourth ($n = 58$) of the restaurants listed as offering table service were randomly selected. Managers at each of the establishments were asked to distribute questionnaires. Fifteen of the restaurants chosen did not actually offer table service or had gone out of business. Of the 43 remaining restaurants, 20 participated (46.5%). Managers requested a total of 277 questionnaires; 90 were completed (77 women, 13 men). Questions about ethnicity were not included, which may represent a potential source of response error. Respondents were paid $10 each.

Variables

The questionnaire covered a variety of topics, including job characteristics, job satisfaction, and emotional labor, measures of which are used in the analyses reported in this chapter. The job reaction variables described below were first regressed on emotional labor; a second set of regressions tested the relation between emotional labor and job well-being when other job characteristics as described below were statistically controlled.

The job-related well-being variables were intercorrelated at magnitudes ranging from 0 to .58 (job satisfaction with growth satisfaction); job characteristics were intercorrelated in the range from .21 to .36. Correlations of job-related well-being with emotional labor ranged from .03 to .37 (for growth satisfaction) and with job characteristics ranged from .07 to .59 (job complexity and growth satisfaction). Finally, emotional labor correlated with other job characteristics in the range from .07 to .37 (growth satisfaction).

Emotional labor. Because waitressing by its nature involves contact with the public, items were developed to approximate the other conditions of emotional labor (Hochschild, 1983). Respondents were asked "To what degree do you think you actually do each of the following as part of your job?" Responses to two phrases following this question ("to make the customer feel important" and "to make the customer like and trust you") were used to assess having to produce an emotional state in another person. Two more pairs of phrases ("to smile and behave in a friendly manner toward the customer" and "to conceal any negative feelings about the customer" vs. "to try to feel sympathy and understanding for the customer" and "to actually feel friendly and warm toward the customer") were used to assess expressive behavior and feeling as controlled by the job, respectively. The emotional labor index was the mean of these items, rated as 1 = *not at all*, 2 = *a little*, 3 = *quite a lot*, and 4 = *very much* (sample M = 3.09, SD = 0.63, internal reliability = .75).

Felt, phony, and masking smiles. To assess frequency of felt, phony, and masking smiles on the job as described by Ekman and Friesen (1982), respondents were asked to rate how often their smile at work is a "genuine reflection of a positive feeling," "is made to appear as though a positive feeling is felt, but in fact nothing much is felt at all," and "is made to appear as though a positive feeling is felt, but in fact conceals strong negative feelings." The response scale for each item was rated as 1 = *always*, 2 = *often*, 3 = *sometimes*, 4 = *rarely*, and 5 = *never*.

The "felt" smile group included those who reported positive felt smiles more often than either neutral or negative felt smiles (n = 55). The "phony" smilers (neutral smiles equal or greater in frequency than positive smiles and neutral smiles more frequent than negative smiles) and "masking" smilers (higher or equal frequency of negative smiles as positive or neutral smiles) were collapsed into a single category of "false" smiles (n = 35) because of small cell sizes.

Job-related well-being. Two job variables were measured with single items asking about job commitment (responses rated from 1 to 5; M = 3.09, SD = 1.68) and performance (responses rated 1 to 4; M = 3.57, SD = 0.60). Multiple items made up a modified Alienation From Work Index (Vallas, 1988; range = 5 to 25, M = 11.70, SD = 3.00, Cronbach's α = .84). Four satisfaction subscales (each with a range from 1 to 7) of the Job Diagnostic Survey (Hackman & Oldham, 1975) were included. These assessed satisfaction with job overall (M = 5.14, SD = 1.19, α = .61), with growth opportunities (M = 4.70, SD = 1.22, α = .77), with social aspects (M = 5.73, SD = 0.88, α = .54), and with supervision (M = 4.94, SD = 1.42, α = .79).

Job characteristics. Job complexity and control measures were derived in previous factor analyses by Adelmann (1987). The job complexity range was from 4 to 20 (M = 13.53, SD = 2.16, α = .73), and for job control, the range was from 5 to 16 (M = 11.54, SD = 1.96, α = .65). Personal income was reported in 25 categories: starting from less than \$2,000 and followed by nine

Table 1. Response of Employees on Emotional Labor Items

Item	M	SD
Induce feelings in others		
Make customer feel important	3.01	0.80
Make customer like–trust you	3.04	0.81
Worker expressive behavior		
Smile–behave in friendly manner	3.49	0.64
Conceal any negative feelings	3.02	0.76
Worker feeling		
Feel sympathy–understanding	2.74	0.80
Feel friendly–warm	2.76	0.88

Note. Response scale: 1 = *not at all,* 2 = *a little,* 3 = *quite a lot,* 4 = *very much.*

levels in $1,000 increments, with remaining categories in larger increments up to $45,000 and over.

Results

Descriptive information on the measure of emotional labor is shown in Table 1. Item means were generally high. Items tapping induction of feeling in others were rated at approximately *quite a lot* (3 on the 4-point scale). Expressive emotional labor was rated similarly high for concealing negative feelings and higher for smiling behavior. The lowest ratings were for the two "feeling emotional" labor items—each with means between *a little* (2) and *quite a lot* (3 on the 4-point scale).

Employees also perceived emotional labor to have generally positive consequences (Table 2). Customer and supervisor effects ("makes customers feel good," "customer has a right," and "pleases supervisor") were rated above the

Table 2. Results for Measure of Perceived Effects of Emotional Labor

Item	M	SD
It makes customers feel good	4.39	0.77
It results in better tips	4.36	0.76
The customer has a right to expect it	3.41	1.18
It pleases your supervisor	4.08	0.96
It helps in getting raises	2.83	1.38
It makes you feel happy	3.84	1.02
It's a sign that you really like people	3.86	1.04
It accurately indicates a friendly personality	3.67	1.25
It makes you feel you are doing your job well	3.48	1.03
It makes you feel false and insincere	2.23	1.21
It makes you feel you are being used by your employer	1.75	0.91
It makes you feel unsure what you really feel	1.71	0.93

Note. Response scale: 1 = *disagree strongly,* 2 = *disagree somewhat,* 3 = *neutral,* 4 = *agree somewhat,* 5 = *agree strongly.*

Table 3. Standardized Regression Coefficients of Job Reactions Regressed on Emotional Labor and With Controls for Complexity, Control, and Income

Job reaction	Without controls	With controls
Job commitment	.21*	.13
Job performance	.07	−.01
Job alienation	−.11	.08
Satisfaction with job	.25**	.02
Satisfaction–growth	.37**	.16*
Satisfaction–social	.08	−.09
Satisfaction–supervision	.18*	.00

*$p < .10$.   **$p < .05$.

item midpoints. Emotional labor was rated as beneficial to amount of tips received but not to getting raises. Agreement was generally high on positive individual consequences ("makes you feel happy" and "are doing job well"), and emotional labor was reported as corresponding with actual feelings and disposition ("like people," "friendly personality") rather than being dissonant with them ("feeling false," "used," or "unsure of true feelings").

Table 3 shows the results of regressions of job reactions on emotional labor. Performing emotional labor was associated with more positive job reactions and was significant on job commitment, job satisfaction, and satisfaction with growth oppportunities.

Controlling for job complexity, control, and personal income eliminated all significant coefficients for emotional labor except on satisfaction with growth opportunities. It appears, then, that most of the apparently positive effects for individuals in jobs with high emotional labor were accounted for by the other desirable characteristics of those jobs.

Finally, the differences in the links between emotional labor and job reactions depending on degree of consonance between expression and feeling are shown in Figure 1. On every job variable except commitment to job, the group reporting predominantly "felt" smiles at work had significantly more favorable job reactions.

Discussion

This study represents a first attempt to assess the reactions of workers to the emotional labor they perform as part of their jobs. The alienation hypothesis, as suggested by Hochschild (1983), predicts that such labor should have negative consequences for employees. The facial-feedback hypothesis, alternatively, predicted beneficial consequences of the positively valenced emotional labor required in this sample of workers. Also explored was the effect of degree of match between emotional expression and subjective experience on these associations.

The results of this study supported the facial-feedback hypothesis to a limited extent. Emotional labor was linked to significantly more positive job evaluations on a number of measures. However, when other desirable job

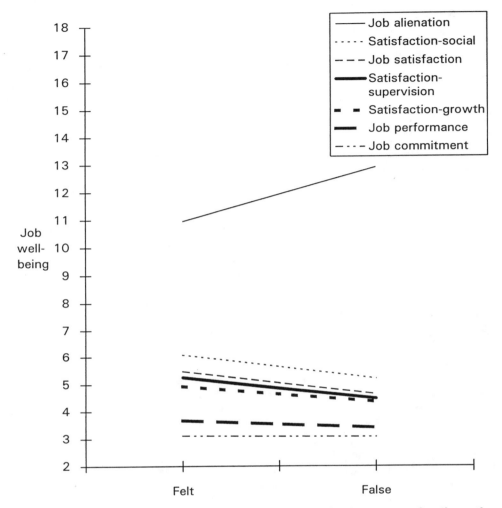

Figure 1. Job well-being graphed according to the predominant type of smile on the job.

characteristics—such as control, complexity, and income—were controlled for, only a single association between emotional labor and job reaction remained significant.

This suggests that desirable jobs, which also happen to demand higher levels of emotional labor, produce high job satisfaction. It may also be that desirable jobs produce greater job satisfaction, which in turn motivates employees to perform a high degree of emotional labor. In either case, it appears that emotional labor per se is not strongly related either positively or negatively to job reactions.

Employees also clearly see a number of good reasons for performing emotional labor. Among these are extrinsic rewards, such as pleasing customers and supervisors and receiving better tips. But workers also report some intrinsic rewards, such as feeling happy and feeling they are doing their jobs well. They also rate potential negative consequences of emotional labor fairly low.

In other respects, there is merit to both hypotheses, however. When employees were divided into groups in which expression was reported as usually consonant with feeling or in which it was not, interesting patterns of job reactions appeared. The former group had more positive reactions than the latter on all job outcomes (although the difference in commitment was not significant). These results support the notion drawn from Ekman and Friesen's (1983) work that it is not emotional labor that is important but the consonance between emotional expression and feeling. In this regard, Hochschild (1983) is supported as well. Although she suggested that emotional labor should be harmful under all circumstances, she was clear in specifying that dissonance between feeling and expression is the locus of much distress.

This study represents an attempt to measure emotional labor as a potential source of job stress in a specific sample of emotional workers. For this purpose, I assessed emotional labor primarily involving expression and feeling of positive emotion. This measure is thus appropriate for the majority of jobs in which the same type of emotional labor is required. To be useful in a wider range of occupations, however, some modifications should be made. These include adapting the measure to assess emotional labor in jobs in which the primary requirement is either concealing emotion (such as physician or psychotherapist) or conveying negative emotion (such as bill collector or prison guard).

From these preliminary explorations of the consequences of emotional labor for workers, some recommendations may be offered. The first is that although workers may perform emotional labor uncomplainingly when it is required by the job, it does not do anything for their satisfaction with their work, their commitment to stay in their jobs, or their reported job performance in the absence of other desirable job characteristics. If an employer especially values worker emotional labor, the way to encourage it may be to offer an enlarged work role and better pay.

An additional question is what to do with workers experiencing distress because of emotional dissonance in their jobs. In the sample I used, a large percentage of workers—two fifths—were experiencing such dissonance on a chronic basis. Quitting did not seem to be an option; they had no greater intention of leaving their jobs than other employees. One solution to this chronic mismatch might be to select out the poorer emotional laborers during hiring. However, it is highly probable given the nature of such jobs that even the most harmonious of emotional laborers experiences an unpleasant degree of dissonance from time to time. A second possibility might be to reduce the demands for emotional labor placed on employees. Given the popular perception that the typical service encounter has already reached an unacceptably low level of civility, this option also seems untenable.

A more fruitful approach may be to provide opportunities and techniques for employees to dissipate emotional dissonance. Strategies reported in descriptive research on other occupations include using humor, depersonalizing the encounter, and talking with coworkers. Employers may need to be creative in tailoring emotional outlets to the workplace. A colleague reported, for example, that in the housewares store where his daughter worked, clerks who had reached the limits of their capacity for emotional dissonance were encouraged to go to the storeroom, where they could smash the chipped and broken stock against the wall until they felt better. Given that emotional labor is becoming more prevalent throughout the labor force, soon more and more workers may need to find their equivalent to throwing dishes at the storeroom wall.

References

Adelmann, P. K. (1987). Occupational complexity, control, and personal income: Their relation to psychological well-being in men and women. *Journal of Applied Psychology*, *72*, 529–537.

Adelmann, P. K., & Zajonc, R. B. (1989). Facial efference and the experience of emotion. *Annual Review of Psychology*, *40*, 249–280.

Albrecht, K. (1988). *At America's service: How corporations can revolutionize the way they treat their customers*. New York: Praeger.

Arther, R. O., & Caputo, R. R. (1959). *Interrogation for investigators*. New York: William C. Copp.

Bell, D. (1973). *The coming of post-industrial society*. New York: Basic Books.

Bell, M. (1984). Teachings of the heart. *Journal of the American Medical Association*, *252*, 2684.

Czepiel, J. A., Solomon, M. R., & Surprenant, C. F. (1985). *The service encounter*. Lexington, MA: Lexington Books.

Ekman, P., & Friesen, W. V. (1982). Felt, false, and miserable smiles. *Journal of Nonverbal Behavior*, *6*, 238–252.

Gellhorn, E. (1964). Motion and emotion: The role of proprioception in the physiology and pathology of the emotions. *Psychological Review*, *71*, 457–472.

George, J. M. (1989). Mood and absence. *Journal of Applied Psychology*, *74*, 317–324.

Hackman, J. R., & Oldham, G. R. (1975). Development of the Job Diagnostic Survey. *Journal of Applied Psychology*, *60*, 159–170.

Hochschild, A. R. (1983). *The managed heart: Commercialization of human feeling*. Berkeley: University of California Press.

Izard, C. E. (1971). *The face of emotion*. New York: Appleton-Century-Crofts.

James, W. (1922). What is an emotion? In K. Dunlap (Ed.), *The emotions* (pp. 11–30). Baltimore: Williams & Wilkins. (Original work published 1884)

Mars, G., & Nicod, M. (1984). *The world of waiters*. London: Allen & Unwin.

Miehlke, A. (1973). *Surgery of the facial nerve*. Philadelphia: WB Saunders.

Payne, R. L., Jabri, M. M., & Pearson, A. W. (1988). On the importance of knowing the affective meaning of job demands. *Journal of Organizational Behavior*, *9*, 149–158.

Rafaeli, A. (1989). When clerks meet customers: A test of variables related to emotional expressions on the job. *Journal of Applied Psychology*, *74*, 385–394.

Rafaeli, A., & Sutton, R. I. (1987). Expression of emotion as part of the work role. *Academy of Management Review*, *12*, 23–37.

Repetti, R. L., & Crosby, F. (1984). Gender and depression: Exploring the adult-role explanation. *Journal of Social and Clinical Psychology*, *2*, 57–70.

Richman, J. A. (1988). Deviance from sex-linked expressivity norms and psychological distress. *Social Forces*, *67*, 208–215.

Riddle, D. I. (1986). *Service-led growth: The role of the service sector in world development*. New York: Praeger.

Shelp, R. K. (1981). *Beyond industrialization: Ascendancy of the global service economy*. New York: Praeger.

Smith, A. C., & Kleinman, S. (1989). Managing emotions in medical school: Students' contacts with the living and the dead. *Social Psychology Quarterly*, *52*, 56–69.

Spector, P. E., Dwyer, D. J., & Jex, S. M. (1988). Relation of job stressors to affective, health, and performance outcomes: A comparison of multiple data sources. *Journal of Applied Psychology, 73*, 11–19.

Stenross, B., & Kleinman, S. (1989). The highs and lows of emotional labor: Detectives' encounters with criminals and victims. *Journal of Contemporary Ethnography, 17*, 435–452.

Sutton, R. I. (1991). Maintaining norms about expressed emotions: The case of bill collectors. *Administrative Science Quarterly, 36*, 245–268.

Sutton, R. I., & Rafaeli, A. (1988). Untangling the relationship between displayed emotions and organizational sales: The case of convenience stores. *Academy of Management Journal, 31*, 461–487.

Tomkins, S. E. (1962). *Affect, imagery, consciousness: Vol. 1. The positive affects.* New York: Springer.

Vallas, S. P. (1988). New technology, job content, and worker alienation. *Work and Occupations, 15*, 148–178.

Author Index

Numbers in italics refer to listings in reference sections.

Subject Index

About the Editors

Steven L. Sauter, PhD, is chief of the Applied Psychology and Ergonomics Branch at the National Institute for Occupational Safety and Health, and an adjunct professor of human factors engineering at the University of Wisconsin. His research interests focus on occupational stress and ergonomics, with special emphasis on office and computer work. He is an associate editor of the *Journal of Occupational Health Psychology* and has prepared numerous articles and books on the psychosocial aspects of occupational health.

Lawrence R. Murphy is a research psychologist with the National Institute for Occupational Safety and Health and an adjunct associate professor of psychology at Xavier University in Cincinnati, Ohio. He received his MA and PhD degrees from DePaul University in Chicago, and postdoctoral training at the Institute for Psychosomatic and Psychiatric Research, Michael Reese Medical Center. He has published many articles in the area of occupational stress and stress management and has coedited several books, including *Stress Management in Work Settings* (1989) and *Stress and Well-Being at Work: Assessments and Interventions for Occupational Mental Health* (1992). His research interests are job stress assessment, stress management interventions, and worker compliance with universal precautions to prevent HIV/AIDS exposure in occupational settings.